# Edexcel
## GCSE Mathematics
*higher*

### book 1

Keith Pledger

Gareth Cole

Peter Jolly

Graham Newman

Joe Petran

Sue Bright

**www.heinemann.co.uk**
✓ Free online support
✓ Useful weblinks
✓ 24 hour online ordering

**01865 888058**

**Heinemann**
*Inspiring generations*

Heinemann Educational Publishers
Halley Court, Jordan Hill, Oxford OX2 8EJ
Part of Harcourt Education Limited

Heinemann is the registered trademark of
Harcourt Education Limited

© Harcourt Education Ltd, 2006

First published 2006

10 09 08 07 06
10 9 8 7 6 5 4 3 2 1

British Library Cataloguing in Publication Data is available from the British Library on request.

10-digit ISBN: 0 435 53365 7
13-digit ISBN: 978 0 435533 65 6

Typeset by Tech-Set Ltd, Gateshead, Tyne and Wear
Original illustrations © Harcourt Education Limited, 2006
Illustrated by Adrian Barclay, Mark Ruffle and HL Studios
Cover design by mccdesign
Printed by CPI Bath Press
Cover photo: Digital Vision ©

**Acknowledgements**
Harcourt Education Ltd would like to thank those schools who helped in the development and trialling of this course.

This high quality material is endorsed by Edexcel and has been through a rigorous quality assurance programme to ensure that it is a suitable companion to the specification for both learners and teachers. This does not mean that its contents will be used verbatim when setting examinations nor is it to be read as being the official specification – a copy of which is available at www.edexcel.org.uk

The publisher's and authors' thanks are due to Edexcel Limited for permission to reproduce questions from past examination papers. These are marked with an [E]. The answers have been provided by the authors and are not the responsibility of Edexcel Limited.

The authors and publisher would like to thank the following individuals and organisations for permission to reproduce photographs:

Harcourt Education Ltd / Peter Morris p1; Getty Images / PhotoDisc pp18, 78, 156, 185; Corbis pp35 left, 214, 276; Alamy Images pp35 right, 216; Empics pp62, 81; Getty Images p68; iStockPhoto.com / Dan Cooper p88; Digital Vision p109; Getty Images / News & Sport p115; Alvey & Towers p144; Science Photo Library pp152, 154; Guillaume Dargaud p184; iStockPhoto.com p212

Every effort has been made to contact copyright holders of material reproduced in this book. Any omissions will be rectified in subsequent printings if notice is given to the publishers.

**Publishing team**

| | |
|---|---|
| Editorial | James Orr, Lindsey Besley, Evan Curnow, Katherine Pate, Nick Sample, Alex Sharpe, Laurice Suess, Elizabeth Bowden, Ian Crane |
| Design | Phil Leafe |
| Production | Siobhan Snowden |
| Picture research | Chrissie Martin |

**Websites**
There are links to relevant websites in this book. In order to ensure that the links are up-to-date, that the links work, and that the sites aren't inadvertently linked to sites that could be considered offensive, we have made the links available on the Heinemann website at www.heinemann.co.uk/hotlinks. When you access the site, the express code is **4092P**.

Tel: 01865 888058   www.heinemann.co.uk

# Quick reference to chapters

# Introduction

## Introduction

These revised and updated editions have been carefully matched to the new two-tier specification for GCSE Maths. Books 1 and 2 cover everything you need to know to achieve success in your exam, up to and including Grade A*. The author team is made up of Senior Examiners, a Chair of Examiners and Senior Moderators, all experienced teachers with an excellent understanding of the requirements of the Edexcel specification.

## Key features

- **Chapters** are divided into **sections**, each with a simple explanation followed by clear examples or a worked exam question. These show you how to tackle questions. Each section also contains practice exercises to develop your understanding and help you consolidate your learning.

- **Key points** are highlighted throughout, like this:

  If $x \times x = A$, then $x$ is the **square root** of $A$, written $\sqrt{A}$

  Each chapter ends with a summary of key points you need to remember.

- **Hint boxes** are used to make explanations clearer. They may also remind you of previously learned facts or tell you where in the book to find more information.

  Remember:
  $(x + 3)^2 = (x + 3)(x + 3)$

- **Mixed exercises** are designed to test your understanding across each chapter. They include past exam questions which are marked with an [E]. You will find a mixed exercise at the end of almost every chapter.

- **Examination practice papers** are included in Book 2 to help you prepare for the exam at the end of your course.

- **Answers** are provided at the back of the book to use as your teacher directs.

## Quick reference and detailed Contents pages

- Use the thumb spots on the edge of the **Quick reference** page to help you turn to the right chapter quickly. Note that Book 1 contains Chapters 1–15 and Book 2 contains Chapters 16–29.

- Use the detailed **Contents** to help you find a section on a particular topic. The summary and reference codes on the right show your teacher the part(s) of the specification covered by each section in the book. (For example, NA 3h refers to Number and Algebra, section 3 Calculations, subsection h.)

## Use of a calculator or a computer

These symbols show you where you must, or must not, use a calculator. Sometimes you may wish to use a spreadsheet package on a computer. There are also links to websites and suggested activities that require an internet search.

## Coursework

A Coursework Guide is available online at www.zebramaths.co.uk

# Contents

Note: *Italic* indicates paragraphs in the Higher tier specification that have been drawn from the Foundation tier.

# 7 Transformations and loci

# 8 Using basic number skills

# 9 Functions, lines, simultaneous equations and regions

# 10 Presenting and analysing data 1

# 11 Estimation and approximation

# 12 Sequences and formulae

# 13 Measure and mensuration

# 14 Simplifying algebraic expressions

# 15 Pythagoras' theorem

# ① Exploring numbers 1

You will need to use and apply numbers in a wide variety of situations throughout your GCSE course and in everyday life.

This chapter deals with some of the terms that describe numbers and their properties.

You should remember these key points from earlier work:

A **factor** of a number is a whole number that divides exactly into the number. The factors include 1 and the number itself.

A **multiple** of a number is the result of multiplying the number by a positive whole number.

Codes based on prime numbers are used to provide the highest level of security for banks and computer systems.

A **prime number** is a number greater than 1 which has only two factors: itself and 1. For example, 7 is a prime number because the only factors of 7 are 7 and 1.

## 1.1 Number facts

### Prime factors

Any factor of a number that is a prime number is a **prime factor**. For example, 2 and 3 are the prime factors of 6.

You can write any whole number as the product of its prime factors.

**Example 1**

Write 720 as the product of its prime factors.

**Method 1**    Split 720 into factors in stages, each time finding the smallest possible prime number that is a factor:

$$720 = 2 \times 360$$
$$= 2 \times 2 \times 180$$
$$= 2 \times 2 \times 2 \times 90$$
$$= 2 \times 2 \times 2 \times 2 \times 45$$
$$= 2 \times 2 \times 2 \times 2 \times 3 \times 15$$
$$= 2 \times 2 \times 2 \times 2 \times 3 \times 3 \times 5$$

This can be written as:    $720 = 2^4 \times 3^2 \times 5$

> Use powers to write $2 \times 2 \times 2 \times 2$ in the shorter form $2^4$.

Here 720 is in **prime factor form**        2, 3 and 5 are **prime factors** of 720

**Method 2**    Use a factor tree to help find the prime factors:

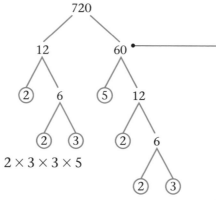

> 12 and 60 is not the only way to split 720. You could use 72 and 10 or 80 and 9, for example. However you start, the factor tree will always end with the same prime factors.

> The circled numbers at the ends of the branches are the prime factors.

So  $720 = 2 \times 2 \times 2 \times 2 \times 3 \times 3 \times 5$
$$= 2^4 \times 3^2 \times 5$$

Writing a number as the product of its prime factors is called writing it in **prime factor form**.

# Finding the highest common factor (HCF)

Sometimes you will need to find the largest factor that two numbers have in common; this is called the **highest common factor** or **HCF**.

For example, to find the highest common factor of 720 and 84:

First write each number in prime factor form:

$720 = $ 2 $\times$ 2 $\times 2 \times 2 \times$ 3 $\times 3 \times 5$

$84 \ = $ 2 $\times$ 2 $\times$ 3 $\times 7$

Then pick out the common factors: those that appear in *both* numbers. These are:

$2 \times 2 \times 3$

The highest common factor of 720 and 84 is $2 \times 2 \times 3 = 12$.

> The **highest common factor** (HCF) of two whole numbers is the highest factor that is common to both of them.

# Finding the lowest common multiple (LCM)

Sometimes you will need to find the lowest multiple that two numbers have in common; this is called the **lowest common multiple** or **LCM**.

The multiples of 6 are:   6  12  18  **24**  30  36  42  **48**  54  60  66  **72** ...

The multiples of 8 are:   8  16  **24**  32  40  **48**  56  64  **72**  80  88  96 ...

6 and 8 have some
common multiples.

The lowest common multiple (LCM) of 6 and 8 is 24.

> The **lowest common multiple (LCM)** of two whole numbers is the lowest number that is a multiple of them both.

You can find the LCM by looking at the prime factor forms of the two numbers.

---

**Example 2** _____

Find the LCM of 6 and 8.

First write the numbers in prime factor form:

$$8 = 2 \times 2 \times 2 \quad \text{and} \quad 6 = 2 \times 3$$

The LCM must contain all the prime factors of 8 *and* all the prime factors of 6:

$$
\begin{array}{c}
8 \\
\overbrace{2 \times 2 \times 2} \times 3 \\
\underbrace{\phantom{2 \times 2} \times 2 \times 3} \\
6
\end{array}
$$

8 and 6 have a common prime factor of 2 which is only counted once.

The LCM of 6 and 8 is $2 \times 2 \times 2 \times 3 = 24$.

---

# Exercise 1A

1   Find all the factors of:

   (a)  24          (b)  36          (c)  308
   (d)  1001        (e)  1400        (f)  53

2   Find all the prime numbers between 1 and 100.

3   Can the sum of two prime numbers be a prime number? Explain your answer.

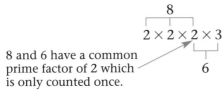

Try adding some pairs of prime numbers.

**4**    Write each number in prime factor form.

(a)   24         (b)   32         (c)   18         (d)   13

(e)   72         (f)   50         (g)   99         (h)   120

**5**    Find the highest common factor (HCF) of

(a)   4 and 8        (b)   9 and 12        (c)   18 and 24

(d)   36 and 48      (e)   720 and 252     (f)   19 600 and 756

**6**    Find the lowest common multiple (LCM) of

(a)   3 and 4        (b)   4 and 6         (c)   7 and 14

(d)   6 and 15       (e)   36 and 16       (f)   85 and 50

**7**    A ship is at anchor between two lighthouses $L$ and $H$.
The light from $L$ shines on the ship every 30 seconds.
The light from $H$ shines on the ship every 40 seconds.
Both lights started at the same moment.
How often do both lights shine on
the ship at once?

> Find the LCM of
> the light times.

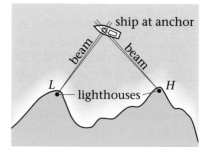

**8**    **The Sigma Function: an investigation**
In this question, $f(n)$ means the sum of the factors of $n$.
So $f(36) = 1 + 2 + 3 + 4 + 6 + 9 + 12 + 18 + 36 = 91$

(a)   Find $f(n)$ when $n$ is
      (i)  24        (ii)  48        (iii)  100        (iv)  256        (v)  32

(b)   Write down an expression for $f(p)$, where $p$ is any prime
      number.

(c)   Show that $f(2^n) = 1 + 2 + 2^2 + 2^3 + \cdots + 2^n$

(d)   Find an expression for $f(p^n)$, where $p$ is any prime number.

# 1.2  Square numbers and cube numbers

These numbers sometimes occur in number patterns in investigations.

> A **square number** is the result of multiplying a whole number by itself.

Square numbers:

$1 \times 1 = 1$ ——————— 1st square number
$2 \times 2 = 4$ ——————— 2nd square number
$3 \times 3 = 9$ ——————— 3rd square number
$4 \times 4 = 16$ —————— 4th square number
$x \times x = x^2$ —————— the square of any number x

$4 \times 4$, for example, can also be written as

- the square of 4
- 4 squared
- $4^2$

1          4          9                16

A square number can be shown as a square pattern.

A **cube number** is the result of multiplying a whole number by itself then multiplying by the number again.

Cube numbers:

$1 \times 1 \times 1 = 1$ ——————— 1st cube number
$2 \times 2 \times 2 = 8$ ——————— 2nd cube number
$3 \times 3 \times 3 = 27$ ——————— 3rd cube number
$4 \times 4 \times 4 = 64$ ——————— 4th cube number
$x \times x \times x = x^3$ ——————— the cube of any number $x$

$4 \times 4 \times 4$, for example, can also be written as

- the cube of 4
- 4 cubed
- $4^3$

A cube number can be shown as a cube pattern.

 1

 8

 27

---

**Example 3**

1, 3, 4, 6, 8, 13, 16, 18, 24, 27, 30

From the list write down

(a) the square numbers          (b) the cube numbers.

(a) 1, 4, 16          (b) 1, 8, 27

---

## Exercise 1B

**1** Find
  (a) the 8th square number          (b) the 7th cube number
  (c) the 12th square number          (d) the 10th cube number
  (e) the first 12 square numbers          (f) the first 8 cube numbers.

**2** From each list write down all the numbers which are
  (i) square numbers          (ii) cube numbers.
  (a) 50, 20, 64, 30, 1, 80, 8, 49, 9
  (b) 10, 21, 57, 4, 60, 125, 7, 27, 48, 16, 90, 35
  (c) 137, 150, 75, 110, 50, 125, 64, 81, 144
  (d) 90, 180, 216, 100, 81, 75, 140, 169, 125

## 1.3 Finding squares and square roots, cubes and cube roots

### Squares

To find the **square** of any number, multiply the number by itself.
The square of $3.7 = 3.7^2 = 3.7 \times 3.7 = 13.69$
The square of $-6.2 = -6.2^2 = -6.2 \times -6.2 = 38.44$

## Square roots

$4 \times 4 = 16$, so we say that 4 is a **square root** of 16. It is a number which multiplied by itself gives 16.

You can write the square root of 16 as $\sqrt{16}$

$1.5 \times 1.5 = 2.25$

So 1.5 is a square root of 2.25, written $\sqrt{2.25}$

In general, for any number $A$:

> If $x \times x = A$, then $x$ is the **square root** of $A$, written $\sqrt{A}$

| Notice that |
|---|
| $-4 \times -4 = 16$ so $-4$ is also a square root of 16. $\sqrt{16} = \pm 4$ |

| Remember: |
|---|
| $\sqrt{2.25}$ can also be $-1.5$ if that is a sensible answer to the problem you are solving. |

You can find the square root of any positive number, though the answer may not be a whole number. Most calculators have a function key that finds the square root of a number. You often need to round the answer on the calculator display. For example

$\sqrt{18} = 4.242\,640\,6\ldots = 4.24$ (to 2 d.p.)

## Cubes

> To find the **cube** of any number, multiply the number by itself then multiply by the number again.
>
> The cube of $5.3 = 5.3^3 = 5.3 \times 5.3 \times 5.3 = 148.877$
>
> The cube of $-2.1 = (-2.1)^3 = -2.1 \times -2.1 \times -2.1 = -9.261$

## Cube roots

$2 \times 2 \times 2 = 8$, so we say that 2 is the **cube root** of 8. It is a number which multiplied by itself, then multiplied by itself again, gives 8.

You can write the cube root of 8 as $\sqrt[3]{8}$.

$3.4 \times 3.4 \times 3.4 = 39.304$

So 3.4 is the cube root of 39.304, written $\sqrt[3]{39.304}$

In general, for any number $A$:

> If $y \times y \times y = A$, then $y$ is the cube root of $A$, written $\sqrt[3]{A}$

You can find the cube root of any positive or negative number, though the answer may not be a whole number. Some calculators have a cube root function key to find the cube root of numbers. As with square roots, you often have to round the answer. For example

$\sqrt[3]{18} = 2.620\,741\,3\ldots = 2.62$ (to 2 d.p.)

| Notice that |
|---|
| $\sqrt[3]{-64} = -4$ because $-4 \times -4 \times -4 = -64$ |

## Exercise 1C

Use your calculator to work out

**1** (a) $13^2$      (b) $3.5^2$      (c) $40^2$

   (d) $8.7^2$      (e) $19.6^2$      (f) $(-57.4)^2$

**2** (a) $6^3$      (b) $2.4^3$      (c) $20^3$

   (d) $(-1.3)^3$      (e) $13.4^3$      (f) $36.2^3$

> Sometimes you are asked to leave an answer as a square root or cube root.
> e.g. $x^2 = 5$
> $x = \sqrt{5}$
> This is called writing your answer in **surd form**.

**3** (a) $\sqrt{121}$      (b) $\sqrt{225}$      (c) $\sqrt{16\,900}$

   (d) $\sqrt{2.89}$      (e) $\sqrt{0.49}$      (f) $\sqrt{33.64}$

**4** In this question give your answers correct to 2 d.p.

   (a) $\sqrt{253}$      (b) $\sqrt{2341}$      (c) $\sqrt{18.4}$

   (d) $\sqrt{8476}$      (e) $\sqrt{29.44}$      (f) $\sqrt{1\,825\,963}$

**5** In this question give your answers correct to 3 s.f.

   (a) $\sqrt[3]{68}$      (b) $\sqrt[3]{3654}$      (c) $\sqrt[3]{26.5}$

   (d) $\sqrt[3]{-9.2}$      (e) $\sqrt[3]{882.5}$      (f) $\sqrt[3]{6\,547\,812}$

## 1.4 Index numbers

In Section 1.2 you saw that

$3 \times 3 = 3^2 = 9$ is a **square number**

and

$4 \times 4 \times 4 = 4^3 = 64$ is a **cube number**

because they can be shown as square and cube patterns.

You cannot draw patterns which go beyond three dimensions, but you can extend the notation for multiplying numbers like this:

$3 \times 3 \times 3 \times 3 = 3^4 = 81$

You say that 81 is **3 raised to the power 4**, or 81 is **3 to the fourth**.

Also:

$2 \times 2 \times 2 \times 2 \times 2 = 2^5 = 32$

You say that 32 is **2 raised to the power 5**, or 32 is **2 to the fifth**, or 32 is **2 to the power 5**.

The $^4$ and the $^5$ are examples of **index numbers**.

32 written in **index form** is $2^5$.

The power a number is raised to is called the **index** (plural **indices**).

## General form for index numbers

You can use algebra to write about index numbers in general. For any number $a$, three lots of $a$ multiplied together can be written:

$$a \times a \times a = a^3$$

and $n$ lots of $a$ multiplied together can be written:

$$a \times a \times a \times \cdots \times a = a^n$$
$$\longleftarrow n \text{ lots of } a \longrightarrow$$

A number written in the form $a^n$ is written in **index form**.

---

**Example 4**

(a) Calculate $4^7$.

(b) Write 243 in index form.

(a) $4^7 = 4 \times 4 \times 4 \times 4 \times 4 \times 4 \times 4$
$= 16\,384$

(b) $243 = 3 \times 81$
$= 3 \times 9 \times 9$
$= 3 \times 3 \times 3 \times 3 \times 3$
$= 3^5$

---

### Exercise 1D

**1** Find the values of these powers.

(a) $2^6$  (b) $10^5$  (c) $5^4$  (d) $7^3$  (e) $12^4$  (f) $(0.9)^5$

**2** Write these numbers in index form.

(a) 1000  (b) 125  (c) 512
(d) 2401  (e) 625  (f) 19 683

**3** Show that 64 can be written as either $2^6$ or $4^3$.
Explain why this is the case.

**4** Which is the greater, and by how much, $2^5$ or $5^2$?

## 1.5 The index laws

There are rules to help you calculate with numbers written in index form.

## Multiplication

$$3^2 \times 3^3 = (3 \times 3) \times (3 \times 3 \times 3) = 3 \times 3 \times 3 \times 3 \times 3$$
$$= 3^5$$

So
$$3^2 \times 3^3 = 3^5 = 3^{2+3}$$

To multiply two powers of the same number add the indices.

$$a^n \times a^m = a^{n+m}$$

## Division

$$2^5 \div 2^3 = \frac{2 \times 2 \times \cancel{2} \times \cancel{2} \times \cancel{2}}{\cancel{2} \times \cancel{2} \times \cancel{2}}$$

$$= 2 \times 2$$
$$= 2^2$$

So    $2^5 \div 2^3 = 2^2 = 2^{5-3}$

To divide two powers of the same number subtract the indices.

$$a^n \div a^m = a^{n-m} \quad \text{or} \quad \frac{a^n}{a^m} = a^{n-m}$$

## Raising to the power 0

Notice that

$$1 = \frac{8}{8} = \frac{2^3}{2^3} = 2^{3-3} = 2^0$$

The 2 could be replaced by any other non-zero number $a$. The result would be the same.

$$a^0 = 1 \text{ (where } a \neq 0)$$

## Negative powers

Sometimes numbers are raised to a negative power.
For example

$$2^2 \div 2^5 = 2^{2-5} = 2^{-3}$$

and   $2^2 \div 2^5 = \dfrac{\cancel{2} \times \cancel{2}}{\cancel{2} \times \cancel{2} \times 2 \times 2 \times 2} = \dfrac{1}{2 \times 2 \times 2} = \dfrac{1}{2^3}$

So                    $2^{-3} = \dfrac{1}{2^3} = \dfrac{1}{2 \times 2 \times 2} = \dfrac{1}{8}$

$$a^{-n} = \frac{1}{a^n} \quad \text{(where } a \neq 0)$$

## Powers raised to further powers

$$(2^3)^2 = (2 \times 2 \times 2)^2$$
$$= (2 \times 2 \times 2) \times (2 \times 2 \times 2)$$
$$= 2 \times 2 \times 2 \times 2 \times 2 \times 2 = 2^6$$

So    $(2^3)^2 = 2^{3 \times 2} = 2^6$

To raise a power to a further power multiply the indices together.

$$(a^n)^m = a^{n \times m}$$

**Example 5**

Calculate each of the following using the index laws. Give your answers both in index form and without using indices (where possible).

(a) $2^5 \times 2^3$    (b) $3^7 \div 3^5$    (c) $(5^3)^2$    (d) $2^{-3}$    (e) $117^0$    (f) $2^2 + 2^3$

(a) $2^5 \times 2^3 = 2^{5+3} = 2^8 = 256$      (b) $3^7 \div 3^5 = 3^{7-5} = 3^2 = 9$

(c) $(5^3)^2 = 5^{3 \times 2} = 5^6 = 15\,625$      (d) $2^{-3} = \dfrac{1}{2^3} = \dfrac{1}{2 \times 2 \times 2} = \dfrac{1}{8} = 0.125$

(e) $117^0 = 1$      (f) $2^2 + 2^3 = 4 + 8 = 12$

## Exercise 1E

**1** Work out each of the following. Give your answer both in index form and without using indices (where possible).

(a) $5^2 \times 5^4$    (b) $5^{10} \div 5^2$    (c) $10^3 \div 10$

(d) $12^2 \times 12$    (e) $3^3 \times 3^4$    (f) $6^0$

(g) $(1.3)^0$    (h) $\dfrac{1}{25}$    (i) $6^{10} \div 6^9$

(j) $5^3 + 5^2$    (k) $2^1 + 2^2 + 2^3$    (l) $(4^3)^2$

(m) $(5^3)^3$    (n) $(2^5)^2$    (o) $\dfrac{3^{-2}}{3^2}$

(p) $\dfrac{4^3}{4^{-2}}$    (q) $\dfrac{6}{6^2}$    (r) $5^2 \div 5^{-3}$

(s) $\dfrac{2^3 \times 2^5}{(2^2)^3}$    (t) $\dfrac{(4^2)^3}{4^2 \times 4^3}$    (u) $(5^{-2})^3$

(v) $(3^2)^{-2}$    (w) $\dfrac{2^3 \times 2^{-3}}{(2^2)^2}$    (x) $\dfrac{(3^{-2})^3}{3^{-2} \times 3^{-6}}$

**2** Investigate to find possible solutions of $n^m = m^n$.

## 1.6 Fractional indices

You should know that      $\sqrt{9} = 3$

So:   $\sqrt{9} \times \sqrt{9} = 3 \times 3 = 9 = 9^1$

We can use this to evaluate $9^{\frac{1}{2}}$.

Using the index law for multiplication:

$9^{\frac{1}{2}} \times 9^{\frac{1}{2}} = 9^{\frac{1}{2} + \frac{1}{2}} = 9^1$

But      $\sqrt{9} \times \sqrt{9} = 9^1$    so   $9^{\frac{1}{2}} = \sqrt{9}$    or   $9^{\frac{1}{2}} = 3$

Similarly,      $27^{\frac{1}{3}} \times 27^{\frac{1}{3}} \times 27^{\frac{1}{3}} = 27^{\frac{1}{3} + \frac{1}{3} + \frac{1}{3}} = 27^1$

But      $\sqrt[3]{27} \times \sqrt[3]{27} \times \sqrt[3]{27} = 27$    so   $27^{\frac{1}{3}} = \sqrt[3]{27}$   or   $27^{\frac{1}{3}} = 3$

$a^{\frac{1}{n}} = \sqrt[n]{a}$

> **Cube roots**
>
> The cube root of 27 is 3 because
>
> $3 \times 3 \times 3 = 27$
>
> The cube root is written
>
> $\sqrt[3]{27}$

**Example 6**

Work out (a) $8^{\frac{1}{3}}$  (b) $8^{\frac{2}{3}}$  (c) $8^{-\frac{1}{3}}$

(a)  $8^{\frac{1}{3}} = \sqrt[3]{8} = 2$  because $8 = 2 \times 2 \times 2$

(b)  $8^{\frac{2}{3}} = 8^{\frac{1}{3}+\frac{1}{3}} = 8^{\frac{1}{3}} \times 8^{\frac{1}{3}} = 2 \times 2 = 4$

(c)  $8^{-\frac{1}{3}} = \dfrac{1}{8^{\frac{1}{3}}} = \dfrac{1}{2}$

**Example 7**

Work out (a) $64^{\frac{1}{3}}$  (b) $64^{-\frac{2}{3}}$

(a)  $64^{\frac{1}{3}} = \sqrt[3]{64} = 4$  because $4 \times 4 \times 4 = 64$

(b)  $64^{-\frac{2}{3}} = 64^{-\frac{1}{3}} \times 64^{-\frac{1}{3}} = \dfrac{1}{64^{\frac{1}{3}}} \times \dfrac{1}{64^{\frac{1}{3}}}$

$\qquad = \dfrac{1}{4} \times \dfrac{1}{4} = \dfrac{1}{16}$

So  $64^{-\frac{2}{3}} = \dfrac{1}{64^{\frac{2}{3}}} = \dfrac{1}{16}$

## Exercise 1F

**1** Work out

(a)  $4^{\frac{1}{2}}$  (b)  $4^{-\frac{1}{2}}$  (c)  $4^{\frac{3}{2}}$

(d)  $125^{-\frac{1}{3}}$  (e)  $16^{\frac{1}{4}}$  (f)  $16^{-\frac{1}{4}}$

(g)  $16^{-\frac{3}{4}}$  (h)  $25^{-\frac{1}{2}}$  (i)  $100^{-\frac{1}{2}}$

(j)  $1000^{\frac{1}{3}}$  (k)  $25^{\frac{3}{2}}$  (l)  $8^{-\frac{2}{3}}$

**2** Work out the following. Write your answers both in index form and without using indices (where possible).

(a)  $2^3 \times 2^7$  (b)  $3^4 \div 3^2$  (c)  $12^0$

(d)  $\dfrac{(5^2)^3}{5^6}$  (e)  $3^0 + 3 + 3^2 + 3^3$  (f)  $(4^2)^{-3}$

(g)  $\dfrac{10^3}{10^5}$  (h)  $(5^{-2})^{-2}$

**3** Work out

(a)  $27^{\frac{1}{3}}$  (b)  $25^{\frac{1}{2}}$  (c)  $49^{-\frac{1}{2}}$

(d)  $(8^{-\frac{1}{3}})^{-2}$  (e)  $16^{\frac{1}{4}} \times 32^{\frac{2}{5}}$  (f)  $1000^{-\frac{2}{3}}$

## 1.7 Powers of 2 and 10

You should be able to recall very quickly the powers of 2 and the powers of 10.

Remember that   $2^3 = 2 \times 2 \times 2 = 8$   and   $2^{-3} = \dfrac{1}{2^3} = \dfrac{1}{8}$

So the powers from $2^{-5}$ to $2^5$ are:

| $2^{-5}$ | $2^{-4}$ | $2^{-3}$ | $2^{-2}$ | $2^{-1}$ | $2^0$ | $2^1$ | $2^2$ | $2^3$ | $2^4$ | $2^5$ |
|---|---|---|---|---|---|---|---|---|---|---|
| $\dfrac{1}{32}$ | $\dfrac{1}{16}$ | $\dfrac{1}{8}$ | $\dfrac{1}{4}$ | $\dfrac{1}{2}$ | $1$ | $2$ | $4$ | $8$ | $16$ | $32$ |

Similarly,

$$10^3 = 10 \times 10 \times 10 = 1000 \quad \text{and} \quad 10^{-3} = \dfrac{1}{10^3} = \dfrac{1}{1000} = 0.001$$

So the powers from $10^{-5}$ to $10^5$ are

| $10^{-5}$ | $10^{-4}$ | $10^{-3}$ | $10^{-2}$ | $10^{-1}$ | $10^0$ | $10^1$ | $10^2$ | $10^3$ | $10^4$ | $10^5$ |
|---|---|---|---|---|---|---|---|---|---|---|
| $\dfrac{1}{100\,000}$ | $\dfrac{1}{10\,000}$ | $\dfrac{1}{1000}$ | $\dfrac{1}{100}$ | $\dfrac{1}{10}$ | $1$ | $10$ | $100$ | $1000$ | $10\,000$ | $100\,000$ |
| $0.000\,01$ | $0.0001$ | $0.001$ | $0.01$ | $0.1$ | | | | | | |

---

**Example 8**

Work out the value of

(a)  $2^6$        (b)  $2^{10}$        (c)  $2^{-10}$        (d)  $10^7$        (e)  $10^{-7}$        (f)  $2^2 \times 10^3$

(a)  $2^6 = 2 \times 2 \times 2 \times 2 \times 2 \times 2$    (b)  $2^{10} = 2 \times 2 \times 2 \times 2 \times 2 \times 2 \times 2 \times 2 \times 2 \times 2 = 1024$
$\phantom{(a)}\quad = 64$

(c)  $2^{-10} = \dfrac{1}{2^{10}} = \dfrac{1}{1024}$    (d)  $10^7 = 10 \times 10 \times 10 \times 10 \times 10 \times 10 \times 10 = 10\,000\,000$

(e)  $10^{-7} = \dfrac{1}{10^7} = \dfrac{1}{10\,000\,000}$    (f)  $2^2 \times 10^3 = (2 \times 2) \times (10 \times 10 \times 10)$
$\phantom{(e)}\qquad\quad = 0.000\,000\,1$    $\phantom{(f)}\qquad\qquad\quad = 4 \times 1000$
$\phantom{(f)}\qquad\qquad\quad = 4000$

---

**Example 9**

Solve the equation   $2^{3n-1} = 64$

First recognise that $64 = 2^6$ so
$\qquad 2^{3n-1} = 2^6$

Hence, equating the indices:
$\qquad 3n - 1 = 6$
$\qquad\quad 3n = 7$ ————————————— Add 1 to both sides.
$\qquad\quad\ n = \tfrac{7}{3}$   or   $n = 2\tfrac{1}{3}$ ————— Divide both sides by 3

---

**Example 10 (Summing a series of powers)**

Find an expression for the sum $S$ of the series

$$1 + 10 + 10^2 + 10^3 + \cdots + 10^n$$

Write $S = 1 + 10 + 10^2 + 10^3 + \cdots + 10^n$

then multiply by 10:

$$10 \times S = 10(1 + 10 + 10^2 + \ldots + 10^n)$$

So      $10S = 10 + 10^2 + 10^3 + \cdots + 10^{n+1}$

and      $S = 1 + 10 + 10^2 + \cdots + 10^n$

Subtract:

$$10S = \qquad 10 + 10^2 + 10^3 + \cdots + 10^n + 10^{n+1}$$
$$-S = -1 - 10 - 10^2 - \cdots - 10^n$$
$$\overline{9S = 10^{n+1} - 1}$$

So      $S = \dfrac{10^{n+1} - 1}{9}$

> You can use this method for other similar series.

## Exercise 1G

**1**  Work out the value of
  (a)  $2^3$
  (b)  $2^{-2}$
  (c)  $10^{-4}$
  (d)  $10^{10}$
  (e)  $2^3 \times 10^5$
  (f)  $2^2 \times 10^2$
  (g)  $2^3 \times 10^{-3}$
  (h)  $2^5 \times 10^5$
  (i)  $10^{-6}$
  (j)  $2^{-8}$

**2**  Round $2^{10}$ to the nearest 100.

**3**  For values of $x$ from $-3$ to 5, draw the graphs of
  (a)  $y = 2^x$
  (b)  $y = 10^x$

> Draw up a table of values.

**4**  Solve these equations
  (a)  $10^{5n-2} = 100$
  (b)  $2^{5-2n} = 8$
  (c)  $10^{2n+3} = 0.00001$

**5**  Find an expression for the sum of the series
$$1 + 2 + 2^2 + 2^3 + \cdots + 2^n$$

## Mixed exercise 1

**1** Write 156 in prime factor form.

**2** Find the HCF and LCM of  (a) 6 and 12  (b) 18 and 30

**3** Work out  (a) $\dfrac{2^4 \times 2^3}{(2^2)^2}$  (b) $(5^2)^{-3}$

**4** Work out  (a) $81^{\frac{1}{2}}$  (b) $216^{\frac{1}{3}}$  (c) $36^{-\frac{1}{2}}$

**5** For any positive whole number $n$ its **Tau Function** $\tau(n)$ is defined as the number of positive whole number factors of $n$.
7 is a prime number. It has two factors, 1 and 7, so $\tau(7) = 2$.

(a) Show that if $p$ is *any* prime number then $\tau(p) = 2$.

(b) For any prime number $p$ and any positive value of $n$ find an expression for $\tau(p^n)$.

(c) **An investigation**

$6 \times 7 = 42$

The factors of 6 are 1, 2, 3, 6 so $\tau(6) = 4$

The factors of 42 are 1, 2, 3, 6, 7, 14, 21 and 42, so 42 has 8 factors and $\tau(42) = 8$.

$6 \times 7 = 42$ and $\tau(42) = 4 \times 2 = \tau(6) \times \tau(7)$,

so  $\tau(6 \times 7) = \tau(6) \times \tau(7)$.

Investigate to see whether or not $\tau(n \times m) = \tau(n) \times \tau(m)$ for other values of $n$ and $m$.

> Remember that $\tau(7) = 2$ (from above).

**6** One way of making the number 5 by adding 1s and 3s is
$5 = 3 + 1 + 1$.
Another different way is $5 = 1 + 3 + 1$.
Investigate the number of different ways of making any number by adding 1s and 3s.

**7** $1^3 + 2^3 + 3^3 \;=\; 1 + 8 + 27 \;=\; 36 \;=\; 6^2 \;=\; (1 + 2 + 3)^2$
$1^3 + 2^3 + 3^3 + 4^3 \;=\; 1 + 8 + 27 + 64 \;=\; 100 \;=\; 10^2$
$\qquad\qquad\qquad\qquad\qquad\quad =\; (1 + 2 + 3 + 4)^2$
Investigate whether this is true for different sets of consecutive numbers.

**8** The **last digit** of 146 is 6. This is written as LD(146) = 6.
What comments can you make about

(a) LD(any square number)  (b) LD($n \times m$)?

(c) Show that $10n + 7$ can never be a square number for any positive whole number value of $n$.

**9** Solve each of these equations.

(a) $2^{5n-2} = 1024$  (b) $2^{3n+1} = 0.125$

(c) $10^{4n+3} = 0.000\,000\,1$

**10** Find an expression for the sum of the series
$$1 + 5 + 25 + 125 + 625 + \cdots + 5^n$$

# Summary of key points

**1**  A **factor** of a number is a whole number that divides exactly into the number. The factors include 1 and the number itself.

**2**  A **multiple** of a number is the result of multiplying the number by a positive whole number.

**3**  A **prime number** is a number greater than 1 which has only two factors: itself and 1.

**4**  Any factor of a number that is a prime number is a **prime factor**.

**5**  Writing a number as the product of its prime factors is called writing it in **prime factor form**.

**6**  The **highest common factor** (HCF) of two whole numbers is the highest factor that is common to both of them.

**7**  The **lowest common multiple** (LCM) of two whole numbers is the lowest number that is a multiple of them both.

**8**  A **square number** is the result of multiplying a whole number by itself.

**9**  A **cube number** is the result of multiplying a whole number by itself, then multiplying by the number again.

**10**  To find the **square** of any number, multiply the number by itself.

**11**  If $x \times x = A$, then $x$ is the **square root** of $A$, written $\sqrt{A}$

**12**  To find the **cube** of any number, multiply the number by itself, then multiply by the number again.

**13**  If $y \times y \times y = A$, then $y$ is the cube root of $A$, written $\sqrt[3]{A}$

**14**  The power a number is raised to is called the **index** (plural **indices**).

**15**  A number written in the form $a^n$ is written in **index form**, where $n$ is the index.

**16**  The **index laws**:

- $a^n \times a^m = a^{n+m}$
- $a^n \div a^m = a^{n-m}$   or   $\dfrac{a^n}{a^m} = a^{n-m}$
- $a^0 = 1$ (where $a \neq 0$)
- $a^{-n} = \dfrac{1}{a^n}$   (where $a \neq 0$)
- $(a^n)^m = a^{n \times m}$

**17**  Fractional indices:  $a^{\frac{1}{n}} = \sqrt[n]{a}$

# 2 Essential algebra

Algebra is the branch of mathematics in which letters are used to represent numbers. This chapter shows you ways of simplifying algebraic expressions and how to solve simple equations.

You should already know that:

$$a + a = 2a \qquad a \times b = ab \qquad ab = ba \qquad a \times a = a^2$$

An **algebraic expression** is a collection of letters, numbers and symbols.

A **function** is a rule which shows how one set of quantities relates to another. A function can be written like this: $n \rightarrow 2n + 3$.

## 2.1 Evaluating algebraic expressions

You need to be able to **evaluate** expressions such as $2n + 3$, $3(n - 2)$ and $3n^2 + 1$ for different values of $n$.

**Remember:**

- Work out the parts in brackets first. ⟶ $2(n + 3)$ means add 3 to $n$ then multiply by 2.

- In an expression such as $\dfrac{n + 3}{2}$ the line acts like a bracket. ⟶ $\dfrac{n + 3}{2}$ means add 3 to $n$ then divide by 2.

- $2n$ means $2 \times n$ and $\dfrac{n}{2}$ means $n \div 2$.

- Do multiplication and division before addition and subtraction. ⟶ $2n + 1$ means multiply $n$ by 2 then add 1.
  $\dfrac{n}{2} - 3$ means divide by 2 then subtract 3.

An algebraic expression can have letters other than $n$. It can also have more than one letter, for example $a + 3b - 2c$.

### Example 1

Evaluate the expression $\dfrac{2a + b}{c}$ when $a = 3$, $b = 4$ and $c = 2$.

$$\dfrac{2a + b}{c} = \dfrac{2 \times 3 + 4}{2} \qquad \text{Work out the part above the line first.}$$

$$= \dfrac{6 + 4}{2}$$

$$= \dfrac{10}{2}$$

$$= 5$$

## Exercise 2A

Work out the value of each algebraic expression using the values given.

**1**  (a)  $4a + 1$ when $a = 3$    (b)  $3b + c$ when $b = 5$, $c = 2$

(c)  $2f - g$ when $f = 1.5$, $g = 4$    (d)  $hg - 2$ when $h = 1.5$, $g = 3$

(e)  $10 + 3x$ when $x = -2$    (f)  $2x - 3y$ when $x = 4$, $y = -2$

(g)  $2x + 3$ when $x = \frac{1}{5}$    (h)  $3ab$ when $a = \frac{1}{4}$, $b = 2$

**2**  (a)  $2(a + 3)$ when $a = 5$    (b)  $3(s - 2)$ when $s = 7$

(c)  $4(p + q)$ when $p = 5$, $q = 3$    (d)  $r(8 - s)$ when $r = 3$, $s = 5$

(e)  $3(b + 7)$ when $b = -2$    (f)  $2(3 - c)$ when $c = -4$

**3**  (a)  $5(a + b)$ when $a = 3$, $b = 4$    (b)  $4(x + y)$ when $x = 5$, $y = -3$

(c)  $\frac{a}{4} + 3$ when $a = 12$    (d)  $\frac{a}{b} + 5$ when $a = 20$, $b = 4$

(e)  $\frac{m - 4}{2}$ when $m = 12$    (f)  $\frac{7 - x}{y}$ when $x = -3$, $y = -2$

**4**  (a)  $\frac{m + n}{r}$ when $m = 8$, $n = 7$, $r = 5$

(b)  $\frac{4q + r}{6}$ when $q = 5$, $r = 4$    (c)  $\frac{3s - r}{t}$ when $s = 8$, $r = 6$, $t = 3$

(d)  $\frac{3s}{4} - r$ when $s = 8$, $r = 3$    (e)  $x - \frac{3y}{6}$ when $x = 3$, $y = -4$

## 2.2  Evaluating algebraic expressions involving squares

**Remember:**

- $n^2$ is called $n$ squared or $n$ to the power of 2. ———————→ $n^2$ means $n$ is multiplied by itself: $n \times n$.

- Squaring is done before multiplying. ———→ $2n^2 + 1$ means work out $n^2$, multiply by 2, then add 1.

A good way to remember the order in which to evaluate an algebraic expression is to use the nonsense word **BIDMAS**.

Use **BIDMAS** to help you remember the order of mathematical operations.

Follow this order:    **B**rackets
**I**ndices
**D**ivide
**M**ultiply
**A**dd
**S**ubtract

Remember:
The index in $x^2$ is $2$.
The plural of *index* is *indices*.

---

**Example 2**

Work out the value of $\dfrac{4r^2 - t}{5}$ when $r = 3$ and $t = 1$.

$$\dfrac{4r^2 - t}{5} = \dfrac{4 \times 3^2 - 1}{5}$$

$$= \dfrac{4 \times 9 - 1}{5} \quad\text{------ Indices} \;\rightharpoondown$$

$$= \dfrac{36 - 1}{5} \quad\text{------ Multiply} \;\left| \begin{array}{l}\text{Work out the top part}\\\text{first.}\end{array}\right.$$

$$= \dfrac{35}{5} \quad\text{------ Subtract} \;\rightharpoonup$$

$$= 7 \quad\text{------ Divide}$$

---

## Exercise 2B

Work out the value of each algebraic expression using the values given.

1  (a)  $4m^2 + 1$ when $m = 5$ 　　　　(b)  $3m^2 - 1$ when $m = 4$

　(c)  $2p^2 - c$ when $p = 3$, $c = 4$ 　　(d)  $4x^2 + d$ when $x = 6$, $d = 3$

　(e)  $2p^2 + 5$ when $p = -3$ 　　　　(f)  $10 - q^2$ when $q = -2$

2  (a)  $ar^2 + t$ when $r = 3$, $a = 2$, $t = 1$ 　(b)  $3m^2 + 2m$ when $m = 3$

　(c)  $p^2q - r$ when $p = 4$, $q = 2$, $r = 5$ 　(d)  $2p^2 - 3p$ when $p = 4$

　(e)  $x^2 - y^2$ when $x = -5$, $y = 3$ 　　(f)  $a^2 - b^2$ when $a = 4$, $b = -3$

3  (a)  $4p^2 + ar$ when $p = 3$, $a = 2$, $r = 4$ 　(b)  $\dfrac{p^2 + 4}{2}$ when $p = 4$

　(c)  $\dfrac{p^2}{3} + 4$ when $p = 6$ 　　　　(d)  $\dfrac{p^2}{2} + \dfrac{q^2}{3}$ when $p = 4$, $q = 6$

　(e)  $2a(b^2 + c^2)$ when $a = 3$, $b = -2$, $c = 1$ 　(f)  $\dfrac{2r^2 - t}{8}$ when $r = -3$, $t = -6$

## 2.3 Indices

A short way of writing a number multiplied by itself is to use an index. You should be used to seeing $a^2$ ($a$ squared or $a$ to the power 2). In the same way,

$$a \times a \times a = a^3 \quad\text{and}\quad a \times a \times a \times a = a^4.$$

The number of times $a$ is multiplied by itself is the index (or power).

---

**Example 3**

Simplify $y^2 \times y^3$.

Using the index law for multiplication: $a^n \times a^m = a^{n+m}$

$$y^2 \times y^3 = (y \times y) \times (y \times y \times y) = y^5$$

---

If the length of each small square on the board is $a$, then the area of each small square is $a^2$. The total area of all the small squares on the board is $64a^2$.

**Example 4**

Simplify $3a^2b \times 4a^4b^3$.

$$3a^2b \times 4a^4b^3 = (3 \times a^2 \times b) \times (4 \times a^4 \times b^3) = (3 \times 4) \times (a^2 \times a^4) \times (b \times b^3) = 12a^6b^4$$

## Exercise 2C

Simplify these algebraic expressions.

**1** (a) $a \times a^3$        (b) $b^3 \times b^2$

    (c) $c^2 \times c \times c^3$     (d) $y \times y \times y^2$

**2** (a) $2ab \times 3ab^3$     (b) $5p^2q^3 \times 2p^4q$

    (c) $3x^2y^2 \times 3x^2y^2$     (d) $st^4 \times 3st$

# 2.4 Removing brackets from algebraic expressions

To remove brackets from an algebraic expression, multiply each term inside the brackets by the term outside.

This is sometimes called **expanding the brackets**.

You can also use the areas of rectangles like these to show the same results:

$$\text{total area} = \text{length} \times \text{width}$$
$$= 2(n + 1)$$
$$\text{sum of separate areas} = 2n + 2$$

so $\qquad\qquad 2(n + 1) = 2n + 2$

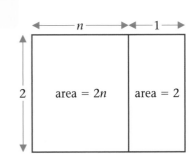

**Example 5**

Remove the brackets from the expression $4(2n - 3)$.

Multiply each term inside the brackets by 4

$$4(2n - 3) = 4 \times 2n + 4 \times -3$$
$$= 8n - 12$$

Or, using rectangles

$$\text{area of left rectangle} = \text{whole area} - \text{area of right rectangle}$$
$$4(2n - 3) = 4 \times 2n - 4 \times 3$$
$$= 8n - 12$$

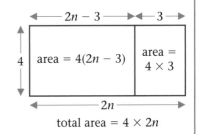

## Exercise 2D

**1** Draw rectangles to find expressions without brackets that are equivalent to these expressions:

    (a) $2(n + 3)$     (b) $4(3p + 2)$     (c) $y(2y + 3)$

    (d) $2x(x + 5)$     (e) $3(n - 2)$     (f) $1(2p - 3)$

**2**    Write these expressions without brackets:
    (a)   $4(n + 3)$           (b)   $2(p - 4)$          (c)   $5(a + 1)$
    (d)   $2(3x - 1)$         (e)   $4(5q - 3)$       (f)   $3(2r + s)$
    (g)   $a(b + 2)$         (h)   $p(p + q)$       (i)   $p(2p - 1)$

**3**    Write these expressions without brackets:
    (a)   $3(x + 6)$          (b)   $4(y - 2)$         (c)   $7(t + 1)$
    (d)   $4(3x + 2)$         (e)   $5(3y - 4)$       (f)   $2(3p + q)$
    (g)   $x(x + 3)$         (h)   $x(x + y)$       (i)   $y(3y - 2)$

**4**    Expand the brackets:
    (a)   $2(m + 5)$         (b)   $9(n - 4)$         (c)   $8(u - 1)$
    (d)   $5(7x + 3)$         (e)   $4y(y - 6)$      (f)   $3x^2(2x^2 + 5)$
    (g)   $4t^3(5t^2 - 3)$      (h)   $4x^2(3x^3 + 7y)$    (i)   $5y(3y^3 - 4x^2)$

## 2.5 Simplifying algebraic expressions

Sometimes you can simplify an algebraic expression by expanding the brackets and collecting **like terms** together.

> Terms with the same power of the same letter(s) are called **like terms**.

---

**Example 6**

Simplify the expression $3(3a + 2b) + 2(a - b)$.

$\quad 3(3a + 2b) + 2(a - b)$
$\quad\quad = 9a + 6b + 2a - 2b$ ——— First expand the brackets.
$\quad\quad = 9a + 2a + 6b - 2b$ ——— Rearrange by collecting like terms
$\quad\quad\quad\quad\quad\quad\quad\quad\quad\quad\quad\quad$ together:
$\quad\quad\quad\quad\quad\quad\quad\quad\quad\quad\quad\quad$ $9a$ and $2a$ are like terms and
$\quad\quad = 11a + 4b$ $\quad\quad\quad\quad\quad\quad$ $6b$ and $-2b$ are like terms.

---

**Example 7**

Simplify the expression $\dfrac{4n + 2}{2}$

$\quad \dfrac{4n + 2}{2}$ •

$\quad\quad = \frac{1}{2}(4n + 2)$

$\quad\quad = \frac{1}{2} \times 4n + \frac{1}{2} \times 2$ ——— Expand the brackets.

$\quad\quad = 2n + 1$

> Remember:
> The line acts like a bracket.

---

**Example 8**

Simplify the expression $x(x + 3y) + 2x(x + y)$.

$\quad x(x + 3y) + 2x(x + y)$
$\quad\quad = x^2 + 3xy + 2x^2 + 2xy$ ——— Expand the brackets.
$\quad\quad = x^2 + 2x^2 + 3xy + 2xy$ ——— Collect like terms.
$\quad\quad = 3x^2 + 5xy$

## Exercise 2E

Expand and simplify the expressions in questions **1–4**.

**1** (a) $2(3r + 1) + 2r$          (b) $3(4p - 2) - 10p$

    (c) $4(2x + y) + 2x - 3y$       (d) $2m - 3n + 3(m + n)$

**2** (a) $4(2a + b) + 2(3a - b)$     (b) $3(p + q) + 2(p - q)$

    (c) $2(3r + s) + 4(r - s)$       (d) $3(2p - q) + 3(p + q)$

**3** (a) $3(x + y) + 4(x - y)$      (b) $4(m - n) + 3(2m - n)$

    (c) $2(p - q) + 2(p - q)$       (d) $3(p - q) + 3(p + q)$

**4** (a) $3(b - a) + 1(6a - 6b)$     (b) $r(r + 2) - r$

    (c) $m(n + m) + m(n - m)$     (d) $m(3 + n) + n(1 - m)$

**5** Write these expressions in a simpler form.

(a) $\dfrac{6n + 4}{2}$      (b) $\dfrac{9n - 6}{3}$      (c) $\dfrac{10n - 20}{5}$

(d) $\dfrac{6p + 10r}{2}$      (e) $\dfrac{4r - 8q}{4}$      (f) $\dfrac{6r - 3s}{3}$

## Dealing with negative numbers

The expression $-2(3a - 2)$ has a negative number outside the brackets. You expand the brackets by multiplying each term inside the brackets by $-2$:

$$-2 \times 3a = -6a$$

$$-2(3a - 2) = -6a + 4$$

$$-2 \times -2 = +4$$

> $-2(3a - 2)$ means
> $-2 \times (3a - 2)$
> $= -6a + 4$

___ **Example 9** ___

Simplify the expression $4(2a + b) - 2(a - b)$.

$4(2a + b) - 2(a - b)$

$= 8a + 4b - 2a + 2b$ ——— Expand the brackets.

$= 8a - 2a + 4b + 2b$ ——— Collect like terms.

$= 6a + 6b$

## Exercise 2F

Simplify these expressions.

**1** (a) $4a - 3(a - b)$       (b) $2(2p + q) - 3(p - q)$

    (c) $3(2n - 3) - 4(n - 2)$    (d) $2(s - r) - 2(r - s)$

    (e) $3(x + y) - 3(x - y)$     (f) $r(s - t) - r(3 - t)$

**2** (a) $3x - 2(x + y)$        (b) $2(6x - y) - (x + y)$

    (c) $x(4x + 5) - 2x(x + 3)$   (d) $5y(4y - 3) - 2(4y - 3)$

    (e) $x(2x - 5) - 2(2x - 5)$   (f) $2y^3(2y - 3) + 3y^2(4y^2 + 5y)$

# 2.6 Factorising

**Factorising** is the opposite of expanding. You write algebraic expressions in a shorter form using brackets. It also helps you solve some algebra problems.

**Factorising** is the opposite of expanding brackets.

Here are some algebraic expressions before and after factorising:

| Before | After |
|--------|-------|
| $6x + 18$ | $6(x + 3)$ |
| $21x - 28$ | $7(3x - 4)$ |
| $x^2 - 9x$ | $x(x - 9)$ |
| $ax + 4a$ | $a(x + 4)$ |
| $x^2y - xy^2$ | $xy(x - y)$ |
| $3x^2 + 12x$ | $3x(x + 4)$ |

To factorise an expression completely, the highest common factor (HCF) must appear outside the brackets.

In $3x^2 + 12x$ the HCF of $3x^2$ and $12x$ is $3x$. The HCF is the largest term which is a factor of $3x^2$ and $12x$.

$3(x^2 + 4x)$ and $x(3x + 12)$ are both ways of factorising $3x^2 + 12x$ but they are *not factorised completely* because the HCF $3x$ does not appear outside the brackets. Factorising completely, $3x^2 + 12x = 3x(x + 4)$.

HCF of $3x^2 + 12x$

$3x^2 = 3 \times x \times x$

$12x = 3 \times 4 \times x$

HCF is $3x$

___ **Example 10** _____

Factorise $8x^2 - 12x$ completely.

$$8x^2 - 12x = 4x(x - 3)$$

$4x$ is the HCF of $8x^2$ and $-12x$

## Exercise 2G

Factorise these expressions completely.

**1**  $5x - 20$    **2**  $8x + 24$    **3**  $12x + 18$

**4**  $20x - 25$    **5**  $8x^2 - 24$    **6**  $9x^2 + 36$

**7**  $10x^2 - 15$    **8**  $x^2 + 6x$    **9**  $x^2 - x$

**10**  $px - 3p$    **11**  $qx + q^2$    **12**  $5x^2 - 15x$

**13**  $6x^2 + 9x$    **14**  $15x^2 - 35x$    **15**  $8x - 12x^2$

**16**  $ax^2 + ax$    **17**  $4ax - 6a$    **18**  $6ax^2 + 15ax$

# 2.7 Multiplying bracketed expressions

Sometimes you will need to multiply bracketed expressions by each other, for example $(e + f)(g + h)$.

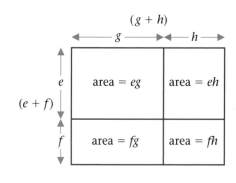

This means $(e + f)$ multiplied by $(g + h)$, or $(e + f) \times (g + h)$.

Look at the rectangles on the right.

The area of the whole rectangle is $(e + f)(g + h)$.

It is the same as the sum of the **four** separate areas so:

$$(e + f)(g + h) = eg + eh + fg + fh$$

Notice that each term in the first bracket is multiplied by each term in the second bracket:

$$e \times h$$
$$e \times g$$
$$(e + f) \ (g + h)$$
$$f \times g$$
$$f \times h$$

You can also think of the area of the rectangle as the sum of **two** separate parts:

$$(e + f)(g + h) = e(g + h) + f(g + h)$$

Think of multiplying each term in the first bracket by the whole of the second bracket.

These are two ways of thinking about the same process. The end result is the same.

This is called **multiplying out** the brackets.

___

**Example 11** ___

Multiply out the brackets in the expression $(2a + 2)(3a - 4)$.

$$(2a + 2)(3a - 4) = 2a(3a - 4) + 2(3a - 4)$$
$$= 6a^2 - 8a + 6a - 8$$
$$= 6a^2 - 2a - 8$$

___

Equations such as

$$(e + f)(g + h) = eg + eh + fg + fh$$

and   $(e + f)(g + h) = e(g + h) + f(g + h)$

which are true for all values of $e$, $f$, $g$ and $h$ are also known as **identities**.

## Exercise 2H

**1**  Expand and simplify these products, drawing rectangles to illustrate your answers.

  **(a)**  $(x + 2)(x + 1)$       **(b)**  $(x + 8)(x + 2)$

  **(c)**  $(x + 3)^2$       **(d)**  $(x + a)(x + b)$

In questions **2–12** multiply out the brackets then simplify your expressions where possible.

**2**  **(a)**  $(a + 4)(b + 3)$       **(b)**  $(c + 5)(d + 4)$

  **(c)**  $(x + 3)(y + 6)$       **(d)**  $(a + 3)(a + 8)$

  **(e)**  $(b + 7)(b + 4)$       **(f)**  $(x + 6)(x + 2)$

**3**  **(a)**  $(2a + 3)(b + 4)$       **(b)**  $(3b + 2)(c + 3)$

  **(c)**  $(4c + 3)(d + 6)$       **(d)**  $(2a + 5)(a + 3)$

  **(e)**  $(3b + 4)(b + 2)$       **(f)**  $(4c + 5)(c + 2)$

**4**  **(a)**  $(a - 4)(b - 3)$       **(b)**  $(c - 5)(d - 4)$

  **(c)**  $(x - 3)(y - 6)$       **(d)**  $(a - 3)(a - 8)$

  **(e)**  $(b - 7)(b - 4)$       **(f)**  $(x - 6)(x - 2)$

**5**  **(a)**  $(a - 4)(b + 3)$       **(b)**  $(c + 5)(d - 4)$

  **(c)**  $(x - 3)(y + 6)$       **(d)**  $(a - 3)(a + 8)$

  **(e)**  $(b - 7)(b + 4)$       **(f)**  $(x + 6)(x - 2)$

**6**  **(a)**  $(2a - 5)(b + 5)$       **(b)**  $(3b + 4)(b - 6)$

  **(c)**  $(3c - 2)(c - 3)$       **(d)**  $(3a - 4)(a - 5)$

  **(e)**  $(3x - 4) (x + 5)$       **(f)**  $(2a + 3)(a - 6)$

**7**  **(a)**  $(x + y)(2x + 3y)$       **(b)**  $(x + y)(3x - 4y)$

  **(c)**  $(x - y)(5x - 3y)$       **(d)**  $(2x + 5y)(3x + 4y)$

  **(e)**  $(3x + 5y)(2x - 5y)$       **(f)**  $(6x - 5y)(2x - 3y)$

**8**  **(a)**  $(x + 3)^2$       **(b)**  $(y - 5)^2$

  **(c)**  $(2x + 1)^2$       **(d)**  $(3y - 4)^2$

  **(e)**  $(3x + 5y)^2$       **(f)**  $(6x - 7y)^2$

> **Remember:**
> $(x + 3)^2 = (x + 3)(x + 3)$

**9**  **(a)**  $(3a + 1)(a - 2)$       **(b)**  $(3p + 2)(4p - 1)$

  **(c)**  $(3a + 2)(a + 1)$       **(d)**  $(4p + 2)(3p + 2)$

  **(e)**  $(2b - 3)(b - 1)$       **(f)**  $(4b - 1)( 2b + 1)$

**10**  **(a)**  $(a + 1)(b + 2) - ab$       **(b)**  $(2p + 1)(q - 2) + 3p - pq$

  **(c)**  $(3r - s)(r - 1) + s - 2r$       **(d)**  $(2p + 3a)(2p - 3a) + 9a^2$

**11**  **(a)**  $(3x + 1)(3x - 1)$       **(b)**  $(1 - 4x)(1 + 4x)$

  **(c)**  $(2x - 5)(2x + 5)$       **(d)**  $(7x + 2)(7x - 2)$

**12**  **(a)**  $5(x + 2)(x - 6)$       **(b)**  $4(x + 1)(x - 1)$

  **(c)**  $2(3x + 1)(5x - 1)$       **(d)**  $3(4x - 3)(3x + 2)$

Wot, no letter z?

# 2.8 Multiplying an expression by itself

You need to be able to square simple expressions.

---
**Example 12**

Expand and simplify   (a) $(x + 6)^2$    (b) $(x - 8)^2$

(a)   $(x + 6)^2 = (x + 6)(x + 6)$
$= x(x + 6) + 6(x + 6)$
$= x^2 + 6x + 6x + 36$
$= x^2 + 12x + 36$

(b)   $(x - 8)^2 = (x - 8)(x - 8)$
$= x(x - 8) - 8(x - 8)$
$= x^2 - 8x - 8x + 64$
$= x^2 - 16x + 64$

---

In general:   $(x + a)^2 = x^2 + 2ax + a^2$
$(x - b)^2 = x^2 - 2bx + b^2$

## Exercise 21

Expand and simplify the expressions in questions **1–9**.

**1**   $(x + 5)^2$         **2**   $(x - 3)^2$         **3**   $(x + 9)^2$

**4**   $(x - 2)^2$         **5**   $(p + q)^2$         **6**   $(p - q)^2$

**7**   $(3 + x)^2$         **8**   $(7 - x)^2$         **9**   $(a - x)^2$

**10**   Copy and complete these expressions by writing an appropriate number in each box.

(a)   $(x + \Box)^2 = x^2 + \Box x + 16$
(b)   $(x - \Box)^2 = x^2 - 20x + \Box$
(c)   $(x + \Box)^2 = x^2 + 2x + \Box$
(d)   $(x - \Box)^2 = x^2 - \Box x + 144$

# 2.9 Solving simple equations

Sometimes you will need to **solve** equations such as $4x + 1 = 7$.
Solving means finding the value or values of $x$ that make the equation true.

To solve an equation like this, rearrange it so that the $x$ term is on its own on one side of the equation.
The $x$ term in $4x + 1 = 7$ is $4x$.

To rearrange an equation you can use the **balancing method**:
- add the same quantity to both sides
- subtract the same quantity from both sides
- multiply both sides by the same quantity
- divide both sides by the same quantity.

Whatever you do to one side of an equation you must also do to the other side.

---

**Example 13**

Solve $4x + 1 = 7$.

$$4x + 1 = 7$$
$$4x = 7 - 1 \qquad \text{Subtract 1 from both sides.}$$
$$4x = 6$$
$$x = 1\tfrac{1}{2} \qquad \text{Divide both sides by 4.}$$

Check by substituting $1\tfrac{1}{2}$ in place of $x$ in $4x + 1 = 7$:

$$(4 \times 1\tfrac{1}{2}) + 1 = 6 + 1 = 7$$

So $1\tfrac{1}{2}$ is the solution.

---

**Example 14**

Solve $5 - 3x = 7$.

$$5 - 3x = 7$$
$$-3x = 2 \qquad \text{Subtract 5 from both sides.}$$
$$x = -\tfrac{2}{3} \qquad \text{Divide both sides by } -3.$$

Check by substituting $-\tfrac{2}{3}$ in place of $x$ in $5 - 3x = 7$:

$$5 - (3 \times -\tfrac{2}{3}) = 5 + 2 = 7$$

---

## Exercise 2J

Solve these equations and check your answers.

| | | | | | |
|---|---|---|---|---|---|
| **1** | $3x + 2 = 17$ | **2** | $5x - 2 = 18$ | **3** | $2x + 5 = 10$ |
| **4** | $5x - 1 = 12$ | **5** | $7x = 3$ | **6** | $4x + 3 = 3$ |
| **7** | $5 + 6x = 10$ | **8** | $9x - 4 = 3$ | **9** | $2x + 7 = 1$ |
| **10** | $3a + 8 = 2$ | **11** | $4b + 17 = 7$ | **12** | $5c - 1 = -13$ |
| **13** | $8d + 7 = 2$ | **14** | $8 + 10e = 3$ | **15** | $10f + 7 = 3$ |
| **16** | $6 - x = 5$ | **17** | $8 - x = 10$ | **18** | $7 - 2y = 3$ |
| **19** | $4 - 3y = 16$ | **20** | $-2a = 12$ | **21** | $-5b = 13$ |
| **22** | $5 - 2c = 2$ | **23** | $2 - 6d = 1$ | **24** | $5 - 8e = 7$ |
| **25** | $3 - 5f = 12$ | | | | |

Don't forget to check your answers by substitution!

**Mixed exercise 2**

1   In each of the following expressions $a = 2$, $b = 9$, $c = 5$.
    Work out the value of each.

   (a)  $2a + 3c$          (b)  $a^2 + c$          (c)  $3ab$

   (d)  $abc$             (e)  $(2c)^2$            (f)  $3b^2$

   (g)  $a\sqrt{b}$          (h)  $(a + b)(b + c)$    (i)  $\dfrac{2b + a}{c}$

   (j)  $\dfrac{2bc}{5a^2}$

2   Simplify
   (a)  $3a + 5b + 6a - 2b$          (b)  $2ab + 3ba$
   (c)  $a^2 + 3a - 4a^2 + a$         (d)  $7p - 4q - 2p - q$
   (e)  $8c + 5d - 9c - d$

3   Expand and simplify
   (a)  $5(3p + 2) - 2(5p - 3)$       (b)  $2(3p + 4) + 3(2p - 1)$
   (c)  $4(3a - 3b) + 5(b - a)$       (d)  $3(2q - 5) - 2(3q - 2)$

4   Expand    $p(q - p^2)$.                                      [E]

5   Expand
   (a)  $(y + 5)(y - 3)$              (b)  $(3x + 2)(4x + 1)$
   (c)  $(5y - 3)^2$                 (d)  $(3a - 2b)^2$

6   Solve
   (a)  $x - 2 = 22$       (b)  $10 - 2x = 2$      (c)  $\dfrac{x}{3} = 4$

   (d)  $5x = 3$          (e)  $8 = 3 - x$        (f)  $4 + 3x = 19$

7   Factorise completely
   (a)  $4p - 6$          (b)  $9q + 3$           (c)  $6a + 4b$
   (d)  $ab + a^2$        (e)  $2ab + 2ac$        (f)  $8a^2 - 6a$

# Summary of key points

1   $a + a = 2a$        $a \times b = ab$        $ab = ba$        $a \times a = a^2$

2   An **algebraic expression** is a collection of letters, numbers and symbols.

3   A **function** is a rule which shows how one set of quantities relates to another.
    A function can be written like this: $n \rightarrow 2n + 3$.

4   Use **BIDMAS** to help you remember the order of mathematical operations.
    Follow this order:    | **B**rackets
                          | **I**ndices
                          | **D**ivide
                          | **M**ultiply
                          | **A**dd
                          ▼ **S**ubtract

**5** To remove brackets from an algebraic expression, multiply each term inside the brackets by the term outside.

This is sometimes called **expanding the brackets**.

**6** Terms with the same power of the same letter(s) are called **like terms**.

**7** **Factorising** is the opposite of removing brackets.

**8** To factorise an expression completely, the highest common factor (HCF) must appear outside the brackets.

**9** Equations such as

$$(e + f)(g + h) = eg + eh + fg + fh$$
$$\text{and } (e + f)(g + h) = e + (g + h) + f(g + h)$$

which are true for all values of $e$, $f$, $g$ and $h$ are also known as **identities**.

**10** In general: $(x + a)^2 = x^2 + 2ax + a^2$
$(x - b)^2 = x^2 - 2bx + b^2$

**11** To rearrange an equation you can use the **balancing method**:

- add the same quantity to both sides
- subtract the same quantity from both sides
- multiply both sides by the same quantity
- divide both sides by the same quantity.

Whatever you do to one side of an equation you must also do to the other side.

# ❸ Shapes

Euclid was a Greek mathematician who lived at Alexandria in Egypt around 300 BC. In his books *The Elements*, he explained everything that was known about 2-D (plane) and 3-D (solid) shapes, like these:

This chapter investigates the properties of 2-D and 3-D shapes.

## 3.1 Angles

You should remember these key points from earlier work:

**Names of types of angles**

A quarter turn is called a right **angle**.

Two lines at right angles are **perpendicular**.

A complete turn is 360°.

The angle on a straight line is 180°.

An angle between 0° and 90° is called an **acute angle**.

An angle between 90° and 180° is called an **obtuse angle**.

An angle between 180° and 360° is called a **reflex angle**.

You need to know these properties of angles:

   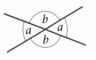

$a + b + c = 180°$

$a + b = 180°$

$a + b + c + d = 360°$

Angles which meet at a point on a straight line add up to 180°.

A pair of angles that add together to make 180° are called **supplementary angles**.

Angles which meet at a point add up to 360°.

Two straight lines which cross at a point form two pairs of **vertically opposite angles**. Vertically opposite angles are **equal**.

Angles formed when a straight line crosses a pair of parallel lines have the following properties:

**Corresponding angles** are equal. So $a = b$. You can find them by looking for an F shape.

**Alternate angles** are equal. So $a = b$. Look for a Z shape.

**Co-interior angles** $x$ and $y$ are supplementary as $x + y = 180°$. Co-interior angles are sometimes called **allied angles**. Look for a C shape.

---

**Example 1**

Find angles $a$ and $b$, giving reasons for your answers.

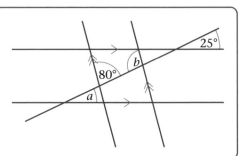

$a$ and 25° are corresponding angles, so $a = 25°$
80° and $b$ are co-interior angles, so:

$$80° + b = 180°$$
$$b = 180° - 80°$$
$$= 100°$$

---

## Exercise 3A

**1** Calculate the size of each lettered angle.

(a)

(b)

(c)

(d)

(e)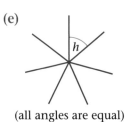

(all angles are equal)

**2** Calculate each of the lettered angles.

(a)

(b)

(c)

## 3.2  2-D shapes

### Triangles

Remember these key points from earlier work:

The **interior angles** in a triangle add up to 180°.

$$a + b + c = 180°$$

An **equilateral triangle** has:
• 3 sides equal
• 3 interior angles equal (60°).

An **isosceles triangle** has:
• 2 sides equal
• base angles equal.

A **right-angled triangle** has:
• 1 angle of 90°.

Triangles without any of these properties are called **scalene triangles**.

---

**Example 2**

Calculate the sizes of the lettered angles, giving reasons for your answers.

$34° + 92° + a = 180°$ (interior angles of a triangle)
$$a = 180° - 126° = 54°$$

$a + b = 180°$ (angles on a straight line)
$$b = 180° - 54° = 126°$$

---

### Exercise 3B

Calculate the size of each lettered angle.
Give reasons for your answers.

**1**

**2**

**3**

**4**

**5**

# Quadrilaterals

Some quadrilaterals have special names and properties:

A **square** has:
- all sides equal
- opposite sides parallel
- all interior angles 90°
- diagonals that bisect at 90°.

A **rectangle** has:
- opposite sides equal
- opposite sides parallel
- all interior angles 90°
- diagonals that bisect each other.

A **parallelogram** has:
- opposite sides equal
- opposite sides parallel
- diagonally opposite angles equal
- adjacent angles are supplementary angles
- diagonals that bisect each other.

A **rhombus** has:
- all sides equal
- opposite sides parallel
- opposite angles equal
- adjacent angles are supplementary angles
- diagonals that bisect at 90°.

A **trapezium** has:
- 1 pair of parallel lines.

An **isosceles trapezium** has:
- 1 pair of parallel lines
- 2 sides equal
- 1 line of symmetry.

A **kite** has:
- 2 pairs of adjacent sides equal
- 1 pair of opposite angles equal
- diagonals cut at 90°
- 1 line of symmetry.

An **arrowhead** has:
- 2 pairs of adjacent sides equal
- 1 line of symmetry

Each special name means the shape has *all* the properties listed.

# The sum of the interior angles of a quadrilateral

The **interior angles** in a quadrilateral add up to 360°.

You can see this by dividing it into two triangles:

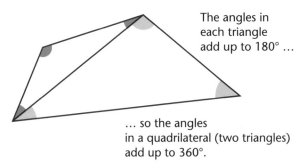

The angles in
each triangle
add up to 180° …

… so the angles
in a quadrilateral (two triangles)
add up to 360°.

# The interior angles of any polygon

The sum of the interior angles of any polygon can be found by
dividing the shape into triangles from one vertex:

**Pentagon**
3 triangles
sum of interior angles:
$3 \times 180° = 540°$

**Hexagon**
4 triangles
sum of interior angles:
$4 \times 180° = 720°$

**Octagon**
6 triangles
sum of interior angles:
$6 \times 180° = 1080°$

The number of triangles is 2 less than the number of sides of the
polygon.

For a polygon with $n$ sides:

   sum of interior angles $= (n - 2) \times 180°$

A **regular polygon** has all its sides and angles equal.

If a polygon is **regular** each interior angle can be calculated from

   interior angle $= \dfrac{(n - 2) \times 180°}{n}$

Sometimes it is simpler to calculate the exterior angle.

The sum of the **exterior angles** of any polygon is 360°.

So for a regular polygon with $n$ sides:

   **exterior angle** $= \dfrac{360°}{n}$

and   **interior angle** $= 180° - $ **exterior angle**

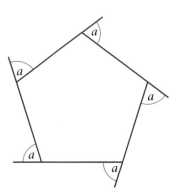

$a + a + a + a + a = 5a = 360°$

For a regular pentagon:
exterior angle $= 72°$
interior angle $= 180° - 72°$
            $= 108°$

LOGO can be used to draw polygons. The exterior angle is used in instructions like these:

```
to pentagon
repeat 5[fd 100 rt 72]
end
```

## Exercise 3C

**1**  Write down the special names of these shapes:
  **(a)**  a triangle with two sides equal
  **(b)**  a quadrilateral with opposite sides equal
  **(c)**  a quadrilateral with one pair of opposite sides parallel and equal
  **(d)**  a quadrilateral with diagonals equal and intersecting at 90°

**2**  **(a)**  Work out the sum of the interior angles of a ten-sided shape (decagon).
  **(b)**  Work out the interior angle of a regular decagon.

# 3.3 Demonstration and proof

You need to understand the difference between demonstration and proof.

## Demonstration

You can **demonstrate** the result that the interior angles of a triangle add up to 180° by drawing a triangle, tearing off the angles $b$ and $c$ and placing them next to angle $a$ to make a straight line as shown:

 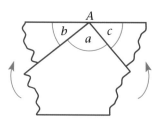

## Proof

For any triangle you can draw a straight line $PQ$ through $A$, parallel to $BC$:

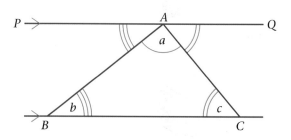

$$P\hat{A}B = b \text{ (alternate angles)}$$
$$C\hat{A}Q = c \text{ (alternate angles)}$$
$$a + b + c = 180° \text{ (angles on a straight line)}$$

So, angles in a triangle add up to 180°.

> The proof applies to **any** triangle.

# Exterior angle of a triangle

Here is another result you should know:

> The **exterior angle** of a triangle is equal to the sum of the interior opposite angles.

To prove this result first draw line $CD$ parallel to $BA$:

$$A\hat{C}D = a \text{ (alternate angles)}$$
$$D\hat{C}X = b \text{ (corresponding angles)}$$
$$A\hat{C}X = A\hat{C}D + D\hat{C}X = a + b$$

Hence,

exterior angle = the sum of the interior opposite angles.

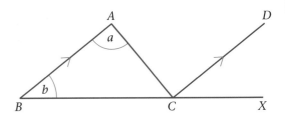

## Exercise 3D

Draw a sketch to demonstrate that the angles of a quadrilateral add up to 360°.

# 3.4  3-D shapes

A solid shape with plane faces and straight edges is called a **polyhedron** (plural: polyhedra).

The picture on the left is of the geodesic domes of the Eden Project. The outer layer of each dome is made up of hexagons and a few pentagons. The picture on the right shows the glass pyramid at the Louvre.

Some polyhedra have special names:

| cube | cuboid | square-based pyramid | triangle-based pyramid |

A **pyramid** takes its name from the shape of its base.

A **prism** is a polyhedron that has the same shape or cross-section wherever you slice it along its length. A prism takes its name from the shape of its cross-section.

triangular prism

hexagonal prism

These solids have some circular edges so they are *not* polyhedra:

circular prism
(usually called a cylinder)

circle-based pyramid
(usually called a cone)

sphere

## Nets: solid shapes unfolded

> The **net** of a 3-D shape is a 2-D shape that can be folded to make the 3-D shape.

To fold up correctly, edges which will touch must be the same length.

Both these nets will make the cuboid shown.

## Plan and elevation

You can show all the details of a 3-D shape by drawing three different 2-D views of it.

- The **plan** of a solid is the view from above.
- The **front elevation** is the view from the front.
- The **side elevation** is the view from the (right-hand) side.

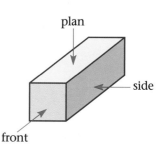

### Example 3

Draw to scale the plan and elevations of this 3-D shape.

> You should link your plans and elevations with dotted lines to show how the different drawings match up.

**Example 4**

Draw the plan and elevations of this
house and garage. Use a scale of 1 cm : 4 m.

0.75 cm — plan — 1.5 cm
0.75 cm
3 cm    0.75 cm

0.5 cm
2 cm    front elevation
1 cm

side elevation
(from the right)
1 cm
1 cm
1.5 cm

2 m
8 m
4 m
6 m
12 m
3 m

Here the scale lengths are
marked. You do not need
to label scale lengths on a
scale drawing in an exam.

## Exercise 3E

1   Sketch six different nets which would make a cube.

2   Sketch a net to make a square-based pyramid.

3   Sketch the net to make the prism
    shown on the right.
    Label the length of each side.

4 cm   7 cm
1 cm
4 cm

4   Sketch a plan, front elevation and side elevation for each of
    these solids.

    (a)

    (b)

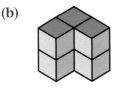

5   Sketch the plans and elevations of these shapes:

    (a)

    (b)

    (c)

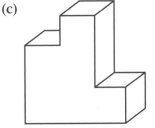

**6**  This regular pyramid has a triangular base.
Each edge of the pyramid is 5 cm long.
Sketch the plan and front elevation.

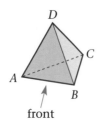

front

**7**  Here are the plan and the front elevation of a prism.
The front elevation shows the cross-section of the prism.

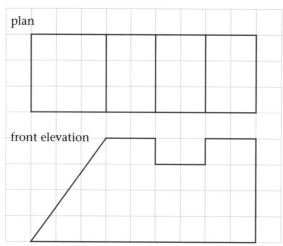

(a)  Draw a side elevation of the prism.

(b)  Draw a 3-D sketch of the prism.

**8**  The diagram shows a scale drawing.
Draw to scale the plan and the
front and side elevations from the
direction of the arrows.

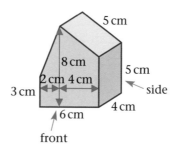

# 3.5 Congruent shapes

When 2-D shapes are exactly the same shape and size they
are **congruent**.

One shape may have to be rotated or turned over to see the match.
Corresponding sides and corresponding angles are identical.

These keys are congruent.

Triangles are congruent if one of these facts is true:

Three pairs of sides are equal (remember this with the abbreviation **SSS** for three sides).

Two pairs of sides are equal and the angles between them (the included angle) are equal (**SAS**).

Two pairs of angles are equal and the sides between them are equal (**ASA**).

Both triangles have a right angle, the hypotenuses are equal and one pair of corresponding sides is equal (**RHS**).

---

**Example 5**

State whether these pairs of shapes are congruent.
List the vertices in corresponding order and give reasons for congruency.

(a)

(b)

(c)

(a)   Yes. *ABC* is congruent to *ZXY* (SAS).

(b)   No. Only the angles are equal. The corresponding sides may not be the same length.

(c)   No. Parallelogram *ABCD* is not congruent with *QRSP*. It is not clear whether *AD* = *PQ* or *BC* = *RS*.

**Example 6**

In the diagram, *ACYX* and *BCQP* are squares.

Prove that triangles *ACQ* and *BCY* are congruent.

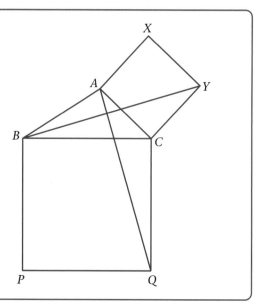

$AC = CY$          (sides of square *ACYX*)

$CQ = BC$          (sides of square *BCQP*)

$\angle ACQ = 90° + \angle ACB$

$\angle BCY = 90° + \angle ACB$

So     $\angle ACQ = \angle BCY$

So triangles *ACQ* and *YCB* are congruent (SAS).

## Exercise 3F

**1**   State whether these pairs of shapes are congruent. List the vertices in corresponding order and give reasons for congruency.

**(a)**

**(b)**

**(c)**

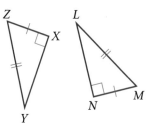

**2**   Which of these pairs of triangles are congruent? Give the vertices in corresponding order and the reason for congruency.

**(a)**

**(b)**

**(c)**

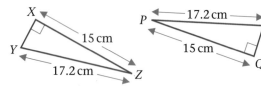

**3** ABCD is a parallelogram.

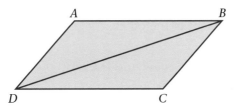

Prove that *ABD* is congruent to *CDB*.

**4** In the diagram, *AC* = *AD* and *BD* = *CE*.
Prove that triangles *ABC* and *ADE* are congruent.

**5**

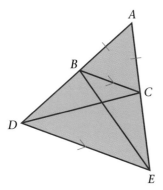

In the diagram, *ABC* is an isosceles triangle with *AB* = *AC*.

Prove that triangles *ACD* and *ABE* are congruent.

**6** In the diagram,

$$AB = BE$$
$$BD = BC$$
$$\angle AEB = \angle BDC$$

Prove that triangles *ABD* and *EBC* are congruent.

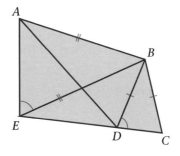

**7** State whether these triangles are congruent. Give reasons for congruency.

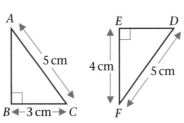

**Activity**
To prove that a statement is incorrect, you need only one **counter example**.
Draw triangles to demonstrate that SSA triangles might not be congruent.

# 3.6 Similar shapes

Shapes are **similar** if one shape is an enlargement of the other.

Polygons are similar if all corresponding angles are *equal* and the ratio of object length to image length is the same for all sides.

The **scale factor** of an enlargement is the ratio

$$\frac{\text{length of a side on one shape}}{\text{length of corresponding side on other shape}}$$

---

**Example 7**

These rectangles are similar. $B$ is an enlargement of $A$.

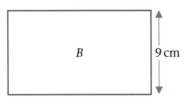

(a)   Find the scale factor of the enlargement.

(b)   Find the missing length on rectangle $B$.

(a)   Using corresponding sides, the scale factor of the enlargement is $\frac{9}{4} = 2.25$

(b)   So the length of $B$ is $7 \times 2.25 = 15.75$ cm

---

To decide whether two triangles are similar, you need to check that all the corresponding angles are equal, or that all the corresponding sides are in the same ratio.

Triangles are similar if one of these facts is true:

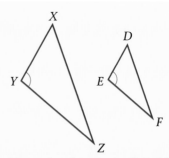

All corresponding angles are equal:

$\hat{A} = \hat{X} \quad \hat{B} = \hat{Y} \quad \hat{C} = \hat{Z}$

All corresponding sides are in the same ratio:

$$\frac{PQ}{AB} = \frac{QR}{BC} = \frac{PR}{AC} = \text{scale factor}$$

Two pairs of corresponding sides are in the same ratio and the included angles are equal:

$$\frac{XY}{DE} = \frac{YZ}{EF} \quad \hat{Y} = \hat{E}$$

**Example 8**

Find the length of the side marked *x*.

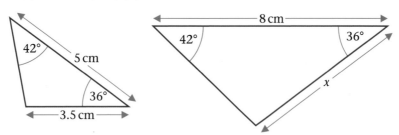

Two pairs of angles are equal, so the third pair must be equal. The triangles are similar.
The scale factor of the enlargement is $\frac{8}{5} = 1.6$

So $x = 3.5 \times 1.6 = 5.6$ cm

## Exercise 3G

1   Each pair of shapes is similar. Calculate each length marked by
    a letter.

(a)

(b)

(c)

(d)

2   Each pair of shapes is similar. Calculate the lengths marked by
    letters.

(a)

(b)

(c)

**3** Match up pairs of similar rectangles.

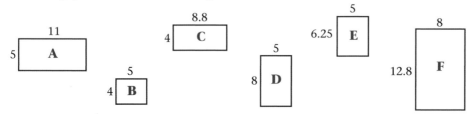

**4** Which of these shape families are always similar?

(a) all squares            (b) all rectangles

(c) all parallelograms      (d) all circles

(e) all equilateral triangles    (f) all isosceles triangles

(g) all regular hexagons      (h) all trapeziums

**5** Which of these solid shape families are always similar?

(a) cubes              (b) cuboids

(c) spheres            (d) tetrahedrons

(e) pyramids          (f) hexagonal prisms

(g) octahedrons       (h) cones

**6** Each group of three triangles has two similar and one 'different' triangle. Which triangle is 'different'?

(a)   (i)              (ii)           (iii)

(b)   (i)              (ii)           (iii)

(c)   (i)              (ii)           (iii)

**7** Write down why these pairs of triangles are similar. Calculate the length of each side marked by a letter.

(a)                 (b)                       (c)

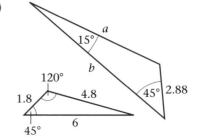

**8 (a)** Explain why the two triangles in this diagram are similar.

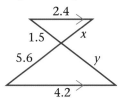

**(b)** Calculate the lengths of *x* and *y*.

## 3.7 Planes of symmetry

Some 3-D shapes can be divided by a plane to produce two identical solid shapes. The plane is called a **plane of symmetry**.

A cuboid has three planes of symmetry:

---

**Example 9**

Copy the house shape. Draw all its planes of symmetry on separate diagrams.

There are two planes of symmetry:

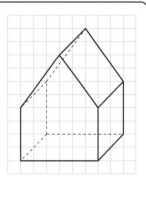

---

## Exercise 3H

**1** Write down the number of planes of symmetry for each of these solids.

**(a)**     **(b)**     **(c)**

2 Write down how many planes of symmetry a regular tetrahedron has. Draw sketches to show them all.

> A regular tetrahedron is a solid shape whose faces are equilateral triangles.

3 Draw sketches to show the planes of symmetry of
(a) a cube
(b) a regular octahedron.
What do you notice?

## Mixed exercise 3

1 (a) *MNOP* is a trapezium.
   $MN = MP$
   $N\hat{P}O = 29°$
   Find (i) $M\hat{N}P$ (ii) $P\hat{M}N$

(b) *ABCD* is a square.
   Triangle *PDC* is equilateral.
   Calculate: (i) $P\hat{C}B$ (ii) $C\hat{P}B$
   (iii) $A\hat{P}D$ (iv) $A\hat{P}B$

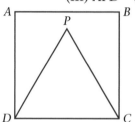

2 $V$ = number of vertices   $F$ = number of faces   $E$ = number of edges
(a) Copy and complete this table for each solid.

| Solid | $V$ | $F$ | $E$ |
|---|---|---|---|
| Cube | 8 | 6 | 12 |
| Cuboid | | | |
| Triangular prism | | | |
| Hexagonal prism | | | |
| Octagonal prism | | | |
| Triangle-based pyramid | | | |
| Square-based pyramid | | | |

> This relationship is known as Euler's theorem after the Swiss mathematician who discovered it.

(b) Write down a relationship between $V$, $F$ and $E$.

3 A regular polyhedron is a solid whose faces are regular polygons.
The same number of these polygons meet at each vertex.

| tetrahedron | cube | octahedron | dodecahedron | icosahedron |

These five regular solids were known to the Greek mathematician and philosopher Plato, and are often called the **Platonic solids**. A tetrahedron is the same as a triangle-based pyramid.

(a)  Check that Euler's theorem (from question **2**) also works for these polyhedra:

| Solid | V | F | E |
|-------|---|---|---|
| Tetrahedron | | | |
| Cube | | | |
| Octahedron | | | |
| Dodecahedron | | | |
| Icosahedron | | | |

(b)  Copy and complete this table:

| Solid | Number of triangular faces meeting at a vertex |
|-------|------------------------------------------------|
| Tetrahedron | |
| Octahedron | |
| Icosahedron | |

(c)  Explain why a regular polyhedron could not have six triangular faces meeting at a vertex.

(d)  Explain why a regular polyhedron cannot be made with regular hexagons as faces.

(e)  Construct these five 3-D solids.

**4**  Which pairs of shapes are congruent?

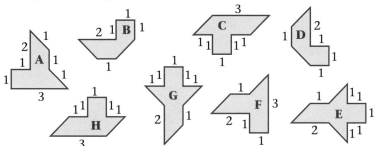

**5**  Each pair of shapes is similar. Calculate each length marked by a letter.

(a)

(b)

(c)

(d)

6  (a)  Explain why the two triangles
        in this diagram are similar.

   (b)  Calculate the lengths of *x* and *y*.

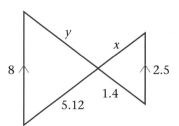

7  (a)  Name the similar triangles.

   (b)  Explain why they are similar.

   (c)  Calculate the length *AB*.

   (d)  Calculate the length *AY*.

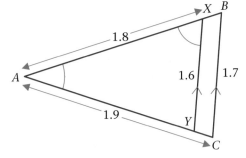

8  *PQRS* is a kite.

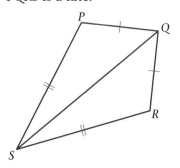

   Prove that triangle *PQS* is congruent to triangle *RSQ*.

9  The diagram shows triangles *ABC* and *ACD*.
   *BCD* is a straight line. The perpendicular
   distance from *A* to the line *BCD* is *h* cm.

   Explain why $\dfrac{\text{area of triangle } ABC}{\text{area of triangle } ACD} = \dfrac{BC}{CD}$

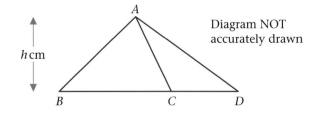

Diagram NOT
accurately drawn

10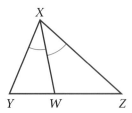

Diagram NOT
accurately drawn

   The diagram shows triangle *XYZ*.
   *W* is the point on *YZ* such that angle *YXW* = angle *WXZ*.

   Using expressions for the area of triangle *YXW* and the area of
   triangle *WXZ*, or otherwise, show that

   $$\frac{XY}{XZ} = \frac{YW}{WZ}$$

# Summary of key points

**1** Properties of angles:

$a + b + c = 180°$

$a + b = 180°$

$a + b + c + d = 360°$

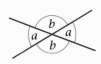

Angles which meet at a point on a straight line add up to 180°.

A pair of angles that add together to make 180° are called **supplementary angles**.

Angles which meet at a point add up to 360°.

Two straight lines which cross at a point form two pairs of **vertically opposite angles**. Vertically opposite angles are **equal**.

**2** Angles formed when a straight line crosses a pair of parallel lines have the following properties:

**Corresponding angles** are equal. So $a = b$. You can find them by looking for an F shape.

**Alternate angles** are equal. So $a = b$. Look for a Z shape.

**Co-interior angles** $x$ and $y$ are supplementary as $x + y = 180°$. Co-interior angles are sometimes called **allied angles**. Look for a C shape.

**3** The **interior angles** in a triangle add up to 180°.

$a + b + c = 180°$

**4**

An **equilateral triangle** has:
• 3 sides equal
• 3 interior angles equal (60°).

An **isosceles triangle** has:
• 2 sides equal
• base angles equal.

A **right-angled triangle** has:
• 1 angle of 90°.

Triangles without any of these properties are called **scalene triangles**.

**5** Some quadrilaterals have special names and properties.

A **square** has:
• all sides equal
• opposite sides parallel
• all interior angles 90°
• diagonals that bisect at 90°.

A **rectangle** has:
• opposite sides equal
• opposite sides parallel
• all interior angles 90°
• diagonals that bisect each other.

A **parallelogram** has:
• opposite sides equal
• opposite sides parallel
• diagonally opposite angles equal
• adjacent angles are supplementary angles
• diagonals that bisect each other.

A **rhombus** has:
• all sides equal
• opposite sides parallel
• opposite angles equal
• adjacent angles are supplementary angles
• diagonals that bisect at 90°.

A **trapezium** has:
• 1 pair of parallel lines.

An **isosceles trapezium** has:
• 1 pair of parallel lines
• 2 sides equal
• 1 line of symmetry.

A **kite** has:
• 2 pairs of adjacent sides equal
• 1 pair of opposite angles equal
• diagonals cut at 90°
• 1 line of symmetry.

An **arrowhead** has:
• 2 pairs of adjacent sides equal
• 1 line of symmetry

Each special name means the shape has all the properties listed.

**6** The **interior angles** in a quadrilateral add up to 360°.

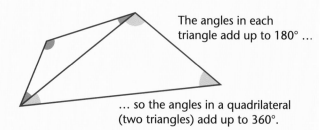

The angles in each triangle add up to 180° …

… so the angles in a quadrilateral (two triangles) add up to 360°.

**7** For a polygon with $n$ sides:

sum of interior angles $= (n - 2) \times 180°$

**8** If a polygon is **regular** each interior angle can be calculated from

interior angle $= \dfrac{(n - 2) \times 180°}{n}$

**9** The sum of the **exterior angles** of any polygon is 360°.

**10** The **exterior angle** of a triangle is equal to the sum of the interior opposite angles.

interior opposite angles

exterior angle

$a + b$

**11** The **net** of a 3-D shape is a 2-D shape that can be folded to make the 3-D shape.

**12** When 2-D shapes are exactly the same shape and size they are **congruent**.

**13** Triangles are congruent if one of these facts is true:

Three pairs of sides are equal (remember this with the abbreviation **SSS** for three sides).

Two pairs of sides are equal and the angles between them (the included angle) are equal (**SAS**).

Two pairs of angles are equal and the sides between them are equal (**ASA**).

Both triangles have a right angle, the hypotenuses are equal and one pair of corresponding sides is equal (**RHS**).

**14** Shapes are **similar** if one shape is an enlargement of the other.

**15** The **scale factor** of an enlargement is the ratio $\dfrac{\text{length of a side on one shape}}{\text{length of corresponding side on other shape}}$

**16**

      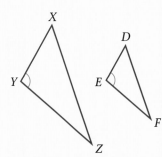

All corresponding angles are equal:

$\hat{A} = \hat{X} \quad \hat{B} = \hat{Y} \quad \hat{C} = \hat{Z}$

All corresponding sides are in the same ratio:

$\dfrac{PQ}{AB} = \dfrac{QR}{BC} = \dfrac{PR}{AC} = \text{scale factor}$

Two pairs of corresponding sides are in the same ratio and the included angles are equal:

$\dfrac{XY}{DE} = \dfrac{YZ}{EF} \quad \hat{Y} = \hat{E}$

**17** Some 3-D shapes can be divided by a plane to produce two identical 2-D shapes. The plane is called a **plane of symmetry**.

# 4 Fractions and decimals

All these things can be divided into parts called **fractions**:

A football pitch has two halves. Each part is $\frac{1}{2}$ the pitch.

This CD has eight equal sectors. Each sector is $\frac{1}{8}$ of the disk.

A chessboard has 64 equal squares. Each square is $\frac{1}{64}$ of the board.

A fraction is a package of information. For example, if $\frac{3}{8}$ of my computer disk is full of data:

The top number shows how many parts are full of data.

The top number is called the **numerator**.

$$\frac{3}{8}$$

The bottom number shows how many parts the disk is divided into.

The bottom number is called the **denominator**.

In your GCSE exam, fractions will usually appear in the context of a number problem, or in questions on probability, areas or volumes.

This chapter shows you how to add, subtract, multiply and divide fractions, to order fractions and decimals, and to use mental and written methods.

You should remember these key points from earlier work:

$\frac{5}{2}$ is called an **improper fraction**. The numerator is greater than the denominator.

$2\frac{1}{2}$ is called a **mixed number**. It contains a whole number part and a fractional part smaller than 1.

Mixed numbers can be written as improper fractions.
Improper fractions can be written as mixed numbers.

## 4.1 Equivalent fractions

You can find **equivalent fractions** by multiplying (or dividing) the top and bottom of a fraction by the same number.

Here are three examples:

$\frac{3}{5} = \frac{6}{10}$ so $\frac{3}{5}$ and $\frac{6}{10}$ are equivalent

$\frac{3}{5} = \frac{9}{15}$ so $\frac{3}{5}$ and $\frac{9}{15}$ are equivalent

$\frac{12}{20} = \frac{3}{5}$ so $\frac{12}{20}$ and $\frac{3}{5}$ are equivalent

So $\frac{3}{5}, \frac{6}{10}, \frac{9}{15}$ and $\frac{12}{20}$ are all equivalent fractions.

**Example 1**

Find the first five equivalent fractions of $\frac{5}{7}$.

$$\frac{5}{7} = \frac{10}{14} = \frac{15}{21} = \frac{20}{28} = \frac{25}{35} = \frac{30}{42}$$

×3
×2
×2
×3

**Example 2**

Complete these equivalent fractions:  (a) $\frac{3}{8} = \frac{?}{16}$  (b) $\frac{4}{5} = \frac{?}{10} = \frac{?}{25}$

(a) $\frac{3}{8} = \frac{?}{16}$  so  $\frac{3}{8} = \frac{6}{16}$  (b) $\frac{4}{5} = \frac{?}{10} = \frac{?}{25}$  so  $\frac{4}{5} = \frac{8}{10} = \frac{20}{25}$

×2  ×5  ×2
×2  ×5

## Exercise 4A

**1**  Copy and complete these sets of equivalent fractions:

   (a) $\frac{3}{4} = \frac{}{8} = \frac{}{12} = \frac{}{16} = \frac{}{20} = \frac{}{24}$

   (b) $\frac{2}{7} = \frac{}{14} = \frac{}{21} = \frac{}{28} = \frac{}{35} = \frac{}{42}$

   (c) $\frac{4}{5} = \frac{}{10} = \frac{}{15} = \frac{}{20} = \frac{}{25} = \frac{}{30}$

   (d) $\frac{3}{9} = \frac{}{18} = \frac{}{27} = \frac{}{36} = \frac{}{45} = \frac{}{54}$

In questions **2** and **3**, copy and complete the pairs of equivalent fractions.

**2**  (a) $\frac{1}{6} = \frac{}{18}$

   (b) $\frac{3}{7} = \frac{}{14}$

   (c) $\frac{3}{8} = \frac{}{48}$

   (d) $\frac{4}{7} = \frac{}{21}$

   (e) $\frac{5}{6} = \frac{}{36}$

   (f) $\frac{2}{3} = \frac{6}{}$

   (g) $\frac{4}{9} = \frac{24}{}$

   (h) $\frac{5}{7} = \frac{}{56}$

**3**  (a) $\frac{9}{10} = \frac{90}{}$

   (b) $\frac{3}{5} = \frac{}{15}$

   (c) $\frac{2}{5} = \frac{}{20}$

   (d) $\frac{5}{8} = \frac{}{40}$

   (e) $\frac{8}{9} = \frac{40}{}$

   (f) $\frac{7}{12} = \frac{84}{}$

   (g) $\frac{7}{8} = \frac{49}{}$

   (h) $\frac{2}{9} = \frac{}{81}$

## 4.2 Ordering fractions

You can **order** fractions by rewriting them as equivalent fractions with a common denominator.

---

**Example 3**

Put the following fractions in order of size, smallest first:

$$\frac{2}{3}, \quad \frac{5}{8}, \quad \frac{7}{12}$$

The smallest number that is a multiple of 3, 8 and 12 is 24. Write them as equivalent fractions with denominator 24:

$$\frac{2}{3} = \frac{2 \times 8}{3 \times 8} = \frac{16}{24}$$

$$\frac{5}{8} = \frac{5 \times 3}{8 \times 3} = \frac{15}{24}$$

$$\frac{7}{12} = \frac{7 \times 2}{12 \times 2} = \frac{14}{24}$$

So, in order of size, smallest first: $\frac{14}{24}, \frac{15}{24}, \frac{16}{24} = \frac{7}{12}, \frac{5}{8}, \frac{2}{3}$

> 24 is the LCM of 3, 8 and 12.

> Compare the three fractions.

---

### Exercise 4B

In each question, put the fractions in order of size, smallest first.

**1** $\frac{1}{2}, \frac{2}{3}, \frac{5}{12}$   **2** $\frac{2}{5}, \frac{5}{8}, \frac{3}{7}$   **3** $\frac{3}{4}, \frac{7}{8}, \frac{8}{12}$   **4** $\frac{2}{15}, \frac{1}{5}, \frac{1}{3}$   **5** $\frac{13}{16}, \frac{7}{8}, \frac{5}{6}$

## 4.3 Ordering decimals

**Decimals** are used for parts of a number that are smaller than 1.

| | Hundreds | Tens | Units | . | tenths | hundredths | thousandths | |
|---|---|---|---|---|---|---|---|---|
| 1.12 | | | 1 | . | 1 | 2 | | This equals $1 + \frac{1}{10} + \frac{2}{100}$ |
| 15.8 | | 1 | 5 | . | 8 | | | This equals $15 + \frac{8}{10}$ |
| 3.576 | | | 3 | . | 5 | 7 | 6 | This equals $3 + \frac{5}{10} + \frac{7}{100} + \frac{6}{1000}$ |

> A place value table is a useful way of relating decimal numbers to fractions.

> This is a decimal point. It separates the whole numbers from the part that is smaller than 1.

**Example 4**

Put the number 7.3208 into a place value table and write it in its separate parts.

You say 'seven point three, two, zero, eight'.

| Hundreds | Tens | Units | . | tenths | hundredths | thousandths | ten thousandths |
|----------|------|-------|---|--------|------------|-------------|------------------|
|          |      | 7     | . | 3      | 2          | 0           | 8                |

7.3208

Separate parts

This equals $7 + \frac{3}{10} + \frac{2}{100} + \frac{8}{10\,000}$

You will often need to sort measurements and other numbers into size order.
You need to be able to sort decimals as well as whole numbers.

**Example 5**

Rearrange these numbers in order of size, largest first:

1.07, 1.7, $1\frac{7}{8}$, 2, 1.085

First write any fractions as decimals. Then compare whole numbers, then digits in the tenths place, then digits in the hundredths place, and so on.

$1\frac{7}{8} = 1.875$

$7 \div 8 = 0.875$

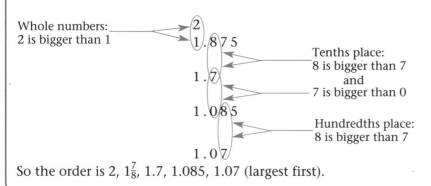

Whole numbers:
2 is bigger than 1

Tenths place:
8 is bigger than 7
and
7 is bigger than 0

Hundredths place:
8 is bigger than 7

So the order is 2, $1\frac{7}{8}$, 1.7, 1.085, 1.07 (largest first).

## Exercise 4C

1 Make a place value table with these headings:

You will need room for 16 answers.

Put each of the numbers into the table and write them in their separate parts.

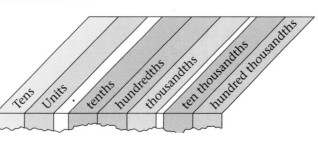

(a) 0.26    (b) 1.79    (c) 38.24    (d) 14.8

(e) 0.0101    (f) 0.033    (g) 2.645    (h) 80.934

(i) 4.398 52    (j) 0.0011    (k) 5.107    (l) 9.8302

(m) 7.457    (n) 13.0306    (o) 54.705    (p) 10.503 01

## Exercise 5F

1 As part of his geography fieldwork, Tony took measurements of the steepness of slopes. The steepness was measured as the angle the slope made with the horizontal. Tony's results are shown below.

15° 16° 9° 21° 32° 37° 25° 36° 40° 8° 32°
13° 21° 32° 29 32° 29° 32° 7° 4° 18° 17°

Copy and complete the frequency distribution table below, using four equal class intervals.

| Class interval (steepness in °) | Tally | Frequency |
|---|---|---|
| 1–10 | | |

[E]

2 Forty people took part in a clay pigeon shooting competition. The points they scored are shown below.

18  24  19   3  24  11  25  10  25  14
25  14  25   9  16  26  21  27  13  23
 5  26  22  12  27  20   7  28  21  20
22  16  12  25   7  25  19  17  15   8

(a) Using the class intervals 1–5, 6–10, 11–15, 16–20, 21–25, 26–30, construct the frequency table.

(b) Use the same data to construct a frequency table with ten class intervals.

(c) Which of your frequency tables do you think is better? Why?

3 Neville weighed 3 dozen hens' eggs to see if there was much difference between them. They all came from boxes marked *Large*. These are his results:

63.1 g  65.4 g  61.9 g  62.2 g  63.4 g  65.1 g  61.7 g  62.2 g
64.9 g  63.5 g  67.1 g  62.8 g  61.9 g  62.6 g  63.1 g  64.3 g
65.0 g  63.7 g  65.2 g  61.8 g  62.1 g  63.5 g  65.1 g  66.3 g
64.4 g  62.3 g  61.5 g  63.7 g  64.7 g  65.1 g  62.3 g  62.8 g
64.7 g  62.2 g  63.6 g  61.4 g

Use class intervals 61.0–61.9, 62.0–62.9, 63.0–63.9, 64.0–64.9, 65.0–65.9, 66.0 and over, to construct a frequency table.

---

**Activity – Hand-span**

(a) Measure the hand-span of each person in your class.

(b) Record the data in a frequency table using class intervals of equal width.

(c) Draw a histogram to display your data.

2   Rearrange each set of measurements in order of size, largest first.

   (a)   4.101 m, 4.009 m, 4.0059 m

   (b)   $\frac{1}{8}$ kg, 0.55 kg, 0.525 kg, 1.25 kg

   (c)   5.202 km, 5.305 km, 5.306 km, 5.204 km

   (d)   $9\frac{9}{10}$ tonnes, 9.904 tonnes, 9.804 tonnes, 9.99 tonnes

   (e)   Times taken in an experiment for a model car to roll down
a slope: $5\frac{3}{4}$ s, 6.556 s, 5.623 s, 6.554 s

   (f)   The capacities of four containers:
2.02 cl,  $\frac{1}{5}$ cl,   2.0 cl,   0.022 cl

   (g)   The distances Barry runs before he is out of breath:
6.202 km, 6.306 km, 6.204 km, 6.305 km

   (h)   The weights of four lorries on a weighbridge:
4.512 tonnes, 6.443 tonnes, 6.448 tonnes, 6.643 tonnes

   (i)   The widths of four machine parts:
1.08 cm, 9.8 cm, 9.08 cm, $10\frac{4}{5}$ cm

   (j)   The lengths of four tubes:
8.701 m, 8.8 m, 8.88 m, 8.801 m

## 4.4  Mental calculations with decimals

You need to be able to calculate with decimals without using a
calculator.

---

**Example 6**

Work out 4.5 + 3.8

$$3.8 = 3 + 0.8$$

So   $4.5 + 3.8 = 4.5 + 3 + 0.8$

$$= 5.3 + 3 \text{———Adding 0.8 to 4.5}$$

$$= 8.3 \text{———Adding 3 to 5.3}$$

> Split into whole number and decimal parts.

> You should be able to do this is in your head.

---

**Example 7**

Work out 54.6 − 6.7

$$54.6 − 6.7 = 54.6 − 6 − 0.7$$

$$= 53.9 − 6 \text{——— Subtracting 0.7 from 54.6}$$

$$= 47.9 \text{——— Subtracting 6 from 53.9}$$

> You should be able to do this in your head.

**Example 8**

Work out $3.8 \times 2$
Rewrite without the decimal point:
$$38 \times 2 = 76$$
Count the number of decimal places in the question: one.
The answer will have one decimal place, 7.6

**Example 9**

Work out $3.2 \div 4$
Rewrite without the decimal point:
$$32 \div 4 = 8$$
Count the number of decimal places in the question: one.
So the answer is 0.8

## Exercise 4D

Write down the answers to the following calculations.

1   $9.7 + 3.4$      2   $8.4 + 11.9 + 7.6$      3   $11.2 - 9.5$      4   $56.3 - 27.5$

5   $3.8 + 2.7 - 1.6$    6   $11.5 + 7.6 - 12.7$    7   $5.3 \times 2$      8   $6.9 \times 4$

9   $4.8 \div 4$      10   $7.8 \div 6$      11   $12.6 \div 2$      12   $25.5 \div 5$

13   Use the information
$$73 \times 154 = 11\,242$$
to write down the value of
(a)   $7.3 \times 1.54$      (b)   $112\,420 \div 0.73$

## 4.5 Written methods for dividing decimals

You need to be able to divide by decimals. It is easier to divide by a whole number, so first multiply the dividing number by a power of ten so that it becomes a whole number. Then multiply the number to be divided by the same power of ten.

**Example 10**

Work out $8.704 \div 0.17$ without using a calculator.
First multiply 0.17 by 100 to give 17. Then multiply 8.704 by 100 to give 870.4.
Here are three ways of setting out the calculation:

**Method 1**   Long division

Follow these steps:

17 divides into 87
5 times remainder 2

17 divides into 20
1 time remainder 3

17 divides into 34
2 times exactly

$$17\overline{)870.4}$$

$$\begin{array}{r} 5 \\ 17\overline{)870.4} \\ -85 \\ \hline 2 \end{array}$$

$$\begin{array}{r} 51 \\ 17\overline{)870.4} \\ -85\downarrow \\ \hline 20 \\ -\ 17 \\ \hline 3 \end{array}$$

$$\begin{array}{r} 51.2 \\ 17\overline{)870.4} \\ -85 \\ \hline 20 \\ -\ 17 \\ \hline 3\ 4 \\ 3\ 4 \\ \hline 0 \end{array}$$

So 17 divides into 870.4 **51.2 times**.

**Method 2**   Short division

This is a shorter way of setting out the steps in method 1:

$$\begin{array}{r} 5\ 1.\ 2 \\ 1\overline{)787^2 0.^3 4} \end{array}$$

**Method 3**   Repeated subtraction

Here you need to multiply both numbers by 1000 to remove the decimals:

$$8704 - 170 = 8534$$
$$8534 - 170 = 8364$$

You would have to do this 512 times – not a practical method – and then sort out the decimal point by dividing by 10.

## Exercise 4E

 Work these out, showing all your working.

**1**  (a)  $4 \div 0.5$          (b)  $12 \div 0.3$          (c)  $1.2 \div 0.5$

**2**  (a)  $3.42 \div 0.2$       (b)  $14.6 \div 0.5$        (c)  $18.2 \div 0.7$

**3**  (a)  $39 \div 1.5$         (b)  $76.85 \div 5.3$       (c)  $356.9 \div 0.86$

   (d)  $813.6 \div 0.18$         (e)  $239.66 \div 0.46$     (f)  $129.26 \div 2.3$

## 4.6 Changing fractions to decimals

A fraction such as $\frac{3}{4}$ can be thought of as $3 \div 4$. You can change fractions into decimals easily using a calculator:

$$3 \div 4 = 0.75$$

You can check this:

$$0.75 \text{ is equal to } \frac{75}{100}$$

$$\frac{75}{100} \text{ simplifies to the equivalent fraction } \frac{3}{4}$$

So the decimal 0.75 is equivalent to the fraction $\frac{3}{4}$.

> You can convert a fraction to a decimal by dividing the numerator by the denominator.

---

**Example 11**

Convert these to decimals.

(a)  $\frac{3}{8}$                          (b)  $4\frac{1}{5}$

(a)  $\frac{3}{8} = 3 \div 8 = 0.375$       (b)  $4\frac{1}{5} = 4 + \frac{1}{5}$

$$\frac{1}{5} = 1 \div 5 = 0.2$$

$$\text{So } 4\frac{1}{5} = 4 + 0.2 = 4.2$$

---

## Exercise 4F

Write these as decimals.

**1**  (a)  $\frac{4}{5}$       (b)  $\frac{1}{4}$       (c)  $1\frac{1}{8}$       (d)  $\frac{19}{100}$

   (e)  $3\frac{3}{5}$          (f)  $\frac{13}{25}$      (g)  $\frac{5}{8}$        (h)  $3\frac{17}{40}$

**2**  (a)  $\frac{7}{50}$      (b)  $4\frac{3}{16}$      (c)  $3\frac{3}{20}$      (d)  $4\frac{5}{16}$

   (e)  $\frac{7}{1000}$        (f)  $1\frac{7}{25}$      (g)  $15\frac{15}{16}$    (h)  $2\frac{7}{20}$

You can convert a decimal to a fraction.

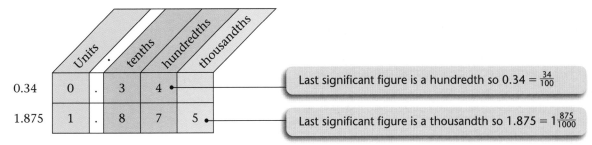

| | Units | . | tenths | hundredths | thousandths | |
|---|---|---|---|---|---|---|
| 0.34 | 0 | . | 3 | 4 | | Last significant figure is a hundredth so $0.34 = \frac{34}{100}$ |
| 1.875 | 1 | . | 8 | 7 | 5 | Last significant figure is a thousandth so $1.875 = 1\frac{875}{1000}$ |

You can write 0.34 as $\frac{34}{100}$ which simplifies to $\frac{17}{50}$.

1.875 is $1\frac{875}{1000}$ which simplifies to $1\frac{7}{8}$.

---

**Example 12**

Write these as fractions in their simplest form.

(a)   0.204             (b)   1.17             (c)   2.4375

(a)   $0.204 = \frac{204}{1000} = \frac{51}{250}$       (b)   $1.17 = \frac{117}{100}$

cannot be simplified further

(c)   $2.4375 = 2\frac{4375}{10\,000} = 2\frac{175}{400} = 2\frac{7}{16}$

---

## Exercise 4G

Write these as fractions in their simplest form.

**1**   (a)   0.48   (b)   0.25   (c)   1.7   (d)   3.406   (e)   4.003

**2**   (a)   2.025   (b)   0.049   (c)   4.875   (d)   3.75   (e)   10.101

**3**   (a)   0.625   (b)   2.512   (c)   0.8125   (d)   14.14   (e)   9.1875

## Recurring decimals

Not all fractions have an exact equivalent decimal.

The fraction $\frac{2}{3}$ is $2 \div 3 = 0.6666666...$ . This is called a **recurring decimal** since one of the digits recurs (repeats).

You usually put a dot over the digits that repeat:

$\frac{2}{3} = 0.6666666... = 0.\dot{6}$    $\frac{5}{12} = 0.4166666... = 0.41\dot{6}$

$\frac{1}{3} = 0.3333333... = 0.\dot{3}$    $\frac{3}{11} = 0.2727272... = 0.\dot{2}\dot{7}$

$\frac{7}{9} = 0.7777777... = 0.\dot{7}$

$\frac{1}{7} = 0.142857142857142857... = 0.\dot{1}4285\dot{7}$

The two dots show that all the digits from 1 to 7 repeat.

**Recurring decimal notation:**
$0.\dot{3}$ means 0.3333333... recurring and
$0.\dot{1}\dot{7}$ means 0.17171717... recurring.

06666667

If you work out $2 \div 3$ or $\frac{2}{3}$ on a calculator the result on the display could be 0.6666667. The result has been corrected to 7 s.f. by the calculator.

You need two dots here since both the 2 and the 7 repeat.

**Example 13**

Write these as recurring decimals.   (a) $\frac{6}{11}$   (b) $3\frac{8}{9}$

Write your answers

(i)   as shown on the calculator display
(ii)  using recurring decimal notation.

(a)  (i)  $\frac{6}{11} = 6 \div 11 = 0.5454545$   (ii) $0.\dot{5}\dot{4}$

(b)  (i)  $3\frac{8}{9} = 3 + (8 \div 9) = 3.8888888$ (or 3.8888889)   (ii) $3.\dot{8}$

Your calculator may round
3.8888888 to 3.8888889

## Exercise 4H

Convert these fractions to recurring decimals.

Write your answers

(i)   as shown on the calculator display
(ii)  using recurring decimal notation.

**1** $\frac{5}{6}$   **2** $1\frac{2}{9}$   **3** $3\frac{1}{6}$   **4** $\frac{11}{12}$   **5** $5\frac{5}{9}$

**6** $4\frac{9}{11}$   **7** $\frac{3}{44}$   **8** $2\frac{7}{11}$   **9** $9\frac{21}{22}$   **10** $\frac{25}{30}$

# 4.7 Adding and subtracting fractions

## Adding fractions with the same denominator

It is easy to add fractions when they have the same denominator.
You add the numerators. You must not add the denominators.

**Example 14**

Work out:   (a) $\frac{4}{9} + \frac{1}{9}$   (b) $\frac{7}{8} + \frac{5}{8}$   (c) $1\frac{1}{5} + 2\frac{3}{5}$

Add the top numbers only

(a)  $\frac{4}{9} + \frac{1}{9} = \frac{4+1}{9} = \frac{5}{9}$

(b)  $\frac{7}{8} + \frac{5}{8} = \frac{7+5}{8} = \frac{12}{8} = \frac{3}{2} = 1\frac{1}{2}$ ←  Change to a mixed number

Simplify

(c)  $1\frac{1}{5} + 2\frac{3}{5} = 3 + \frac{1}{5} + \frac{3}{5} = 3 + \frac{1+3}{5} = 3\frac{4}{5}$

Add the whole numbers first

**Why you don't add denominators**

$\frac{1}{8}$ + $\frac{3}{8}$ = $\frac{4}{8}$

not $\frac{4}{16}$ !

## Adding fractions with different denominators

$$\frac{3}{4} + \frac{1}{8} = ?$$

The denominators of these fractions are different.

---

**Example 15**

Work out  (a) $1\frac{3}{4} + 2\frac{1}{8}$   (b) $\frac{2}{3} + \frac{1}{5}$   (c) $\frac{5}{6} + \frac{3}{4}$

Add the whole numbers first

(a)  $1\frac{3}{4} + 2\frac{1}{8} = 3 + \frac{3}{4} + \frac{1}{8}$

To add $\frac{3}{4}$ and $\frac{1}{8}$ find equivalent fractions with the same denominator.

$\frac{3}{4}$ is equivalent to $\frac{6}{8}$

$\frac{3}{4} + \frac{1}{8} = \frac{6}{8} + \frac{1}{8} = \frac{7}{8}$ •————— Write $\frac{3}{4}$ as an equivalent fraction with denominator 8.

So  $1\frac{3}{4} + 2\frac{1}{8} = 3\frac{7}{8}$

(b)  $\frac{2}{3} + \frac{1}{5}$ •————— The smallest number that is a multiple of both 3 and 5 is 15, so change both the $\frac{2}{3}$ and the $\frac{1}{5}$ to equivalent fractions with denominator 15.

$\frac{2}{3}$ is equivalent to $\frac{10}{15}$, and $\frac{1}{5}$ is equivalent to $\frac{3}{15}$.

So  $\frac{2}{3} + \frac{1}{5} = \frac{10}{15} + \frac{3}{15} = \frac{13}{15}$

(c)  $\frac{5}{6} + \frac{3}{4} = \frac{10}{12} + \frac{9}{12} = \frac{19}{12} = 1\frac{7}{12}$ •————— The smallest number that is a multiple of both 6 and 4 is 12, so change both fractions to equivalent fractions with denominator 12.
You could use any multiple of 12 as the denominator.

---

To **add** fractions, change them to equivalent fractions that have the same denominator (bottom). Then add the numerators.

## Exercise 4I

Work out the additions in questions **1–3**.

**1**  (a) $\frac{1}{8} + \frac{3}{8}$    (b) $\frac{2}{7} + \frac{4}{7}$    (c) $\frac{2}{5} + \frac{4}{5}$    (d) $\frac{9}{10} + \frac{7}{10}$

   (e) $\frac{7}{9} + 2\frac{4}{9}$    (f) $\frac{5}{6} + 1\frac{5}{6}$    (g) $\frac{3}{4} + \frac{3}{4} + \frac{1}{4}$    (h) $\frac{3}{8} + \frac{5}{8} + \frac{7}{8}$

**2**  (a) $\frac{5}{8} + \frac{1}{4}$    (b) $1\frac{1}{2} + 2\frac{1}{8}$    (c) $\frac{1}{2} + \frac{7}{8}$    (d) $2\frac{3}{4} + 3\frac{7}{8}$

   (e) $1\frac{3}{4} + 2\frac{5}{16}$    (f) $\frac{3}{4} + 3\frac{5}{8}$    (g) $\frac{3}{8} + \frac{11}{16}$    (h) $2\frac{9}{16} + 1\frac{5}{8}$

**3**  (a) $\frac{1}{5} + \frac{3}{8}$    (b) $\frac{1}{5} + \frac{1}{6}$    (c) $1\frac{3}{10} + 1\frac{2}{3}$    (d) $\frac{2}{3} + \frac{2}{7}$

   (e) $3\frac{1}{6} + \frac{2}{7}$    (f) $2\frac{5}{6} + 1\frac{1}{7}$    (g) $3\frac{2}{5} + 2\frac{7}{15}$    (h) $1\frac{2}{3} + 1\frac{2}{9}$

**4**  Becky cycled $2\frac{3}{4}$ miles to one village then a further $4\frac{1}{3}$ miles to her home. What is the total distance Becky cycled?

**5** Work out the perimeter of this photograph.

**6** Two pieces of wood are fixed together, one on top of the other. One piece has thickness $2\frac{3}{8}$ inches and the other has thickness $1\frac{5}{16}$ inches.
What is the total thickness of the two pieces of wood?

**7** In a class, $\frac{1}{6}$ of the pupils own one pet, and $\frac{2}{5}$ of the pupils own more than one pet.
What total fraction of the pupils own at least one pet?

**8** A bag weighs $\frac{3}{7}$ lb. The contents weigh $1\frac{1}{5}$ lb.
What is the total weight of the bag and its contents?

$5\frac{1}{4}$ in

$\longleftarrow 3\frac{1}{2}$ in $\longrightarrow$

## Subtracting fractions

It is easy to subtract fractions when they have the same denominator.
You subtract the numerators. You must not subtract the denominators.

**Example 16**

Work out  (a) $\frac{7}{8} - \frac{11}{16}$   (b) $7\frac{3}{5} - 3\frac{1}{2}$

(a) $\dfrac{7}{8} - \dfrac{11}{16}$

$= \dfrac{14}{16} - \dfrac{11}{16} = \dfrac{3}{16}$

> Here there are different denominators. Change the eighths ($\frac{7}{8}$) to sixteenths to match the $\frac{11}{16}$.
> $\frac{7}{8}$ is equivalent to $\frac{14}{16}$.

(b)  **Method 1**

$7\dfrac{3}{5} - 3\dfrac{1}{2}$

> Subtract the whole numbers first.

$= 7 - 3 + \left( \dfrac{3}{5} - \dfrac{1}{2} \right)$

$= 4 + \left( \dfrac{6}{10} - \dfrac{5}{10} \right) = 4\dfrac{1}{10}$

> Change both the $\frac{3}{5}$ and the $\frac{1}{2}$ to equivalent fractions with denominator 10. The lowest number that is a multiple of both 5 and 2 is 10.

$\frac{3}{5}$ is equivalent to $\frac{6}{10}$   $\frac{1}{2}$ is equivalent to $\frac{5}{10}$

**Method 2**

Change to improper fractions first:

$7\dfrac{3}{5} - 3\dfrac{1}{2} = \dfrac{38}{5} - \dfrac{7}{2}$

> $7 = \frac{35}{5}$
> $3 = \frac{6}{2}$

$= \dfrac{76}{10} - \dfrac{35}{10} = \dfrac{41}{10} = 4\dfrac{1}{10}$

To subtract fractions, change them into equivalent fractions that have the same denominator. Then subtract the numerators.

## Exercise 4J

Work out the subtractions in questions **1–4**.

**1** (a) $\frac{3}{4} - \frac{1}{4}$   (b) $\frac{5}{8} - \frac{3}{8}$   (c) $\frac{15}{16} - \frac{7}{16}$   (d) $\frac{6}{7} - \frac{3}{7}$

**2** (a) $\frac{1}{2} - \frac{3}{8}$   (b) $\frac{7}{8} - \frac{1}{2}$   (c) $\frac{7}{8} - \frac{3}{4}$   (d) $4\frac{5}{8} - 2\frac{1}{4}$

**3** (a) $2\frac{3}{4} - \frac{3}{5}$    (b) $4\frac{4}{5} - 2\frac{2}{7}$    (c) $8\frac{2}{3} - 3\frac{2}{5}$    (d) $4\frac{5}{8} - 1\frac{2}{9}$

**4** (a) $4\frac{7}{8} - 1\frac{2}{3}$    (b) $5\frac{7}{9} - 3\frac{1}{3}$    (c) $3\frac{4}{5} - \frac{3}{8}$    (d) $7\frac{4}{7} - 4\frac{2}{5}$

**5** A box containing vegetables has a total weight of $5\frac{7}{8}$ kg. The empty box has a weight of $1\frac{1}{4}$ kg. What is the weight of the vegetables?

**6** A tin contains $7\frac{1}{2}$ pints of oil. Julie pours out $4\frac{3}{8}$ pints from the tin. How much oil remains?

**7** A plank of wood is $6\frac{1}{2}$ feet long. A $4\frac{3}{8}$ foot length is cut from one end of the plank. What length of wood remains?

**8** Carol spends $\frac{2}{3}$ of her salary on food for her family. She spends $\frac{1}{4}$ of her salary on bills. What fraction of her salary is left?

**9** Amarjit travels $5\frac{3}{8}$ km due North in his car, then $3\frac{1}{4}$ km due South. How far is he from his starting point?

## 4.8 Multiplying fractions

### How to multiply a fraction by a whole number

To work out $\frac{7}{10} \times 4$ first write 4 as an improper fraction: $\frac{4}{1}$.

$$\frac{7}{10} \times \frac{4}{1} \quad \text{is} \quad \frac{7 \times \overset{2}{\cancel{4}}}{\underset{5}{\cancel{10}} \times 1} = \frac{7 \times 2}{5 \times 1} = \frac{14}{5}$$

So $\frac{7}{10} \times 4 = \frac{14}{5}$ which as a mixed number is $2\frac{4}{5}$.

> To multiply a fraction by a whole number, write the whole number as an improper fraction, then multiply the numerators and denominators.

**Example 17**

Find $\frac{2}{5}$ of 65 metres.

$$\frac{2}{5} \text{ of 65 m is } \frac{2}{5} \times \frac{65}{1} = \frac{2 \times 65}{5 \times 1}$$

Simplify by dividing top and bottom by 5

$$= \frac{2 \times \overset{13}{65}}{\underset{1}{5} \times 1} = 26 \text{ m}$$

**Worked examination question**

Work out $\frac{3}{8}$ of 6 metres.

$$\frac{3}{8} \times \frac{6}{1} = \frac{3 \times \overset{3}{6}}{\underset{4}{8} \times 1} = \frac{9}{4} = 2\frac{1}{4} \text{ or 2.25 metres}$$

# How to multiply two fractions

Finding $\frac{2}{3}$ of $\frac{6}{7}$ is equivalent to $\frac{2}{3} \times \frac{6}{7}$.

The blue part represents $\frac{6}{7}$

The pink part represents $\frac{2}{3}$ of $\frac{6}{7}$

So $\frac{2}{3}$ of $\frac{6}{7} = \frac{4}{7}$.

In this context the word **of** means **multiplied by**.

Multiply the numerators (top).

$$\frac{2}{3} \times \frac{6}{7} = \frac{12}{21} = \frac{4}{7}$$

Multiply the denominators (bottom).

It can be useful to simplify before multiplying:

$$\frac{2}{3} \times \frac{6}{7} = \frac{2 \times \cancel{6}^2}{\cancel{3}_1 \times 7}$$

Simplify by dividing top and bottom by 3

$$= \frac{4}{7}$$

> To **multiply** two fractions, multiply the numerators (top) then multiply the denominators (bottom).
>
> To multiply or divide mixed numbers, change them to improper (top-heavy) fractions first.

## Example 18

(a) Find the weight of a quarter of a $\frac{3}{5}$ kg packet of biscuits.

(b) Work out $2\frac{1}{2} \times 1\frac{2}{5}$

> Multiplying by $\frac{1}{4}$ is the same as dividing by 4.
> $\frac{1}{4}$ is called the **reciprocal** of 4.
> The reciprocal of $a$ is $1 \div a$.

(a) $\frac{1}{4}$ of $\frac{3}{5}$ kg is $\frac{1}{4} \times \frac{3}{5}$ kg $= \frac{3}{20}$ kg

First multiply the numerators, then multiply the denominators.

(b) $2\frac{1}{2} \times 1\frac{2}{5} = \frac{5}{2} \times \frac{7}{5}$ ← First change mixed numbers to improper fractions.

$= \frac{\cancel{5}^1 \times 7}{2 \times \cancel{5}_1}$ ← Simplify by dividing top and bottom by 5

$= \frac{7}{2} = 3\frac{1}{2}$ ← Always write the answer in its simplest form.

## Exercise 4K

Work out the quantities in questions **1–4**.

**1** (a) $\frac{1}{8}$ of 72     (b) $\frac{5}{6}$ of 36     (c) $\frac{4}{9}$ of 63 litres     (d) $\frac{7}{16}$ of 48 pints

**2** (a) $\frac{1}{12}$ of £180     (b) $\frac{4}{5}$ of 4.63 kg     (c) $\frac{2}{3}$ of £3.96     (d) $\frac{17}{20}$ of 73 litres

**3** (a) $\frac{3}{4}$ of 36 kg     (b) $\frac{2}{5}$ of £5.55     (c) $\frac{11}{12}$ of 714 km     (d) $\frac{4}{7}$ of 490 people

**4** (a) $\frac{4}{9}$ of £38.25     (b) $\frac{4}{15}$ of 630 toys     (c) $\frac{4}{9}$ of 1620 cars     (d) $\frac{5}{7}$ of £52.01

**5** During a 28-week holiday season, $\frac{2}{7}$ of the days were wet. How many dry days were there?

**6** Jomo delivers 56 newspapers on his round. On Fridays $\frac{3}{8}$ of the newspapers have a magazine supplement. How many supplements does he deliver?

Work out the multiplications in questions **7–9**.

**7** (a) $\frac{1}{2} \times \frac{3}{8}$     (b) $\frac{4}{5} \times \frac{2}{3}$     (c) $\frac{4}{7} \times \frac{1}{3}$     (d) $\frac{2}{3} \times \frac{2}{5}$

    (e) $\frac{2}{7} \times \frac{1}{5}$     (f) $\frac{2}{3} \times \frac{5}{7}$     (g) $\frac{1}{2} \times \frac{3}{4}$     (h) $\frac{3}{5} \times \frac{1}{3}$

**8** (a) $\frac{1}{3} \times \frac{6}{7}$     (b) $\frac{6}{7} \times \frac{5}{12}$     (c) $\frac{1}{2} \times \frac{4}{5}$     (d) $\frac{2}{3} \times \frac{1}{4}$

    (e) $\frac{3}{7} \times \frac{2}{6}$     (f) $\frac{6}{5} \times \frac{1}{3}$     (g) $5 \times \frac{7}{10}$     (h) $\frac{9}{10} \times \frac{13}{18}$

**9** (a) $\frac{2}{3} \times 1\frac{1}{3}$     (b) $\frac{2}{5} \times 2\frac{1}{3}$     (c) $1\frac{1}{2} \times \frac{1}{4}$     (d) $1\frac{1}{2} \times 2\frac{1}{2}$

    (e) $2\frac{1}{2} \times \frac{1}{4}$     (f) $1\frac{1}{5} \times 1\frac{1}{3}$     (g) $6 \times 2\frac{2}{3}$     (h) $2\frac{1}{7} \times 1\frac{2}{5}$

**10** Barry earns £130.60 in one week. He pays $\frac{1}{4}$ of this in tax. How much money does he pay in tax each week?

**11** Sara receives £2.70 pocket money each week. She saves $\frac{2}{5}$ of it. How much money does she save each week?

**12** A melon weighs $2\frac{1}{2}$ lb. Work out the total weight of $8\frac{1}{4}$ melons.

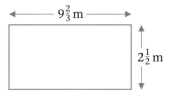

**13** Kieran takes $2\frac{1}{4}$ minutes to complete one lap at the Go Kart Centre. How long will it take him to complete $6\frac{1}{2}$ laps?

**14** Find the area of this rectangle. Leave your answer as a fraction.

$9\frac{2}{3}$ m

$2\frac{1}{2}$ m

# 4.9 Dividing fractions

Here is a problem that you can solve if you divide by a fraction:

> The length of a relay race is 2 laps of a running track.
> Each member of a team runs $\frac{1}{5}$ of a lap.
> How many runners are there in a team?

You can easily work out in your head that there are 10 runners in a team. To show your method you need to find how many fifths of a lap there are in 2 whole laps.

You could work this out by dividing 2 by $\frac{1}{5}$.

To get the answer 10 you could work out $\dfrac{2}{1} \times \dfrac{5}{1}$.

You get this expression from $\dfrac{2}{1} \div \dfrac{1}{5}$ if you invert the second fraction (turn it upside down) and change the ÷ sign to a × sign.

> **Why inverting works**
> A fraction like $\frac{3}{4}$ is the same as
> $$3 \div 4 \quad \text{or} \quad 3 \times \tfrac{1}{4}$$
> But $\frac{1}{4}$ is $\frac{4}{1}$ inverted.
>
> So dividing is the same as multiplying by the inverted number:
> $$12 \div 3 = 4$$
> $$12 \times \tfrac{1}{3} = 4 \text{ too}$$

**Example 19**

$\frac{1}{4} \div \frac{3}{5} = ?$ — Turn the fraction you are dividing by upside down. This is called inverting the fraction.

$\frac{1}{4} \times \frac{5}{3} = \frac{5}{12}$ — Change the $\div$ sign to a $\times$ sign.

To **divide** by a fraction, invert the dividing fraction (turn it upside down) and change the division sign to multiplication.

To divide mixed numbers, change to improper fractions first.

**Example 20**

Work out    (a) $\frac{2}{5} \div \frac{1}{2}$    (b) $\frac{4}{9} \div 6$    (c) $3\frac{1}{2} \div 2\frac{2}{3}$

(a)  $\frac{2}{5} \div \frac{1}{2} = \frac{2}{5} \times \frac{2}{1} = \frac{4}{5}$ — The $\frac{1}{2}$ becomes $\frac{2}{1}$. The $\div$ becomes $\times$

(b)  $\frac{4}{9} \div 6 = \frac{4}{9} \div \frac{6}{1}$ — The 6 can be written $\frac{6}{1}$, which becomes $\frac{1}{6}$ when you invert it.

$\qquad = \frac{4}{9} \times \frac{1}{6} = \frac{4}{54} = \frac{2}{27}$

(c)  $3\frac{1}{2} \div 2\frac{2}{3} = \frac{7}{2} \div \frac{8}{3}$ — First write the mixed numbers as improper fractions.

$\qquad = \frac{7}{2} \times \frac{3}{8} = \frac{21}{16} = 1\frac{5}{16}$ — Remember to simplify the final answer.

## Exercise 4L

Work out the divisions in questions **1–3**.

**1**  (a) $\frac{2}{9} \div \frac{1}{2}$    (b) $\frac{2}{5} \div \frac{3}{4}$    (c) $\frac{3}{8} \div \frac{2}{3}$    (d) $\frac{1}{2} \div \frac{1}{4}$

**2**  (a) $\frac{8}{9} \div 4$    (b) $\frac{2}{3} \div 6$    (c) $4\frac{2}{3} \div 4$    (d) $5\frac{1}{4} \div 3$

**3**  (a) $1\frac{1}{3} \div 1\frac{1}{2}$    (b) $2\frac{1}{2} \div \frac{1}{3}$    (c) $4\frac{3}{5} \div \frac{2}{3}$    (d) $2\frac{1}{5} \div 1\frac{1}{3}$

 (e) $1\frac{1}{3} \div 2\frac{2}{9}$    (f) $2\frac{2}{3} \div 2\frac{2}{5}$    (g) $3\frac{1}{3} \div 7\frac{1}{2}$    (h) $4\frac{4}{5} \div 5\frac{1}{3}$

**4**  A tin holds $10\frac{2}{3}$ litres of methylated spirit for a lamp. How many times will it fill a lamp holding $\frac{2}{3}$ litre?

**5**  A metal rod is $10\frac{4}{5}$ metres long. How many short rods $\frac{3}{10}$ metre long can be cut from the longer rod?

**6**  Tar & Stone Ltd can resurface $2\frac{1}{5}$ km of road in a day. How many days will it take them to resurface a road of length $24\frac{3}{5}$ km?

# 4.10 Solving problems involving fractions

Fractions are used in many different situations. The problems in this section are some of the types that are included in GCSE exams.

**Example 21**

A bag of flour weighs 2.25 kg. More flour is added and the weight of the bag of flour is increased by three fifths.
What is the new weight of the bag of flour?

$$\frac{3}{5} \text{ of } 2.25 \text{ kg is } \frac{3}{5} \times 2.25 = \frac{3 \times 2.25}{5} = \frac{6.75}{5} = 1.35 \text{ kg}$$

The new weight is 2.25 kg + 1.35 kg = 3.6 kg

**Example 22**

A 5 litre tin of paint is filled with blue and yellow paint to make a shade of green. The tin contains $1\frac{1}{2}$ litres of blue paint.
What fraction of the paint in the 5 litre tin is blue?

The fraction of paint that is blue is

$$\frac{\text{blue paint}}{\text{whole tin}} = \frac{1\frac{1}{2}}{5}$$

$$= 1\frac{1}{2} \div \frac{5}{1} = \frac{3}{2} \times \frac{1}{5} = \frac{3}{10}$$

## Exercise 4M

1   A loaded lorry has a total weight of 13.2 tonnes. This weight is decreased by five eighths when the load is removed.
Find the weight of the lorry without the load.

2   Last year 204 cars were imported by a garage. This year the number of cars imported has increased by five twelfths.
How many cars have been imported this year?

3   Of 144 rail passengers surveyed, 32 claimed their train was regularly late.
What fraction of the total number of passengers was this?

4   There are 225 houses on an estate. Of these houses, 85 have no garage.
What fraction of houses have no garage?

5   Find the difference between $\frac{3}{5}$ of 36 miles and $\frac{2}{3}$ of 30 miles.

6   A tin contains approximately 440 beans. The manufacturer increases the volume of the tin by three eighths.
Approximately how many beans would you expect to find in the larger tin?

**7**    A newspaper has 14 columns of photographs and 18 columns of advertisements.
What fraction of the paper is advertisements?

**8**    144 men, 80 women and 216 children went on the rollercoaster.
What fraction of the total number is made up of children?

## Mixed exercise 4

**1**    Complete these sets of equivalent fractions:

(a)  $\dfrac{5}{9} = \dfrac{}{18} = \dfrac{}{27} = \dfrac{}{36} = \dfrac{}{45}$    (b)  $\dfrac{2}{5} = \dfrac{}{10}$

(c)  $\dfrac{3}{} = \dfrac{24}{64}$    (d)  $\dfrac{}{7} = \dfrac{40}{35}$

**2**    Order these fractions, starting with the smallest.

$\dfrac{3}{4}, \quad \dfrac{7}{8}, \quad \dfrac{2}{5}, \quad \dfrac{7}{10}$

**3**    Express these as decimals.

(a)  $\dfrac{7}{8}$    (b)  $2\dfrac{3}{4}$    (c)  $4\dfrac{9}{25}$    (d)  $\dfrac{7}{9}$    (e)  $2\dfrac{5}{6}$

**4**    Express these as fractions.

(a)  0.04    (b)  2.725    (c)  5.68    (d)  0.3    (e)  0.45

**5**    Find the difference between $\frac{2}{3}$ of 15 kg and $\frac{3}{5}$ of 18 kg.

**6**    Two pipes of length $4\frac{5}{8}$ ft and $3\frac{3}{4}$ ft are put end to end.
What is their total length?

**7**    Work out

(a)  $11.7 + 73.4$    (b)  $4.9 \times 5$

(c)  $28.5 \div 5$    (d)  $4.8 - 5.9 + 2.3$

(e)  $15 \div 0.2$    (f)  $106.8 \div 0.15$

**8**    A length of wire is $5\frac{7}{8}$ feet long. A length of $1\frac{3}{16}$ feet is cut off.
What length of wire is left?

**9**    There are 70 ounces of sweets in a jar.
How many $4\frac{1}{4}$ ounce bags can be filled from the jar?

**10**    Derek spent £2 on motor oil and £16 on petrol.
What fraction of the total amount did he spend on petrol?

11 Two rods are fixed together to make a part
for a motor.

←— $1\frac{2}{3}$ inches —→ ←——— $3\frac{1}{4}$ inches ———→

Work out the total length of the two rods.
Write your answer as a mixed number in its
simplest form.                                   [E]

12 A personal stereo was priced at £48. In a sale it was reduced to
£42. By what fraction was the original price reduced?        [E]

13 Work out $\frac{3}{4}$ of £24.                          [E]

14 Six distances have been recorded:

   3.451 km,  3.506 km,  3.9 km,  3.008 km,  3.671 km,  3.91 km

Rewrite these distances in order, starting with the largest.

## Summary of key points

1  $\frac{5}{2}$ is called an **improper fraction**. The numerator is greater than the denominator.

2  $2\frac{1}{2}$ is called a **mixed number**. It contains a whole number part and a fractional part smaller
   than 1.

3  Mixed numbers can be written as improper fractions.
   Improper fractions can be written as mixed numbers.

4  You can find **equivalent fractions** by
   multiplying (or dividing) the top and
   bottom of a fraction by the same number.

$$\frac{6}{18} = \frac{1}{3}$$

5  You can **order** fractions by rewriting them as equivalent fractions with a common denominator.

6  **Decimals** are used for parts of a number that are smaller than 1.

7  You can convert a fraction to a decimal by dividing the numerator by the denominator:
   $\frac{4}{5} = 4 \div 5 = 0.8$

8  0.6666666… is called a **recurring decimal** since one of the digits recurs (repeats).
   **Recurring decimal notation:**
       0.$\dot{3}$ means 0.3333333… recurring
       0.$\dot{1}\dot{7}$ means 0.17171717… recurring
       0.$\dot{2}15\dot{4}$ means 0.215421542154… recurring.

**9** To **add** fractions, change them to equivalent fractions that have the same denominator (bottom). Then add the numerators:

$$\frac{1}{2} + \frac{2}{6} \;=\; \frac{3}{6} + \frac{2}{6} \;=\; \frac{3+2}{6} \;=\; \frac{5}{6}$$

equivalent fractions

**10** To **multiply** two fractions, multiply the numerators (top) then multiply the denominators (bottom):

$$\frac{3}{4} \times \frac{1}{7} \;=\; \frac{3 \times 1}{4 \times 7} \;=\; \frac{3}{28}$$

**11** To multiply or divide **mixed numbers**, change them to improper (top-heavy) fractions first.

**12** To **divide** by a fraction, invert the dividing fraction (turn it upside down) and change the division sign to multiplication:

$$\frac{1}{4} \div \frac{2}{5} \;=\; \frac{1}{4} \times \frac{5}{2} \;=\; \frac{1 \times 5}{4 \times 2} \;=\; \frac{5}{8}$$

# 5 Collecting and recording data

Every day you are surrounded by a sea of information.

This chapter is about the ways that information can be collected.

The information collected is called **data**.

## 5.1 Different types of data

Data is either qualitative or quantitative.

> **Qualitative data** is described using words.
> Place names such as North Wales, activities such as mountain biking, and colours such as red and green are **qualitative data**.

> **Quantitative data** consists of numbers.
> Data that can be counted or measured, such as the number of days in a holiday, temperatures and weights, are **quantitative data**.

Quantitative data can be **discrete** or **continuous**.

**Discrete data** can only take particular values. For example, you can buy shoes in these sizes:

$$6 \quad 6\tfrac{1}{2} \quad 7 \quad 7\tfrac{1}{2} \quad 8$$

These values are **discrete** (meaning separate).

There are *no* values in between them. Discrete data has an *exact* value.

**Continuous data** can take any value. For example, your foot could be:

18 cm long    21 cm long

or *any* value in between, such as 19.1573 cm long.

Continuous data *cannot be measured exactly*. The accuracy of a measurement depends on the accuracy of the measuring device.

## Exercise 5A

For each type of data below, write down whether it is qualitative, quantitative and discrete, or quantitative and continuous.

(a)  length of a nail
(b)  colour of a flower
(c)  time taken to play a CD
(d)  weight of a packet of sugar
(e)  number of goals scored in a hockey match
(f)  age of a tree
(g)  taste of a drink
(h)  smell of a scent
(i)  number of buses per day
(j)  score on a dice
(k)  temperature of an oven

## Reasons for collecting data

There are lots of reasons for collecting data. For example:
- market research prior to launching a new product
- quality control to make sure a product is up to standard
- collecting information for reference.

## Market research

A company is about to launch a new product, for example a new soap powder.

It wants to know what to call its product and which type of advertising campaign is most likely to be successful.

It conducts a survey using interviews and a questionnaire.

## Quality control

A fireworks company needs to be sure that its products will perform well.

Every day they take a batch of 20 of each type of firework and test them. The fireworks are graded 'excellent', 'good' or 'poor', depending on the number in the sample that perform well.

The production manager studies the results and decides what action to take.

Information collected directly at first hand is called **primary data**.

## Information and reference

A tourist office in a holiday resort keeps daily records of sunshine, rainfall and maximum and minimum temperatures.

Hotels in the resort may use this information in their brochures.

Information taken from existing records is called **secondary data**.

# 5.2 Sampling

When collecting data you may have to restrict the number of items you survey. This could be because of the time available, the cost, or because taking a large survey is not practical.

> The **population** is the complete set of items under consideration.

> A **sample** is part of the population selected for surveying.

Selecting a suitable sample is crucial for reliable survey results. You would hardly expect to get a fair picture if you only asked your friends what they thought.

> A **biased sample** is one which would be likely to have an undue influence on the outcome.

For example, a boys-only sample might well give a totally different picture to a girls-only sample.

> In a **random sample** every member of the population has an equal chance of being chosen.

> A **random process** must be unpredictable.

The sample size should be small enough to be manageable, but large enough to be representative of the whole population. In most cases a random sample of around 5% to 10% of the population should be sufficient.

## Random sampling

If there are 600 students in your school, a manageable and representative sample size would be 30 students.

It is important that your sample is random. If you only ask Radiohead fans about their favourite band, your sample's views will not be representative of those of the whole population.

To take your random sample of 30:

1   List all 600 students in any order and label their names from 000 to 599.

| 000 | C.J. Adams |
| 001 | P.E. Ash |
| 002 | C.R. Ashbee |

2　Choose a way of generating random numbers from 000 to 599. Here are two possible methods:

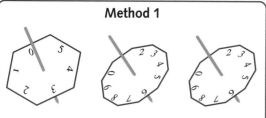

**Method 1**

Use one 6-sided and two 10-sided spinners to generate the three digits.

**Method 2**

Use the RND function on a scientific calculator.

> Random numbers are generated by a random process – they cannot be predicted.

## Stratified sampling

In a school survey on favourite bands it is likely that the students' age will influence their choices. Some bands have more appeal to younger students, some to older ones.

You might want to look at the popularity of the various bands according to the ages of students. To do this you can put the students in groups called **strata**, according to their ages.

> A **stratified sample** is one in which the population is divided into groups called strata and each of the strata is randomly sampled.

A convenient way of doing this in a school would be to use the year groups of the students as the strata.

For example, the table shows the numbers in each year group in a school of 600 students.

There are more students in Year 7 than in Year 10, so the sample should include more students from Year 7 than Year 10. Year 7 students are $\frac{150}{600} = \frac{1}{4}$ of the whole school, so they should make up $\frac{1}{4}$ of the sample.

For example you could take a 6% sample of each of Years 7 to 11.

A 6% sample is in the range 5%–10% and gives whole numbers of students in each of the strata:

| Year group | Number of students |
|:---:|:---:|
| 7 | 150 |
| 8 | 150 |
| 9 | 100 |
| 10 | 100 |
| 11 | 100 |

| Year group | Number of students | Number in 6% sample |
|:---:|:---:|:---:|
| 7 | 150 | 9 |
| 8 | 150 | 9 |
| 9 | 100 | 6 |
| 10 | 100 | 6 |
| 11 | 100 | 6 |

> Sample size = 36
> Year 7 = $\frac{9}{36} = \frac{1}{4}$ of sample
> Year 10 = $\frac{6}{36} = \frac{1}{6}$ of sample

For each of the strata the sample you take must be random.

## Systematic sampling

Systematic sampling is often used in quality control, where items such as light bulbs, batteries, computer chips and tinned food need to be tested at the factory to ensure that they have been made to satisfactory standards.

A **systematic sample** is one in which every $n$th item is chosen.

To take a 5% sample you select 1 in every 20 items.

$5\% = \frac{5}{100} = \frac{1}{20}$

You could take a 5% systematic sample of the students at your school. To do this you would list all the names. Randomly select any number from 1 to 20, for example 8. Then from your list choose the 8th, 28th, 48th, 68th… student names.

---

**Example 1**

There are 1200 students at Lucea High School. This table shows how students are distributed by year group and gender.

| Year group | Number of boys | Number of girls |
|:---:|:---:|:---:|
| 7 | 144 | 156 |
| 8 | 150 | 150 |
| 9 | 87 | 113 |
| 10 | 102 | 96 |
| 11 | 100 | 102 |

Jamilla is conducting a survey about the students' favourite school subject. She decides to use a stratified random sample of 100 students according to year group and gender.

How many Year 7 girls should there be in her sample?

The number of girls in Year 7 is 156.

As a proportion of the total of 1200 students, this is $\frac{156}{1200} = 0.13$

Jamilla's total sample is to be 100 so she should sample

$\qquad 0.13 \times 100 = 13$ girls from Year 7

---

## Exercise 5B

1   For each method, say whether it would give a random sample or whether it is likely to be biased.

   (a)   Take every 10th name from a list.

   (b)   Interview all the people in a launderette.

   (c)   Put all the names into a hat and pick without looking.

   (d)   Test the first article produced each hour by a machine.

   (e)   Number all the items and then select by using random number tables.

Random number tables give lists of numbers generated at random by a computer.

2    Use the data in Example 1 on page 75 for this question.

    **(a)**    Work out the number of students Jamilla should sample from
        **(i)** Year 8                **(ii)** boys in Year 10.

    **(b)**    Explain why the correct answer to **(ii)** above will create a
        problem for Jamilla. How could Jamilla resolve this problem?

    **(c)**    Work out the number of students Jamilla should sample
        from boys in Year 9.

    **(d)**    Comment on your answers to **(b)** and **(c)**.

3    Just before a local election a market research company makes a survey of the voting intentions of the electorate. There

| Age range (years) | Number of males | Number of females |
|---|---|---|
| Under 30 | 5800 | 6200 |
| 30 or over | 9500 | 8500 |

are 30 000 people who can vote in the election. They are categorised according to age and gender as in the table above.

The market research company will try to obtain the views of a 2000-person sample.

Work out the number in the sample who should be

**(a)**   aged under 30   **(b)**   male   **(c)**   female and aged 30 or more.

4    Explain how you could take a systematic sample of 2% of the names in a telephone directory.

## 5.3  Collecting primary data

### Questionnaires

One way of collecting data is to use a **questionnaire**.

> When you are writing questions for a **questionnaire**:
> • be clear about what you want to find out, and what data you need
> • ask short, simple questions.

Here are some good examples:

Are you:

Male ☐

Female ☐

    This has a clear choice of two answers.

What age are you?

Under 17 ☐

17–20 ☐

21–30 ☐

Over 30 ☐

Which of these styles of music do you like best?

Metal ☐

House ☐

Grunge ☐

None of them ☐

These both offer four choices.

Avoid questions that are vague, personal or **biased** (which may influence the answer).

> How often do you go swimming?
>
> Sometimes ☐     Occasionally ☐     Often ☐

*Sometimes, occasionally* and *often* may mean different things to different people.

> Have you ever stolen anything from a shop?
>
> Yes ☐     No ☐

Even a hardened criminal is unlikely to answer this question honestly!

> Do you agree that the UK should have the euro?
>
> Yes ☐     No ☐

This question suggests that the right answer is Yes. It is **biased**.

Test your questionnaire on a few people first to see if it works or needs to be improved. This is called a **pilot survey**.

---

**Example 2**

The Governors of Lucea High School want to find out whether parents think that girls attending the school should wear ties. Design a question to obtain parents' views on this which could be used in a questionnaire.

Several designs are possible. Here is one example:

> Please tick the box which most accurately reflects your view on this statement:
>
> *Girls attending Lucea High School should wear ties.*
>
> ☐ Strongly agree     ☐ Agree     ☐ Not sure     ☐ Disagree     ☐ Strongly disagree

You could use only the middle three boxes. Using any more than the five boxes shown here would make it harder to find a pattern in the responses.

---

## Avoiding bias

When you are collecting data you need to make sure that your survey or experiment is **fair** and avoids **bias**. A bias is anything that might make the data unrepresentative.

For example, if you want to find out which sport is most popular amongst 14–16 year olds in the UK, you will not be able to ask everyone in this age group. You will have to ask a **sample** of 14–16 year olds and treat their views as being representative of all people of their age.

If you only asked 14–16 year old boys at a football match, your survey would be biased because you would be collecting the views of male football enthusiasts.

The question 'Do you agree that running is good for you?' is biased too, because it suggests that a particular answer is correct.

## Exercise 5C

1   Look at these pairs of questions. Choose whether Question X or
    Question Y is better to do the job in the *To find out* column.

|     | To find out: | Question X | Question Y |
|-----|--------------|------------|------------|
| (a) | if people like the Labour party | Do you like the Labour party? Yes/No | Do you agree that New Labour is the best party? Yes/No |
| (b) | which age group a person is in | How old are you? | Are you under 21, 21 to 40, 41 to 60, over 60? |
| (c) | the most popular soap on TV | Do you watch *Eastenders*? Yes/No | Do you watch *Eastenders/ Coronation Street/ Emmerdale/Hollyoaks/ Other*? |
| (d) | if they watched the film | Did you see the film *War of the Worlds*? Yes/No | Do you like Steven Spielberg? |
| (e) | if someone is short sighted | How good is your eyesight? | Can you read that sign without glasses? Yes/No |
| (f) | if people give money to charity | Do you give money to charity? Yes/No | Everyone gives money to charity, don't they? Yes/No |
| (g) | if the hotel was satisfactory | Was everything in the hotel all right? Yes/No | Did you enjoy your stay? Yes/No |
| (h) | if newspapers should be censored | Newspapers should be censored: Agree/Disagree/Don't know | What do you think about censoring newspapers? |

2   Here are some questions that are not suitable for a questionnaire.
    For each one, say why and write a more suitable question.

   (a)  Do you agree that the UK should have a monarchy?
        Yes ☐   No ☐   Don't know ☐

   (b)  What was the weather like on your holiday?
        Terrible ☐   Quite good ☐   OK ☐

   (c)  Most people approve of corporal punishment. Do you?
        Yes ☐   No ☐

   (d)  Do you still play football?
        Yes ☐   No ☐

   (e)  How many hours of TV do you watch?
        1 ☐   2 ☐   3 ☐

   (f)  Does your local library have wheelchair access?
        Yes ☐   No ☐

**3** Finn wants to find out about people's mobile phones. He has designed the following questionnaire for his web page.

(a) How could you improve part **4** of the questionnaire?

(b) Finn also wants to write a question about how people buy their call time. Design a question he could use. Include tick boxes for a response.

> # Questionnaire: Mobile phones
>
> **1** Do you have a mobile phone?
> Yes ☐　No ☐
>
> **2** Who is your service provider?
> Mobile P ☐　　　　H$_4$ ☐　Five ☐
> Fonavode ☐　Pineapple ☐　Other ☐
>
> **3** Do you:　Pay monthly ☐
> 　　　　　　Pay-As-You-Go ☐
>
> **4** How much do you spend on your phone each month?
> £5 ☐　£10 ☐　£15 ☐　£20 ☐

---

**Activity – Holidays**

Design a questionnaire to find out about the kind of holidays people had last year.

Test your questions by asking some of your friends.

---

## Observation and measurement

Data can also be collected by observation (e.g. a traffic survey) or by measurement (e.g. weighing bars of chocolate produced). This method is suitable for quality control.

**Example 3**

You are commissioned to do a survey on traffic flows on a particular road to see whether parking restrictions are required. What factors might affect traffic flow? Design a data capture sheet for this survey.

Things which might make a difference to traffic flow include:

- day of the week
- types of vehicle using the road
- time of day
- direction of flow.

> A data capture sheet can be used to record primary data.

Here is a possible data capture sheet to record results:

| Monday | | 7 am – 10 am | 10 am – 1 pm | 1 pm – 4 pm | 4 pm – 7 pm |
|---|---|---|---|---|---|
| North/ South | cars vans lorries others | | | | |
| South/ North | cars vans lorries other | | | | |

## Exercise 5D

1  Prepare data capture sheets for surveys to find out two of the following by observation:
   (a)  the make of people's MP3 player
   (b)  the colour of people's eyes
   (c)  the most popular brand of sports shoe of people in your school
   (d)  the CPU speed and hard disk space on people's computers
   (e)  the age and gender of people entering a supermarket.

2  Design a suitable data capture sheet for quality control at a fireworks factory. There is a day shift and a night shift and five machines. Since testing means that the firework cannot be sold, you are only allowed to test 1000 fireworks each week.

3  A supermarket wishes to conduct research to follow the sales trends of five items over a period of 3 months. There are 2045 branches, and 200 branches are going to run cut-price promotion offers on the five items.
   Plan the data collection.

# 5.4 Secondary data

Secondary data is information that has already been collected and recorded. It is quick, cheap and ready for you to use. If such data is adequate for your research, it makes sense to use it.

For example, suppose you want to know if there is any evidence to suggest that homes are becoming safer places. You would need to collect records first hand for years before you could make any comment.

However, the *Annual Abstract of Statistics,* available at libraries and online, will give you details of deaths in the home and accidents at home that needed hospital treatment. This provides information going back 20 years or more.

> Data like these are obtained from the National Census, held every ten years.

The internet is a good place for finding secondary data.

## Obtaining data from the internet

The internet can be a very useful source of data. But remember that data collected from the internet may be inaccurate or out of date.

When you collect data from the internet make sure that
 • the data comes from a reliable source
 • the data is accurate – check against other sources.

**Activity – Internet search**

Use the internet to find the following information.
Give two reliable sources for each answer.

(a) The members of the European Union.

(b) The heights of the five highest mountains in the world.

(c) The average life expectancy of people in the UK.

(d) The number of gold, silver and bronze medals won by Great Britain in the Paralympic Games in 2004.

## Obtaining data from a database

A **database** is an organised collection of information. It can be stored on paper or on a computer.

Here is a spreadsheet showing part of a database stored on a computer:

|   | A | B | C | D | E | F | G | H |
|---|---|---|---|---|---|---|---|---|
| **1** | Year group | Surname | Years | Months | Gender | Sport | Height (m) | Weight (kg) |
| **2** | 10 | Abejurouge | 15 | 3 | Male | Rugby | 1.63 | 60 |
| **3** | 10 | Aberdeen | 15 | 0 | Male | Rounders | 1.75 | 45 |
| **4** | 11 | Ableson | 16 | 6 | Female | Table tennis | 1.83 | 60 |
| **5** | 11 | Acton | 16 | 3 | Female | Basketball | 1.67 | 52 |
| **6** | 10 | Adam | 15 | 1 | Male | Judo | 1.80 | 49 |
| **7** | 10 | Agha | 15 | 7 | Male | Cricket | 1.66 | 70 |

A computer database allows you to obtain information quickly and in a variety of forms, for example:

- in alphabetical order
- girls' results only
- in numerical order
- male students over a certain height.

### Exercise 5E

1 Say whether you would collect primary data or use secondary data for the following research. Explain your answers.

(a) a survey on train punctuality

(b) research into wildlife in an African National Park

(c) investigating levels of student attendance at your school

(d) market research into sales at the school tuck shop

(e) compiling a report on the major tourist attractions in the UK

2  (a)  Give one example of
          **(i)**  a project where you would use primary data
          **(ii)** a project where you would use secondary data.
   (b)  Give an example of a situation where you could collect primary
        data and then compare it with secondary data.

---

**Activity – Mayfield School database (Go to www.heinemann.co.uk/hotlinks, insert the express code 4092P and click on this activity.)**

Use the Mayfield school database to answer these questions:

**(a)**  How tall is David Hazelwood (Year 9)?

**(b)**  How many KS4 students were born in April?

**(c)**  How many KS3 students said their favourite TV programme
        is *The Simpsons*? Which one of these said their favourite sport is running?

**(d)**  How many KS3 students are right handed and have dark brown eyes? Which of these said
        their favourite TV programme is *Eastenders*?

**(e)**  Which female KS4 student has 5 pets and said her favourite subject is PE?

---

# 5.5 Recording and presenting grouped data

When quantitative data has a wide range of values, it makes sense to group
sets of values together. This makes it easier to record the data and to spot
any patterns or trends.

For example, scores out of 50 in a test might be grouped:

    0–10,   11–20,   21–30,   31–40,   41–50

It often makes life easier if all the groups are the same size, but they do not
have to be. In this case the first group has 11 members and the others have 10.

The groupings 0–10, 11–20 and so on are called **class intervals**.

   **Class intervals** are groupings of quantitative data.

Here is a frequency table for a test taken by some pupils:

| Score | Tally | Frequency |
|-------|-------|-----------|
| 0–10  | \|\|  | 2 |
| 11–20 | JHT \|\|\| | 8 |
| 21–30 | JHT JHT \|\|\|\| | 14 |
| 31–40 | JHT | 5 |
| 41–50 | \| | 1 |

The class intervals must not overlap.
Each score can only be in one class interval.

The test scores are discrete data.
You can score 31 or 32, but *not* 31.4

You can also group continuous data. Here is some data
from a traffic study. Kuljit has timed the interval in
seconds between successive vehicles passing her school
for 50 vehicles. The times are correct to the nearest 0.1 second.

```
 3.3   21.0   23.5    9.4   14.6   46.8   34.3   45.8   56.1   50.4   12.2    7.6   14.4
16.5   34.5   35.7    3.5    2.8    5.7   10.0   45.1   46.2   23.6   17.1    9.7   38.4
 3.5    7.3   28.7   32.1   51.7   21.3    6.1   17.4   12.2   43.2   56.3   34.5   37.9
12.0   17.3    3.2   15.3    4.2   24.4   35.6   29.8    7.1    3.7   10.2
```

To record this data in a frequency table you need to group it into class intervals. If the class intervals are too narrow there will be too many groups to show up any pattern in the data. If the class intervals are too wide there will be too few groups to show up a pattern.

There is no golden rule for choosing the sizes of the class intervals or the number of groups, but it is usually best to have no fewer than five groups and no more than ten.

Here is a frequency table for the data grouped into class intervals of width 10 seconds:

This means 0 up to but not including 10

This means 50 up to but not including 60

| Class interval (seconds) | Tally | Frequency |
|---|---|---|
| $0 \leqslant t < 10$ | ⦸⦸ ‖‖ | 14 |
| $10 \leqslant t < 20$ | ⦸⦸ ‖ | 12 |
| $20 \leqslant t < 30$ | ⦸ ‖ | 7 |
| $30 \leqslant t < 40$ | ⦸ ‖‖ | 8 |
| $40 \leqslant t < 50$ | ⦸ | 5 |
| $50 \leqslant t < 60$ | ‖‖‖ | 4 |

## Presenting grouped data

Data that is grouped and continuous can be displayed in a **histogram**.

Here is a histogram for the traffic data from the frequency table:

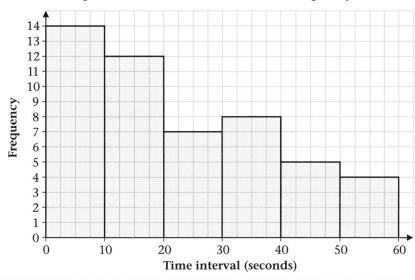

A histogram *looks* like a bar chart but:
- the data is continuous so there can be no gaps between the bars
- the *area* of the bars represents the frequency, so the data must be grouped into class intervals of equal width if you want to use the *lengths* of the bars to represent data values.

There is more about histograms in Chapter 20 (in Book 2).

## Grouped data in two-way tables

Daniel wants to find out if the amount of pocket money school students receive is related to their age. For each student in his survey he needs to record two variables – age and amount of pockey money.

> A two-way table records two variables.

He records the data in a two-way table:

|  |  | Amount of pocket money | | |
|---|---|---|---|---|
|  |  | £0–£3.00 | £3.01–£6.00 | £6.01–£9.00 |
| Age | $11 \leqslant x < 12$ |  |  |  |
|  | $12 \leqslant x < 13$ |  |  |  |
|  | $13 \leqslant x < 14$ |  |  |  |
|  | $14 \leqslant x < 15$ |  |  |  |
|  | $15 \leqslant x < 16$ |  |  |  |

> The variables can be either discrete (e.g. money) or continuous (e.g. age).

---

**Example 4**

The tourist office at a holiday resort records the hours of sunshine and the maximum daily temperature for publicity purposes. Design a suitable two-way table for collecting the data.

|  |  | Hours of sunshine | | | | |
|---|---|---|---|---|---|---|
|  |  | $0 \leqslant y < 3$ | $3 \leqslant y < 6$ | $6 \leqslant y < 9$ | $9 \leqslant y < 12$ | over 12 |
| Maximum daily temperature (°C) | $15 \leqslant x < 20$ |  |  |  |  |  |
|  | $20 \leqslant x < 25$ |  |  |  |  |  |
|  | $25 \leqslant x < 30$ |  |  |  |  |  |
|  | over 30 |  |  |  |  |  |

---

## Exercise 5G

Design two-way tables to record the data in questions **1–3**.

1   Height (ranging from 160 cm to 200 cm).
    Waist measurement (ranging from 65 cm to 100 cm).

2   Average speed of a journey (ranging from 30 km/h to 60 km/h).
    Length of journey (ranging from 10 km to 100 km).

3   Height of a nest above the ground (ranging from 0 cm to 400 cm).
    Number of eggs in the nest (between 1 and 7 inclusive).

4   Thirty pupils were asked about their lunch one day. The table gives some information about their answers.

    (a)   Copy and complete the table.

    (b)   How many of the girls had sandwiches?   [E]

|  | School dinner | Sandwiches | Other | Total |
|---|---|---|---|---|
| Boys | 12 | 3 |  | 16 |
| Girls | 8 |  | 2 |  |
| Total |  |  |  | 30 |

## 5.6 Frequency polygons

A **frequency polygon** can be used to show the general pattern of data. Plot the frequency for each class interval against the mid-point of that interval.

This table shows the frequency distribution of marks in a test:

| Mark | 0–9 | 10–19 | 20–29 | 30–39 | 40–49 | 50–60 |
|------|-----|-------|-------|-------|-------|-------|
| Frequency | 16 | 14 | 18 | 9 | 6 | 2 |

This is discrete data grouped into class intervals 0–9, 10–19 and so on.

One way of presenting this data is to plot a graph of frequency against mark. For each class interval, plot the mid-point against the frequency. Join the points with straight lines.

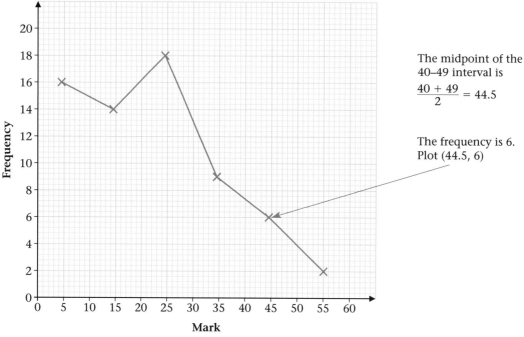

The midpoint of the 40–49 interval is
$$\frac{40 + 49}{2} = 44.5$$

The frequency is 6. Plot (44.5, 6)

The resulting graph is called a **frequency polygon**. Here the mid-point of each class interval is treated as being representative of all the points in that interval.

## Exercise 5H

1 James asked people to draw a line 5 cm long using a straight edge without any markings on it. Here are the lengths in centimetres of the lines they drew.

> 4.3  3.2  3.9  4.7  5.8  6.1  5.7  6.2  6.5  3.7  4.2
> 5.1  6.5  7.2  7.4  3.7  5.8  4.2  4.1  5.0  5.1  4.7
> 3.2  3.5  5.2  2.9  2.8  4.3  5.1  4.8

(a) Organise these results in a grouped frequency table. Use a class interval of 1 centimetre.

(b) Draw a frequency polygon for the data.

2   This frequency polygon shows the times of 25 girls who each had
    to sew on two buttons with standard lengths of thread.

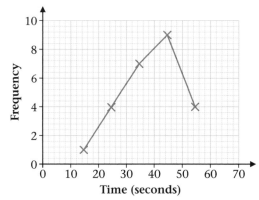

    A group of 25 boys was challenged to do the same task. Here are
    their times, to the nearest second.

    25   32   46   32   57   46   51   28   49   68   55   78   32
    44   89   22   56   67   77   40   41   48   60   *    *

    The stars represent two boys who gave up.

    (a)   How will you deal with the two boys who gave up?

    (b)   Group the data and draw a frequency polygon.

    (c)   Compare the two frequency polygons. What conclusions
          can you draw from the two frequency polygons?

## Mixed exercise 5

1   Grace and Gemma were carrying out a survey on the food people
    eat in the school canteen. Grace wrote the question 'Which food
    do you eat?' Gemma said this question was too vague.

    Write down two ways in which this question could be improved.
                                                                    [E]

2   Fred is conducting a survey into television viewing habits. One
    of the questions on his survey is 'How much television do you
    watch?' His friend, Sheila, tells him that it is not a very good
    question.
    Write down two ways in which Fred could improve this
    question.                                                       [E]

3   Nazia is going to carry out a survey of the types of DVD her
    friends have watched.
    Draw a suitable data collection sheet that Nazia could use.     [E]

> 'Data collection sheet' is
> another name for 'data
> capture sheet'.

4   Rachel and Terry were collecting information on the types of
    meals bought by students in the school canteen.
    Draw a suitable data collection sheet for this information.     [E]

5   There are 1000 students in Nigel and Sonia's school.
    Explain how Nigel could take a random sample of students to
    carry out a survey.                                             [E]

**6** Categorise these sampling methods as random, not random but unlikely to be biased, or biased.

    **(a)** Take every 20th name from a telephone directory.

    **(b)** Use all those with a birthday in June.

    **(c)** Use married men for a survey on football.

    **(d)** Give all members of a tennis club a number and use random number tables.

**7** Luca is trying to find out which weekly magazines are read most by students in his school. He decides to ask 10 of his friends.

    **(a)** Explain why this is not a reliable method.

    **(b)** Suggest two steps that Luca could take to get more reliable results.

**8** There are 1200 students at Russell High School.

Maria wishes to take a random sample of 60 of these students for her humanities project.

Describe at least three different ways in which Maria could take such a sample.

**9** The table shows the number of students in each year group at a school.

| Year group | Number of students |
|:---:|:---:|
| 7 | 270 |
| 8 | 270 |
| 9 | 240 |
| 10 | 200 |
| 11 | 180 |

Mrs Fox is the music teacher. She is carrying out a survey about the students' favourite radio channel. She uses a stratified sample of 40 students according to year group.
Calculate how many Year 10 students should be in her sample. [E]

**10** Bob carried out a survey of 100 people who buy tea. He asked them about the tea they buy most. The two-way table gives some information about his results.

| | Tea bags | Packet tea | Instant tea | Total |
|:---:|:---:|:---:|:---:|:---:|
| 50 g 100 g 200 g | 2 35 15 | 0 20 | 5 | 60 |
| Total | | 25 | | 100 |

Copy and complete the two-way table. [E]

Sales of Fairtrade tea are increasing in Britain. Fairtrade initiatives should ensure workers earn fair wages.

11  This table gives information on the sales of petrol and diesel in a garage last week.

| Day | Number of litres of petrol sold | Number of litres of diesel sold |
|---|---|---|
| Monday | 400 | 400 |
| Tuesday | 600 | 200 |
| Wednesday | 700 | 300 |
| Thursday | 450 | 700 |
| Friday | 200 | 900 |
| Saturday | 700 | 800 |
| Sunday | 600 | 700 |

(a)  Draw two frequency polygons on the same axes to represent this data.

(b)  Comment on the sales of petrol and diesel last week.

12  The table shows the frequency distribution of the ages of members of a sports club in 2000 and 2005.

| Age | 0–9 | 10–19 | 20–29 | 30–39 | 40–49 | 50–59 |
|---|---|---|---|---|---|---|
| 2000 | 6 | 16 | 22 | 29 | 18 | 9 |
| 2005 | 9 | 23 | 27 | 21 | 10 | 7 |

Draw two frequency polygons on the same axes and compare the ages of members in 2000 and 2005.

# Summary of key points

1   There are two types of data:
   • **Qualitative data** is described using words. For example, Sheffield, blue, euro...
   • **Quantitative data** consists of numbers: it is data that can be counted or measured.

2   **Quantitative data** can be discrete or continuous:
   • **Discrete data** can take only particular values. For example, shoe sizes 6, $6\frac{1}{2}$, 7...
   • **Continuous data** can take any value. For example, lengths 1.5 cm, 2.54 cm, 62.643 cm...

3   Information collected directly at first hand is called **primary data**.
   Information taken from existing records is called **secondary data**.

4   The **population** is the complete set of items under consideration.
   A **sample** is part of the population selected for surveying.
   A **biased sample** is one which would be likely to have an undue influence on the outcome.
   In a **random sample** every member of the population has an equal chance of being chosen.
   A **random process** must be unpredictable.

**5**   A **stratified sample** is one in which the population is divided into groups called strata and each of the strata is randomly sampled. It must have the same proportion from each of the strata as occurs in the whole population.

**6**   A **systematic sample** is one in which every *n*th item is chosen.

**7**   When you are writing questions for a **questionnaire**:
- be clear about what you want to find out, and what data you need
- ask short, simple questions
- avoid questions that are vague, personal, or **biased** (which may influence the answer).

Test your questionnaire on a few people first to see if it works or needs to be improved. This is called a **pilot survey**.

**8**   When you collect data from the internet make sure that:
- the data comes from a reliable source
- the data is accurate – check against other sources.

**9**   A **database** is an organised collection of information. It can be stored on paper or on a computer.

**10**   **Class intervals** are groupings of quantitative data.

**11**   Data that is grouped and continuous can be displayed in a **histogram**.

**12**   A histogram looks like a bar chart but:
- the data is continuous so there can be no gaps between the bars
- the *area* of the bars represents the frequency, so the data must be grouped into class intervals of equal width if you want to use the *lengths* of the bars to represent data values.

**13**   A **frequency polygon** can be used to show the general pattern of data. Plot the frequency for each class interval against the mid-point of that interval.

# ⑥ Solving equations and inequalities

In this chapter you will learn more about solving equations.

## 6.1 Solving simple equations

In Section 2.9 you solved simple equations using the balancing method.
Remember this key point from that section:

> Whatever you do to one side of an equation you must also do to the other side.

**Example 1**

Solve $14 = 9 - 2x$.

$$14 = 9 - 2x \bullet$$
$$14 - 9 = -2x \quad \text{——— Subtract 9 from both sides.}$$
$$5 = -2x$$
$$-2\tfrac{1}{2} = x \quad \text{——— Divide both sides by } -2.$$

Check by substituting $x = -2\tfrac{1}{2}$ into the original equation:
$$14 = 9 - 2(-2\tfrac{1}{2}) = 9 + 5 = 14$$

So $x = -2\tfrac{1}{2}$ is the solution.

> You need to collect the number terms on one side of the equation and the letter terms on the other.

### Exercise 6A

Solve these equations. Check your answers by substitution.

**1** $2 - 3x = 17$  **2** $4x + 3 = -5$  **3** $7 = 2x + 2$  **4** $16 = 5 - 2x$  **5** $2a + 7 = 1$

**6** $11 - 5b = 3$  **7** $9 = 16 + 2c$  **8** $-13 = 5 - 6p$  **9** $14 - 3q = 2$  **10** $23 = 3 - 5s$

## 6.2 When the $x$ term includes a fraction

Sometimes the coefficient of $x$ is a fraction, for example in $\tfrac{1}{4}x - 5 = 2$.
Here are two ways of solving the equation:

**Method 1**

$$\tfrac{1}{4}x - 5 = 2$$
$$\tfrac{1}{4}x = 2 + 5 \quad \text{——— Add 5 to both sides.}$$
$$\tfrac{1}{4}x = 7$$
$$x = 28 \quad \text{——— Multiply both sides by 4.}$$

**Method 2**

$$\tfrac{1}{4}x - 5 = 2$$
$$x - 20 = 8 \quad \text{——— Multiply both sides by 4.}$$
$$x = 8 + 20 \quad \text{——— Add 20 to both sides.}$$
$$x = 28$$

Check by substituting $x = 28$ in $\tfrac{1}{4}x - 5 = 2$: $\tfrac{1}{4} \times 28 - 5 = 7 - 5 = 2$

So $x = 28$ is the solution.

## Exercise 6B

Solve these equations and check your answers.

**1** $\frac{1}{3}x - 4 = 2$      **2** $\frac{1}{2}x + 7 = 4$

**3** $\frac{x}{4} - 5 = 1$      **4** $\frac{3}{4}x + 2 = 9$

**5** $\frac{2}{3}x - 4 = -1$      **6** $9 - \frac{x}{2} = 2$

**7** $7 - \frac{x}{3} = 9$      **8** $6 - \frac{x}{4} = 9$

**9** $5 - \frac{2}{3}x = 1$      **10** $3 - \frac{3x}{4} = 8$

# 6.3 When the 'unknown' $x$ is on both sides

In some equations, for example in $5x - 4 = 3x - 10$, there is an $x$ term on both sides. To solve this, rearrange the equation so that all the $x$ terms are on one side.

**Example 2**

Solve $5x - 4 = 3x - 10$.

$$5x - 3x - 4 = -10 \quad\text{——— Subtract } 3x \text{ from both sides.}$$
$$2x - 4 = -10$$
$$2x = -10 + 4 \quad\text{——— Add 4 to both sides.}$$
$$2x = -6$$
$$x = -3 \quad\text{——— Divide both sides by 2.}$$

Check by substituting $x = -3$ in $5x - 4 = 3x - 10$

Left side:      $(5 \times -3) - 4 \ = -15 - 4 \ = \ -19$

Right side:      $(3 \times -3) - 10 = -9 - 10 \ = \ -19$

So $x = -3$ is the solution.

For equations with the unknown on both sides, rearrange so the unknowns are on one side of the equation and the numbers are on the other.

## Exercise 6C

Solve these equations and check your answers by substitution.

**1** $2a + 5 = a + 9$      **2** $6b - 5 = 4b + 1$

**3** $6c + 1 = 4c + 2$      **4** $2d + 3 = 7d - 1$

**5** $5e + 1 = 2e - 5$      **6** $3f - 2 = 8f + 3$

**7** $4g - 5 = 8g - 11$      **8** $7h - 3 = 4h + 8$

**9** $2j - 9 = 8j - 1$      **10** $9k + 8 = 4k - 3$

# 6.4 Unknown on both sides and negative coefficients

Some equations, for example $5x + 4 = 2 - 3x$, have the 'unknown' $x$ on both sides and one of the $x$ terms has a negative coefficient, in this case $-3x$.

To solve this type of equation, rearrange it so that the unknown appears on only one side.

**Example 3**

Solve $5x + 4 = 2 - 3x$.

$5x + 3x + 4 = 2$ ———————— Add $3x$ to both sides.

$8x + 4 = 2$

$8x = 2 - 4$ ———————— Subtract 4 from both sides.

$8x = -2$

$x = -\frac{2}{8}$ ———————— Divide both sides by 8.

$= -\frac{1}{4}$

**Example 4**

Solve $1 - 5x = 10 - 2x$.

$1 = 10 - 2x + 5x$ ———— Add $5x$ to both sides.

$1 = 10 + 3x$

$1 - 10 = 3x$ ———————— Subtract 10 from both sides.

$-9 = 3x$

$-3 = x$ ———————— Divide both sides by 3.

So $x = -3$

> Here both $x$ terms have negative coefficients.

## Exercise 6D

Solve these equations. Check your answers by substitution.

1   $4x + 3 = 8 - x$      2   $3x + 4 = 7 - 3x$      3   $2 - 5x = 3x + 14$

4   $9 - 2x = 3 - 4x$     5   $7 - 8a = 4 - 3a$      6   $5 - 6b = 8 - 2b$

7   $9 - 7c = 3 - 2c$     8   $5d - 7 = 2 - 4d$      9   $9 - 4e = 9 + 3e$

10   $8 - 3f = 1 - 6f$

# 6.5 Solving equations involving brackets

Sometimes you will need to solve equations involving brackets.

> See Section 2.4 to remind yourself how to multiply out brackets.

**Example 5**

Solve $3(x + 2) = 10$.

$3x + 6 = 10$ ———————— Expand the brackets.

$3x = 4$ ———————— Subtract 6 from both sides.

$x = \frac{4}{3} = 1\frac{1}{3}$ ———————— Divide both sides by 3.

**Example 6**

Solve $3(x + 8) = 27x - 6$.

You could always multiply out the brackets first and then continue as before. Here, the quicker thing to do is to divide both sides by 3 (as both the terms on the RHS are divisible by 3).

$$x + 8 = 9x - 2 \text{ ———————— Divide both sides by 3.}$$
$$x + 8 + 2 = 9x \text{ ———————— Add 2 to both sides.}$$
$$x + 10 = 9x$$
$$10 = 9x - x \text{ ———————— Subtract } x \text{ from both sides.}$$
$$10 = 8x$$
$$x = 1.25 \text{ ———————— Divide both sides by 8.}$$

## Exercise 6E

Solve these equations.

**1** $5(x + 2) = 30$      **2** $2(x + 7) = 8$

**3** $6(x - 2) = 1$      **4** $3(x - 1) = 7$

**5** $4(x + 1) = 9x$      **6** $5(x - 4) = 3x - 7$

**7** $3(2h + 1) = h - 2$      **8** $2(3p - 3) = 5(p - 1)$

**9** $2(2q + 3) = 3(4q - 2)$      **10** $4(9 - 3r) = 3(r + 2)$

**11** $4 - 2t = 2(8 + t)$      **12** $2(13 - 2x) = 9(9 + 2x)$

**13** $3(4x - 5) - 5(2x - 3) = 4(x - 1)$

**14** $6 + (5x - 7) - 2(3x + 4) = 7(x + 1)$

**15** $4(3x - 2) - (7x + 8) = 2(x - 5)$

**16** $6(x + 5) - 5(3x - 4) = 11 + 3(2x - 7)$

**17** $2(7x - 4) + (5 - 9x) = 1 - 3x$

**18** $3(5x + 2) - (9x - 8) = 7(x - 4) + (x + 12)$

**19** $8x - 5(2x + 3) - (1 - 6x) = 8 + (4 + 6x)$

**20** $5(3x - 7) + 2(9 - 2x) = 8x - (2x + 1) - 16$

**21** $3(5x - 4) - 7(2x - 3) = 3(x + 1) + 5$

# 6.6 Equations involving algebraic fractions

**Example 7**

Solve the equation $\dfrac{p}{4} - 2 = \dfrac{p + 4}{6}$

$\dfrac{p + 4}{6}$ is an algebraic fraction.

Multiply both sides of the equation by the LCM of the denominators.

The LCM of 4 and 6 is 12.

$$12\left(\dfrac{p}{4} - 2\right) = 12\left(\dfrac{p + 4}{6}\right) \quad\text{— Multiply both sides by 12.}$$
$$3p - 24 = 2p + 8 \quad\text{— Expand the brackets.}$$
$$p - 24 = 8 \quad\text{— Subtract } 2p \text{ from both sides.}$$
$$p = 32 \quad\text{— Add 24 to both sides.}$$

$$12\left(\dfrac{p}{4} - 2\right) = \dfrac{12 \times p}{4} - 24$$
$$= 3p - 24$$
$$12\left(\dfrac{p + 4}{6}\right) = 2(p + 4)$$
$$= 2p + 8$$

## Exercise 6F

Solve these equations.

**1** $\dfrac{h}{5} + 4 = 16$      **2** $\dfrac{p - 4}{8} = 7$      **3** $\dfrac{m + 7}{5} = 7$      **4** $\dfrac{m}{3} + 2 = \dfrac{m}{4} + 3$

**5** $\dfrac{g}{2} - 1 = \dfrac{g}{4} + 1$      **6** $\dfrac{n + 3}{3} = \dfrac{n}{5} + 3$      **7** $\dfrac{x}{6} + 1 = \dfrac{x - 4}{4}$      **8** $3(2p - 10) = \dfrac{4p - 7}{2}$

**9** $5\left(\dfrac{r}{3} - 3\right) = 40$      **10** $\dfrac{x}{4} - 6 = 1 - 2x$

# 6.7 Using equations to help solve problems

To solve 'mystery number' problems:

- Use a letter to represent the unknown number.
- Write the problem as an equation.
- Solve the equation.
- Write the answer.

Mystery Number Challenge

**Example 8**

I add 3 to a mystery number and multiply the result by 5. My answer is 55. Find the mystery number.

Write the problem as an equation with $x$ as the mystery number:

$$(x + 3) \times 5 = 55$$
$$5(x + 3) = 55$$
$$x + 3 = 11 \quad\text{— Divide both sides by 5.}$$
$$x = 11 - 3 \quad\text{— Subtract 3 from both sides.}$$
$$x = 8$$

The mystery number is 8.

## Exercise 6G

Solve the problems in questions **1** and **2** by writing and solving an equation.

**1**   I subtract 9 from a number and multiply the result by 4.
My answer is 36. Find the number.

**2**   I add 2 to a number and multiply the result by 5. The answer is
the same as when I add 8 to the number and multiply the result
by 3. Find the number.

**3**

(a)   The diagram shows an equilateral triangle.
Write down an equation in $p$ that must be true.

(b)   Solve your equation to find the value of $p$.

(c)   What is the length of a side of the triangle?

**4**   (a)   The diagram shows a square.
Write down an equation in $x$ that must be true.

(b)   Solve your equation to find the value of $x$.

(c)   What is the length of a side of the square?

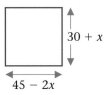

**5**   Priya has £15 at the start of half-term holiday. During the
holiday she goes to the cinema three times. Serena starts
with £12 and goes to the cinema twice. Neither of them
spends any other money. At the end of the week they
have equal amounts of money left. Let $c$ stand for the
cost of going to the cinema.

(a)   Write down an equation in $c$ that must be true.

(b)   Solve your equation to find the cost of going to
the cinema.

**6**   A cafe sells orange juice and apple juice.
At the start of one day there are 70 litres of orange juice and 60
litres of apple juice. During the day the cafe sells 60 glasses of
orange juice and 20 glasses of apple juice.
At the end of the day there are equal amounts of orange and
apple juice left.
Let $g$ stand for the amount of juice in a glass.

(a)   Write down an equation in $g$ that must be true.

(b)   Solve your equation to find the amount of juice in a glass.

# 6.8 Showing inequalities on a number line

An expression in which the left hand side and the right hand side are *not* equal is called an **inequality**. For example $x > 2$

You can use a number line to show an inequality such as $x > 2$:

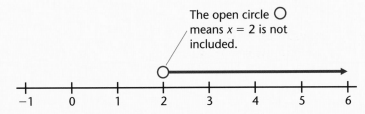

The open circle ◯ means $x = 2$ is not included.

| > | greater than |
| < | less than |
| ⩾ | greater than or equal to |
| ⩽ | less than or equal to |

Here is $x \leqslant 3$:

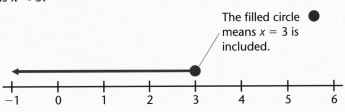

The filled circle ● means $x = 3$ is included.

And this shows $-2 \leqslant x < 1$:

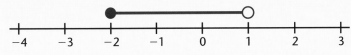

## Exercise 6H

Write down the inequalities shown in questions **1–4**.

**1**

**2**

**3**

**4**

Draw number lines to show the inequalities in questions **5–10**.

**5**  $x < 4$          **6**  $x \geqslant -2$          **7**  $x \leqslant -1$

**8**  $1 < x < 5$          **9**  $-2 < x \leqslant 0$          **10**  $-3 \leqslant x < -1$

# 6.9 Solving inequalities

$3 > -6$ is an inequality. It is also a true statement, so $3 > -6$ is a true inequality.

But does the inequality remain true when you do the following things to it?

(a) Add 4 to both sides:

$$3 + 4 > -6 + 4$$
$$7 > -2 \text{ is still true}$$

(b) Subtract 2 from both sides:

$$3 - 2 > -6 - 2$$
$$1 > -8 \text{ is still true}$$

(c) Multiply both sides by 2:

$$3 \times 2 > -6 \times 2$$
$$6 > -12 \text{ is still true}$$

(d) Divide both sides by 3:

$$3 \div 3 > -6 \div 3$$
$$1 > -2 \text{ is still true}$$

(e) Multiply both sides by $-5$:

$$3 \times -5 > -6 \times -5$$
$$-15 > 30 \text{ is \textbf{not true}}$$

(f) Divide both sides by $-3$:

$$3 \div -3 > -6 \div -3$$
$$-1 > 2 \text{ is \textbf{not true}}$$

> You can solve inequalities in the same way as solving equations **except** that you must not multiply or divide by a *negative* number.

To solve an inequality, rearrange it so that $x$ is on one side of the inequality, to give a range of values for $x$.

> To solve an inequality you **can**:
> - add the same quantity to both sides
> - subtract the same quantity from both sides
> - multiply both sides by the same *positive* quantity
> - divide both sides by the same *positive* quantity.
>
> But you **must not**:
> - multiply both sides by a *negative* quantity
> - divide both sides by a *negative* quantity.

**Example 9**

Solve $3x + 4 > 22$.

$3x > 18$ ———————— Subtract 4 from both sides.

$x > 6$ ———————— Divide both sides by 3.

**Example 10**

Solve $6 - 5x \geq 3x + 2$.

$6 \geq 3x + 5x + 2$ ———————— Add $5x$ to both sides.

$6 \geq 8x + 2$

$6 - 2 \geq 8x$ ———————— Subtract 2 from both sides.

$4 \geq 8x$

$\frac{1}{2} \geq x$ ———————— Divide both sides by 8.

Another way of writing $\frac{1}{2} \geq x$ is $x \leq \frac{1}{2}$.

## Exercise 6I

Solve these inequalities.

**1** $3x - 5 \leqslant 4$      **2** $5x + 2 > 4$      **3** $4x + 7 \geqslant 7x + 2$

**4** $7x + 2 < 5x - 4$      **5** $8 - 3a \leqslant 5$      **6** $1 - 6b > 7$

**7** $-5c < 20$      **8** $-2d \geqslant -3$      **9** $\frac{1}{2}e + 3 \leqslant 1$

**10** $5 - \frac{1}{4}f > 12$      **11** $2 - \frac{1}{2}g \geqslant 1$      **12** $4 - 5h \leqslant 3h$

**13** $8 - 3j < 2j + 13$      **14** $7 - 5k \leqslant 12 - 8k$      **15** $8 - 2m \geqslant 1 - 4m$

**16** $4 - 9n > 1 - 11n$

## Solving two-sided inequalities

To solve a two-sided inequality, treat it as two inequalities. Solve each inequality separately, then combine the two solutions.

---
**Example 11**

Solve $7 \leqslant 3x - 2 < 9$.

Treat this as two inequalities:

$$7 \leqslant 3x - 2 \quad \text{and} \quad 3x - 2 < 9$$
$$9 \leqslant 3x \qquad\qquad\qquad 3x < 11$$
$$3 \leqslant x \qquad\qquad\qquad x < 3\tfrac{2}{3}$$

Write the answer as $3 \leqslant x < 3\tfrac{2}{3}$.

---

## Exercise 6J

Solve these inequalities.

**1** $7 < 4p + 3 \leqslant 27$      **2** $3 < 2q - 7 < 8$

**3** $1 \leqslant 3r + 4 \leqslant 10$      **4** $-2 < \frac{1}{2}s + 1 < 3$

## Giving integer solutions to inequalities

**Integers** are the positive and negative whole numbers and 0:

$$\dots -3 \quad -2 \quad -1 \quad 0 \quad 1 \quad 2 \quad 3 \dots$$

Some questions will ask you for only the integer solutions of an inequality.

---
**Worked examination question 1**

List all the possible integer values of $n$ such that $-3 \leqslant n < 2$.

$$n = -3, \quad -2, \quad -1, \quad 0, \quad 1$$

---

---

**Worked examination question 2**

Given that $n$ is an integer, find the greatest value for $n$ for which $4n + 3 < 18$.

$$4n + 3 < 18$$
$$4n < 15$$
$$n < 3\tfrac{3}{4}$$

The greatest integer value less than $3\tfrac{3}{4}$ is 3. So $n = 3$

---

## Exercise 6K

**1**   List the possible integer values of $n$.

   (a)   $-2 \leqslant n \leqslant 1$        (b)   $0 < n < 5$

   (c)   $-3 \leqslant n < 0$        (d)   $-1 < n \leqslant 3$

**2**   Write down an inequality satisfied by the integers listed.

   (a)   2, 3, 4, 5        (b)   0, 1, 2, 3

   (c)   $-3, -2, -1$        (d)   $-2, -1, 0, 1, 2$

**3**   Find the greatest integer value of $n$.

   (a)   $3n + 2 < 10$        (b)   $8 - 5n \geqslant 2$

   (c)   $4n + 7 < 5$        (d)   $1 - 3n > 9$

**4**   Find the lowest integer value of $n$.

   (a)   $4n + 5 \geqslant 1$        (b)   $7 - 2n < 4$

   (c)   $6n + 7 > 2$        (d)   $5 - 4n < -2$

**5**   Find all the possible integer values of $n$.

   (a)   $5 \leqslant 2n + 1 < 9$        (b)   $4 < 5n - 1 \leqslant 14$

   (c)   $-4 < 3n + 5 < 12$        (d)   $-2 \leqslant 1 - 2n < 3$

# 6.10 Solving inequalities involving brackets

Remember that inequalities can be solved in the same way as equations except that you must not multiply or divide both sides by a *negative* number.

---

**Example 12**

Solve $3(x - 2) \leqslant 20$.

$$3x - 6 \leqslant 20 \text{ ———— Expand the brackets.}$$
$$3x \leqslant 26 \text{ ———— Add 6 to both sides.}$$
$$x \leqslant 8\tfrac{2}{3} \text{ ———— Divide both sides by 3.}$$

---

> Another way of solving $3(x - 2) < 20$ is to divide by 3 first.
>
> You can do this because 3 is positive.

**Example 13**

Solve $2(x + 2) + 3(2x - 3) > 2$.

$2x + 4 + 6x - 9 > 2$ —————— Expand the brackets.

$8x - 5 > 2$ —————— Simplify.

$8x > 7$ —————— Add 5 to both sides.

$x > \frac{7}{8}$ —————— Divide both sides by 8.

**Example 14**

Solve $2(3x - 2) + 3(4 - 3x) > 12 - (5x + 7)$.

$6x - 4 + 12 - 9x > 12 - 5x - 7$ ——— Expand the brackets.

$8 - 3x > 5 - 5x$ ——— Simplify.

$8 + 2x > 5$ ——— Add $5x$ to both sides.

$2x > -3$ ——— Subtract 8 from both sides.

$x > -1\frac{1}{2}$ ——— Divide both sides by 2.

## Exercise 6L

Solve these inequalities.

**1**   $3(x - 7) > 14$

**2**   $5(x + 4) > 40$

> Divide both sides by 5.

**3**   $4(x + 1) \leqslant 2x - 3$

**4**   $2(3x - 5) \geqslant 8 - 3x$

**5**   $3(x + 2) - 5(x - 4) < 27$

**6**   $5 - (3x + 4) \geqslant 4$

**7**   $7(x - 2) - (5x - 9) > 0$

**8**   $3x + 4(2x + 3) < 1$

**9**   $4(2x - 1) \leqslant 3(x + 4)$

**10**   $3 - (2x - 3) > 6$

**11**   $6(3x + 1) - 2(5x - 4) < 5(x + 2)$

**12**   $3(4x + 5) + (8 - 10x) \leqslant 4(x + 6)$

**13**   $7(3x - 4) - (12x - 5) > 5(2x - 3)$

**14**   $8x + 7(2 - x) < 9 - 3(x + 1)$

## Mixed exercise 6

In questions **1–14** solve the equations.

**1**   $6a - 5 = 13$

**2**   $5b + 2 = 9$

**3**   $8c + 10 = 2$

**4**   $4d + 5 = 3d + 9$

**5**   $7e + 4 = 5e - 8$

**6**   $6f - 1 = 3f + 1$

**7**   $8 - g = 10$

**8**   $-4h = 10$

**9**   $7 - 5i = 4$

**10**   $\dfrac{j}{2} + 3 = 7$

**11**   $9 - \frac{1}{4}k = 11$

**12**   $\dfrac{2m}{3} + 5 = 9$

**13**   $7n - 6 = 14 - 3n$

**14**   $8 - 3p = 13 - 5p$

**15** I multiply a number by 5 and add 3. The result is the same as when I multiply the number by 8 and subtract 18. Find the number.

**16** Pineapples cost six times as much as lemons.
The cost of 20 pineapples and 200 lemons is £86.40.
Find the cost of a lemon.

**17** (a)

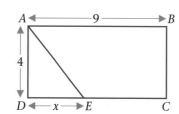

ABCD is a rectangle, measuring 4 cm by 9 cm.
E is a point on DC with DE = x cm.

The area of trapezium ABCE is 26 cm². Find the value of x.

(b)

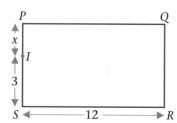

The area of rectangle PQRS is 60 cm². Find the value of x.

**18** Draw number lines to show these inequalities:
(a)  $x > 5$          (b)  $x \leqslant -3$
(c)  $3 < x \leqslant 5$        (d)  $-4 \leqslant x < 0$

**19** Solve these inequalities:
(a)  $8x + 3 < 19$      (b)  $6 - 5x \geqslant 16$      (c)  $3 - 2x < 7 - 5x$

**20** Find (i) the greatest and (ii) the lowest integer values of n for which these inequalities are true:
(a)  $4 \leqslant 3n - 2 < 10$          (b)  $1 < 4n + 5 < 20$

**21** The diagram shows the lengths, in cm, of the sides of a rectangle. The perimeter of the rectangle is P cm.
Work out the value of P.          [E]

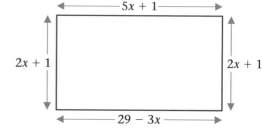

**22** Solve the inequality
$6(x + 4) - 7 - (3x + 10) \geqslant 2(4x - 5)$

**23** Solve the equation $\dfrac{y + 5}{3} = 6 - 2y$

# Summary of key points

**1** Whatever you do to one side of an equation you must also do to the other side.

**2** For equations with the unknown on both sides, rearrange so the unknowns are on one side of the equation and the numbers are on the other.

**3** An expression in which the left hand side and the right hand side are *not* equal is called an **inequality**. For example $x > 2$

**4** You can use a number line to show an inequality such as $x > 2$:

Here is $x \leqslant 3$:

And this shows $-2 \leqslant x < 1$:

**5** To solve an inequality you **can**:
- add the same quantity to both sides
- subtract the same quantity from both sides
- multiply both sides by the same *positive* quantity
- divide both sides by the same *positive* quantity.

But you **must not**:
- multiply both sides by a *negative* quantity
- divide both sides by a *negative* quantity.

**6** **Integers** are the positive and negative whole numbers and 0:

$$... -3 \quad -2 \quad -1 \quad 0 \quad 1 \quad 2 \quad 3 ...$$

# 7 Transformations and loci

This chapter shows you how to translate, rotate, reflect and enlarge shapes on a grid, and how to make accurate constructions and scale drawings.

Translations, rotations and reflections change the position of the object, but not its size or shape. The image and object are **congruent**.

## 7.1 Transformations

A **transformation** is a change in an object's position or size. You need to know the four kinds of transformation – translation, reflection, rotation and enlargement.

### Translation

> A **translation** moves every point on a shape the same distance and direction.

In this diagram triangle $A$ is translated to $B$. $B$ is the **image** of $A$. All the points on $A$ are moved $+3$ units parallel to the $x$-axis followed by $-2$ units parallel to the $y$-axis.

This translation is described by the **vector** $\begin{pmatrix} 3 \\ -2 \end{pmatrix}$.

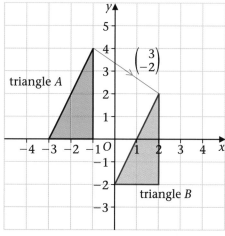

We say that triangle **A** 'maps onto' triangle **B**.

> In the vector $\begin{pmatrix} x \\ y \end{pmatrix}$
> - $x$ gives the movement parallel to the $x$-axis
> - $y$ gives the movement parallel to the $y$-axis.

> To describe a translation fully you need to give the distance moved and the direction of the movement. You can do this by giving the vector of the translation.

---

**Example 1**

Triangle $B$ is a translation of triangle $A$.
Describe the translation that takes $A$ to $B$.

Triangle $A$ has moved 2 squares in the $x$-direction
                   1 square in the $y$-direction.

The translation has vector $\begin{pmatrix} 2 \\ 1 \end{pmatrix}$.

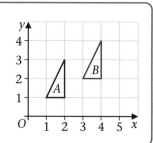

## Exercise 7A

1   Write the vectors describing these translations:

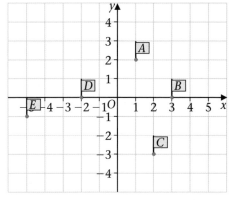

(a) flag $A$ to flag $B$

(b) flag $B$ to flag $A$

(c) flag $D$ to flag $B$

(d) flag $C$ to flag $E$

(e) flag $A$ to flag $E$.

2   Use graph paper or squared paper. Draw a set of axes and label each one from $-5$ to 5. Use the same scale for each axis. Draw a trapezium $A$, with vertices at $(-5, 3)$, $(-4, 3)$, $(-3, 2)$ and $(-3, 1)$.

(a) Transform $A$ by the translation $\begin{pmatrix} 7 \\ 1 \end{pmatrix}$.
    Label the new trapezium $B$.

(b) Transform $B$ by the translation $\begin{pmatrix} -1 \\ -6 \end{pmatrix}$.
    Label the new trapezium $C$.

(c) Write the single translation required to transform $A$ to $C$.

(d) Write the single translation required to transform $C$ back to $A$.

3   Use graph paper or squared paper. Draw a set of axes and label each one from $-5$ to 5. Plot points $A$ $(0, 1)$ and $B$ $(3, 2)$.

$T_1$ describes a translation of $\begin{pmatrix} 3 \\ 2 \end{pmatrix}$. $T_2$ describes a translation of $\begin{pmatrix} -2 \\ 1 \end{pmatrix}$. Write down the coordinates of $A$ and $B$ after these translations:

(a) $T_1$                         (b) $T_1$ followed by $T_1$ again

(c) Write down a single translation for **(b)**

(d) $T_1$ followed by $T_2$       (e) $T_2$ followed by $T_1$

(f) Write down what you notice about the images in **(d)** and **(e)**.

## Reflection

Stand directly in front of a mirror. You see your reflected **image**. The image appears to be the same distance away from the mirror as you are. Move closer to the mirror and the image moves closer. The mirror acts as a plane of symmetry.

> A **reflection** in a line produces a mirror image.
> The mirror line is a line of symmetry.

The diagram on the right shows a point $A$ reflected in a line.

The original shape $A$ and the image $A'$ are the same distance from the line, but on opposite sides.

If you draw a line from $A$ to $A'$ to cross the line of reflection at $M$. $AM = A'M$ and $AA'$ is at right angles to the line of reflection

Notice that $A'$ is a reflection of $A$ and $A$ is a reflection of $A'$.

You can draw the reflection of a shape by using these facts to find the images of different points on the shape.

___

**Example 2** _____

Copy the diagram on squared paper.

(a) Draw the reflection of the shape in the line $y = x$.

(b) Reflect the image back in the line $y = x$.
   What do you notice?

(a) Take each vertex on the object and locate its image.
   Imagine a line perpendicular to the line of symmetry.
   Join the points to produce the image.

   > For a sloping line of reflection, it is easier to draw a reflection if you turn the paper until the line is vertical.

(b) The image reflected in the line $y = x$ returns back to the object position.

___

A point on the mirror line remains unchanged by reflection.

A **repeated reflection** in the same mirror line returns the image to the original object.

To describe a reflection fully you need to give the equation of the mirror line.

## Exercise 7B

1  Draw a coordinate grid with both $x$- and $y$-axes going from $-4$ to 4.

   (a) Plot the points $P(-2, 1)$, $Q(0, 1)$, $R(1, 0)$, $S(3, 4)$ and $T(-2, 4)$ and join them in order to form the closed shape $PQRST$.

   (b) Draw the image of $PQRST$ after a reflection in the $x$-axis.

2   Describe fully the transformation that maps shape *A* onto *B*.

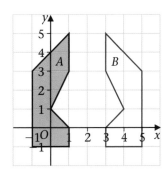

3   Use graph paper or squared paper. Draw a set of axes and label each axis from −5 to 5. Use the same scale for each axis.
Draw a rectangle with vertices (3, 1), (3, 2), (5, 2), (5, 1).
Label the rectangle *A*.

   (a)    (i)   Draw the reflection of *A* in the *x*-axis.
Label the image *B*.

          (ii)   Write the coordinates of the vertices of *B*.

         (iii)   Describe how the coordinates of *A* are changed by the transformation.

   (b)    (i)   Draw the reflection of *A* in the *y*-axis. Label the image *C*.

          (ii)   Write the coordinates of the vertices of *C*.

         (iii)   Describe how the coordinates of *A* are changed by the transformation.

   (c)   Draw the reflection of *A* in the line *y* = *x*. Label the image *D*.

   (d)   Draw the reflection of *D* in the *y*-axis. Label the image *E*.

   (e)   Describe fully the reflection that transforms *E* to *C*.

4   (a)   Copy this diagram. Extend the *x*- and *y*-axes to −5.
Reflect the object in the line *x* = 3.

   (b)   Reflect the image in the line *y* = 2.

   (c)   Reflect the object in the line *y* = −*x*.

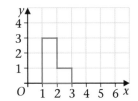

## Rotation

An object can be turned about a point.
This point is called the centre of rotation.

Triangle *A* is turned 120° clockwise about a **centre of rotation**.

To describe a **rotation** fully you need to give the
- centre of rotation
- amount of turn
- direction of turn.

(A clockwise direction may be indicated by a negative sign, and an anticlockwise direction by a positive sign.)

**Example 3**

Describe fully the transformation which maps shape $P$ onto shape $Q$.

Rotation of 90° clockwise about (0, 0).

Each vertex of the rectangle has been rotated 90° clockwise.

> You can use tracing paper to help you find the angle and centre of rotation.

The transformation in Example 3 could also be described as a rotation of 270° anticlockwise about the origin.

## Exercise 7C

1 Use graph paper or squared paper. Draw a set of axes and label each axis from −5 to 5. Use the same scale for each axis. Draw a triangle with vertices (3, 1), (5, 1) and (5, 3). Label the triangle $A$.

   (a) Rotate $A$ about the origin through 90° anticlockwise. Label the image $B$. Write the coordinates of the vertices of $B$.

   (b) Rotate $B$ about the origin through 90° anticlockwise. Label the image $C$. Write the coordinates of the vertices of $C$.

   (c) Write a single rotation to transform $A$ to $C$.

   (d) Rotate $A$ about the origin through 90° clockwise. Label the image $D$. Write the coordinates of the vertices of $D$.

   (e) Write a single rotation to transform $B$ to $D$.

   (f) Rotate $A$ about the point (3, 0) through 90° clockwise. Label the image $E$.

2 Describe fully the transformation which maps shape $A$ onto shape $B$.

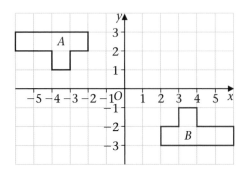

# Enlargement

Different sized photographs can be printed from the same negative. In each photograph the dimensions are in the same proportion as in the original. The images are not distorted. Each length is enlarged or reduced by a **scale factor**.

> An **enlargement** changes the size but not the shape of an object. The **scale factor** of the enlargement is the number of times the lengths of the original object have been enlarged.

The sides of shape $B$ are all twice as long as the corresponding sides of shape $A$. You can say that $B$ is an enlargement of $A$ with scale factor 2. All the corresponding angles are equal so $A$ and $B$ are **similar** (they are the same shape). $A$ and $B$ are the same way up.

Each line of $B$ is parallel to the corresponding line of $A$.

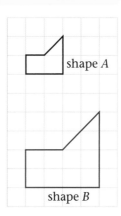

shape $A$

shape $B$

The scale factor can be positive, fractional or negative. In the diagram below, triangle $ABC$ has been enlarged by scale factor 2, using $X$ as the centre of enlargement.

For an enlargement about a centre $X$:

length $XA'$ = scale factor × length $XA$
length $XB'$ = scale factor × length $XB$,  etc.

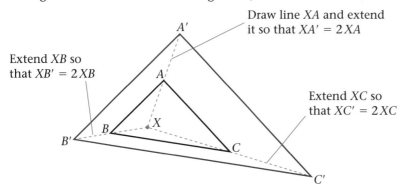

Draw line $XA$ and extend it so that $XA' = 2XA$

Extend $XB$ so that $XB' = 2XB$

Extend $XC$ so that $XC' = 2XC$

The enlarged triangle $A'B'C'$ is similar to triangle $ABC$. Each side of $A'B'C'$ is twice as long as the corresponding side in $ABC$. This is because the scale factor of the enlargement is 2. Corresponding angles are identical. Each of the lines in the enlarged shape is parallel to the corresponding original side.

> To describe an enlargement fully you need to give its centre and the scale factor.

**Example 4**

(a) Enlarge triangle $ABC$ with scale factor $\frac{1}{2}$ using $O$ as the centre of enlargement.

(b) Enlarge triangle $ABC$ with scale factor $-1$ using $O$ as the centre of enlargement.

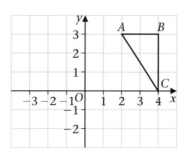

(a) $OA \times \frac{1}{2} = OA'$  $OB \times \frac{1}{2} = OB'$  $OC \times \frac{1}{2} = OC'$

An enlargement of scale factor $\frac{1}{2}$ has reduced each side of the triangle $ABC$. Triangles $ABC$ and $A'B'C'$ are similar.

The ratio of corresponding sides is $1 : \frac{1}{2}$ or $2 : 1$

(b) $OA \times -1 = OA''$  $OB \times -1 = OB''$  $OC \times -1 = OC''$

A negative scale factor indicates measuring from the centre of the enlargement in the opposite direction.

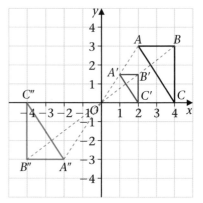

An enlargement by a scale factor smaller than 1 gives a reduced image.

An enlargement by a negative scale factor indicates that the measuring from the centre of the enlargement must be in the opposite direction.

**Example 5**

Describe fully the transformation that maps $ABCD$ onto $PQRS$.

$PQRS$ is the same shape as $ABCD$. The sides of $PQRS$ are all 2 times the lengths of the corresponding sides of $ABCD$.
So the transformation is an enlargement by a scale factor 2.

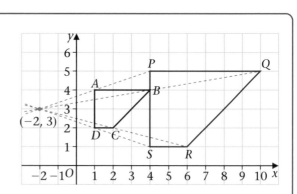

To find the centre of enlargement:
Join $P$ to $A$ and continue the line.
Join $Q$ to $B$ and continue the line.
In the same way, join $R$ to $C$ and $S$ to $D$ and continue the lines.

The lines all pass through the same point $(-2, 3)$, so this is the centre of enlargement.

The transformation is an enlargement by scale factor 2 with centre of enlargement $(-2, 3)$.

## Exercise 7D

1   Copy this shape on squared paper and then draw these enlargements:

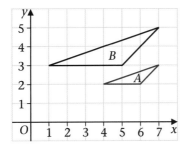

(a)   centre of enlargement at the origin and scale factor of enlargement 2

(b)   centre of enlargement at point (2, 1) and scale factor of enlargement 2

(c)   centre of enlargement at point (0, 0) and scale factor of enlargement $\frac{1}{2}$.

(d)   centre of enlargement at point (0, 4) and scale factor of enlargement $\frac{1}{2}$

2   Describe fully the transformation that maps shape $B$ onto shape $A$.

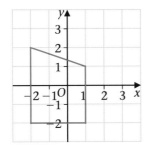

3   Copy this shape on squared paper and then draw the enlargement with centre of enlargement at the origin and scale factor of enlargement $\frac{1}{2}$.

4   Copy this shape on squared paper and then draw the enlargement with centre of enlargement at the origin and scale factor of enlargement $-3$.

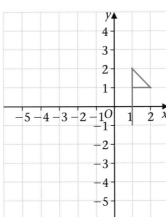

**5** State the centre of enlargement and scale factor of enlargement for

    (a) shape *A* to shape *B*

    (b) shape *A* to shape *C*

    (c) shape *C* to shape *A*

    (d) shape *A* to shape *D*.

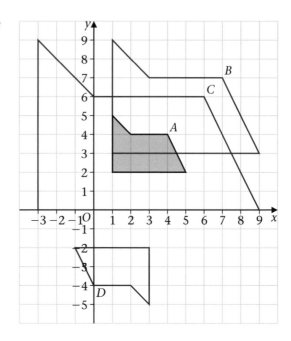

**6** These LOGO instructions produce a square:

Alter these instructions to enlarge the square by scale factor 3 with centre of enlargement at the starting position.

```
repeat 4 [fd 15 rt 90]
end
```

**7** Describe fully the enlargement that

    (a) maps *A* onto *B*

    (b) maps *B* onto *A*.

    (c) What do you notice about the scale factors?

**8**

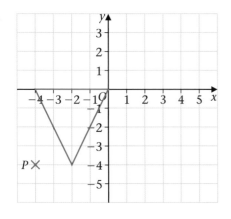

Draw a copy of the diagram on squared paper.
Enlarge the triangle by a scale factor $1\frac{1}{2}$, centre *P*.

9 Describe fully the single transformation which maps triangle $P$ onto triangle $Q$.

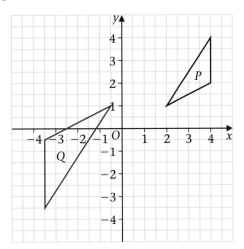

# 7.2 Combined transformations

Transformations can be combined by performing one transformation and then performing another transformation on the image.

**Example 6**

(a) Reflect the flag in the $y$-axis.

(b) Reflect the image in the line $y = x$.

(c) Describe the single transformation to replace (a) and (b).

(d) Reflect the image from (a) in the line $x = 2$.

(e) Describe the single transformation to replace (a) and (d).

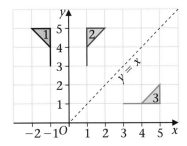

(a) Flag 2 is the image of flag 1.

(b) Flag 3 is the image of flag 2.

(c) Single transformation: rotate flag 1 through 90° clockwise about the origin.

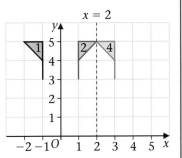

(d) The image from (a) is flag 2. Flag 4 is the image of flag 2.

(e) Single transformation: translate flag 1 by $\begin{pmatrix} 4 \\ 0 \end{pmatrix}$.

A reflection followed by a reflection can be replaced by a single transformation of
• a rotation if the reflection lines are *not* parallel
• a translation if the reflection lines are parallel.

## Exercise 7E

**1** (a) Reflect the triangle in the *x*-axis.

(b) Reflect the image in the *y*-axis.

(c) Describe the single transformation that replaces (a) and (b).

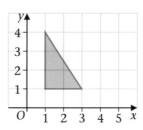

**2** (a) Reflect the shape in the line $x = 3$.

(b) Reflect the image in the line $x = 6$.

(c) Describe the single transformation that replaces (a) and (b).

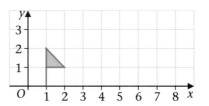

**3** (a) Reflect the rectangle in the line $y = -x$.

(b) Rotate the image 90° clockwise about the origin.

(c) Describe the single transformation that replaces (a) and (b).

**4** (a) Start with the same rectangle as in question **3**.
Rotate the rectangle 90° clockwise about the origin.

(b) Reflect the image in the line $y = -x$.

(c) Describe the single transformation that replaces (a) and (b).

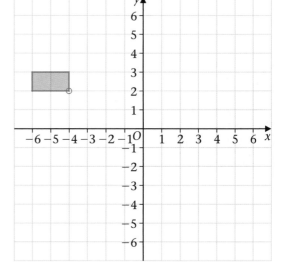

**5** (a) Enlarge the shape in question **2** with centre of enlargement at the point (2, 1) and scale factor −1.

(b) Describe this transformation in another way.

**6** (a) Rotate the rectangle 90° anticlockwise (+90°) about the point (1, 0).

(b) Enlarge the image with centre of enlargement at the point (−1, 3) and scale factor 2.

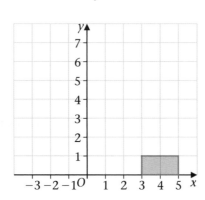

7 (a) Describe fully the single transformation that maps shape *P* onto shape *Q*.

(b) On a copy of the diagram, reflect shape *P* in the line $x = 1$.

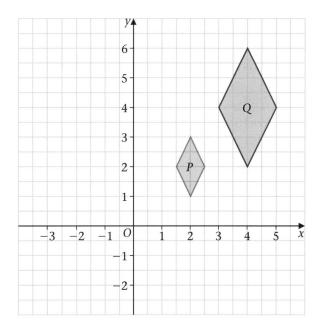

## 7.3 Scale drawings and scale models

The model racing car on the left is a small replica of the real racing car on the right. Each part of the model is a smaller version of the corresponding part on the real car.

Each length of 1 cm on the model represents 18 cm on the real car.
The model is built to a scale of 1:18.
The racing car is an enlargement of the model using a scale factor of 18.

    width of model × 18 = real width
    length of model × 18 = real length

To check the model steering wheel is in the correct scale:

    real steering wheel = 28.8 cm
   model steering wheel = 1.6 cm

Comparing measurements    1.6 : 28.8
                  1 : 18

> 28.8 ÷ 1.6 = 18

The model steering wheel is correctly made to a scale of 1 : 18.

> Scale drawings (or models) of objects are enlargements of a real object. The size of enlargement is given by the scale factor.

> The enlargement has a fractional scale factor.

**Example 7**

A map has a scale of 1 : 500 000.

(a) Complete this sentence: 1 cm on the map represents
_____ km in real life.

(b) The distance between Arken and Blorcastle is 4 cm on the map.
How far is Arken from Blorcastle in real life?

(c) Blorcastle is 12 km from Clarkwood. How far is this on the map?

(a) 1 : 500 000 is shorthand for '1 unit on the map represents 500 000 units in real life'. 1 cm on the map represents 5 km in real life.

(b) Arken and Blorcastle are 20 km apart.

(c) 12 km is represented on the map by 2.4 cm.

> Both parts of the ratio 1 : 500 000 have the same units. 500 000 cm = 5 km

> $4 \times 500\,000$ cm = 20 km
> $\frac{12}{5}$ km = $\frac{1\,200\,000}{500\,000}$ cm

## Exercise 7F

**1** A model boat is made using a scale 1:10.

    (a) The model is 76 cm long. How long is the real boat?

    (b) The model is 43 cm wide. How wide is the real boat?

**2** A model aeroplane is built using a scale of 1:50.

    (a) The model is 1.60 m wide. How wide is the real aeroplane?

    (b) The real aeroplane is 75 m long. How long is the model?

**3** This map of the Norfolk Broads is drawn to a scale of 1:600 000.

    (a) Calculate the approximate distance in kilometres between the centres of Acle and Great Yarmouth.

    (b) Calculate the approximate distance in kilometres between the centres of Norwich and Great Yarmouth.

    (c) Lowestoft is 16.25 km from Great Yarmouth. How far would this be on the map?

**4**　This is a scale drawing of Shardia's bedroom: She has drawn it so that 1 cm on the diagram represents 2 m in her bedroom.

(a)　Write this as a scale.

(b)　Measure the length and width of the bedroom on the plan.

Hint: 1 : ___ ___ ___

(c)　What are the length and width of the real bedroom?

(d)　How long is the real desk in metres?

**5**　This is a sketch of Arfan's bedroom. It is *not* drawn to scale. Draw an accurate scale drawing on cm squared paper of Arfan's bedroom. Use a scale of 1 : 50.

## 7.4 Constructions

A **construction** is an accurate drawing carried out using a straight edge (ruler), a pencil and a pair of compasses.

### Constructing a triangle

**Example 8**

Construct a triangle with sides of length 3 cm, 4 cm and 6 cm.

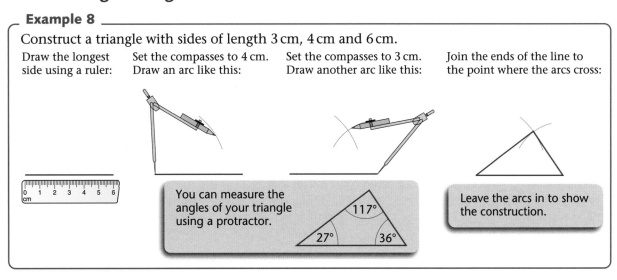

Draw the longest side using a ruler:

Set the compasses to 4 cm. Draw an arc like this:

Set the compasses to 3 cm. Draw another arc like this:

Join the ends of the line to the point where the arcs cross:

You can measure the angles of your triangle using a protractor.

Leave the arcs in to show the construction.

**Example 9**

Use triangle constructions to draw an angle of 60° without using a protractor.

An equilateral triangle has angles of 60°.
Construct an equilateral triangle by keeping your compasses set to the same length throughout.

Each angle of the equilateral triangle is 60°.

# Constructing a regular hexagon

**Example 10**

Construct a regular hexagon.
Keep your compasses set to the same length throughout.

| Draw a circle of any radius: | With the point of the compasses on the circumference, draw an arc: | Place your compass point where the first arc crossed the circle. Draw another arc: | Draw four more arcs like this and join them up to make a regular hexagon: |

Constructing a regular hexagon is another way of constructing a 60° angle. Each angle at the centre of the hexagon is 60°.

# Constructing perpendiculars

Perpendicular lines meet at right angles.
The green line is the perpendicular bisector of the blue one.

**Bisect** means 'cut in half'.

**Example 11**

Draw a line segment *AB* of length 8 cm and construct its perpendicular bisector.

You need to set your compasses to more than half the length of the line segment, say 6 cm.

| With the compass point at *B*, draw a large arc: | Place the compass point at *A*. Draw this arc: | Join the points where the arcs cross. This is the perpendicular bisector of *AB*. |

 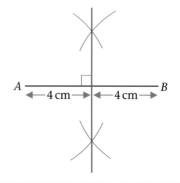

## Example 12

Construct a perpendicular to *AB* that passes
through the point *P*.
This is called constructing the perpendicular
**from *P* to *AB***.

Place your compass point at *P*.
Draw two arcs to cut the line
*AB*:

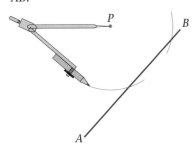

With the compass point at
the points where the arcs cut
the line, draw these arcs:

Join the point where the arcs
cross to *P*. This line is the
perpendicular from *P* to *AB*.

## Example 13

Construct a perpendicular to *AB* that passes through the point *P*.
This is called constructing the perpendicular **to *AB* at *P***.

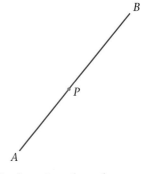

Place your compass point at *P*.
Draw two arcs to cut the line
*AB*:

Open the compasses more.
With the compass point at
the points where the arcs cut
the line, draw these arcs:

Join the point where the arcs
cross to *P*. This line is the
perpendicular to *AB* at *P*.

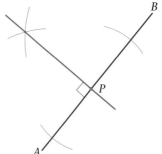

Examples 11, 12 and 13 all show methods of constructing right angles.

You could also construct a right angle using your knowledge of Pythagoras' theorem.

$3^2 + 4^2 = 5^2$, so you can create a right-angle by constructing a triangle with sides of length 3 cm, 4 cm and 5 cm.

> You will learn more about Pythagoras' theorem in Chapter 15.

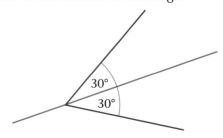

## Bisecting an angle

The bisector of an angle is the line that divides the angle into two equal parts. The green line is the bisector of this angle:

30°
30°

---

**Example 14**

Draw a 50° angle and construct its bisector.

Keep your compasses set to the same distance throughout.

Use a protractor to draw an angle of 50°. With your compass point at the vertex of the angle, draw two arcs to cut the sides of the angle:

Place your compass point at the points where the arcs cut the sides of the angle. Draw these arcs:

Join the point where the arcs cross to the vertex of the angle. This line is the bisector of the angle.

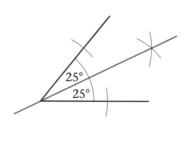

25°
25°

---

The bisector is a line of symmetry for the angle. The perpendicular distances from the bisector to both sides of the angle are the same.

$x$

$x$

## Exercise 7G

**1** Using a ruler, a pair of compasses and pencil only, construct triangles with sides of length

(a) 4 cm, 10 cm and 9 cm    (b) 8 cm, 7 cm and 12 cm.

**2** Use a ruler and protractor to draw triangles with the following lengths and angles.

(a) 6 cm, 50°, 7 cm    (b) 80°, 5.5 cm, 58°

(c) 6 cm, 5 cm, 40°

> Draw a sketch first.

**3** Draw a line segment of length 10 cm.
Using a straight edge, a pair of compasses and pencil only, construct the perpendicular bisector of this line segment.

**4** Draw this line accurately.
Construct the perpendicular to *XY* at *P*.

**5** Draw a line segment *AB* and a point below it, *Q*.
Construct the perpendicular from *Q* to *AB*.

**6** Construct an equilateral triangle with sides of length 8 cm.
What is the size of each angle of your construction?

**7** Draw an angle of any size.
Without using any form of angle measurer, construct the bisector of the angle.

**8** The diagram shows a construction of a regular hexagon.
What is the size of

(a) angle *x*    (b) angle *y*?

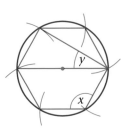

**9** Without using any form of angle measurer, construct an angle of

(a) 90°    (b) 45°    (c) 135°    (d) 60°

(e) 30°    (f) 15°    (g) 120°

**10** This diagram is a sketch of a triangle *ABC*.

(a) Without using any form of angle measurer, construct the triangle *ABC*.

(b) Measure the length of *BC*.

# 7.5 Locus of a point

When Michael throws a cricket ball to his friend
Simon, the ball moves along the path shown in
the diagram on the right.

As this merry-go-round turns, the horses move
up and down.

Michael                                    Simon

The mechanism on the merry-go-round makes a point on the tip of a
horse's nose (or any point on a horse) obey a particular rule which
takes the same path every rotation:

360°

0°

Path of the tip of the horse's
nose during one revolution
of the merry-go-round.

This path is called the **locus** of the point.

> A **locus** is a set of points which obey a particular rule (plural : loci).

A locus may be produced by something moving (such as a cricket ball
or a merry-go-round) according to a set of rules, or by a set of points
which follow a mathematical rule.

## Locus around a fixed point

**Example 15**

Draw the locus of a point which moves so that it is
always 3 cm from a fixed point.

*A* is the fixed point. Draw a circle, radius 3 cm and
centre at *A*. The locus of points satisfying the rule is
the circumference of the circle.

3 cm

*A*

The locus of a point which moves so that it is always a fixed distance from a point $A$ is a circle, centre $A$.

---

**Example 16** _____

The diagram shows a rectangular lawn.

A garden sprinkler rotates from a fixed position on the lawn. Water from the sprinkler reaches a maximum distance of 4 m from the sprinkler.

Complete the diagram and shade the parts of the lawn watered by the sprinkler.

The sprinkler waters the area within a circle, centre the sprinkler, radius 4 m.

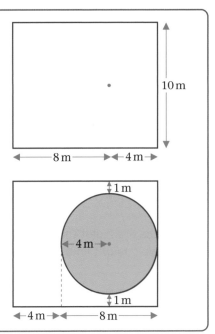

---

## Locus around a fixed line

**Example 17** _____

(a) Sketch the locus of a point which moves so that it is always 2 cm from a straight line 3 cm long.

(b) A goat is tethered in a field by a 10 m rope. The other end of the rope is allowed to slide along a horizontal bar 12 m long. Make a scale drawing to show the parts of the field the goat can graze.

(a) The locus is two parallel lines (2 cm either side of $AB$ and the same length as $AB$) with a semicircle of radius 2 cm drawn at each end.

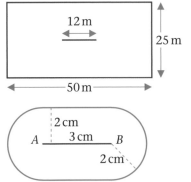

(b) The goat can graze any of the shaded area.

---

The locus of a point that moves so that it is always the same distance from a straight line is two parallel lines with a semicircle at each end.

# Locus of a point the same distance from two lines at an angle

### Example 18

Draw the locus of a point which moves so that it is always the same distance from two straight lines.

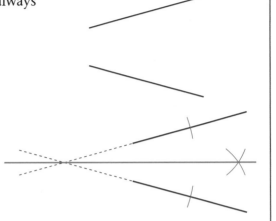

The perpendicular distances from two lines to their angle bisector are always equal.

Continue the two lines and bisect the angle between them.

The locus of a point that moves so that it is always the same distance from two straight lines is the bisector of the angle between the lines.

# Locus of a point the same distance from two points

### Example 19

Draw the locus of a point that moves so that it is always the same distance from points $A$ and $B$.

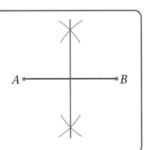

Draw the perpendicular bisector of $AB$.

The locus of a point which moves so that it is always the same distance from two points $A$ and $B$ is the perpendicular bisector of the line $AB$.

## Exercise 7H

**1** Mark two points *A* and *B* roughly 4 cm apart. Draw a path equidistant from *A* and *B*.

**2** Draw the locus of a point that moves so that it is always 2.5 cm from a line 4 cm long.

**3** A heavy cuboid box is moved by tipping it over on each edge. Draw the locus of any point *P* on the box as it makes a whole turn.

> You could model this using a cube.

**4** A running track is designed so that any point on the track is 22.3 m from a fixed line 150 m long.

(a) Draw the locus of the point.

(b) Calculate the distance once round the running track.

**5** A bicycle has wheels of radius 45 cm. It has a reflector on the front wheel attached 30 cm from the centre.

(a) Write the shortest distance the reflector can be from the road.

(b) Sketch the locus of the reflector as the bicycle moves forward through one complete wheel turn.

**6** Baby Susan is placed inside a rectangular playpen measuring 1.2 m by 0.8 m. She can reach 30 cm outside the playpen. Draw the locus of the points Susan can reach beyond the edge of the playpen.

**7** Daniel lives at the point marked *X*. There are schools at Ayleton, Bankbury and Corley. Each school allows pupils to attend provided they live in the catchment area. This is a particular distance from the school.

Ayleton

Bankbury

*X*

Corley

**Scale: 1 cm = 1 mile**

Ayleton accepts pupils who live less than 5 miles away. Bankbury accepts pupils who live less than 4 miles away, and Corley accepts pupils who live less than 3 miles away. Trace the diagram. Shade the catchment area for each school. Write down which school(s) Daniel could attend.

**8** Samia enters a rectangular field 40 m by 30 m by a gate in one corner. She crosses the field by taking a path equidistant from the hedges at the side of the gate. Construct the locus of her path accurately.

**9** *A* and *B* are two fixed points.
A point *P* moves in the plane such that $A\hat{P}B = 45°$.
Sketch the complete locus of *P* above and below the line *AB*.

**10** Repeat question **9** for $A\hat{P}B = 30°$.

# 7.6 Bearings

Imagine your boat is in the harbour at point *H*. There is a ship out at sea at point *S*, 5 km away. You can describe the position of the ship by giving its bearing and distance from you.

The **bearing** is the angle measured from North in a clockwise direction.

It is a 3-figure angle measured in degrees.

The ship's bearing from you is 065°. It is 5 km from you, on a bearing of 065°.

A **bearing** is an angle expressed in three digits to indicate direction.

___ **Example 20** _____

Fred lives at *F*. His friend Winston lives 1 km away on a bearing of 210°.

**(a)** Show this on a diagram.

Fred visits Winston. After a while Fred returns home.

**(b)** Calculate the bearing Fred takes from Winston's home to arrive back home.

**(a)**

The bearing of *W* from *F* is 210°

N

210°

F

1 km

W

**(b)  Method 1**

*W* is on a bearing of 210° from *F*. Fred needs to turn through half a turn (180°) to face home again. The bearing of *F* from *W* is

210° − 180° = 030°

The bearing of *F* from *W* is 030°.

**Method 2**

Draw another North line at *F* and use alternate angles:

The bearing of *F* from W is 030°.

A bearing giving the reverse direction is called a **back-bearing**.

## Exercise 7I

**1**  Draw diagrams to show these bearings:

    (a)  016°          (b)  200°          (c)  325°

    (d)  009°          (e)  168°

**2**  Write

    (a)  the bearing of *A* from *O*.

    (b)  the bearing of *B* from *O*.

    (c)  the bearing of *C* from *O*.

**3**  Three friends live near each other. Their homes are shown by *X*, *Y* and *Z*. *Y* is on a bearing of 055° from *X*. Angle *XYZ* = 120° as shown on the diagram.

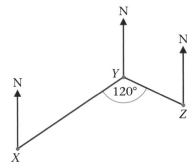

Remember:
Co-interior angles

*x* + *y* = 180°

Calculate the bearing of

    (a)  *X* from *Y*          (b)  *Z* from *Y*          (c)  *Y* from Z.

**4** The bearing of *B* from *A* is 060°.
What is the bearing of *A* from *B*?

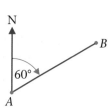

**5** The bearing of *E* from *D* is 145°.
What is the bearing of *D* from *E*?

**6** Investigate bearings and back-bearings where the bearing of *B* from *A* is

(a) less than 180°

(b) greater than 180°.

## Mixed exercise 7

**1** A ship, *S*, leaves a harbour, *H*, and travels 40 km due North to reach a marker buoy, *B*.
At *B* the ship turns and travels for a further 30 km on a bearing of 075° from *B* to reach a lighthouse, *L*.
At *L* it turns again and travels back to *H* in a straight line.

(a) Sketch the locus of the ship's path.

(b) Make an accurate scale drawing of the path taken by the ship.

(c) Measure the bearing of *L* from *H*.

(d) Use your scale drawing to find the distance *HL*.

**2** Make a copy on squared paper of the diagram below.

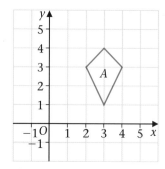

Reflect shape *A* in the *x*-axis to give shape *B*.
Draw and label shape *B*.

Enlarge shape *A* by scale factor 2, centre *O*, to give shape *C*.
Draw and label shape *C*.

3   Make a copy on squared paper of the diagram below.

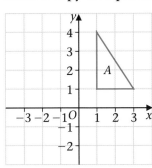

Shape *A* is rotated 90° anticlockwise, centre (0, 1), to shape *B*.

Shape *B* is rotated 90° anticlockwise, centre (0, 1), to shape *C*.

Shape *C* is rotated 90° anticlockwise, centre (0, 1), to shape *D*.

(a)   Mark the positions of shapes *B*, *C* and *D*.

(b)   Describe the single transformation that takes shape *C* to shape *A*.

4   Make a copy on squared paper of the diagram on the right.

(a)   Rotate triangle *A* 180° about *O*. Label your new triangle *B*.

(b)   Enlarge triangle *A* by scale factor $\frac{1}{2}$, centre *O*. Label your new triangle *C*.

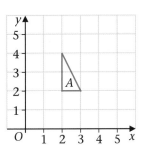

5   Triangle B is a reflection of triangle A.

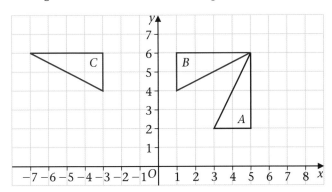

(a)   Copy the diagram on squared paper and draw the line of reflection.

(b)   Write down the equation of the line of reflection.

(c)   Describe fully the single transformation that maps triangle *A* onto triangle *C*.                                                                 [E]

6   A map is drawn to scale of 1 : 25 000.

Two schools *A* and *B* are 12 cm apart on the map.

(a)   Work out the actual distance from *A* to *B*. Give your answer in kilometres.

*B* is due East of *A*.

*C* is another school. The bearing of *C* from *A* is 064°. The bearing of *C* from *B* is 312°.

(b) On a copy of the scale drawing below, mark, with a cross, the position of the school *C*.

N

*A* ————————————————————————— *B*

**7** Make a copy of the line *XY*.
Draw the locus of all points which
are 3 cm away from the line *XY*.

*Y*

*X*

**8** The diagram represents a triangular garden *ABC*.

The scale of the diagram is 1 cm to represent 1 m.

A tree is to be planted in the garden so that it is
• nearer to *AB* than to *AC*
• within 5 m of point *A*.

On a copy of the diagram, shade the
region where the tree may be planted.

*A*

*B*

*C*

**9** Draw a line and mark the point *A* at one end.
Use a ruler and a pair of compasses to construct
an angle of 45° at *A*.

You must show all construction lines.

Draw a circle and divide
the angle at the centre by
the number of sides.

**10** Construct a regular pentagon and a regular octagon of any size.

**11** The diagram shows the position of each of three buildings in a
town.

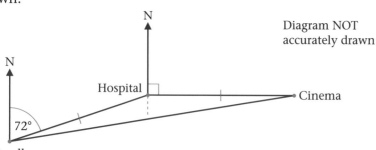

N

Diagram NOT
accurately drawn

N

Hospital

Cinema

72°

Art gallery

The bearing of the hospital from the art gallery is 072°.
The cinema is due East of the hospital.
The distance from the hospital to the art gallery is equal to the
distance from the hospital to the cinema.

Work out the bearing of the cinema from the art gallery.     [E]

# Summary of key points

**1** A **translation** moves every point on a shape the same distance and direction.

**2** To describe a translation fully you need to give the distance moved and the direction of the movement. You can do this by giving the vector of the translation.

**3** In the vector $\begin{pmatrix} x \\ y \end{pmatrix}$

- $x$ gives the movement parallel to the $x$-axis
- $y$ gives the movement parallel to the $y$-axis.

**4** A **reflection** in a line produces a mirror image. The mirror line is a line of symmetry.

**5** A point on the mirror line remains unchanged by reflection. A **repeated reflection** in the same mirror line returns the image to the original object.

**6** To describe a reflection fully you need to give the equation of the mirror line.

**7** To describe a **rotation** fully you need to give the
- centre of rotation
- amount of turn
- direction of turn.

(A clockwise direction may be indicated by a negative sign, and an anticlockwise direction by a positive sign.)

**8** An **enlargement** changes the size but not the shape of an object. The **scale factor** of the enlargement is the number of times the lengths of the original object have been enlarged.

**9** To describe an enlargement fully you need to give its centre and the scale factor.

**10** An enlargement made with a scale factor smaller than 1 gives a reduced image.

**11** An enlargement made with a negative scale factor indicates that the measuring from the centre of the enlargement must be in the opposite direction.

**12** A reflection followed by a reflection can be replaced by a single transformation of
- a rotation if the reflection lines are *not* parallel
- a translation if the reflection lines are parallel.

**13** Scale drawings (or models) of objects are enlargements of a real object. The size of enlargement is given by the scale factor.

**14** A **construction** is an accurate drawing carried out using a straight edge (ruler), a pencil and a pair of compasses.

**15**   A **locus** is a set of points which obey a particular rule (plural : loci).

**16**   The locus of a point which moves so that it is always a fixed distance from a point $A$ is a circle, centre $A$.

**17**   The locus of a point that moves so that it is always the same distance from a straight line is two parallel lines with a semicircle at each end.

**18**   The locus of a point that moves so that it is always the same distance from two straight lines is the bisector of the angle between the lines.

**19**   The locus of a point which moves so that it is always the same distance from two points $A$ and $B$ is the perpendicular bisector of the line $AB$.

**20**   The position of a point $P$ with reference to a fixed point $O$ can be identified by the **bearing** of $P$ (bearings are angles measured clockwise from the North line and expressed in three digits), together with the distance $OP$.

**21**   A bearing giving the reverse direction is called a **back-bearing**. It is the outward bearing plus 180°.

# 8 Using basic number skills

You need to use number skills in a wide range of mathematical calculations. In this chapter you will calculate percentages and rates, and learn the notation for very large or very small numbers.

## 8.1 Percentage increases

2003 was a 'boom year' for house prices in the UK. Prices went up by an average of 24% during the first quarter.

If this bar represents the price of a house at the beginning of the year,

then this bar represents the price at the end of March.

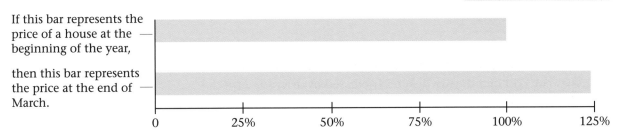

As a percentage the new value is

100% + 24% = 124% of the old value.

**Example 1**

Jenny earns £26 000 a year. She gets a 12.5% increase. Calculate her new salary.

A 12.5% increase means that her new salary will be (100 + 12.5)% of her old salary.

112.5% as a decimal is 1.125 •————

1.125 is called the multiplier.

Her new salary is 1.125 × 26 000 = £29 250

**Example 2**

Tom gets a 15% rise in pay.

He was earning £9500 a year. What is his new salary?

As a percentage of his old salary his new salary is

(100 + 15)% = 115%

As a decimal, 115% is 1.15

Tom's new salary is 1.15 × £9500 = £10 925

If an amount is increased by $x$% the new amount is (100 + $x$)% of the original amount. So the new amount = the old amount × (100 + $x$)%.

## Exercise 8A

1   Write the new value as a percentage of the old value if
   (a)   a house increases in value by 12%
   (b)   the balance in a bank account increases by 17%
   (c)   the weight of a man goes up by 30%
   (d)   the cost of a car goes up by 11%
   (e)   the cost of a washing machine increases by 8.5%.

2   (a)   If you want to increase a quantity by 24%, what do you multiply by?
   (b)   Graham's salary of £10 850 is increased by 24%. What is his new salary?

3   (a)   In order to increase an amount by 40%, what do you multiply by?
   (b)   The cost of a theatre ticket is increased by 40% for a special concert. What is the new price if the normal price was £15.40?

4   Katherine buys a woodburning stove for £1298 plus VAT at $17\frac{1}{2}$%. Work out the total price including VAT.

5   Gail wants to work out what her weight will be if it increases by 4%.
   What should she multiply her present weight by?

6   (a)   Increase £120 by 20%.
   (b)   Increase 56 kg by 25%.
   (c)   Increase 2.4 m by 16%.
   (d)   Increase £1240 by 10.5%.
   (e)   Increase 126 cm by 2%.

## 8.2 Percentage decreases

During 1993 house prices in the UK fell by an average of 5% during the first quarter.

If this bar represents the price of a house at the beginning of the year,

then this bar represents the price at the end of March.

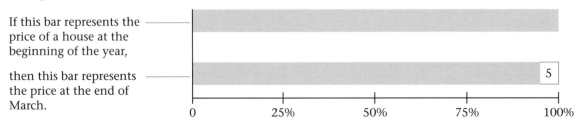

As a percentage the new value is
   $(100 - 5)\% = 95\%$ of the old value.

> If an amount is decreased by $x$% the new amount is $(100 - x)$% of the original amount. So the new amount = the old amount $\times (100 - x)$%.

## Exercise 8B

**1**  Write the new value as a percentage of the old value if
  (a)  a house decreases in value by 16%
  (b)  the balance in a bank account decreases by 11%
  (c)  the weight of a man goes down by 5%
  (d)  the value of a car goes down by 22%.

**2**  (a)  If you want to decrease a quantity by 34%, what do you multiply by?
  (b)  The value of a company's shares falls by 34%. Before the drop the shares cost £5.25 each. What is the new price?

**3**  Alan weighs 82 kg before going on a diet. He sets himself a target of losing 5% of his original weight. What is his target weight?

**4**  (a)  Decrease £120 by 20%.   (b)  Decrease 56 kg by 25%.
  (c)  Decrease 2.4 m by 16%.   (d)  Decrease £1240 by 10.5%.
  (e)  Decrease 126 cm by 2%.

**5**  Carla invested £100 in a savings account on 1 January 1999. The interest paid was 6% per annum.
  (a)  What do you multiply by to find the total amount in her savings account at the end of the first year?
  (b)  How much money did she have in her account at the end of the first year?
  (c)  Copy and complete this table. Give the amounts to the nearest pound.

| Date | 1/1/99 | 1/1/00 | 1/1/01 | 1/1/02 | 1/1/03 |
|---|---|---|---|---|---|
| Amount | £100 | | | | |

**6**  A car costing £14 000 depreciates (loses value) by
  • 12% in its first year
  • 18% in its second year
  • 5% each year thereafter.
  (a)  Find the value of the car after 1 year.
  (b)  Copy and complete this table. Give your answers to the nearest pound.

| New price | £14 000 |
|---|---|
| Value after 1 year | |
| Value after 2 years | |
| Value after 3 years | |
| Value after 4 years | |
| Value after 5 years | |

7    The amount in an investment account increases by 10% in the first year and a further 8% in the second.

   (a)    What should you multiply by to find the value after the first year?

   (b)    What should you multiply by to find the value after two years?

> Be careful: it is not 1.18.

## 8.3 Finding percentage increases

The **percentage increase** is $\dfrac{\text{actual increase}}{\text{original price}} \times 100\%$

### Example 3

In 2000 a box of tissues cost 60p.
In 2004 a similar box cost 80p.
What was the percentage increase in price?

The actual increase is $80 - 60 = 20$p.

The fractional increase is $\dfrac{\text{actual increase}}{\text{original price}} = \dfrac{20}{60}$

$\frac{20}{60}$ as a decimal is $0.3\dot{3}$

Percentage increase is $0.3\dot{3} \times 100 = 33\frac{1}{3}\%$

> Remember:
> To change a decimal to a percentage multiply by 100.

## Exercise 8C

1    The box of tissues in Example 3 had increased in price from 45p in 1998 to 80p in 2004. Find

   (a)    the fractional increase from the 1998 cost of 45p to the 2004 price

   (b)    the fractional increase from the 1995 cost of 40p to the 2004 price

   (c)    the percentage increase from 1998 to the 2004 price

   (d)    the percentage increase from 1995 to the 2004 price.

2    Calculate the percentage increase from

   (a)    £24 to £36           (b)    12.5 kg to 20 kg

   (c)    2.45 m to 2.86 m     (d)    50 s to 1 minute.

3    Before fitting a 'fuel-saver' Jamie's car travelled 36 km on 4.5 litres of petrol. After fitting the fuel-saver it travelled 58.3 km on 5.5 litres. Find

   (a)    the distance travelled on 1 litre of fuel before the fuel saver was fitted

   (b)    the distance travelled on 1 litre of fuel after it was fitted

   (c)    the percentage increase in distance travelled.

4    Siamak buys an old car for £8400. He spends £1040 on repairs, then sells the car on eBay for £14 900. Find

   (a)   his actual profit

   (b)   his percentage profit to the nearest 1%.

5    A mechanic at a garage pours 1.5 litres of oil into a 24 litre oil drum which was exactly $\frac{1}{4}$ full.

   (a)   Find the amount of oil now in the drum.

   (b)   By what percentage has the amount of oil in the drum increased?

# 8.4 Finding percentage decreases

The **percentage decrease** is $\dfrac{\text{actual decrease}}{\text{original price}} \times 100\%$

---

**Example 4**

Josie invests £800 in a company called Spec-U-Late Ltd.
One year later she finds her investment is only worth £680.
Find   (a)  her actual loss       (b)  her percentage loss.

(a)    Her actual loss is £800 − £680 = £120

(b)    Her fractional loss is $\frac{120}{800}$

       $\frac{120}{800}$ as a decimal is 0.15

       So her percentage loss is $0.15 \times 100 = 15\%$

---

## Exercise 8D

1    Josie invested £800. One year later this investment was only worth £680 (see Example 4). After a further year Josie's investment had fallen to £540. Find

   (a)   her actual loss over the two years

   (b)   her percentage loss over the two years

   (c)   her percentage loss between the end of the first year and the end of the second year of her investment.

2    Find the percentage decrease to the nearest 1% of

   (a)   a decrease from £48 to £32

   (b)   a decrease from 5.2 kg to 3.8 kg

   (c)   a decrease from 45 cm to 39.5 cm

   (d)   a decrease from 2 min to 110 s

   (e)   a decrease from 1 m to 45 cm.

3   This table shows the value of a car after different numbers of years from new.

| New price | £12 500 |
|---|---|
| after 1 year | £10 000 |
| after 2 years | £8 600 |
| after 3 years | £7 500 |
| after 4 years | £6 600 |

(a)   Calculate the percentage loss from new to the end of each year.

(b)   Calculate the percentage loss between the second and third years.

## 8.5 Mixing percentage increases and decreases

**Example 5**

In 1997, Mr Peck's flat was valued at £60 000.
The value of the flat increased by 20% during 1998.
During 1999 the value of the flat decreased by $12\frac{1}{2}$%.

Work out the value of the flat at the end of 1999.

By the end of 1998, the value of the flat, in pounds, was

$$60\,000 + 20\% \text{ of } 60\,000$$
or      $60\,000 \times (1 + 0.2)$
or      $60\,000 \times 1.2$
         $= 72\,000$

By the end of 1999, the value of the flat, again in pounds, had fallen by 12.5% of the £72 000.

So by the end of 1999, the value of the flat was

$$72\,000 - 12.5\% \text{ of } 72\,000$$
or      $72\,000 \times (1 - 0.125)$
or      $72\,000 \times 0.875$
         $= 63\,000$

## Exercise 8E

1   The price of a holiday in 2004 was £450.
    The same holiday cost an extra 12% in 2005.
    In 2006 the same holiday was reduced by 15% of its price in 2005.
    Work out the price of this holiday in 2006.

2   Jenny bought a flat in September 2002.
    The value of the flat then was £52 000.
    During the first year, the value of the flat decreased by 8%.
    Over the next year the value of the flat increased by 14%.
    Work out the value of the flat in September 2004 to the nearest pound.

3   Erica bought £10 000 worth of shares in May 2002.
    By May 2003 the value of the shares had increased by 15%.
    By May 2004 the value of the shares had decreased by $n$% of
    their value in May 2003.
    The value of the shares in May 2004 was again £10 000.
    Work out the value of $n$.

4   Sanjit bought a house in 1994 for £84 000. In 1999 he sold it to
    James for £120 000. In 2004 James had to sell the house for
    £80 000. Calculate

    (a)   Sanjit's percentage profit

    (b)   James's percentage loss

    (c)   the percentage change in the value of the house between
          1994 and 2004.

## 8.6 More percentage calculations

### Example 6

The price of a carpet is reduced by 20% in the sale. It now costs
£60. What was the pre-sale price?

The sale price is $(100 - 20)$% = 80% of the pre-sale price

$$= 0.8 \text{ in decimal form}$$

A flow diagram can be used to represent the information in the
question:

$$\text{pre-sale price} \xrightarrow{\times 0.8} \text{£60}$$

To solve this type of flow diagram problem, draw a second flow
diagram reversing the direction and using the inverse operation:

$$\text{£75} \xleftarrow{\div 0.8} \text{£60}$$

The pre-sale price of the carpet was £75.

Remember:
In this type of question
you are *not* finding 80%
of the *given* price, but
80% of the *unknown*
price.

### Example 7

A gas bill of £47.25 includes VAT at 5%. How much VAT is paid?

**Method 1**

$$£47.25 = 105\%$$

So        $1\% = 47.25 \div 105$

$$= £0.45$$

So   5% VAT $= 5 \times 0.45 = £2.25$

**Method 2**

Use the multiplier method:

Bill without VAT

$$= 47.25 \div 1.05$$

$$= £45$$

So VAT $= 47.25 - 45 = £2.25$

## Exercise 8F

1   A television is reduced by 10% in a sale. The sale price is £540.

   (a)   What percentage of the pre-sale price is the sale price?

   (b)   Draw a flow diagram to show this information.

   (c)   Find the pre-sale price.

2   An electricity bill of £58.38 includes VAT at 5%.
    How much VAT is paid?

3   A dining room table costs £699, including VAT at $17\frac{1}{2}$%.
    How much VAT is paid?

4   The total price of a winter holiday includes VAT at 17.5%.
    In the brochure the total price is quoted as £320 per person.

   (a)   What percentage of the pre-VAT price is the total price?

   (b)   Draw a flow diagram to show this information.

   (c)   Find the price before VAT is added.

5   Due to falling orders, Jonson's Electrical Company decreases
    its workforce by 8%, down to 161 employees. Find

   (a)   the number of employees before the decrease

   (b)   the actual decrease in the number of employees.

6   After two years the value of a new drilling machine has fallen to
    £12 000. The depreciation is estimated at 10% per year. Find, to
    the nearest penny,

   (a)   the value of the drilling machine after the first year

   (b)   the original price.

# 8.7 Compound interest

Tessa invests £250 in a bank's internet account. The account
pays an annual interest rate of 6% per annum. She wants
to know how much her money will be worth in 6 years.

This problem would be easy if the bank paid **simple interest**
of 6% of the original amount for each of the 6 years:

   6% interest on £250 for 1 year is £15

   6% interest on £250 for 6 years is £15 × 6 = £90

Tessa's investment after 6 years would then be worth

   £250 + £90 = £340.

But banks usually pay **compound interest**, meaning they pay interest
on the interest too. So at the end of the second year Tessa will get 6%
interest on both her original investment and the first year's interest.

This table shows how her investment will grow over 6 years.

| Year | Amount at start of year | Interest | Total amount at year end |
|------|------------------------|----------|--------------------------|
| 1 | £250 | $250 \times 0.06$ | £265 |
| 2 | £265 | $265 \times 0.06 = 250 \times 0.06^2$ | £280.90 |
| 3 | £280.90 | $280.90 \times 0.06 = 250 \times 0.06^3$ | £297.75 |
| 4 | £297.75 | $297.75 \times 0.06 = 250 \times 0.06^4$ | £315.62 |
| 5 | £315.62 | $315.62 \times 0.06 = 250 \times 0.06^5$ | £334.56 |
| 6 | £334.56 | $334.56 \times 0.06 = 250 \times 0.06^6$ | £354.63 |

After 6 years' compound interest, Tessa's investment will have grown to £354.63 to the nearest penny, compared with £340 if simple interest only had been paid.

**Compound interest** is interest paid on an amount and on the interest already earned.

To calculate compound interest, find the multiplier:

Amount after $n$ years = original amount $\times$ multiplier$^n$

___ **Example 8** ___

A student borrows £600 to buy a laptop. Interest is added to the loan each year at the rate of 5% per annum.
How much does the student owe after 3 years if no repayments are made?

Each year the loan is increased by 5% to 105%, which is 1.05 times the previous value.

$£600 \times 1.05^3 = £694.58$

## Exercise 8G

Use the table in Section 8.7 for questions **1–4**.

**1** (a) How much more interest does Tessa receive over the six years if compound interest is paid, rather than simple interest?

(b) What percentage of the original investment is the extra interest?

**2** Copy the table showing Tessa's compound interest and extend it to find how much the original investment would have grown to after ten years.

**3**  **(a)**  How much more interest does £250 invested at 6% compound interest for 10 years gain than £250 invested at 6% simple interest?

  **(b)**  What percentage of the £250 is the extra interest?

  **(c)**  What annual simple interest rate over the 10 year investment period would give the same amount of interest as the 6% compound interest rate?

**4**  How many years will it take £250 to double in value when invested

  **(a)**  at 6% compound interest

  **(b)**  at 6% simple interest?

**5**  On 1 January Surjit invests £1000 in an investment account that pays compound interest at a rate of 8.2%.
Calculate the value at

  **(a)**  the end of the first year

  **(b)**  the end of the fourth year

  **(c)**  the end of the eighth year.

**6**  The Bank of Nirvana pays compound interest at an annual rate such that an investment doubles in value every two years.
Claire thinks that the interest rate paid per annum must be 50%.
Explain why she must be wrong.

**7**  Colin rents a house at a monthly rent of £620. In the rent agreement it states that the rent will be reviewed annually and will be increased by the annual inflation rate.
Assuming an annual inflation rate of 4%, find

  **(a)**  the amount of rent paid in the first year

  **(b)**  the rent increase at the end of the first year

  **(c)**  the monthly rent paid during the second year

  **(d)**  the monthly rent to be paid during the seventh year.

**8**  A car costs £12 000 when bought new. It depreciates (loses value) at an annual rate of 10%. Find

  **(a)**  the value of the car at the end of the first year

  **(b)**  the value at the end of the second year

  **(c)**  the value at the end of the fifth year

  **(d)**  the time it takes for the value of the car to reach £6000.

> The value goes down each year so do the opposite of compound interest: take the amount off each year. The amount each year will be different.

**9**  By what factor will an investment increase if compound interest is paid at a rate of 12.5% per annum over a period of

  **(a)**  4 years          **(b)**  6 years          **(c)**  10 years?

Write your answers as decimals or percentages.

10  For insurance purposes the value of house contents depreciate by
    8% each year once purchased. What is the value of the following
    items for insurance purposes?

    (a)  A television bought for £650 and 2 years old

    (b)  A dining room table and chairs bought for £2450 and
         4 years old

    (c)  A three piece suite bought for £1250 and 3 years old

## 8.8 Compound measures

Compound measures combine measurements of two or more
different types. For example, a speed is a measurement of a *distance*
and the *time* taken to travel it. You need to know how to use a variety
of compound measures.

### Average speed (rate of travel)

Lisa travelled from Nottingham to London, a distance of 205 km. She
started at 07.00 and arrived in London two and a half hours later.

She did not travel at a constant speed throughout the journey, but her
average speed can be found from:

**Average speed** $= \dfrac{\text{distance travelled}}{\text{time taken}}$

So average speed $= \dfrac{205}{2.5} = 82$ km/h

> In travel problems, times
> are often given in hours
> and minutes. To make
> calculations easier, change
> the minutes into a decimal
> fraction of an hour.
>
> To do this, divide the
> minutes by 60.
> For example:
> 42 minutes $= 42 \div 60$
> $\qquad\qquad\quad = 0.7$ hour

___ Example 9 ___

Jacki takes 36 minutes to walk to school, a distance of 1.8 km.
Find her average speed in

(a) metres per minute    (b) km per hour    (c) miles per hour.

(a)  Distance travelled = 1800 m
     Time taken = 36 minutes

     Average speed $= \dfrac{1800}{36} = 50$ m/min

(b)  Distance travelled = 1.8 km
     Time taken $= 36 \div 60 = 0.6$ hour

     Average speed $= \dfrac{1.8}{0.6} = 3$ km/h

(c)  Distance travelled $= 1.8 \times 0.625 = 1.125$ miles
     Time taken $= 36 \div 60 = 0.6$ hour

     Average speed $= \dfrac{1.125}{0.6} = 1.88$ mph

> You can use this triangle
> to help you remember the
> formulae.

> Cover the value you wish
> to find with your thumb:
> e.g. to find speed cover S.
> You are left with D over T,
> that is
> $\dfrac{\text{distance}}{\text{time}}$

> 1 km $= \frac{5}{8}$ mile
> 1 km = 0.625 mile

## Exercise 8H

1 *The Flying Scotsman* took 7 hours 15 minutes to travel from Edinburgh to London, a distance of 632 km.

   (a) Calculate the average speed of the train in km per hour.

   (b) Given that 1 km is approximately equal to 0.62 miles, calculate the average speed in miles per hour.

*The Flying Scotsman* first broke the 100 mph speed barrier in 1934.

2 Paul travelled by coach from Derby to Birmingham, a distance of 45 miles.
   The journey took 1 hour 45 minutes.
   Calculate the average speed of the coach.

3 Change these times into hours, giving your answers correct to 2 d.p. where appropriate.

   (a) 75 minutes    (b) 24 minutes    (c) 6 minutes

   (d) 25 minutes    (e) 45 minutes    (f) 10 minutes

4 A car travelled 50 km in 2 hours 42 minutes. How long was the journey in

   (a) minutes      (b) hours?

   (c) Calculate the average speed for the journey.

5 Shannon took 1 hour 40 minutes to complete a science experiment. Jack took 1.6 hours to complete the same experiment. Work out

   (a) who took the longer time, and by how much, to complete the experiment

   (b) the average (mean) time taken by the two students.

> To change a decimal fraction of an hour into minutes, multiply by 60. For example:
> 0.6 hour = 0.6 × 60
> = 36 minutes

6 Change these times into hours and minutes.

   (a) 0.4 hour      (b) 5.3 hours      (c) 3.25 hours

   (d) 6.29 hours    (e) 3.9 hours      (f) 9.88 hours

7 Ron and Garth set out at 1200 hours for a 25 km walk. They walked for 2 hours 18 minutes, then had a 30 minute rest before completing their walk in a further 2.2 hours. Calculate

   (a) the time it took to complete the 25 km walk

   (b) the average speed for the journey.

8 A train travelled at 80 km per hour for 2.25 hours, then at 60 km per hour for a further 4 hours 36 minutes. Find

   (a) how far the train travelled altogether

   (b) how long the journey took in total

   (c) the average speed for the journey.

## Other rates

**Example 10**

The average fuel consumption of a car can be measured in kilometres per litre.

A car uses 17.6 litres (*l*) of petrol in travelling 220 km. What is its average fuel consumption?

$$\text{Average fuel consumption} = \frac{220}{17.6} = 12.5 \text{ km per litre or km/}l$$

## Exercise 8I

1   What is the average fuel consumption (in km per litre) of a car which travels 464 km on 32 litres of petrol?

2   Mr Robson sets out with a full tank of petrol on a business trip of 588 km. When he arrives, his petrol gauge indicates that his tank is $\frac{1}{8}$ full.

   (a)   If a full tank holds 48 litres of petrol, calculate
      (i)   how much petrol it took to complete the journey
      (ii)   the average fuel consumption.

   (b)   If the average fuel consumption remains the same, how much further can he travel before he runs out of petrol?

3   Carol fits a *regular* 4.5 V battery into her radio. The battery costs £2.60 and lasts for 320 hours. She replaces it with a *long life* battery which costs £4.68 but lasts for 600 hours.

   (a)   Find   (i)   the cost per hour for each battery
          (ii)   the time per pound for each battery.

   (b)   Which type of battery is the better buy, and why?

4   Kay found these exchange rates in a newspaper:
      £1 was equivalent to 2.25 Swiss francs
      £1 was equivalent to 1.58 US dollars
   Calculate the exchange rate between the USA and Switzerland in

   (a)   francs per dollar      (b)   dollars per franc.

5   If this bath is filled from the cold tap only, it takes 5 minutes to fill. If filled from the hot tap only, it takes 8 minutes to fill. The bath holds 920 litres. Calculate

   (a)   the flow rate in litres per minute for each tap

   (b)   how long it would take to fill the bath if both taps were turned fully on.

**6**    A lorry travelling at 40 km per hour uses diesel fuel at an
average consumption of 6.25 km per litre.

    **(a)**    What is the consumption:
        **(i)**  in litres per km   **(ii)**  in litres per hour?

    **(b)**    **(i)**  How far will the lorry travel in 15 minutes?
         **(ii)**  How much diesel will it use?

## Measuring flow

For liquid flowing through a pipe:
volume flowing per second = cross-sectional area × speed

### Example 11

Roger is watering his vegetable patch with a hosepipe
which has a cross-sectional area of $1.6\,\text{cm}^2$.
Water flows out of the pipe at a speed of 5 cm per second.

Find the amount of water flowing out of the pipe in

**(a)**  $\text{cm}^3$ per second      **(b)**  litres per hour.

**(a)**    Volume flowing = cross-sectional area × speed

$$= 1.6 \times 5$$
$$= 8 \text{ cm}^3/\text{second}$$

> In one second a cylinder of water
> 5 cm long and $1.6\,\text{cm}^2$ in cross-
> section flows out of the pipe.

**(b)**    If $8\,\text{cm}^3$ flow per second then

$60 \times 8\,\text{cm}^3$ will flow per minute $= 480\,\text{cm}^3/\text{minute}$

and $60 \times 480\,\text{cm}^3$ will flow per hour $= 28\,800\,\text{cm}^3/\text{hour}$

$$= \frac{28\,800}{1000}$$

$1000\,\text{cm}^3 = 1$ litre ⎯⎯⎯ $= 28.8$ litres/hour

## Exercise 8J

**1**    A water butt holds $1.5\,\text{m}^3$ when full. It is leaking at a rate of
0.25 litres/minute.
How long will it take in hours and minutes for a full butt of water
to leak away?

**2**    Water flows through a plastic pipe at a rate of $260\,\text{cm}^3$ per
second. Find

    **(a)**    the amount of water discharged in
        **(i)**  cubic metres per second   **(ii)**  litres per minute

    **(b)**    the time it takes to discharge one cubic metre of water

    **(c)**    the time it would take to fill a water tank holding
        800 litres of water.

# Density

The density of a substance is its mass per unit volume:

$$\textbf{density} = \frac{\text{mass}}{\text{volume}}$$

Densities are often given in g/cm³ (i.e. grams per cubic centimetre).

---

**Example 12**

This block of lead has a volume of 540 cm³ and a mass of 6.156 kg.
Find its density in g/cm³.

$$\text{Density} = \frac{\text{mass}}{\text{volume}} = \frac{6156\,\text{g}}{540\,\text{cm}^3} = 11.4\,\text{g/cm}^3$$

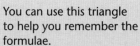

---

**Example 13**

A gold bar has a density of 19.3 g/cm³.
Its mass is 57 900 g.
Calculate the volume of the bar.

$$\text{Volume} = \frac{\text{mass}}{\text{density}} = \frac{57\,900}{19.3} = 3000\,\text{cm}^3$$

You can use this triangle
to help you remember the
formulae.

## Exercise 8K

1 A cast iron rod has a mass of 240 kg. Its cross-sectional area
   is 10 cm² and its density is 7.5 g/cm³. Calculate
   (a) the volume of the rod
   (b) the length of the rod in metres.

2 A cast iron rod 2 metres long has a cross-sectional area of 14 cm².
   The mass of the rod is 210 kg. Calculate
   (a) the volume of metal in the rod
   (b) the density of cast iron in g/cm³.

3 The density of aluminium is 2590 kg/m³. Find
   (a) the mass of a piece of aluminium which has a volume of
       2.5 m³
   (b) the volume of a piece of aluminium whose mass is 1200 kg.

4 This is the cross-section of a prism 12 cm long. It has a mass of
   3.5 kg. Calculate
   (a) its volume
   (b) the density in g/cm³ of the material from which it is made.

## 8.9 Ratios

You can use **ratios** to show how things are divided or shared.

---

**Example 14**

Tony and Kamiljit bought a pack of five recordable
DVDs. They shared the DVDs and the cost.
Tony took two DVDs and Kamiljit took three.

(a)  In what ratio did they share the DVDs?

(b)  What fraction of the DVDs did Tony take?

(c)  The pack cost £3. What was a fair amount for Tony to pay?

(a)  They shared the DVDs in the ratio $2:3$

(b)  Tony took $\frac{2}{5}$ of the DVDs.

(c)  Tony should pay $\frac{2}{5} \times £3 = £1.20$

> ratio:     $2:3$
> fraction: $\frac{2}{5}$  $\frac{3}{5}$

---

**Example 15**

Barbara and Peter inherit £4000 in their aunt's will. The money is to be shared $3:2$ in favour of
Barbara. How much does each receive?

**Method 1**

Sharing in the ratio $3:2$ means
that the money is divided into
5 parts, with Barbara getting
3 parts and Peter getting 2 parts.

So Barbara gets  $\frac{3}{5} \times £4000 = £2400$
and Peter gets  $\frac{2}{5} \times £4000 = £1600$

**Method 2**

Use the unitary method.
Find the value of one part:

5 parts = £4000
  1 part = £4000 ÷ 5 = £800

So Barbara gets $3 \times £800 = £2400$
and Peter gets $2 = £800 = £1600$

> Check this by adding:
> £2400 + £1600 = £4000

---

## Exercise 8L

1   Errol, Jane and Karl open a bag of chocolate and find it contains
    12 bars. They decide to share them in the ratio $1:2:3$. In turn
    Errol takes one bar, Jane two and Karl three. They keep doing
    this until they have shared out all the bars.

(a)  How many chocolate bars will
     (i) Errol have   (ii) Jane have   (iii) Karl have?

(b)  When all the chocolate bars have been shared out, what
     fraction of the total will
     (i) Errol have   (ii) Jane have   (iii) Karl have?

     Write each fraction in its simplest form.

2   Sally, Brian and Mark want to share £40 in the ratio $2:3:5$.

(a)  What fraction of the £40 will each person receive?

(b)  How much will each person receive?

**3** Donna and Shirley share £270 in the ratio 3:5, respectively.

   **(a)** To work out how much each receives, how many parts should £270 be divided into?

   **(b)** What fraction of £270 does Donna receive?

   **(c)** How much does Donna receive?

   **(d)** What fraction does Shirley receive?

   **(e)** How much does Shirley receive?

**4** Danny and Melissa work in a café. Danny works five days a week but Melissa only works two days a week.

   To be fair they agree to share their tips in the ratio of the numbers of days they work.

   **(a)** In what ratio do they share their tips?

   **(b)** What fraction of the tips should Danny receive?

   **(c)** If the tips in one week came to £66.50, how much did Melissa receive?

   **(d)** The following week the tips came to £84. How much did Danny receive?

   **(e)** One week Danny received £25 in tips. How much did Melissa receive?

**5** In a GCSE maths course, 80 of the final marks are for written exam papers. The other 20 are from coursework assignments.

   **(a)** Write the ratio of exam marks to coursework marks in its simplest form.

   **(b)** Daly got a final percentage of 66. The ratio of his exam marks to coursework marks was 8:3. How many coursework marks did he get?

**6** Tom sells three types of soap powder in his shop: New Mold, New Drift and New Purr. In one week he sells 476 boxes of soap powder in the ratio 1:2:4, respectively.

   **(a)** What fraction of the total sales are New Drift?

   **(b)** How many boxes of New Mold does he sell?

   **(c)** If he makes 8p profit on each box sold, how much profit does he make altogether from the two best-selling powders?

**7** Val and Bill run The Grange Residential Home. They held a fund raising morning and raised £360. Val raised £240 from selling raffle tickets. The rest was raised by Bill selling refreshments.

   **(a)** How much did Bill raise from the sale of refreshments?

   **(b)** What is the ratio of the amount raised from selling raffle tickets to the amount raised from refreshments? Write your ratio in its simplest form.

   **(c)** The following year a second fund raising morning was held and a total of £423 raised. The amounts raised were in the same ratio as in the previous year. How much was raised from selling raffle tickets?

**8** Four darts players each threw three rounds of three darts to raise money for charity. The charity received £1 for each point scored. The players scored a total of 1728 between them. Their individual scores were in the ratio 3:4:4:5.

(a) What score did the best player obtain?

(b) What must the best player have scored each round to achieve this total score?

(c) What was the lowest total score?

(d) What was the difference in score between the highest scorer and the lowest?

> The highest possible score for one dart is 60.

**9** In Midgrove School the ratio of pupils to teachers is 17.2 to 1.

(a) Multiply 17.2 by 5.

(b) Rewrite the ratio in the form $m:n$ where $m$ and $n$ are both whole numbers.

(c) What is the smallest possible number of pupils in the college?

(d) If the actual total of pupils and teachers is 1456, how many teachers are there?

> Use part **(a)** to help you.

# 8.10 More ratios

**Example 16**

In a bottle of Pepsea two secret ingredients are added in the ratio 5:8. If 5.2 ml of the first ingredient is added

(a) how much of the second ingredient is added

(b) how much in total is added?

(a) Of the total amount added, $\frac{5}{13}$ is the first ingredient and $\frac{8}{13}$ the second.

$\frac{5}{13}$ of the total amount added is 5.2 ml.

Find 1 part from 5 parts:

$\frac{1}{13}$ of the total amount added is $5.2 \div 5 = 1.04$ ml

so $\frac{8}{13}$ of the total amount is $8 \times 1.04 = 8.32$ ml.

8.32 ml of the second ingredient is added.

(b) There are 5.2 ml of the first ingredient and 8.32 ml of the second so a total of $5.2 + 8.32 = 13.52$ ml of the two ingredients are added.

## Exercise 8M

**1** At Christmas Darren, Nathan and Joe received Christmas cards in the ratio 4:4:5, respectively. Joe received 75 cards.

(a) What fraction of the cards did Joe receive?

(b) What fraction did Darren and Nathan receive between them?

(c) How many cards did Darren receive?

(d) How many cards did they receive altogether?

2 A petrol company carried out a fuel consumption test and found that the winter to summer ratio for the same car over the same test track was 3.5:4. The winter fuel consumption rate was 8.2 km per litre. Find the summer consumption rate.

5 miles is approximately equal to 8 km.

3 When driving in France the speed limit in towns is 60 km/h.

   (a) Write the distance in miles to the distance in kilometres as a ratio.

   (b) Kevin drives through a French town at 35 mph. Is he breaking the speed limit?

   (c) The maximum speed allowed on British roads is 70 mph. What is this speed in km/h?

4 The average marks of three teaching groups at Midgrove School were in the ratio 4:5:7. The average mark of the middle group was 62.5. Find

   (a) the lowest average mark

   (b) the difference between the highest and lowest average marks

   (c) the ratio of the lowest average mark to the highest average mark, expressing your answer in the form 1:$n$.

5 Ben and Catherine win the National Lottery and have a motoring holiday in Europe. They visit Paris, Rome, Berlin and Oslo, and spend time in each city in the ratio 4:5:7:9, respectively. They spend 12 days in Paris. Find

   (a) how many days they spend in Oslo

   (b) how many days they spend in Berlin

   (c) how much longer they spend in Berlin than in Rome

   (d) how many days they spend away altogether.

6 During one season East Ham Rovers, Muncaster United and Sheffield Thursday scored a total of 270 goals between them. East Ham Rovers scored twice as many as Muncaster United, who scored 3 times as many as Sheffield Thursday. Find

   (a) the scoring ratio between the three football clubs

   (b) how many goals Muncaster United scored

   (c) the difference between the number of goals scored by East Ham Rovers and by Sheffield Thursday.

7 A gang of four villains robbed a bank but got caught. On passing sentence the judge told the first villain: 'You are the gang leader and will serve the longest sentence'. To the next: 'You were second in charge so you will serve the next longest sentence'. To the fourth robber he said, 'You were led astray by the others so I will give you the shortest sentence. I sentence you all to a total of 122 years in prison to be served in the ratio $1:\frac{1}{2}:\frac{1}{3}:\frac{1}{5}$.' Work out how long each person's prison sentence was.

# 8.11 Standard form

Standard form is a convenient kind of shorthand for writing large and small numbers. To use it you need to know how to write powers of 10 in index form.

For example:

$$10 = 10^1$$
$$100 = 10 \times 10 = 10^2$$
$$1000 = 10 \times 10 \times 10 = 10^3$$

This **power** or **index** means multiply 10 by itself 3 times. It does not mean $3 \times 10$.

## Numbers greater than 1

Here are some numbers greater than 1 written in standard form:

| number | | | in standard form | |
|---|---|---|---|---|
| 3000 | = | $3 \times 1000$ | = | $3 \times 10^3$ |
| 5 000 000 | = | $5 \times 1\,000\,000$ | = | $5 \times 10^6$ |
| 7 200 000 | = | $7.2 \times 1\,000\,000$ | = | $7.2 \times 10^6$ |

Astronomers use standard form to record large measurements. The Sun's diameter is about 1 392 000 km or $1.392 \times 10^6$ km.

A number is in **standard form** when:

$$7.2 \times 10^6$$

This part is written as a number between 1 and 10

This part is written as a power of 10

$72 \times 10^5$ is *not* in standard form.

This part has *not* been written as a number between 1 and 10.

Make sure you know how to enter numbers in standard form on your calculator.

## Exercise 8N

**1** Express these numbers as powers of 10.
  (a)  $10 \times 10$
  (b)  $10 \times 10 \times 10$
  (c)  $10 \times 10 \times 10 \times 10 \times 10 \times 10$
  (d)  $10 \times 10 \times 10 \times 10 \times 10 \times 10 \times 10 \times 10 \times 10 \times 10$

For example, $10 \times 10 \times 10 \times 10 = 10^4$.

**2** Write each number as a number of millions using decimals where necessary.
  (a)  6 000 000
  (b)  3 400 000
  (c)  7 800 000
  (d)  5 500 000
  (e)  2 650 000
  (f)  7 642 000

For example, 8 650 000 is 8.65 million.

**3** Write these numbers in standard form.
  (a)  3.1 million
  (b)  4.3 million
  (c)  0.5 million
  (d)  2 400 000
  (e)  7 800 000
  (f)  8 600 000
  (g)  4 000 000
  (h)  9 000 000
  (i)  400 000

**4** Write these numbers as powers of 10.

- (a) 1 thousand
- (b) ten thousand
- (c) ten
- (d) 1 million
- (e) 1 hundred thousand
- (f) ten × ten × ten

> For example,
> $100 = 10 \times 10 = 10^2$.

**5** Copy and complete this table.

| | $10^6$ | $10^5$ | $10^4$ | $10^3$ | $10^2$ | $10^1$ | $10^0$ | Standard form |
|---|---|---|---|---|---|---|---|---|
| (a) | | | 7 | 4 | 0 | 0 | 0 | $7.4 \times 10^4$ |
| (b) | | | | | 2 | 6 | 0 | |
| (c) | | 6 | 8 | 0 | 0 | 0 | 0 | |
| (d) | | | | | | 4 | 5 | |
| (e) | 9 | 9 | 0 | 0 | 0 | 0 | 0 | |
| (f) | | | | | | 6 | 2 | |
| (g) | | | | | | | 8 | |

> The first row is done for you.

**6** Write these numbers in standard form.

- (a) 16
- (b) 4300
- (c) 650 000
- (d) 87 000 000
- (e) 670
- (f) 865
- (g) 9 870 000
- (h) 98 500
- (i) 805 000 000 000

## Changing from standard form to an ordinary number

Here is how to change $5.2 \times 10^4$ from standard form into an ordinary number:

$$
\begin{aligned}
5.2 \times 10^4 &= 5.2 \times 10 \times 10 \times 10 \times 10 \\
&= 52 \times 10 \times 10 \times 10 \\
&= 520 \times 10 \times 10 \\
&= 5200 \times 10 \\
&= 52\,000
\end{aligned}
$$

So $5.2 \times 10^4 = 52\,000$ as an ordinary number.

## Exercise 8O

**1** Change these numbers from standard form to ordinary numbers.

- (a) $4.2 \times 10^2$
- (b) $6.7 \times 10^4$
- (c) $5.5 \times 10^3$
- (d) $7.5 \times 10^6$
- (e) $6.2 \times 10^5$
- (f) $7.3 \times 10^4$
- (g) $2.4 \times 10^7$
- (h) $1.1 \times 10^1$
- (i) $7.25 \times 10^0$

**2** Evaluate these expressions, giving your answers in standard form.

- (a) $25 \times 36$
- (b) $640 \times 15$
- (c) $45 \times 900$
- (d) $25^4$

# Numbers less than 1

Very small numbers can also be written more conveniently in standard form.

You need to know how to write these as powers of 10:

$$0.1 = \frac{1}{10} \qquad = \qquad = 10^{-1}$$

$$0.01 = \frac{1}{100} = \frac{1}{10 \times 10} = 10^{-2}$$

$$0.001 = \frac{1}{1000} = \frac{1}{10 \times 10 \times 10} = 10^{-3}$$

$$0.0001 = \frac{1}{10\,000} = \frac{1}{10 \times 10 \times 10 \times 10} = 10^{-4}$$

Here is how to write 0.041 in standard form:

$$0.041 = \frac{4.1}{100} = 4.1 \times \frac{1}{100} = 4.1 \times \frac{1}{10^2} = 4.1 \times 10^{-2}$$

0.041 in standard form is $4.1 \times 10^{-2}$.

Here is how to change a number in standard form back to an ordinary decimal number:

$$2.4 \times 10^{-3} = \frac{2.4}{10^3} = \frac{2.4}{1000} = 0.0024$$

$$10^{-3} = \frac{1}{10^3}$$

Biologists working with micro-organisms sometimes use standard form to record their sizes.
This bacterium is 0.000 21 cm long or $2.1 \times 10^{-4}$ cm.
Magnification: ×14 400.

> Start by writing 0.041 as a fraction with a numerator between 1 and 10.
> Remember:
> $$10^{-2} = \frac{1}{10^2}$$

## Exercise 8P

**1** Copy and complete this table.

|  | $10^0$ | $10^{-1}$ | $10^{-2}$ | $10^{-3}$ | $10^{-4}$ | $10^{-5}$ | Standard form |
|---|---|---|---|---|---|---|---|
| (a) | 0 | 0 | 0 | 2 | 4 |  | $2.4 \times 10^{-3}$ |
| (b) | 0 | 2 |  |  |  |  |  |
| (c) | 0 | 0 | 0 | 0 | 0 | 6 |  |
| (d) | 0 | 1 | 5 |  |  |  |  |
| (e) | 0 | 0 | 0 | 7 |  |  |  |
| (f) | 0 | 0 | 0 | 0 | 4 | 5 |  |
| (g) | 0 | 0 | 3 | 4 | 6 |  |  |
| (h) | 0 | 0 | 0 | 1 | 2 | 5 |  |

> The first row is done for you.

**2** Write these numbers in standard form.

     (a)   0.002        (b)   0.15        (c)   0.0004

     (d)   0.054        (e)   0.000 008        (f)   0.000 000 000 068

     (g)   0.346        (h)   0.09        (i)   0.0056

**3** Change these numbers back to ordinary decimal number form.

(a) $3.5 \times 10^{-1}$  (b) $6.0 \times 10^{-2}$  (c) $7.2 \times 10^{-4}$

(d) $2.2 \times 10^{-3}$  (e) $1.35 \times 10^{-5}$  (f) $5.33 \times 10^{-6}$

(g) $8.8 \times 10^{-10}$  (h) $4.4 \times 10^{-7}$  (i) $4.999 \times 10^{-1}$

# 8.12 Calculations in standard form

## Example 17

Evaluate $(2.95 \times 10^5) \times (4.0 \times 10^3)$, giving your answer in standard form.

$2.95 \times 4.0 \times 10^5 \times 10^3$ ——— Rearrange the expression with the powers of 10 on the right.

$= 11.8 \times 10^8$ ——— Multiply the numbers on the left and the tens on the right.

11.8 is not between 1 and 10, so the answer is not in standard form yet.

11.8 is $1.18 \times 10$

so $(1.18 \times 10) \times 10^8 = 1.18 \times 10^9$

> Remember:
> The index rule for multiplying powers is:
> $10^m \times 10^n = 10^{m+n}$
> So
> $10^5 \times 10^3 = 10^8$

## Worked examination question

(a) The distance from the Earth to the Moon is approximately 250 000 miles. Express this number in standard form.

(b) The distance from the Earth to the Sun is approximately $9.3 \times 10^7$ miles. Calculate the value of the expression

$$\frac{\text{distance from the Earth to the Moon}}{\text{distance from the Earth to the Sun}}$$

giving your answer in standard form.

(a) $250\,000 = 2.5 \times 10^5$

(b) Substituting the distances in the expression gives $\dfrac{2.5 \times 10^5}{9.3 \times 10^7}$.

Here are two ways of evaluating this:

**Method 1**
$$\frac{2.5 \times 10^5}{9.3 \times 10^7}$$

$\div 10\,000$

$$= \frac{250\,000}{93\,000\,000} = \frac{25}{9300}$$

$\div 10\,000$

$= 0.002\,69$ (to 3 s.f.)

$= 2.69 \times 10^{-3}$

**Method 2**
$$\frac{2.5 \times 10^5}{9.3 \times 10^7}$$

$$= \frac{2.5 \times 1}{9.3 \times 10^2}$$

$= 0.269 \times \dfrac{1}{10^2}$

$= 0.269 \times 10^{-2}$

$= 2.69 \times 10^{-3}$

> Remember:
> The index rule for dividing powers is
> $10^m \div 10^n = 10^{m-n}$
> So
> $10^5 \div 10^7 = 10^{(5-7)} = 10^{-2}$

You can use standard form to help you make approximations and estimates.

___ **Example 18** _____

The distance from the Earth to the Sun is 93 000 000 miles. The Earth moves around the Sun in an approximately circular orbit. One complete orbit of the Sun takes 365 days.

Use standard form to help work out an estimate of the average speed of the Earth as it orbits the Sun.

The Earth orbits the Sun at a distance of approximately 90 000 000 or $9 \times 10^7$ miles.

The distance travelled by the Earth as it makes one orbit of the Sun is roughly equal to the circumference of a circle of radius $9 \times 10^7$ miles.

Using circumference = $2\pi r$, the total distance travelled by the Earth in 365 days is

$$2 \times \pi \times 9 \times 10^7$$

> You should remember from previous work that $C = 2\pi r$

But $\pi$ is about 3.1, so $2 \times \pi$ is just over 6.

$$2 \times \pi \times 9 \text{ is about } 55.$$

Hence the distance travelled by the Earth in 365 days is approximately

$$55 \times 10^7 = 5.5 \times 10 \times 10^7$$
$$= 5.5 \times 10^8 \text{ miles}$$

365 days is $365 \times 24$ hours, or approximately

$$350 \times 20 = 7000$$
$$= 7 \times 10^3 \text{ hours}$$

So the Earth travels approximately $5.5 \times 10^8$ miles in approximately $7 \times 10^3$ hours.

Using the formula   **average speed** $= \dfrac{\textbf{distance}}{\textbf{time}}$,

the speed of the Earth as it orbits the Sun is

$$\text{average speed} = \frac{5.5 \times 10^8}{7 \times 10^3}$$
$$= \frac{55}{7} \times \frac{10^7}{10^3}$$
$$= \frac{55}{7} \times 10^4$$

This sort of division should be done **mentally**.

$\dfrac{55}{7}$ is approximately 8

> A good method for approximating $55 \div 7$ mentally is to think of the number closest to 55 in the 7 times table.
> $7 \times 8 = 56$.

So the speed is approximately $8 \times 10^4$ miles per hour.

You could use different approximations to get your answer. For example, you could have approximated the distance from the Earth to the Sun as 100 000 000 miles, or $1 \times 10^8$ miles. This would give you a different answer.

In your exam you should make sure that you clearly state what approximations you are using.

## Exercise 8Q

1   Evaluate these expressions, giving your answers in standard form.

(a)  $(6.4 \times 10^8) \times (1.5 \times 10^5)$       (b)  $(8.2 \times 10^7) \times (2.1 \times 10^{-4})$

(c)  $(5.25 \times 10^2) \times (1.6 \times 10^{-5})$    (d)  $(4.1 \times 10^{-6}) \times (3.6 \times 10^{-7})$

(e)  $\dfrac{6.4 \times 10^4}{2.2 \times 10^5}$    (f)  $\dfrac{5.6 \times 10^{-2}}{3.8 \times 10^7}$    (g)  $\dfrac{3.4 \times 10^{24}}{1.2 \times 10^{-6}}$

(h)  $\dfrac{8.8 \times 10^{25}}{8.8 \times 10^{22}}$    (i)  $(2.8 \times 10^3)^2$    (j)  $(2.2 \times 10^{-2})^3$

2   Evaluate these expressions, giving your answers in standard form.

(a)  $500 \times 600 \times 700$          (b)  $0.006 \times 0.004$

(c)  $\dfrac{0.08 \times 480}{180}$          (d)  $\dfrac{89\,000 \times 0.0086}{48 \times 0.25}$

(e)  $\dfrac{65 \times 120}{1500}$          (f)  $\dfrac{8.82 \times 5.007}{10\,000}$

(g)  $(12.8)^4$          (h)  $(36.4 \times 24.2)^{-3}$

3   The distance from the Earth to the Sun is approximately 93 000 000 miles. Light travels at a speed of approximately 300 000 kilometres per second.

> 1 mile is approximately 1.6 kilometres.

Use standard form to work out an estimate of the time it takes light to travel from the Sun to the Earth.

4   The Earth's diameter is $1.27 \times 10^4$ km and the diameter of Mars is $6.79 \times 10^3$ km.

(a)   Which planet has the larger diameter?

(b)   What is the difference between their diameters?

(c)   What is the total if the two diameters are added?

(d)   How many times bigger is one planet than the other? (Hint: consider their volumes.)

## Mixed exercise 8

1   The auction price of a second hand car is 25% less than the retail price of the same car.

(a)   Calculate the auction price of a car which has a retail price of £4200.

(b)   Calculate the retail price of a car which has an auction price of £5400.

2   The price of a shirt has been reduced by $12\frac{1}{2}$% to £21 in a sale.
    What was the original selling price?

3   Asif puts £200 into a building society savings account. He leaves
    the money in the account for three years without withdrawing
    any money or adding any to his savings. The building society
    pays a compound interest rate of 4% per annum. How much
    money will Asif have in his account at the end of the three years?

4   On a test drive, a new car travels 307 miles on 37.7 litres of petrol.
    Work out the average number of miles the car travels on each litre
    of petrol. Give your answer correct to two significant figures.

5   In a competition, the total prize money is £2000.
    This is divided between the winners of the first, second and third
    prizes in the ratio 5 : 3 : 1 respectively.
    Calculate the value of the first prize.

6   The prices below include VAT at $17\frac{1}{2}$%.
    Calculate each price exclusive of VAT.

    (a)   £135 for a mountain bike

    (b)   £209 for a hammer drill

    (c)   £49 for a grill

7   A motorbike originally cost £2800. Its value has depreciated by
    35%. What is the new value?

8   Dinosaurs roamed the Earth about
    140 million years ago.

    (a)   Express 140 million in standard form.

    (b)   The average human life span is 72 years.
          How many average human life spans
          is 140 million years? Give your answer
          in standard form, correct to three
          significant figures.

9   In 2005, 623 118 students sat GCSE English. The entry fee for
    each GCSE student was £22.50. Use standard form to work out
    an estimate for the total entry fee in 2005 for all the GCSE
    English students.

10  The density of oak is 720 kg/m³.
    Calculate the mass of a rectangular block of oak measuring 6 m
    by 0.7 m by 0.12 m.

11  Approximately $\frac{2}{3}$ of the Earth's surface is covered with water.
    The Earth can be assumed to be a sphere with a radius of
    6350 km. Use standard form and the formula

        surface area of sphere = $4 \times \pi \times$ radius²

    to work out an estimate of the area of the surface of the Earth
    covered by water.

# Summary of key points

**1** If an amount is increased by $x\%$ the new amount is $(100 + x)\%$ of the original amount. So the new amount = the old amount $\times (100 + x)\%$.

**2** If an amount is decreased by $x\%$ the new amount is $(100 - x)\%$ of the original amount. So the new amount = the old amount $\times (100 - x)\%$.

**3** The **percentage increase** is $\dfrac{\text{actual increase}}{\text{original price}} \times 100\%$

**4** The **percentage decrease** is $\dfrac{\text{actual decrease}}{\text{original price}} \times 100\%$

**5** **Compound interest** is interest paid on an amount and on the interest already earned.

**6** To calculate compound interest, find the multiplier:

Amount after $n$ years = original amount $\times$ multiplier$^n$

**7** **Average speed** $= \dfrac{\text{distance travelled}}{\text{time taken}}$ (typical units: km/h)

**8** Volume flowing per second = cross-sectional area $\times$ speed (typical units: cm$^3$/s)

**9** **Density** $= \dfrac{\text{mass}}{\text{volume}}$ (typical units: kg/m$^3$)

**10** You can use **ratios** (such as $2:3$ and $5:4:7$) to show how things are divided or shared.

**11** Large and small numbers can conveniently be represented in **standard form**. A number is in standard form when:

$$7.2 \times 10^6$$

This part is written as a number between 1 and 10

This part is written as a power of 10

# 9 Functions, lines, simultaneous equations and regions

In this chapter you will draw straight line graphs for functions, and use graphs to represent inequalities and simultaneous equations.

## 9.1 Functions

Here is a pattern sequence:

6 sticks        11 sticks              16 sticks                    21 sticks

To work out the number of sticks in the pattern, the rule is:

> There is more on number sequences in Chapter 12.

'Multiply the pattern number by 5, then add 1'

You can show how the rule works by using a flowchart like this:

$$\text{Input} \rightarrow \boxed{\times 5} \rightarrow \boxed{+1} \rightarrow \text{Output}$$

$$1 \rightarrow 5 \rightarrow 6$$
$$2 \rightarrow 10 \rightarrow 11$$
$$3 \rightarrow 15 \rightarrow 16$$
$$4 \rightarrow 20 \rightarrow 21$$

$$n \rightarrow 5n \rightarrow 5n + 1$$

Instead of using the flow chart you can write $n \rightarrow 5n + 1$

You can say that $n$ maps onto $5n + 1$

> You can let the letter $n$ stand for any number. For this function, $n$ must be a positive whole number.

$n \rightarrow 5n + 1$ is called a function.

> A **function** is a rule which shows how one set of numbers relates to another set.

## Exercise 9A

**1**  Work out the outputs for each function using the inputs 1, 2, 3 and 10.

> Remember the order of operations.

(a)  $n \rightarrow 2n - 2$

(b)  $n \rightarrow 3n + 2$

(c)  $n \rightarrow 2(n + 3)$

(d)  $n \rightarrow 3(n - 1)$

(e)  $n \rightarrow \dfrac{n}{2} + 1$

(f)  $n \rightarrow \dfrac{n + 3}{2}$

# 9.2 Graphs of linear functions with positive whole number inputs

Here is a simple function: $n \to 2n + 1$

Another way to look at a function is to let $x$ stand for the input and $y$ stand for the output, so $x \to y$

But using $n \to 2n + 1$ we know that $x \to 2x + 1$

So $y$ and $2x + 1$ must be worth the same and you can write $y = 2x + 1$

> $y = 2x + 1$ is called an **equation**. The value of $y$ is *always* equal to the value of $2x + 1$.

You now have two ways of showing the same rule or function:

$n \to 2n + 1$    or    $y = 2x + 1$

$0 \to 1$
$1 \to 3$
$2 \to 5$
$3 \to 7$
$4 \to 9$
$5 \to 11$

| $x$ | 0 | 1 | 2 | 3 | 4 | 5 |
|---|---|---|---|---|---|---|
| $y$ | 1 | 3 | 5 | 7 | 9 | 11 |

This is called a **table of values**.

You can show the numbers in the table as coordinates on a graph.

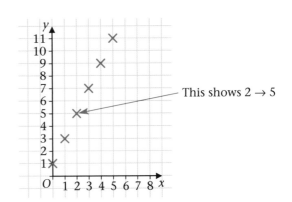

This shows $2 \to 5$

## Exercise 9B

You will need graph paper for this exercise.

1  (a)  Write the function $n \to n + 2$ as an equation using $x$ and $y$.

   (b)  Make a table of values for your equation using the values 0, 1, 2, 3, 4, 5 for $x$.

   (c)  Draw a graph to show the numbers from your table of values.

2  Do the same as in question **1** for each of these functions:

   (a)  $n \to n + 4$          (b)  $n \to 2n + 3$

   (c)  $n \to 3n + 2$          (d)  $n \to 2n$

**3** **(a)** Complete the table of values for this sequence of matchstick patterns.

| Number of squares $x$ | 1 | 2 | 3 | 4 | 5 |
|---|---|---|---|---|---|
| Number of matchsticks $y$ | 4 | 7 | | | |

**(b)** Draw the graph for this table of values.

**(c)** Write down the equation of the graph passing through these points.

**4** **(a)** Complete the table of values for this sequence of matchstick patterns.

| Number of triangles $x$ | 1 | 2 | 3 | 4 | 5 |
|---|---|---|---|---|---|
| Number of matchsticks $y$ | 3 | | | | |

**(b)** Draw the graph for the table of values.

**(c)** Write down the equation of the graph passing through these points.

**5** **(a)** Invent and draw a sequence of stick patterns for each of these graphs:

> Draw up a table of values for each graph.

**(i)**                    **(ii)**

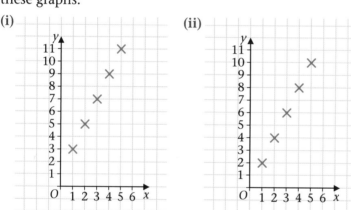

**(b)** Write an equation for each graph in part (a).

## 9.3 Graphs of linear functions with continuous positive inputs

In questions **3** and **4** of Exercise 9B, $x$ was the number of matchsticks. So $x$ could take only whole number values. You cannot not join the points in those graphs because there are no values of $x$ and $y$ between those points.

If $x$ can take any values, either whole numbers or decimals, we say $x$ is **continuous**.

> The input values of $x$ are **continuous** if $x$ can take any value (whole numbers or decimals).

Look at the graph for $y = 2x + 1$.

The points lie on a straight line.

| $x$ | 0 | 1 | 2 | 3 | 4 | 5 |
|---|---|---|---|---|---|---|
| $y$ | 1 | 3 | 5 | 7 | 9 | 11 |

You can draw the straight line in this graph because $x$ is continuous.

The $x$ and $y$ values for the point marked ● are 2 and 5.
So the point ● has coordinates (2, 5).

You say the coordinates (2, 5) 'satisfy' the equation $y = 2x + 1$.

Look at the point ▲ which has coordinates $(1\frac{1}{2}, 4)$.
Put $x = 1\frac{1}{2}$ in the equation $y = 2x + 1$.
You get $y = 2 \times 1\frac{1}{2} + 1 = 4$.
So when $x = 1\frac{1}{2}$, $y = 4$.

Do the same for other points on the straight line.

> $y = 2x + 1$ is the equation of a straight line. The coordinates of any point
> on the straight line 'satisfy' the equation.

> $x \rightarrow 2x + 1$ is called a **linear function** because its graph is a straight line.

You can draw graphs to solve real-life problems.

### Example 1

Water flows steadily from a pipe into a storage tank. Every minute the depth of the water in the tank increases by 2 cm. When the water starts to flow the depth of water in the tank is already 3 cm.

(a)  Draw a graph to show the relationship between the depth, $y$ cm, of the water in the tank and the time, $x$ minutes, after the water starts to flow.

(b)  Use the graph to find the depth of water $3\frac{1}{2}$ minutes after the water starts to flow.

(a)  Draw up a table of values for whole number values of $x$:

| Time in minutes $x$ | 0 | 1 | 2 | 3 | 4 |
|---|---|---|---|---|---|
| Depth in cm $y$ | 3 | 5 | 7 | 9 | 11 |

Draw the graph.

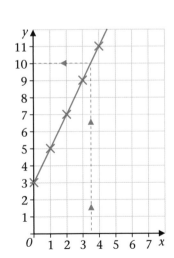

(b)  Find $3\frac{1}{2}$ on the $x$-axis.
Go up to the line and across to find the corresponding value of $y$, which is 10.
The depth of the water $3\frac{1}{2}$ minutes after the water starts to flow is 10 cm.

## Exercise 9C

You will need graph paper for these questions.

**1**   A narrow boat travels on a canal at a speed of 4 miles per hour.

   **(a)**   Complete this table of values:

| Time travelled in hours $x$ | 0 | 1 | 2 | 3 | 4 |
|---|---|---|---|---|---|
| Distance travelled in miles $y$ | 0 | 4 | | | |

   **(b)**   Draw the graph for the table of values.

   **(c)**   Use your graph to find how far the boat travels in $3\frac{1}{2}$ hours.

**2**   In Britain miles are used to measure large distances. In the rest of Europe kilometres are used. A good approximation to use to change miles into kilometres is 5 miles = 8 kilometres.

   **(a)**   Complete this table of values:

| Distance in miles $x$ | 0 | 5 | 10 | 15 | 20 | 25 |
|---|---|---|---|---|---|---|
| Distance in kilometres $y$ | 0 | 8 | | | | |

   **(b)**   Draw the graph for the table of values.

   **(c)**   Use your graph to find how many kilometres are approximately the same as 13 miles.

   **(d)**   How many miles are approximately the same as 14 kilometres?

> Find 14 on the $y$-axis, go across to the line and down to the $x$-axis.

**3**   Mortar is used to stick bricks together. To mix mortar you put 1 bucket of cement with 3 buckets of sand.

> I always use 3 buckets of sand to every bucket of cement.

   **(a)**   Complete this table of values:

| Buckets of cement $x$ | 0 | 1 | 2 | 3 | 4 | 5 | 6 |
|---|---|---|---|---|---|---|---|
| Buckets of sand $y$ | 0 | 3 | | | | | |

   **(b)**   Draw the graph for the table of values.

   **(c)**   Use your graph to find how many buckets of cement you should put with 14 buckets of sand.

**4**   A cookery book gives this rule for cooking joints of lamb:

   Cook for half an hour per 500 g plus half an hour.

   **(a)**   Complete this table of values:

| Weight in kg $x$ | $\frac{1}{2}$ | 1 | $1\frac{1}{2}$ | 2 | $2\frac{1}{2}$ | 3 | $3\frac{1}{2}$ |
|---|---|---|---|---|---|---|---|
| Cooking time in hours $y$ | 1 | $1\frac{1}{2}$ | | | | | |

   **(b)**   Why isn't it sensible to start the values of $x$ at 0? What is the biggest value you think it would be sensible to put for $x$?

   **(c)**   Draw the graph for the table of values.

   **(d)**   Use your graph to estimate how long it would take to cook a 2.3 kg joint of lamb.

# 9.4 Lines and parallel lines

The diagram shows the lines with equations
$y = 2x + 3$, $y = 2x + 1$ and $y = 2x - 1$.

In all three equations the number in front
of $x$ (the **coefficient** of $x$) is 2, and the three
lines are all **parallel**.

The number term in each equation gives the
$y$-coordinate of the point where the line cuts
the $y$-axis.

For example, the line with equation
$y = 2x + 3$ cuts the $y$-axis at $(0, 3)$.

This point is called its **intercept** on the $y$-axis.
So, the intercept on the $y$-axis of the line with
equation $y = 2x + 1$ is $(0, 1)$ and the intercept on
the $y$-axis of the line with equation $y = 2x - 1$ is $(0, -1)$.

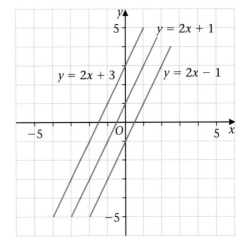

An **intercept** is a point at which a line cuts the $y$-axis or
the $x$-axis.

---

**Example 2**

(a) Draw the line with equation $y = 3x + 2$.

(b) Write its intercept on the $y$-axis.

(c) Write the equation of the line parallel to $y = 3x + 2$ whose
intercept is $(0, -1)$.

(a) If you plot two points on the line, you can draw it,
but a third point is a useful check. All three points
should lie on the same straight line.

Here is a table of values:

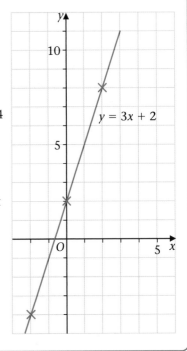

| $x$ | $-2$ | $0$ | $2$ |
|---|---|---|---|
| $y$ | $-4$ | $2$ | $8$ |

When $x = -2$, $y = 3 \times -2 + 2 = -6 + 2 = -4$
When $x = 0$, $y = 3 \times 0 + 2 = 0 + 2 = 2$
When $x = 2$, $y = 3 \times 2 + 2 = 6 + 2 = 8$

(b) The intercept on the $y$-axis is $(0, 2)$.

(c) The line parallel to $y = 3x + 2$ will have the same coefficient
of $x$, which is 3.

The equation is $y = 3x - 1$.

## Exercise 9D

1   On separate diagrams, draw lines with these equations.

(a)   $y = x + 6$  (b)   $y = 2x + 5$

(c)   $y = 3x + 1$  (d)   $y = 3x - 4$

(e)   $y = -2x + 3$  (f)   $y = \frac{1}{2}x - 2$

2   Write the equations of the two parallel lines in question **1**.

3   (a)   Without drawing the lines, write the equations of the two parallel lines in the following.

(i)   $y = 4x - 1$  (ii)   $y = \frac{1}{4}x + 1$

(iii)   $y = x - 4$  (iv)   $y = -4x + 1$

(v)   $y = \frac{1}{4}x - 1$  (vi)   $y = -x + 4$

(b)   Explain how you found your answer.

4   Write the intercepts on the $y$-axis of lines with these equations.

(a)   $y = 7x + 5$  (b)   $y = 5x - 2$

(c)   $y = -3x - 5$  (d)   $y = \frac{1}{4}x + 4$

5   A line is parallel to the line $y = 4x + 5$ and its intercept on the $y$-axis is (0, 3). Write the equation of the line.

6   A line is parallel to the line $y = 5x + 7$ and its intercept on the $y$-axis is (0, −3). Write the equation of the line.

7   A line is parallel to the line $y = 3x$ and its intercept on the $y$-axis is (0, 5). Write the equation of the line.

8   A line is parallel to the line $y = mx$ and its intercept on the $y$-axis is (0, $c$). Write the equation of the line.

9   The point with coordinates (2, 14) lies on the line with equation $y = 5x + c$. Find the value of $c$ and write the line's intercept on the $y$-axis.

10   The point with coordinates (8, 1) lies on the line with equation $y = \frac{1}{2}x + c$. Find the value of $c$ and write the line's intercept on the $y$-axis.

11   A line has equation $y = mx + 1$.

(a)   Write the line's intercept on the $y$-axis.

The point with coordinates (3, 16) lies on the line.

(b)   Find the value of $m$.

12   A line is parallel to the line with equation $y = \frac{1}{3}x + 2$ and passes through the point with coordinates (12, 0).

(a)   Find the equation of the line.

(b)   Write its intercept on the $y$-axis.

13 (a) On the same diagram, draw lines with these equations.

(i) $y = x + 4$      (ii) $y = 2x + 4$      (iii) $y = 3x + 4$

(b) Write the intercept on the $y$-axis of each of the lines.

(c) How does the coefficient of $x$ in the equations affect the lines?

14 The diagram below shows the line $y = 3x - 4$.
Calculate the value of

(a) $\dfrac{AB}{BC}$    (b) $\dfrac{DE}{EF}$

This is the **gradient** of the line.

15 The diagram below shows the line $y = \frac{1}{2}x + 1$.
Calculate the value of

(a) $\dfrac{AB}{BC}$

(b) $\dfrac{DE}{EF}$

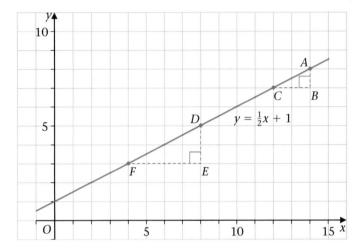

# 9.5 $y = mx + c$

Following on from Exercise 9D you should now see that

$$\text{gradient} = \frac{\text{change in } y\text{-direction}}{\text{change in } x\text{-direction}}$$

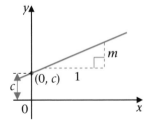

The straight line with equation $y = mx + c$ has a gradient of $m$ and its intercept on the $y$-axis is $(0, c)$.

**Example 3**

Write down (a) the gradient and (b) the intercept on the $y$-axis of the line with equation $y = 7x - 3$.

(a) The gradient is 7.    (b) The intercept on the $y$-axis is $(0, -3)$.

**Example 4**

Write down (a) the gradient and (b) the intercept on the $y$-axis of the line with equation $y = -2x + 5$.

(a)   The gradient is $-2$.    (b)   The intercept on the $y$-axis is $(0, 5)$.

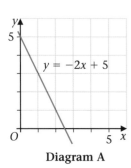

**Diagram A**

Diagram A shows the direction of the slope of a line with a **negative** gradient.

Diagram B shows lines with various gradients.

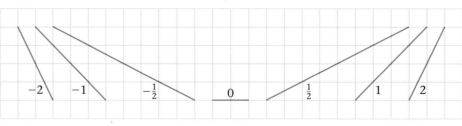

**Diagram B**

Lines with equation $y = mx + c$, with the same gradient ($m$), are parallel.

**Example 5**

Find (a) the gradient and (b) the intercept on the $y$-axis of the line with equation $2x - 3y = 18$.

Here the equation must be rearranged in the form $y = mx + c$

$$3y = 2x - 18$$
$$y = \tfrac{2}{3}x - 6$$

(a)   The gradient is $\tfrac{2}{3}$.    (b)   The intercept on the $y$-axis is $(0, -6)$.

> Rearrange
> $2x - 3y = 18$
> to $2x - 18 = 3y$
> So $3y = 2x - 18$
> Then divide by 3.

**Example 6**

The graph shows the cost, $C$ pounds, of staying in a hotel for $n$ nights. $C$ is given by the formula $C = an + b$.

Find the values of $a$ and $b$.

Gradient $= \dfrac{PQ}{QR} = \dfrac{40}{1}$

$\qquad\quad = 40$

so    $a = 40$

Intercept on $C$-axis is $(0, 20)$

so    $b = 20$

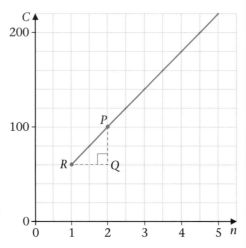

> Although $n$ is not continuous you can draw the line to help work out the gradient.

> $PQ = £40$
> $QR = 1$ night

> If you put your ruler on the graph you will see that it would cross the C-axis at $(0, 20)$.

## Exercise 9E

1   Write (i) the gradient and (ii) the intercept on the $y$-axis of lines
    with the equations
    (a)   $y = 5x + 4$               (b)   $y = 2x - 7$
    (c)   $y = \frac{1}{4}x + 9$      (d)   $y = -4x - 3$
    (e)   $y = 8 + 9x$               (f)   $y = 7 - 2x$

2   Find (i) the gradient and (ii) the intercept on the $y$-axis of lines
    with the equations
    (a)   $2x + y = 3$               (b)   $3x - y = 5$
    (c)   $x - 2y = 8$               (d)   $x + 3y = 6$
    (e)   $3x - 5y = 10$             (f)   $3x + 4y - 12 = 0$

3   The gradient of a line is 6 and its intercept on the $y$-axis is $(0, 7)$.
    Write the equation of the line.

4   Find the equations of the lines shown on the diagram.

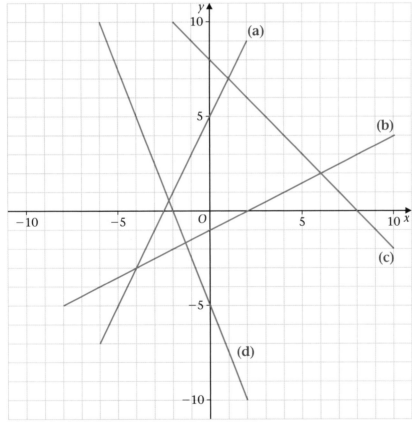

5   A line passes through the points with
    coordinates $(0, 2)$ and $(2, 8)$.
    (a)   Find the gradient of the line.
    (b)   Write the equation of the line.

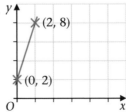

6 The gradient of a line is 4.
The point with coordinates (4, 23) lies on the line.
Find the equation of the line.

> It may help to draw a diagram for these questions.

7 The intercept on the $y$-axis of a line is (0, 11).
The point with coordinates $(-2, 17)$ lies on the line.
Find the equation of the line.

8 A line passes through the points with coordinates (2, 11) and (5, 23).

(a) Find the gradient of the line.

(b) Find the equation of the line.

## 9.6 Perpendicular lines

The diagram shows two pairs of perpendicular lines.

The gradient of line $a$ is 2 and the gradient of line $b$ is $-\frac{1}{2}$.

The gradient of line $c$ is $-\frac{2}{3}$ and the gradient of line $d$ is $1\frac{1}{2}$ or $\frac{3}{2}$.

In both cases, to obtain the second gradient, find the reciprocal of the first gradient and change its sign.

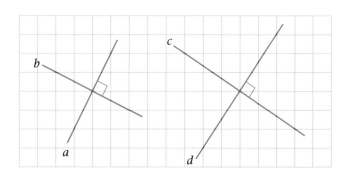

> If a line has a gradient $m$, a line perpendicular to it has a gradient $-\dfrac{1}{m}$

> Reciprocal of
> $m = 1 \div m = \dfrac{1}{m}$

Notice that $2 \times -\frac{1}{2} = -1$  and  $-\frac{2}{3} \times \frac{3}{2} = -1$.

> If two lines are perpendicular, the product of their gradients is $-1$.
>
> $m \times \dfrac{1}{m} = -1$

### Example 7

A line is perpendicular to the line with equation $y = 4x + 7$ and its intercept on the $y$-axis is (0, 3). Find the equation of the line.

The line with equation $y = 4x + 7$ has a gradient of 4.

So a line perpendicular to it has a gradient of $-\frac{1}{4}$.

Its intercept on the $y$-axis is (0, 3).

The equation of the line is $y = -\frac{1}{4}x + 3$.

> $y = -\frac{1}{4}x + 3$ can also be written as $x + 4y = 12$.

**Example 8**

A line passes through the point with coordinates $(10, -6)$ and is perpendicular to the line with equation $5x - 4y = 20$.
Find the equation of the line.

Make $y$ the subject of the equation $5x - 4y = 20$

$$y = \tfrac{5}{4}x - 5$$

The gradient of this line is $\tfrac{5}{4}$.

The gradient of the perpendicular is $-\tfrac{4}{5}$.

The equation of the perpendicular line is $y = -\tfrac{4}{5}x + c$ and it passes through $(10, -6)$ so $y = -6$ and $x = 10$ satisfy the equation

$$-6 = -\tfrac{4}{5}(10) + c$$
$$-6 = -8 + c$$
$$c = 2$$

The required equation is $y = -\tfrac{4}{5}x + 2$.

> $y = -\tfrac{4}{5}x + 2$ can also be written as $4x + 5y = 10$.

## Exercise 9F

**1** Write down the gradient of a line which is perpendicular to a line with gradient

   (a)  5            (b)  2            (c)  1

   (d)  $\tfrac{3}{4}$         (e)  $-2\tfrac{1}{2}$       (f)  $-\tfrac{2}{7}$

**2** Which of these lines is perpendicular to the line with equation $y = 5x - 3$? Give reasons for your answers.

   (a)  $y = \tfrac{1}{5}x + 2$       (b)  $y = -\tfrac{1}{5}x + 2$

   (c)  $y = -5x - 2$       (d)  $y = 5x + 2$

**3** A line passes through the origin and is perpendicular to the line with equation $y = 3x - 2$. Find the equation of the line.

**4** A line is perpendicular to the line with equation $y = x + 4$ and its intercept on the $y$-axis is $(0, 6)$. Find the equation of the line.

**5** A line passes through the point with coordinates $(4, 1)$ and is perpendicular to the line with equation $y = -\tfrac{2}{5}x + 3$.
Find the equation of the line.

**6** Which of these lines is perpendicular to the line with equation $3x + 5y = 15$? Give reasons for your answer.

   (a)  $3x - 5y = 30$     (b)  $5x + 3y = 30$     (c)  $5x - 3y = 30$

**7** A line passes through the point with coordinates $(6, 1)$ and is perpendicular to the line with equation $2x - 3y = 6$.
Find the equation of the line.

**8** A line passes through the point with coordinates $(8, 1)$ and is perpendicular to the line with equation $4x + 3y = 12$.
Find the equation of the line.

Remember, if two lines are perpendicular, then they are at right angles to each other.

## 9.7 The mid-point of a line segment *AB*

Here is a straight line *AB*.
The straight line is called the line segment *AB*.

*A* has coordinates (1, 1), *B* has coordinates (3, 6).

*M* is halfway along the line segment *AB*.
*M* is called the **mid-point of the line segment *AB***.

You can find the coordinates of the mid-point.

**Step 1** Add the *x*-coordinates and divide by 2

$$\frac{1 + 3}{2} = \frac{4}{2} = 2$$

**Step 2** Add the *y*-coordinates and divide by 2

$$\frac{1 + 6}{2} = \frac{7}{2} = 3\frac{1}{2}$$

So the coordinates of the mid-point are $(2, 3\frac{1}{2})$.

AB is a segment of the line through A and B. This line continues infinitely in either direction.

> The **mid-point of the line segment *AB*** between $A(x_1, y_1)$ and
> $B(x_2, y_2)$ is $\left(\dfrac{x_1 + x_2}{2}, \dfrac{y_1 + y_2}{2}\right)$.

---

**Example 9**

Work out the coordinates of the mid-point of the line segment *AB* where *A* is (2, 3) and *B* is (7, 11).

Mid-point *x*-coordinate is

$$\frac{2 + 7}{2} = \frac{9}{2} = 4\frac{1}{2}$$

Mid-point *y*-coordinate is

$$\frac{3 + 11}{2} = \frac{14}{2} = 7$$

So mid-point is $(4\frac{1}{2}, 7)$.

---

### Exercise 9G

1   Work out the coordinates of the mid-point of the line segments:

(a)   *A*(0, 0) and *B*(4, 5)      (b)   *C*(3, 1) and *D*(4, 9)

(c)   *E*(5, 7) and *F*(1, 6)      (d)   *G*(1, 0) and *H*(5, 8)

(e)   *I*(9, 10) and *J*(3, 7)

## 9.8 Simultaneous equations – graphical solutions

An *infinite number* of pairs of values of *x* and *y* will make the equation $2x + y = 6$ true.

$x = 0$ and $y = 6$, for example, satisfy this equation.

The coordinates of every point on the line represent a possible solution.

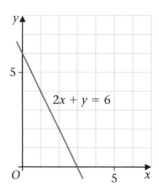

Similarly, an infinite number of pairs of values of $x$ and $y$ satisfy the equation $x + y = 5$.

The coordinates of the points on the line represent these solutions.

But there is only *one* pair of values which makes both $2x + y = 6$ and $x + y = 5$ true.

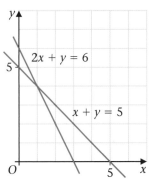

The diagram above shows a graphical solution to finding the pair.

The pair of values are the $x$ and $y$ coordinates of the point of intersection of the two lines:

$x = 1$   and   $y = 4$

$2x + y = 6$   and   $x + y = 5$   are called **simultaneous equations** and their solution is $x = 1$, $y = 4$.

> Check by substituting into the original equations:
> $2 \times 1 + 4 = 6$ ✓
> $1 + 4 = 5$ ✓

---

**Example 10**

Solve these simultaneous equations
$$x + 2y = 10$$
$$x - y = 1$$

Here are the tables of values:

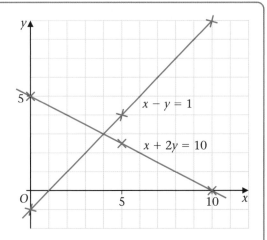

$x + 2y = 10$

| $x$ | 0 | 5 | 10 |
|---|---|---|---|
| $y$ | 5 | 2.5 | 0 |

$x - y = 1$

| $x$ | 0 | 5 | 10 |
|---|---|---|---|
| $y$ | -1 | 4 | 9 |

Plot three points for each equation and draw straight lines.

The coordinates of the point of intersection of the lines gives the solution

$x = 4$   and   $y = 3$

Check by substituting into the original equations:
$$4 + 2 \times 3 = 10 \quad ✓$$
$$4 - 3 = 1 \quad ✓$$

---

**Simultaneous equations** can be solved graphically, by drawing the graphs for the two equations and finding the coordinates of their point of intersection.

## Exercise 9H

**1**   Write down four pairs of integer values of $x$ and $y$ which satisfy the equation $x + y = 10$.

**2**   Which of the following points lies on the line with equation $2x + 3y = 6$?

   (a)  $(2, 0)$     (b)  $(3, 0)$     (c)  $(6, -2)$     (d)  $(-3, 4)$

**3**   Write four pairs of integer values of $x$ and $y$ which satisfy the equation $2x - y = 8$.

**4**   Which two of the following equations are satisfied by $x = 3$ and $y = 5$?

   (a)  $2x + 3y = 20$     (b)  $3x - y = 4$

   (c)  $5x - 2y = 5$     (d)  $4x + 3y = 25$

**5**   Use the diagram to solve these simultaneous equations

$$x + 3y = 6$$
$$x + y = 4$$

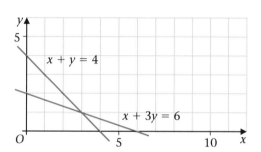

**6**   Draw appropriate straight lines to solve these simultaneous equations

   (a)  $x + y = 3$       (b)  $x + y = 6$

       $x - y = 1$          $x + 2y = 8$

   (c)  $x + 2y = 6$     (d)  $2x + 3y = 6$

       $x - y = 3$          $x + 2y = 5$

   (e)  $x + y = 2$       (f)  $3x - y = 9$

       $x - 3y = 6$        $x - 2y = -2$

> Draw a separate diagram for each part.

> Remember to draw the lines by plotting three points.

## 9.9 Simultaneous equations – algebraic solutions

Simultaneous equations can also be solved algebraically.

---

**Example 11**

Solve these simultaneous equations

$$2x + y = 12$$
$$x - y = 3$$

Here the two equations may be added together in order to eliminate $y$

$$
\begin{array}{r}
2x + y = 12 \\
\text{ADD} \quad \underline{x - y = \phantom{0}3} \\
3x \phantom{+ y} = 15 \\
\hline
x = 5
\end{array}
$$

> $+y$ ADD $-y = 0$

To find $y$, substitute $x = 5$ into one of the equations.

$$5 - y = 3$$
$$y = 2$$

The solution is $x = 5$, $y = 2$.

When the coefficients of $x$ or $y$ in the two equations are equal, you may eliminate one of the unknowns by **subtracting** one equation from the other.

___ **Example 12** ___

Solve these simultaneous equations

$$4x + 3y = 5 \quad (1)$$
$$4x - 5y = 13 \quad (2)$$

> Call the equations (1) and (2).

In this case, adding equations (1) and (2) will not help.
Try subtracting:

$$4x + 3y = \phantom{1}5 \quad (1)$$
SUBTRACT
$$\underline{4x - 5y = 13} \quad (2)$$
$$8y = -8$$
$$\overline{\phantom{8}y = -1}$$

> $+3y - (-5y)$
> $= +3y + 5y$
> $= 8y$

Substitute $y = -1$ into equation (1).

$$4x - 3 = 5$$
$$4x = 8$$
$$x = 2$$

> Check:
> $4 \times 2 + 3 \times -1 = 5$ ✓
> $4 \times 2 - 5 \times -1 = 13$ ✓

The solution is $x = 2$, $y = -1$.

It doesn't matter which of the two original equations you substitute into, but you should always remember to check that your values fit the other one as well.

## Exercise 9I

Solve these simultaneous equations.

**1** $x + 4y = 11$
$\phantom{1}x - y = 1$

**2** $3x + 2y = 14$
$\phantom{2}5x - 2y = 18$

**3** $5x + 4y = 6$
$\phantom{3}3x - 4y = 10$

**4** $3x - 4y = 6$
$\phantom{4}5x - 4y = 2$

**5** $4x + 2y = 5$
$\phantom{5}8x - 2y = 1$

**6** $2x + 3y = 2$
$\phantom{6}8x + 3y = 17$

**7** $\phantom{1}x - 6y = 16$
$\phantom{7}2x + 6y = 5$

**8** $4x - 2y = 9$
$\phantom{8}4x - 5y = 18$

**9** $2x - 3y = 4$
$\phantom{9}2x + 3y = -8$

## More algebraic solutions

When the equations do not have equal $x$ or $y$ coefficients, you need to multiply one or both of the equations before adding or subtracting.

**Example 13**

Solve these simultaneous equations.

$6x - 7y = 16$    (1)

$3x - 2y = 5$    (2)

Try multiplying equation (2) by 2. This gives:

$6x - 4y = 10$    (3)

Now subtract (1) from (3):

$6x - 4y = 10$    (3)

$6x - 7y = 16$    (1)

(1) − (3):    $3y = -6$

$y = -2$

Substitute $y = -2$ into (2):

$3x + 4 = 5$

$3x \quad = 1$

$x \quad = \frac{1}{3}$

The solution is $x = \frac{1}{3}$, $y = -2$.

> This gives the same coefficient of $x$ in two equations.

> $-4y - (-7y) = 3y$

**Example 14**

Solve these simultaneous equations.

$2x + 3y = 12$    (1)

$3x - 4y = 1$    (2)

(1) × 4:   $8x + 12y = 48$    (3)

(2) × 3:   $9x - 12y = 3$    (4)

(3) + (4):    $17x = 51$

$x = 3$

Substitute $x = 3$ into (1):

$6 + 3y = 12$

$3y = 6$

$y = 2$

The solution is $x = 3$, $y = 2$.

> Multiply equation (1) by 4 and equation (2) by 3 to get $12y$ in each equation.

> Add, since the $12y$ terms have different signs.

Simultaneous equations can be solved algebraically by
- multiplying one or both equations by a number, if necessary
- adding or subtracting, and solving the resulting equation
- substituting this value back into the original equation.

## Exercise 9J

Solve these simultaneous equations.

**1**   $8x + 3y = 35$
        $2x - 5y = 3$

**2**   $7x + 2y = 17$
        $5x + 6y = 3$

**3**   $5x - 4y = 5$
        $7x - 12y = 39$

**4**  $2x + 3y = 12$
   $3x - 4y = 1$

**5**  $6x - 5y = 23$
   $4x - 3y = 14$

**6**  $2x + 7y = 31$
   $5x - 3y = 16$

**7**  $3x - 8y = 11$
   $2x - 5y = 6$

**8**  $9x + 4y = 7$
   $8x - 5y = 49$

**9**  $6x + 7y = 22$
   $8x + 9y = 29$

**10**  $9x + 4y = 8$
    $6x + 5y = 3$

## 9.10 Solving problems using simultaneous equations

**Example 15**

The total cost of 4 small radiators and 3 large radiators is £159.
The total cost of 5 small radiators and 2 large radiators is £134.
Find the cost of one small radiator.

Let the cost of a small radiator be $x$ pounds and the cost of a large radiator be $y$ pounds.

> Define any letters you introduce.

The cost, in pounds, of 4 small radiators is $4x$.
The cost, in pounds, of 3 large radiators is $3y$.
The total cost, in pounds, is therefore $4x + 3y$.

> Express the information in two equations.

So            $4x + 3y = 159$    (1)
Similarly    $5x + 2y = 134$    (2)
(1) × 2:      $8x + 6y = 318$    (3)
(2) × 3:    $15x + 6y = 402$    (4)
(4) − (3):         $7x = 84$
                     $x = 12$

> Solve the equations.

One small radiator costs £12.

> Remember to answer the original question.

**Worked examination question**

Mrs Rogers bought 3 blouses and 2 scarves. She paid £26. Miss Summers bought 4 blouses and 1 scarf. She paid £28. The cost of a blouse was $x$ pounds. The cost of a scarf was $y$ pounds.

(a)  Use the information to write down two equations in $x$ and $y$.

(b)  Solve these equations to find the cost of one blouse.

(a)                $3x + 2y = 26$    (1)
                   $4x + y = 28$    (2)

(b)  (2) × 2:      $8x + 2y = 56$    (3)
    (3) − (1):         $5x = 30$
                        $x = 6$

One blouse costs £6.

## Exercise 9K

**1**  The cost, $C$ pounds, for a group of $n$ students to visit the aquarium is given by the formula $C = a + bn$.
It costs £25 for 5 students and £43 for 9 students.
Find the values of $a$ and $b$.

**2** For 6 hours of work at the normal rate of pay and one hour at the overtime rate, Mr Chung is paid £37. For 4 hours at normal rate and 3 hours at the overtime rate, he is paid £41. Find his normal rate of pay.

**3** The sum of two numbers is 66. Their difference is 8. Find both numbers.

**4** The total cost of a meal and a bottle of wine is £12.50. The meal costs £6.10 more than the bottle of wine. Find the cost of the meal.

Work in pence.

**5** Heather has 23 coins in her pocket. Some of them are 5p coins and the rest are 10p coins. The total value of the coins is £2.05. Find the number of 10p coins.

**6** The cost, $C$ pounds, of artificial Christmas trees is given by the formula $C = ah + b$, where $h$ is the height in feet. A 3 foot tree costs £10 and a 6 foot tree costs £25. Find the values of $a$ and $b$.

**7** Cinema tickets for 2 adults and 3 children cost £12. The cost for 3 adults and 5 children is £19. Find the cost of an adult's ticket.

**8** The total cost of 3 biros and 4 pencils is 98p. The total cost of 2 biros and 5 pencils is 91p. Find the cost of a pencil.

**9** The total weight of 2 giraffes and 3 zebras is 2.5 tonnes. The total weight of 5 giraffes and 4 zebras is 5.2 tonnes. Find the weight, in kg, of a zebra.

**10** The points with coordinates (3, 5) and (5, 12) lie on the line with equation $ax + by = 11$.
   (a) Find the values of $a$ and $b$.
   (b) Find (i) the gradient of the line and
         (ii) its intercept on the $y$-axis.

1 tonne = 1000 kg

# 9.11 Regions

In Chapter 6 inequalities were represented on a number line.

An inequality may also be represented by a region on a graph.

___ **Example 16** _____

Sketch the region defined by the inequality $x > 3$.

First draw the line $x = 3$. The region for $x > 3$ is the **shaded part** to the right of the line $x = 3$.

Every point to the right of the line $x = 3$ satisfies this inequality.

The unshaded region is the unwanted part for $x > 3$. Because $x = 3$ is also in the unwanted region, the line is dotted.

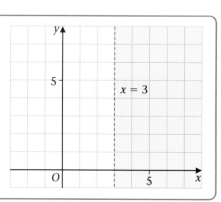

**Example 17**

Sketch the region defined by the inequality $2x + y \geqslant 6$.

First draw the line $2x + y = 6$. If it is not obvious which side of the line satisfies the inequality, substitute the $x$ and $y$ coordinates of a point (often the origin) into the inequality.

In this case, letting $x = 0$ and $y = 0$ does not satisfy the inequality and so the origin lies in the unwanted (unshaded) region.

In this case, because the inequality is '**greater than or equal to**', the line is included in the region required. Hence it is drawn as a solid line.

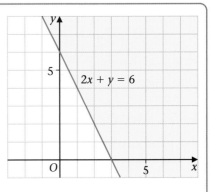

**Example 18**

Sketch the region defined by the inequality $y < 3x$.

First draw the line $y = 3x$. Test with a point not on the line, for example $(1, 0)$.

Letting $x = 1$ and $y = 0$ does satisfy the inequality and so $(1, 0)$ lies in the required (shaded) region.

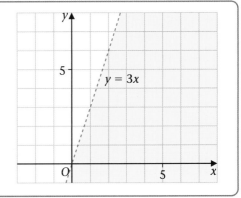

**Example 19**

Sketch the region which is defined by all of the inequalities

$$y < x + 1, \quad y < 7 - 2x \quad \text{and} \quad y > 2$$

Draw each of the lines

$$y = x + 1, \quad y = 7 - 2x \quad \text{and} \quad y = 2$$

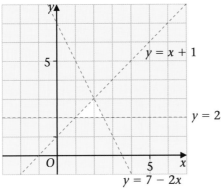

The region needed is     below $y = x + 1$

            below $y = 7 - 2x$

and            above $y = 2$

So it is the unshaded region.

> When you have more than one inequality, if you shade the parts that are **not needed**, then the blank region is the region required.

> Note: the region does not include the boundary lines.

## Exercise 9L

In questions **1–12**, draw diagrams and shade the regions which satisfy the inequalities.

**1**  $x < 4$

**2**  $y \geqslant 2$

**3**  $x \geqslant 0$

**4**  $-2 < y \leqslant 3$

**5**  $x + y \leqslant 5$

**6**  $x + 2y > 6$

**7**  $3x + 4y < 12$

**8**  $2x - 5y < 10$

**9**  $y \geqslant 2x$

**10**  $y \leqslant 3x - 2$

**11**  $2x + 3y \geqslant 12$

**12**  $3x - 2y > 6$

> Remember to draw dotted or solid lines depending on the inequality.

In questions **13–16**, write the inequalities which describe the **unshaded** regions.

**13**

**14**

**15**

**16**
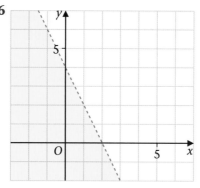

In questions **17–20**, draw diagrams and shade the regions which are not required, leaving unshaded regions which satisfy **all** the inequalities.

**17**  $x \geqslant 1, y \leqslant 4, y \geqslant x - 1$

**18**  $x \geqslant 0, y \geqslant 0, x + y \leqslant 6$

**19**  $x < 5, y < \frac{1}{2}x, y \geqslant 0$

**20**  $x \geqslant 0, y > 2x, 3x + 4y \leqslant 24$

**21**  Sketch the region defined by the inequalities
$$y > x + 1, \quad y > 7 - 2x \quad \text{and} \quad y < 5$$

**22**  Sketch the region defined by the inequalities
$$y \leqslant 2x + 1, \quad 2x + y \leqslant 9 \quad \text{and} \quad y \geqslant 3$$

**23** Work out the three inequalities which define the shaded region in the diagram.

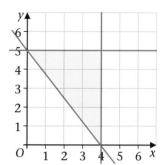

Note: the region should include the boundaries.

## Mixed exercise 9

**1**

Pattern 1          Pattern 2                    Pattern 3

| Pattern number | 1 | 2 | 3 | 4 | 5 |
|---|---|---|---|---|---|
| Number of rods | 5 | 9 | 13 | | |

Copy and complete the table of values.
Draw the graph for the table of values.
Write down the equation of the graph.

**2** On separate diagrams, draw lines with these equations

(a)  $y = 3x - 2$          (b)  $y = \frac{1}{2}x + 1$          (c)  $y = 5 - 2x$

**3** For each of the lines in question **2**, write down the equation of a line that is parallel to it.

**4** Work out the coordinates of the mid-point of the line segment $AB$, where $A$ is the point $(-2, 5)$ and $B$ is the point $(3, 5)$.

**5** Find the equation of the line which is perpendicular to $y = 3x - 5$ and which passes through

(a)  $(0, 9)$          (b)  $(3, 5)$

**6** Find the gradient and the $y$-intercept for the lines with these equations

(a)  $y = 7x + 3.5$      (b)  $3x + 2y = 6$

(c)  $3y - 6x = 15$      (d)  $x + y + 2 = 0$

**7** Solve these simultaneous equations algebraically

(a)  $3p + q = 11$      (b)  $6x - 2y = 33$

   $p + q = 3$              $4x + 3y = 9$

**8**   $ABCD$ is a rectangle. $A$ is the point $(0, 1)$.
$C$ is the point $(0, 6)$.

The equation of the straight line
through $A$ and $B$ is $y = 2x + 1$.

(a)   Find the equation of the
straight line through $D$ and $C$.

(b)   Find the equation of the
straight line through $B$ and $C$.

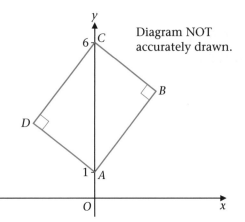

Diagram NOT
accurately drawn.

**9**   (a)   On a copy of the grid draw straight lines and use
shading to show the region **R** that satisfies
the inequalities

$x \geqslant 2, \quad y \geqslant x \quad$ and $\quad x + y \leqslant 6$

(b)   The point $P$ with coordinates $(x, y)$ lies inside
the region **R**. $x$ and $y$ are **integers**.

Write down all the possible points $P$ could be.

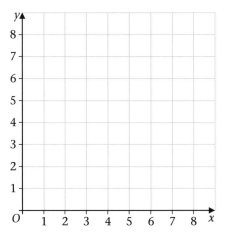

**10**   The line with equation $6y + 5x = 15$ is drawn on
the graph below.

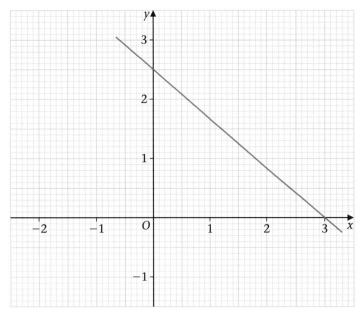

(a)   Rearrange the equation $6y + 5x = 15$ to make $y$ the subject.

(b)   The point $(-21, k)$ lies on the line. Find the value of $k$.

(c)   (i)   On a copy of the grid, shade the region of points whose
coordinates satisfy these four inequalities:

$y > 0, \quad x > 0, \quad 2x < 3, \quad 6y + 5x < 15$

Label this region **R**. $P$ is a point in the region **R**. The coordinates of $P$ are both integers.

(ii)   Write down the coordinates of $P$.

'Make $y$ the subject'
means 'put in the
form $y = \ldots$'

# Summary of key points

**1** A **function** is a rule which shows how one set of numbers relates to another.

**2** $y = 2x + 1$ is called an **equation**. The value of $y$ is always equal to the value of $2x + 1$.

**3** The input values of $x$ are **continuous** if $x$ can take any value (whole numbers or decimals).

**4** $y = 2x + 1$ is the equation of a straight line. The coordinates of any point on the straight line 'satisfy' the equation.

**5** $x \rightarrow 2x + 1$ is called a **linear function** because its graph is a straight line.

**6** An **intercept** is a point at which a line cuts the $y$-axis or the $x$-axis.

**7** $\text{Gradient} = \dfrac{\text{change in } y\text{-direction}}{\text{change in } x\text{-direction}}$

**8** The straight line with equation $y = mx + c$ has a gradient of $m$ and its intercept on the $y$-axis is $(0, c)$.

**9** Lines with equation $y = mx + c$, with the same gradient ($m$), are parallel.

**10** If a line has a gradient of $m$, a line perpendicular to it has a gradient of $-\dfrac{1}{m}$.

**11** If two lines are perpendicular, the product of their gradients is $-1$.

$$m \times \frac{1}{m} = -1$$

**12** The **mid-point of the line segment** $AB$ between $A(x_1, y_1)$ and $B(x_2, y_2)$ is $\left(\dfrac{x_1 + x_2}{2}, \dfrac{y_1 + y_2}{2}\right)$.

**13** **Simultaneous equations** can be solved
- graphically, by drawing the graphs for the two equations and finding the coordinates of their point of intersection
- algebraically, by multiplying one or both of the equations by a number, if necessary, and then adding or subtracting before dividing by the coefficient.

**14** Regions on a graph can be used to represent inequalities.
For example, the shaded region represents the inequality $5x + 3y > 15$.

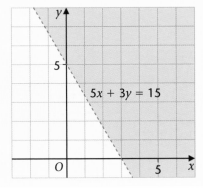

# 10 Presenting and analysing data 1

In this chapter you will calculate averages and measures of the spread of data and draw conclusions from them. The second part shows you how to draw and interpret time series and scatter diagrams.

## 10.1 Averages for discrete data

### The mean

The **mean** of a set of data is the sum of the values divided by the number of values:

$$\text{mean} = \frac{\text{sum of values}}{\text{number of values}}$$

A short way of writing the mean uses the Greek letter sigma $\Sigma$ to represent the sum of a set of values:

$$\bar{x} = \frac{\Sigma x}{n}$$

where $\bar{x}$ is the mean of the values, $\Sigma x$ is the sum of the values and $n$ is the number of values.

A male Emperor penguin goes without food for an average of 115 days each winter, while it looks after the egg or newly hatched chick and waits for the female to return.

### The median

The **median** is the middle value when the data is arranged in order of size.

If there is an even number of values in the data then the median is the mean of the middle two values.

For a data set with $n$ data values, the median is the $\frac{n+1}{2}$th value.

If there is an even number of data values in the set, $\frac{n+1}{2}$ will not give a whole number. For 30 data values, for example, $\frac{n+1}{2} = 15\frac{1}{2}$. The median is the mean of the data values either side, in this case the mean of the 15th and 16th values.

### The mode

The **mode** of a set of data is the value which occurs most often.

There can be more than one mode for a set of data.

**Example 1**

Here are the CPU speeds, in GHz, of eight computers in an office:

    1.5   1.9   2.4   1.7   2.7   1.7   1.6   2.1

Calculate

(a)  the mean      (b) the median      (c) the mode.

(a)  Calculate the **mean** by adding all the speeds and dividing by the number of computers

$$\text{mean} = \frac{1.5 + 1.9 + 2.4 + 1.7 + 2.7 + 1.7 + 1.6 + 2.1}{8} = \frac{15.6}{8} = 1.95$$

(b)  Calculate the **median** by putting the speeds in order of increasing size and then calculating the mean of the two middle values:

       1.5   1.6   1.7   1.7   1.9   2.1   2.4   2.7

$$\text{median} = \frac{1.7 + 1.9}{2} = 1.8$$

(c)  Find the **mode** by selecting the speed that appears most often:

       mode = 1.7

## 10.2 Stem and leaf diagrams

The ages of the 30 members of an aerobics class are:

| 19 | 22 | 31 | 17 | 8  | 12 | 23 | 47 | 53 | 47 |
|----|----|----|----|----|----|----|----|----|----|
| 19 | 46 | 38 | 59 | 47 | 52 | 21 | 58 | 54 | 26 |
| 32 | 47 | 55 | 62 | 64 | 36 | 37 | 43 | 15 | 51 |

These are presented as a stem and leaf diagram by using the first digit as stem, and the second digit as leaf:

19 is written 1 | 9
22 is written 2 | 2
31 is written 3 | 1

17 is then   1 | 9, 7

and 8 is   0 | 8

```
0 | 8
1 | 9, 7
2 | 2
3 | 1
4 |
5 |
6 |
```

So the complete diagram is:

```
0 | 8
1 | 9, 7, 2, 9, 5
2 | 2, 3, 1, 6
3 | 1, 8, 2, 6, 7
4 | 7, 7, 6, 7, 7, 3
5 | 3, 9, 2, 8, 4, 5, 1
6 | 2, 4
```

Now put the 'leaves' in order:

```
0 | 8
1 | 2, 5, 7, 9, 9
2 | 1, 2, 3, 6
3 | 1, 2, 6, 7, 8
4 | 3, 6, 7, 7, 7, 7
5 | 1, 2, 3, 4, 5, 8, 9
6 | 2, 4
```

15th value

16th value

mode

> You should include a key with a stem and leaf diagram.

Key:  6 | 2 means 62 years

From this you can pick out the mode and identify the median.

> The average of the 15th and 16th values is
> $$\frac{38 + 43}{2} = 40.5$$

Mode = 47

The median is the $\frac{30 + 1}{2} = 15\frac{1}{2}$th value = 40.5

## Exercise 10A

**1**  Here are the ages of a random sample of people on holiday in Spain in October.

53  55  45  65  68  60  57  75  62  58
57  74  60  55  49  54  64  82  70  58
64  73  67  62  56  66  83  60  77  63

Draw a stem and leaf diagram for this data (remember to use a key). Find the mode, median and mean.

**2**  Here are the masses (in kg) of 24 babies born in a hospital.

4.1  3.7  2.8  4.3  4.7  4.6  2.8  5.2  3.9  3.7  3.7  4.6
3.8  3.4  4.9  4.6  4.7  4.2  3.0  3.1  2.5  5.0  4.5  4.5

Draw a stem and leaf diagram for this data. Find the mean, median and mode.

**3**  The data shows an athlete's times in seconds, over a season, in the 400 m track event.

44.9  45.3  45.2  45.7  45.6  45.0  45.1  46.2  45.9
45.3  44.8  44.9  46.3  44.8  46.3  46.1  45.4  44.7
45.3  45.7  44.7  46.2  45.7  44.9  45.0  45.5  46.0

Use 44, 45 and 46 as the stem to produce a stem and leaf diagram. Work out the mode and median.

## 10.3 Using appropriate averages

The three different types of average are useful in different situations. The choice of which average you use or quote can be crucial; this is especially true when you do statistics-based coursework.

The **mean** is very useful when you need to quote a 'typical' value, provided that the data is quite closely grouped around the mean.

The mean can, however, be seriously influenced by extreme values. For example, consider the situation below.

Bob is the Director of a small company which employs 10 people, including himself. The salaries of the 10 people are:

| | |
|---|---|
| Director | £80 000 per year |
| 7 people earning | £20 000 per year |
| 2 people earning | £12 000 per year. |

The mean of these salaries is

$$\frac{80\,000 + 7 \times 20\,000 + 2 \times 12\,000}{10}$$

or $\quad \dfrac{80\,000 + 140\,000 + 24\,000}{10} = £24\,400$

It would be silly to say that a 'typical' salary is £24 400 when in fact nobody at the company earns that amount and only one person earns above, and considerably above, that amount.

In a situation such as this, it would be far more sensible to use the **median** salary as the 'typical' value, i.e. £20 000.

The **mode** is useful in situations such as when you want to know:

- Which dress size is most common?
- Which brand of dog food is most popular?

The mode is an average which shops use when they calculate the stock they need.

> The **median** and **mode** are not influenced by extreme values, but the **mean** is influenced by extremes.

**Example 2**

There are 10 houses in Streetfield Close.

On Monday, the numbers of letters delivered to the houses are:

   0   2   5   3   34   4   0   1   0   2

Calculate the mean, mode and median of the number of letters.

Comment on your results.

$$\text{Mean} = \frac{0 + 2 + 5 + 3 + 34 + 4 + 0 + 1 + 0 + 2}{10}$$

$$= 5.1$$

$$\text{Mode} = 0$$

$$\text{Median} = 2$$

In this case the mean has been distorted by the large number of letters delivered to one of the houses. It is, therefore, not a good measure of a 'typical' number of letters delivered to any house in the close.

The mode (0) is also not a good measure of a 'typical' number of letters delivered to a house, since 7 out of the 10 houses do actually receive some letters.

The median (2) is perhaps the best measure of the 'typical' number of letters delivered to each house, since half of the houses received 2 or more letters and the other half received 2 or fewer letters.

## Exercise 10B

1  Ten students submitted their Design portfolios which were marked out of 40. The marks they obtained were

    37   34   34   34   29   27   27   10   4   28

   (a)  For these marks find
        (i) the mode   (ii) the median   (iii) the mean.

   (b)  Comment on your results.

   (c)  An external moderator reduced all the marks by 3.

        Find the mode, median and mean of the moderated marks.

2  The ages of the people in the Jones family are

        Grandpa         79
        John            42
        Mary            44
        Sarah           16
        Peter           12
        Lucy             3

   (a)  Calculate the mean age of the Jones family.

   (b)  State, with a reason, whether the mean age is a sensible measure of the age of a 'typical' member of the Jones family.

3  A newspaper headline reads:

        'The average weekly wage in the UK is in excess of £250'

   Explain why this headline could be misleading.

> **Activity – Citius, Altius, Fortius (Swifter, Higher, Stronger)**
>
> Use the internet to find out the total number of medals won by Great Britain in each of the Olympic Games since 1894.
>
> Work out the mode, median and mean of the data.
>
> Which is the best measure of average to use? Explain your answer.

# 10.4 The quartiles

The median divides a set of data arranged in order of size into two halves. The data can also be divided into four quarters.

When the data is arranged in ascending order of size:
- the **lower quartile** is the value one quarter of the way into the data
- the **upper quartile** is the value three quarters of the way into the data

For example, here are the results of asking 15 people how many cousins they have. The data is arranged in order of size.

Number
of        0  2  4  5  7  18  10  12  12  12  13  14  14  15  16
cousins

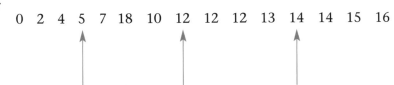

The lower quartile    The median is    The upper quartile
is the 4th value.     the 8th value.   is the 12th value.

So the lower quartile is 5 cousins, the median is 12 cousins, and the upper quartile is 14 cousins.

For a set of $n$ data values arranged in order of size:

$$\text{lower quartile} = \left(\frac{n+1}{4}\right)\text{th value}$$

$$\text{median} = \left(\frac{n+1}{2}\right)\text{th value}$$

$$\text{upper quartile} = \frac{3(n+1)}{4}\text{th value}$$

---

**Example 3**

Shah records the numbers of hits on his web page for each of 11 consecutive days. Here are his results.

> 63   96   67   99   87   68   61   85   91   102   89

Work out  (a) the lower quartile   (b) the upper quartile.

(a)  First arrange the numbers of hits in order of size

> 61   63   67   68   85   87   89   91   96   99   102

The lower quartile is the $\left(\frac{11+1}{4}\right)$ = 3rd value, so it is 67.

(b)  The upper quartile is the $\frac{3(11+1)}{4}$ = 9th value, so it is 96.

**Example 4**

The table shows the life expectancy of people in South America.

| Country | Argentina | Bolivia | Brazil | Chile | Colombia | Ecuador |
|---|---|---|---|---|---|---|
| Life expectancy (years) | 75.5 | 71.1 | 71.1 | 76.8 | 71.1 | 71.9 |

| F. Guiana | Guyana | Surinam | Paraguay | Peru | Uruguay | Venezuela |
|---|---|---|---|---|---|---|
| 76.7 | 63.1 | 69.2 | 74.4 | 70.9 | 75.9 | 73.8 |

Work out (a) the median  (b) the lower quartile  (c) the upper quartile of the data.

(a)  First arrange the values in order of size:

63.1   69.2   70.9   71.1   71.1   71.1   71.9   73.8   74.4   75.5   75.9   76.7   76.8

There are 13 values. The median is the $\frac{13+1}{2}$ = 7th value, so it is 71.9 years.

(b)  The lower quartile is the $\frac{13+1}{4}$ = $3\frac{1}{2}$th value.

You treat this as being the value halfway between the 3rd value (70.9) and the 4th value (71.1), so the lower quartile is 71 years.

(c)  The upper quartile is the $\frac{3(13+1)}{4}$ = $10\frac{1}{2}$th value.

You treat this as being the value halfway between the 10th value (75.5) and the 11th value (75.9), so the lower quartile is 75.7 years.

## Exercise 10C

For each set of data below work out

(a) the median  (b) the lower quartile  (c) the upper quartile.

1  The numbers of seats won by the Labour party in General Elections from 1959 to 1998

258   317   363   287   301   319   269   209   229   271   418

2  The numbers of delegates for each country in the European parliament

18   25   6   24   14   6   14   78   99   24   13   78   9

13   6   5   27   54   24   14   7   54   19   78   24

3  The masses (in g) of a random sample of watch batteries

Mass of batteries

| 50.7 | 3, 5, 7 |
|---|---|
| 50.8 | 6, 9 |
| 50.9 | 0, 2, 3, 6 |
| 51.0 | 6 |
| 51.1 | 3, 6, 8, 9, 9 |
| 51.2 | 5 |
| 51.3 | 6, 8, 9 |

Key: 50.9 | 2 means 50.92 grams

# 10.5 Measures of spread

## The range

The **range** is a measure of **spread**.

> The **range** of a set of data is the difference between the highest and lowest values
>
> range = highest value − lowest value

The range can be **greatly** affected by extreme (very large or very small) values.

## The interquartile range

The quartiles are useful because together they can be used to give a better idea of the spread of a set of data than the range can.

> The **interquartile range** is the difference between the upper and lower quartiles:
>
> interquartile range = upper quartile − lower quartile

Unlike the range, the interquartile range is not distorted by extreme data values. It also tells you whether the data values are spread evenly throughout the range, or concentrated in the middle of the range.

For example, there are 12 houses in a close. The numbers of letters delivered to the houses one day are, in order:

1   2   2   2   3   3   3   3   5   5   5   30

The range of these numbers is $30 − 1 = 29$.

The interquartile range is

upper quartile − lower quartile = $5 − 2 = 3$

If the house that received 30 letters instead had received 8 letters then the range would have been $8 − 1 = 7$. This change in the extreme value from 30 to 8 makes no change to the interquartile range.

Because it is not affected by extreme values, the interquartile range is a good measure of the spread of the data as a whole, and particularly the spread either side of the median.

A large range tells you very little about how the data is spread.

A large interquartile range tells you that the middle 50% of the data is widely spread about the median.

A small interquartile range tells you that the middle 50% of the data is highly concentrated about the median.

> One house receives a lot of letters.

# 10.6 Averages from frequency distributions

This section shows you how to find the mean, mode and median where the information is given in a frequency table.

A frequency table with the totals included is called a **frequency distribution**.

For a frequency distribution:

- the **mode** = the item of data which has the highest frequency

- the **median** = the middle value of the data = the $\dfrac{\Sigma f + 1}{2}$th value ← the sum of the frequencies

- the **mean**, $\bar{x} = \dfrac{\Sigma fx}{\Sigma f}$ ← the sum of all the $(f \times x)$ values in the distribution
  ← the sum of the frequencies

---

**Example 5**

In a survey, the number of eggs in seagulls' nests in June was counted. The table shows the results.

Find

(a) the mode

(b) the median

(c) the mean number of eggs.

| Number of eggs $x$ | Frequency $f$ |
|:---:|:---:|
| 0 | 17 |
| 1 | 12 |
| 2 | 23 |
| 3 | 37 |
| 4 | 18 |
| Total | 107 |

(a) The mode is the value which occurs most often. In a frequency table this is the item of data which has the highest frequency. For this data the mode is 3 eggs. There are more nests with 3 eggs than with any other number of eggs.

(b) The median is the middle value of the data = the $\dfrac{\Sigma f + 1}{2}$th value.

There are 107 nests altogether. So the middle nest is the $\dfrac{107 + 1}{2} = 54$th nest.

      Nests 1–17 have 0 eggs

      Nests 18–29 have 1 egg

      Nests 30–52 have 2 eggs

      Nests 53–89 have 3 eggs

So nest 54 is a 3-egg nest. The median is 3 eggs.

(c) The mean is the total number of eggs divided by the
total number of nests (the total frequency) $= \dfrac{\Sigma fx}{\Sigma f}$

| Number of eggs<br>$x$ | Frequency<br>$f$ | Frequency × number of eggs<br>$fx$ |
|:---:|:---:|:---:|
| 0 | 17 | 0 |
| 1 | 12 | 12 |
| 2 | 23 | 46 |
| 3 | 37 | 111 |
| 4 | 18 | 72 |
| Totals | 107 | 241 |

> Add a column to the table for $fx$.

> The number of eggs in 2-egg nests is $23 \times 2 = 46$

> The total number of eggs is the sum of all the $fx$ values.

The mean $= \dfrac{\Sigma fx}{\Sigma f}$

$\qquad = \dfrac{241}{107} = 2.25$ eggs

## Exercise 10D

**1** For the data given, calculate the mean, mode and median number of cars per household. Use a table like this:

| Cars per household<br>$x$ | Frequency<br>$f$ | $fx$ |
|:---:|:---:|:---:|
| 0 | 6 | |
| 1 | 20 | |
| 2 | 13 | |
| 3 | 4 | |
| 4 | 2 | |
| Totals | | |

The frequency tables in questions **2–3** are written sideways in rows. You might find it easier to rewrite them in columns.

**2** A factory takes random samples of 102 items and tests them for faults. Here are their results for last week:

| Number of faults per sample | 0 | 1 | 2 | 3 | 4 | 5 |
|:---|:---:|:---:|:---:|:---:|:---:|:---:|
| Number of samples | 76 | 13 | 6 | 3 | 3 | 1 |

> 'Per sample' tells you that you need to divide the total number of faults by the total number of samples. So the 'number of samples' is the frequency.

Work out the mode, median and mean number of faults per sample.

**3** The table shows the number of goals Lucy scored in matches during the netball season.

| Number of goals | 0 | 1 | 2 | 3 | 4 | 5 | 6 | 7 | 8 |
|---|---|---|---|---|---|---|---|---|---|
| Frequency | 4 | 0 | 6 | 5 | 3 | 2 | 1 | 3 | 0 |

(a) How many goals scored is the mode?

(b) Work out the median number of goals scored

(c) Calculate the mean number of goals scored correct to 1 d.p.

## 10.7 Spread from frequency distributions

This section shows you how to work out the interquartile range from information given in a frequency distribution.

---

**Example 6**

The table shows the number of complaints per day to Ofcom about a popular TV soap.

| Number of complaints per day | 3 | 4 | 5 | 6 | 7 | 8 | 9 | 10 | 11 | Total |
|---|---|---|---|---|---|---|---|---|---|---|
| Frequency | 1 | 2 | 4 | 7 | 17 | 23 | 24 | 16 | 1 | 95 |

Work out **(a)** the range **(b)** the interquartile range.

(a) Range = highest value − lowest value = 11 − 3 = 8 complaints

(b) The lower quartile is the $\dfrac{95 + 1}{4}$ = 24th value.

Adding up the frequencies in order:

$$1 + 2 + 4 + 7 = 14$$
and $\qquad 1 + 2 + 4 + 7 + 17 = 31$

As the 24th value is between the 14th and 31st values, it is one of the 17 values recorded as 7 complaints. So the lower quartile is 7 complaints.

Using the same method, the upper quartile is the $\dfrac{3(95 + 1)}{4}$ = 72nd value.

Adding up the frequencies in order:

$$1 + 2 + 4 + 7 + 17 + 23 = 54$$
and $\qquad 1 + 2 + 4 + 7 + 17 + 23 + 24 = 78$

As the 72nd value is between the 54th and 78th values, it is one of the 24 values recorded as 9 complaints. So the upper quartile is 9 complaints.

The interquartile range is

upper quartile − lower quartile = 9 − 7 = 2 complaints

## Exercise 10E

For each set of data below work out

(a)  the range          (b)  the interquartile range.

**1**  The numbers of emails received in a day by 31 people in an office

| Number of emails | 0 | 1 | 2 | 3 | 4 | 5 | 6 | 7 |
|---|---|---|---|---|---|---|---|---|
| Frequency (number of people) | 4 | 11 | 8 | 6 | 1 | 0 | 0 | 1 |

**2**  The amounts received from the sale of £1 lottery tickets to 93 people

| Amount (£) | 1 | 2 | 3 | 4 | 5 | 6 | 7 | 8 | 9 | 10 |
|---|---|---|---|---|---|---|---|---|---|---|
| Frequency | 32 | 16 | 3 | 2 | 21 | 4 | 2 | 3 | 0 | 10 |

**3**  The sizes of shoes for hire at a bowling alley

| Size | 6 | $6\frac{1}{2}$ | 7 | $7\frac{1}{2}$ | 8 | $8\frac{1}{2}$ | 9 | $9\frac{1}{2}$ | 10 | $10\frac{1}{2}$ |
|---|---|---|---|---|---|---|---|---|---|---|
| Frequency | 4 | 5 | 7 | 8 | 6 | 5 | 4 | 6 | 8 | 4 |

## 10.8 Averages from grouped data

Data in a frequency distribution may be grouped. You can **estimate** averages from grouped data.

The manager of a hotel checks the cost of telephone calls made by each guest by looking at the number of units used per call. She summarises the data about the phone calls in a frequency table, grouping it in class intervals.

| Number of units | Frequency |
|---|---|
| 1–5 | 73 |
| 6–10 | 161 |
| 11–15 ⌐ | 294 |
| 16–20 | 186 |
| 21–25 | 65 |
| over 25 | 11 |
| Total | 790 |

The $395\frac{1}{2}$th value is in this class interval.

**The median:** There were 790 phone calls so the position of the median data value is the $(790 + 1) \div 2 = 395\frac{1}{2}$th value.
It is in the class interval 11–15.
You cannot give an exact value for the median.

For grouped data, you can state the class interval that contains the median.

**The modal class:** The class interval 11–15 units per call has the highest frequency.

> For grouped data, the class interval with the highest frequency is called the **modal class**.

The modal class only makes sense as a measure of the average if the class intervals are the same.

**The mean:** Each class interval contains calls using different numbers of units, so you have not got the exact data you need to calculate the mean. But you can calculate an **estimate of the mean**. This is *not* a guess, but a calculation. Here is how to do it.

Assume each call in a class interval uses the number of units given by the middle value of the class interval the call is in.

> The middle value of the class interval 1–5 is 3. The middle value of class interval 6–10 is 8 and so on.

| Number of units used per call | Frequency $f$ | Middle value $x$ | $fx$ |
|---|---|---|---|
| 1–5 | 73 | 3 | 219 |
| 6–10 | 161 | 8 | 1288 |
| 11–15 | 294 | 13 | 3822 |
| 16–20 | 186 | 18 | 3348 |
| 21–25 | 65 | 23 | 1495 |
| over 25 | 11 | 28 | 308 |
| Total, $\Sigma f$ | 790 | Total, $\Sigma fx$ | 10 480 |

> The 161 calls did not all use 8 units each. The errors made by overestimating approximately balance those made by underestimating.

> A middle value must be chosen for calls over 25 units. This is a matter of judgement depending on the raw data. Here 28 is used.

Now you can calculate an estimate of the mean in a similar way to calculating the mean for ungrouped data (Section 10.6):

$$\text{estimate of mean} = \frac{\text{sum of (middle values} \times \text{frequencies)}}{\text{sum of frequencies}}$$

$$= \frac{\Sigma fx}{\Sigma f}$$

$$= \frac{10\,480}{790} = 13.3$$

> For grouped data you can **calculate an estimate of the mean** using the middle value of each class interval.

In the telephone calls example the data is discrete. You can use exactly the same method to find an estimate of the mean of continuous data. The method works even if the class intervals are not the same size and the middle values are not whole numbers.

> The estimate of the mean for grouped data is
> $$\bar{x} = \frac{\Sigma fx}{\Sigma f}$$
> where $x$ is the mid-point of each class interval.

**Example 7**

A saleswoman kept a record of the mileage she travelled each day. Calculate an estimate for the mean distance travelled from the data in this table:

| Mileage $m$ (miles) | Frequency |
|---|---|
| $0 \leqslant m < 50$ | 2 |
| $50 \leqslant m < 100$ | 8 |
| $100 \leqslant m < 150$ | 17 |
| $150 \leqslant m < 200$ | 21 |
| $200 \leqslant m \leqslant 300$ | 2 |

This is 0 up to but not including 50.

First draw up a table of frequencies and mid-points.

| Mileage | $f$ | Mid-point $x$ | $fx$ |
|---|---|---|---|
| $0 \leqslant m < 50$ | 2 | 25 | 50 |
| $50 \leqslant m < 100$ | 8 | 75 | 600 |
| $100 \leqslant m < 150$ | 17 | 125 | 2125 |
| $150 \leqslant m < 200$ | 21 | 175 | 3675 |
| $200 \leqslant m \leqslant 300$ | 2 | 250 | 500 |
| | $\Sigma f = 50$ | | $\Sigma fx = 6950$ |

The mid-point of the interval from 0 to 50 is
$\dfrac{0 + 50}{2} = 25$

The estimate of the mean $\bar{x}$ is

$$\bar{x} = \frac{\Sigma fx}{\Sigma f}$$

$$= \frac{6950}{50} = 139 \text{ miles}$$

## Exercise 10F

1  Hajra looked at a passage from a book. She recorded the number of words in each sentence in a frequency table using class intervals of 1–5, 6–10, 11–15, etc.

   (a) Copy and complete the table.

   (b) Work out an estimate for the mean number of words in a sentence.

| Class interval | Frequency $f$ | Middle value $x$ | $f \times x$ |
|---|---|---|---|
| 1–5 | 16 | | 48 |
| 6–10 | 28 | | |
| 11–15 | 26 | 13 | |
| 16–20 | 14 | | |
| 21–25 | 10 | | 230 |
| 26–30 | 3 | | |
| 31–35 | 1 | | |
| 36–40 | 0 | | |
| 41–45 | 2 | | 86 |
| Total, $\Sigma f$ | | Total, $\Sigma fx$ | |

**2**    The table shows how long couples had been married whose marriage ended in a divorce in 2005.

| Length of marriage in completed years | 0–2 | 3–4 | 5–9 | 10–14 | 15–19 | 20–24 | 25–29 | 30–40 |
|---|---|---|---|---|---|---|---|---|
| Frequency as a % | 9 | 14 | 27 | 18 | 13 | 10 | 5 | 4 |

Work out an estimate for the mean length of a marriage that ended in divorce in 2005.

**3**    In a darts match a record is kept of the scores for each throw of three darts.

| Score | 1–20 | 21–40 | 41–60 | 61–100 | 101–140 | 141–180 |
|---|---|---|---|---|---|---|
| Frequency | 3 | 17 | 25 | 56 | 8 | 3 |

(a)   Write down the modal class.

(b)   Write down the class interval in which the median lies.

(c)   Work out an estimate for the mean score.

**Activity – Maze**

How long does it take you to get through this maze?

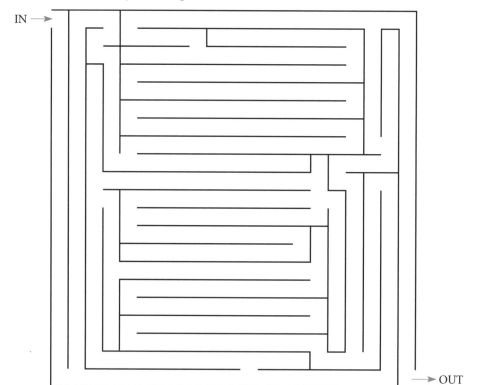

(a)   Design your own maze and time how long it takes your friends to do it.

(b)   Record the data in a frequency table using class intervals of equal width.

(c)   Work out an estimate for the mean.

## 10.9 Drawing conclusions from data

In statistics it is easy to draw incorrect conclusions from data, especially if you do not have sufficient information.

For example, suppose that a group of girls and a group of boys took the same test marked out of 20. You are told that:

- the mean mark for the girls was 10
- the mean mark for the boys was 8

Can you now conclude that the girls have on the whole done better in the test than the boys?

It would be easy to conclude this because the mean mark for the girls is higher than for the boys. But a closer look shows that this conclusion need not be true.

Suppose only three girls and three boys took the test and that the marks were:

girls  9  10  11          boys  0  12  12

The mean for the girls is          The mean for the boys is

$$\frac{9 + 10 + 11}{3} = 10 \qquad \frac{0 + 12 + 12}{3} = 8$$

Although the mean for the girls is greater, it would not be valid to say that the girls did better than the boys. In fact two-thirds of the boys scored a mark higher than any of the girls.

To say whether the girls did better than the boys, you need further information. You need to know how the marks were distributed or spread out.

> To compare two sets of data you should use a measure of average and a measure of spread.

To help you see why, you can represent the scores in the test along an axis:

The red marks show the positions of the average marks for boys and girls. Here it looks as if the girls have done better than the boys.

But if we add brackets to show the measure of spread of the scores, the diagrams now look like this:

> Boys: range = 12 − 0 = 12
> Girls: range = 11 − 9 = 2

While the average score for the girls is greater than that for the boys, the **measures of spread** mean that many boys may have done better than any of the girls.

In the test results:

- if the mean mark for the girls had been greater than the mean mark for the boys

  *and*

- if the spread of marks for the girls had been about the same as the spread of marks for the boys

you would be justified in concluding that the girls did better in the test than the boys.

___ **Example 8** ___

A group of students took a science examination consisting of two papers, Paper 1 and Paper 2.

The table gives the median marks and the interquartile ranges of the marks on those papers.

| Paper | Median (%) | Interquartile range (%) |
|-------|-----------|-------------------------|
| 1 | 63 | 12 |
| 2 | 51 | 38 |

Comment on these results.

Because the median mark on Paper 1 was greater than the median mark on Paper 2, it looks as if Paper 1 was easier than Paper 2 (or as if more students scored higher marks on Paper 1 than on Paper 2).

However, the interquartile range for Paper 2 was much greater than that for Paper 1.

So it could be that many students obtained a higher mark on Paper 2 than on Paper 1 – and so found Paper 2 to be the easier paper.

## Exercise 10G

1   The mean weekly wage at Cromby and Sons is £300.

The mean weekly wage at Drapeway Ltd is £350.

Is it fair to say that the people at Drapeway Ltd are better paid than those at Cromby and Sons? Explain your answer.

2   The Year 11 students at Lucea High School sat a French exam consisting of two papers, Paper A and Paper B.

The table shows the median marks and the interquartile ranges of the marks on the two papers.

| Paper | Median (%) | Interquartile range (%) |
|-------|-----------|-------------------------|
| A | 72 | 32 |
| B | 60 | 12 |

Comment on this data.

**3**   In the town of Reddshaw there are two golf clubs.

The table shows the median ages and the interquartile ranges of the ages of the club members.

| Club | Median age | Interquartile range of ages |
|------|-----------|------------------------------|
| 1 | 34 | 17 |
| 2 | 42 | 12 |

Explain whether or not it would be fair to say that the members of Club 2 are, in general, older than the members of Club 1.

## 10.10 Moving averages

This section shows you how to calculate moving averages and interpret time series.

> A graph showing how a given value changes over time is called a **time series graph**.

This graph shows the variation in the number of job vacancies in a district over three years.

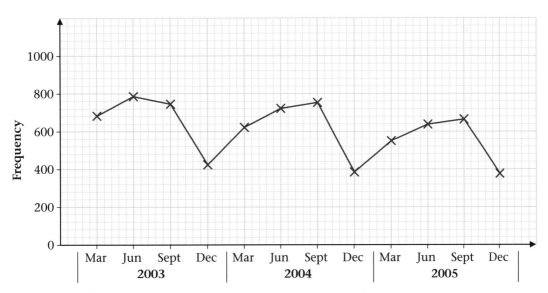

It is difficult to see from the graph whether the trend in the number of job vacancies has risen or fallen over the three years. There is too much variation within each year.

You can take account of this variation by working out a **moving average**. This takes the average of consecutive pieces of data.

Here is the table of results for the graph on the previous page:

| Year | March | June | September | December |
|------|-------|------|-----------|----------|
| 2003 | 682 | 785 | 742 | 423 |
| 2004 | 622 | 722 | 752 | 385 |
| 2005 | 550 | 639 | 661 | 376 |

There are four values for each year, so look at groups of four.

> If you consider groups of four you are finding a **four-point moving average**.

The first moving average, $M_1$, is the mean of the first four values:

$$M_1 = \frac{682 + 785 + 742 + 423}{4} = 658$$

The next moving average, $M_2$, is found by 'moving up one place'.
It is the mean of the values from June 2003 to March 2004:

$$M_2 = \frac{785 + 742 + 423 + 622}{4} = 643$$

The four-point moving averages for the whole data set are:

| $M_1$ | $M_2$ | $M_3$ | $M_4$ | $M_5$ | $M_6$ | $M_7$ | $M_8$ | $M_9$ |
|-------|-------|-------|-------|-------|-------|-------|-------|-------|
| 658 | 643 | 627 | 630 | 620 | 602 | 582 | 559 | 557 |

You can plot the four-point moving averages on the same graph as your original data. Each average should be plotted at the mid-point of the values from which it was generated.

You can now see that the number of job vacancies fell between the beginning of 2003 and the end of 2005.

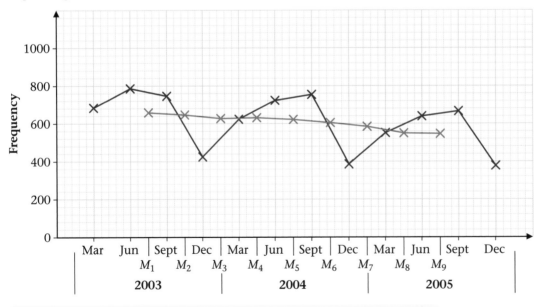

A moving average 'smooths out' the data to show the trend on a time series graph.

## Exercise 10H

1   Dr Singh keeps a record of the number of patients he treats for shingles. Here are his results for eight months:

| Month | June | July | Aug | Sept | Oct | Nov | Dec | Jan |
|---|---|---|---|---|---|---|---|---|
| Number of patients | 7 | 8 | 6 | 10 | 5 | 9 | 7 | 8 |

(a)   Plot the time series graph.

(b)   Calculate the three-point moving averages for the data and plot them on the same graph.

(c)   Dr Singh says 'Shingles appears to be in decline'.
Do you agree? Give a reason for your answer.

2   The table shows information about the quarterly gas bills for Alice's house, over a period of two years.

| Year | Quarter | | | |
|---|---|---|---|---|
| | 1 | 2 | 3 | 4 |
| 1 | £196 | £158 | £80 | £138 |
| 2 | £216 | £162 | £96 | £146 |

(a)   Plot the data and the four-point moving averages on the same graph.

(b)   Comment on your graph.

3   The table shows information about the numbers of passengers travelling by fast ferry to Jersey.

| Year | 2003 | | | | 2004 | | | | 2005 | | | |
|---|---|---|---|---|---|---|---|---|---|---|---|---|
| Season | Sp | Su | Au | Wi | Sp | Su | Au | Wi | Sp | Su | Au | Wi |
| Number of passengers (thousands) | 21 | 50 | 33 | 16 | 17 | 46 | 25 | 16 | 21 | 42 | 25 | 12 |

Draw suitable graphs and comment on the trend of the data.

Use four-point moving averages.

# 10.11 Scatter diagrams

Statements such as 'Smoking can cause lung cancer' and 'Drink driving causes accidents' are often made in the media. Sometimes they are supported by data showing, for example, whether there is a relationship between a smoking habit and the chance of getting lung cancer.

This section shows you how to compare two sets of data to see whether there is a relationship between them.

For example, is there a relationship between the number of ice-creams sold at a kiosk and the average daytime temperature?
James collected data to find out:

| Average temperature (°C) | 13 | 14 | 21 | 22 | 16 | 18 | 13 | 20 | 21 | 18 | 15 | 16 | 14 |
|---|---|---|---|---|---|---|---|---|---|---|---|---|---|
| No. of ice-creams sold | 5 | 9 | 51 | 48 | 20 | 30 | 15 | 32 | 42 | 37 | 23 | 25 | 14 |

He plotted each pair of values (13, 5), (14, 9), and so on, on a graph.
This is called a **scatter diagram** or **scatter graph**.

There does appear to be a relationship between the average daytime temperature and the number of ice-creams sold: the hotter it is, the more ice-creams are sold.

Here is another example. On a journey Chandra noted down how many miles there were still to go. She did this every ten minutes:

| Time (min) | 10 | 20 | 30 | 40 | 50 | 60 | 70 | 80 | 90 | 100 |
|---|---|---|---|---|---|---|---|---|---|---|
| Miles to go | 72 | 60 | 54 | 42 | 40 | 35 | 24 | 18 | 10 | 0 |

Here is a scatter diagram showing this data:

There is a relationship between the time she has been travelling and the number of miles still to go: the greater the travelling time, the fewer miles there are to go.

Sometimes there is no relationship between two sets of data.
Every Monday Trish recorded the temperature in °F and the rainfall in mm.
Her results were:

| Temperature (°F) | 74 | 70 | 63 | 68 | 65 | 64 | 60 | 51 | 54 | 56 | 50 |
|---|---|---|---|---|---|---|---|---|---|---|---|
| Rainfall (mm) | 1 | 0 | 2 | 7 | 5 | 1 | 8 | 2 | 11 | 4 | 6 |

A scatter graph of this data looks like this:

There does not appear to be any relationship.

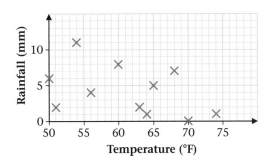

You can use a **scatter diagram** to show whether two sets of data are related.

## Exercise 10I

1   The table shows the distance travelled and the depth of tread of a sample of motorcycle tyres.

| Tyre | A | B | C | D | E | F | G | H | I |
|---|---|---|---|---|---|---|---|---|---|
| Distance travelled (1000 km) | 15 | 9 | 2 | 23 | 30 | 45 | 19 | 6 | 36 |
| Depth of tread (mm) | 8.9 | 9.6 | 10.7 | 8.2 | 7.9 | 6.8 | 7.9 | 9.2 | 7.7 |

Draw a scatter diagram for the data and comment on any relationship between the depth of tread and the distance travelled.

2   The table below shows the number of hours of sunshine and the maximum temperature in ten British towns, on one particular day.

| Maximum temperature (°C) | 13 | 20 | 19 | 15 | 16 | 12 | 14 | 14 | 17 |
|---|---|---|---|---|---|---|---|---|---|
| Number of hours of sunshine | 11.7 | 15.2 | 15.4 | 13.2 | 11.8 | 9.8 | 10.2 | 12.4 | 13.7 |

(a)   Plot this information as a scatter diagram.

(b)   What does your diagram tell you about change in the maximum temperature as the number of hours of sunshine increases?

---

**Activity – Height and arm-span**
Is there a relationship between a person's height and their arm-span?

(a)   Collect data for your class.

(b)   Draw a scatter diagram to represent your data.

(c)   Describe the relationship.

# 10.12 Correlation and lines of best fit

Scatter diagrams can be used to show whether there is a relationship between two sets of data. Such a relationship is called a **correlation**.

> If the points on a scatter diagram are very nearly along a straight line there is a high **correlation** between the variables.

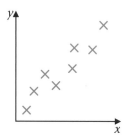

Positive correlation

When the values in one set increase as the values in the other set increase, the relationship between them is called **positive correlation**.

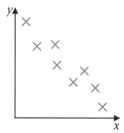

Negative correlation

When the values in one set increase as the values in the other set decrease the relationship between them is called **negative correlation**.

No correlation

When there is no linear relationship between the two sets of values, there is **no correlation**.

## Line of best fit

When there is a relationship between two sets of data there is some correlation. You can show this on a scatter diagram by drawing the **line of best fit**. This is a line that shows the general trend of the relationship between the two sets of data. It may or may not pass through any of the data points themselves.

> A line that is drawn to pass as close as possible to all the plotted points on a scatter diagram is called the **line of best fit**.

This scatter diagram (from the data on page 204) shows the average daytime temperature plotted against the numbers of ice-creams sold:

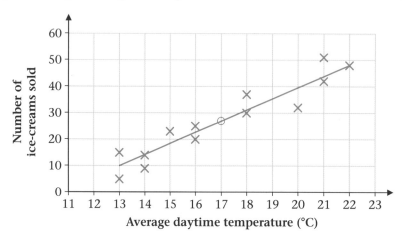

The line of best fit should really be drawn through the point with coordinates (mean average daytime temperature, mean number of ice-creams sold). Here this is (17, 27) and the point is circled on the graph. However, you would not be expected to do this in your exam. Drawing the line 'by eye' would be suggested.

The line of best fit has been drawn by eye. You should draw the line so that there are about the same number of plotted points on either side of it. Position the line so that the distances of the plotted points from it on each side balance each other out as much as possible.

The closer the points are to this line of best fit, the higher the correlation. The gradient of the line is not important, except that a vertical or horizontal line of best fit means that the variables are not connected. Here are some typical examples and their interpretation:

| high or strong positive correlation | low positive correlation – not a strong relationship | no correlation – no linear relationship | low negative correlation – not a strong relationship | high or strong negative correlation |

**Example 9**

The table shows the acidity of seven lakes near to an industrial plant and their distance from it.

| Distance (km) | 4 | 34 | 17 | 60 | 6 | 52 | 42 |
|---|---|---|---|---|---|---|---|
| Acidity (pH) | 3.0 | 4.4 | 3.3 | 7.0 | 3.2 | 6.8 | 5.2 |

(a) Draw a scatter graph to illustrate this data.

(b) Draw and label the line of best fit on your scatter graph.

(c) Use your line of best fit to predict the acidity of a lake at a distance of 25 km.

(d) For what range of values could you use your line of best fit to predict the acidity of a lake?

(a), (b)

(c) Read up from 25 on the distance axis to the line of best fit, and across to the acidity axis. Using your line of best fit you can predict that the pH will be 4.3.

(d) Look at the range of the line of best fit. This is approximately from 4 km to 60 km.

## Exercise 10J

**1**　The table shows the engine sizes of various cars and the distance they travel on one litre of petrol.

| Engine size (litres) | 0.9 | 1.2 | 2.0 | 1.0 | 1.9 | 1.3 | 1.5 |
|---|---|---|---|---|---|---|---|
| Distance travelled (km) | 13 | 10 | 8 | 12 | 7 | 11 | 9 |

   **(a)**　Draw a scatter diagram to represent this data.

   **(b)**　What type of correlation do you find?

   **(c)**　Draw a line of best fit and use it to estimate the distance travelled on one litre of petrol by a car with an engine size of 1.7 litres.

**2**　An anemometer is used to measure wind speed. The table gives the rotational speed of an anemometer for different wind speeds.

| Wind speed (m/s) | 1.0 | 1.2 | 1.4 | 1.6 | 1.8 | 2.0 | 2.2 |
|---|---|---|---|---|---|---|---|
| Rotational speed (rev/min) | 20 | 40 | 65 | 85 | 110 | 130 | 155 |

   **(a)**　Plot a scatter diagram and draw a line of best fit for the data.

   **(b)**　Comment on the relationship between the rotational speed of the anemometer and the wind speed.

   **(c)**　Use your graph to estimate the rotational speed of the anemometer when the wind speed is 1.5 m/s.

   **(d)**　Explain why it may not be appropriate to use your graph to estimate the rotational speed of the anemometer when the wind speed is 4 m/s.

> The reason is not that your graph is too small.

**3**　The scatter diagram shows the number of hours of sunshine and the maximum temperature in ten British towns on one day.

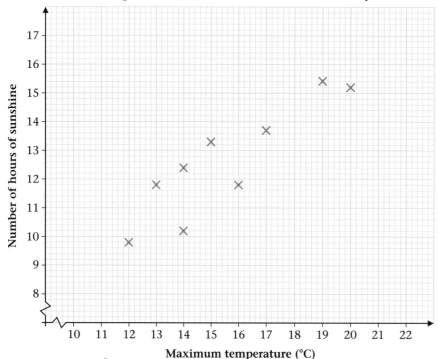

(a)  Copy the scatter diagram and draw a line of best fit on it.

(b)  Use your line of best fit to estimate
   (i)   the number of hours of sunshine when the maximum
         temperature was 18°C
   (ii)  the maximum temperature when the number of hours
         of sunshine recorded in the day was 12 hours.      [E]

---

**Activity – Country area and population**

Is there a correlation between the area of a country and the size of its population?

(a)  Use the internet to collect data for European countries.

(b)  Draw a scatter diagram to represent your data.

(c)  Comment on your findings.

---

## Mixed exercise 10

**1**  In an experiment, 35 people were asked to guess the weight,
in kg, of the lead singer in a rock group. Here are their guesses:

| 76 | 80 | 90 | 100 | 83 | 95 | 106 | 95 | 95 |
|----|----|----|-----|----|----|-----|----|----|
| 77 | 80 | 87 | 108 | 78 | 90 | 85 | 88 | 95 |
| 108 | 80 | 77 | 105 | 98 | 95 | 82 | 79 | 80 |
| 86 | 101 | 78 | 106 | 95 | 95 | 77 | 87 |  |

The total of these weights is 3137 kg

(a)  Draw a stem and leaf diagram for the data.

(b)  For this data work out
   (i)   the mode      (ii)  the median      (iii)  the mean
   (iv)  the range     (v)   the interquartile range.

**2**  The numbers 4, 8, 12, 17 and $N$ are arranged in ascending order.
The mean of the numbers is equal to the median. Find $N$.

**3**  A farmer wants to sell her sheep. Their weights,
in kg, are given in the stem and leaf diagram.

Weight of sheep (kg)

| 15 | 0 2 3 3 7 |
|----|-----------|
| 16 | 0 1 3 9 |
| 17 | 5 7 |
| 18 | 7 8 |
| 19 | 5 |

The total weight is 2340 kg

Key: 19 | 5 means 195 kg

(a)  Find the median weight and the mean weight.

(b)  In an advertisement the farmer claims that 'The average
weight is 162 kg'.
   (i)   Which 'average' has the farmer used to describe her
         sheep?
   (ii)  Does this average describe the sheep fairly? Explain
         your answer.

**4** The table gives information about the numbers of letters delivered one day to the houses in a street.

(a) How many houses are there in the street?

(b) Work out the range and the interquartile range for the data.

(c) Work out the mean number of letters delivered to each house in the street.

(d) Is this a sensible measure of average to describe the number of letters delivered to each house in the street?

| Number of letters delivered | Number of houses (frequency) |
|---|---|
| 0 | 3 |
| 1 | 14 |
| 2 | 2 |
| 3 | 7 |
| 4 | 0 |
| 5 | 3 |
| 6 | 1 |

**5** Malvika is doing a geology project. She weighs 40 rock samples from her test site. Her results are summarised in the table.

| Weight (grams) | $100 < w \leqslant 300$ | $300 < w \leqslant 500$ | $500 < w \leqslant 700$ | $700 < w \leqslant 900$ |
|---|---|---|---|---|
| Frequency | 9 | 16 | 7 | 8 |

(a) Write down the modal class.

(b) Calculate an estimate of the total weight of the rock samples.

(c) Explain why this is an *estimate* of the total weight of the rock samples.

(d) Calculate an estimate for the mean.

**6** The graph gives information about the quarterly gas bills of a householder.

(a) Using the information in the graph, calculate the four-point moving averages for the data.

(b) Comment on the trend of the gas bills.

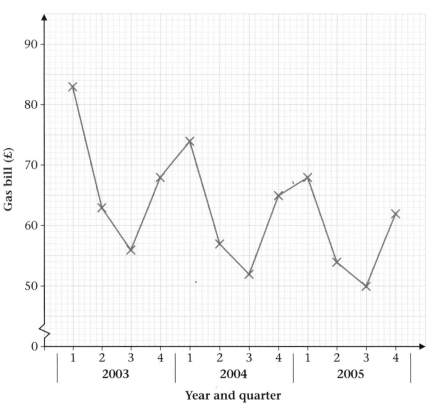

**7** The table gives the numbers of text messages received by a student over a weekend.

|          | Morning | Afternoon | Evening |
|----------|---------|-----------|---------|
| Friday   |         |           | 12      |
| Saturday | 15      | 9         | 17      |
| Sunday   | 19      | 18        | 11      |
| Monday   | 1       |           |         |

(a) Calculate the values of a suitable moving average.

(b) Plot the data and the moving averages on the same graph.

(c) Comment on your graph.

**8** The table shows information about the age and cranial capacity of eight fossils of a particular species of ape.

| Fossil                    | A   | B   | C   | D   | E   | F   | G   | H   |
|---------------------------|-----|-----|-----|-----|-----|-----|-----|-----|
| Age (millions of years)   | 2.3 | 1.9 | 0.7 | 1   | 1.5 | 0.6 | 0.3 | 1.3 |
| Cranial capacity ($cm^3$) | 37  | 81  | 173 | 170 | 88  | 158 | 205 | 128 |

Cranial capacity is a measure of the volume of the interior of the skull.

(a) Draw a scatter diagram to represent this data.

(b) Is there any evidence from the scatter diagram to suggest that there is a correlation between the age of a fossil and the cranial capacity for this species of ape? Explain your answer.

(c) Draw a line of best fit and use it to estimate the cranial capacity of a fossil ape that is 1.75 million years old.

**9** The table gives information about eight types of aircraft.

| Aircraft    | Wingspan ($x$ metres) | Maximum take-off weight ($y$ tonnes) |
|-------------|-----------------------|--------------------------------------|
| B747-400    | 64.30                 | 394.0                                |
| B747-200    | 38.00                 | 108.8                                |
| DC10-30     | 50.40                 | 263.5                                |
| LT-1011-200 | 47.35                 | 219.0                                |
| CRJ-200 ER  | 21.21                 | 23.1                                 |
| VC10        | 44.55                 | 114.5                                |
| A300 B4     | 44.84                 | 165.0                                |
| HS Com 4    | 34.98                 | 70.7                                 |

(a) Plot the data on a scatter diagram.

(b) Calculate the mean wingspan, $\bar{x}$ metres, and the mean maximum take-off weight, $\bar{y}$ tonnes, of these eight aircraft.

(c) On your scatter diagram
(i) plot the point $(\bar{x}, \bar{y})$
(ii) draw a line of best fit through the point $(\bar{x}, \bar{y})$.

(d) For what range of values of the wingspan is it suitable to use your line of best fit to predict the maximum take-off weight?

**10** This back-to-back stem and leaf diagram gives information about the numbers of lessons needed by a group of students to pass their driving test:

| Male students | | Female students |
|---|---|---|
| 8 6 3 2 2 | 1 | 3 6 7 9 |
| 7 6 4 3 3 2 1 0 | 2 | 3 3 4 5 5 6 7 8 9 9 |
| 6 6 | 3 | 1 2 5 |

Key for males:
6 | 3 means 36

Key for females:
3 | 1 means 31

(a) Copy and complete the following table.

|  | Median | Interquartile range |
|---|---|---|
| Male students |  |  |
| Female students |  |  |

(b) Explain whether or not it would be fair to say that, in general, the male students passed their driving test after fewer lessons than the female students.

## Summary of key points

**1** The **mean** of a set of data is the sum of the values divided by the number of values:

$$\text{mean} = \frac{\text{sum of values}}{\text{number of values}} = \bar{x} = \frac{\Sigma x}{n}$$

where $\Sigma x$ is the sum of the values and $n$ is the number of values.

**2** The **median** is the middle value when the data is arranged in order of size.

**3** For a data set with $n$ data values, the median is the $\frac{n+1}{2}$th value.

**4** The **mode** of a set of data is the value which occurs most often.

**5** The **median** and **mode** are not influenced by extreme values, but the **mean** is influenced by extreme values.

**6** When the data is arranged in ascending order of size:
- the **lower quartile** is the value one quarter of the way into the data
- the **upper quartile** is the value three quarters of the way into the data.

**7** The **range** of a set of data is the difference between the highest and lowest values:

range = highest value − lowest value

**8** The **interquartile range** is the difference between the upper and lower quartiles:

interquartile range = upper quartile − lower quartile

9  For a frequency distribution:
   - the **mode** = the item of data which has the highest frequency
   - the **median** = the middle value of the data = the $\dfrac{\Sigma f + 1}{2}$th value
   - the **mean** = $\dfrac{\Sigma fx}{\Sigma f}$

   where $\Sigma f$ is the sum of the frequencies and $\Sigma fx$ is the sum of all the $(f \times x)$ values in the distribution.

10  For grouped data:
   - you can state the class interval that contains the median
   - the class interval with the highest frequency is called the **modal class**
   - you can **calculate an estimate of the mean** using the middle value of each class interval
   - the estimate of the mean for grouped data is

   $\bar{x} = \dfrac{\Sigma fx}{\Sigma f}$, where $x$ is the mid-point of each class interval.

11  To compare two sets of data you should use a measure of average and a measure of spread.

12  A graph showing how a given value changes over time is called a **time series graph**.

13  A moving average 'smooths out' the data to show the trend on a time series graph.

14  You can use a **scatter diagram** to show whether two sets of data are related.

15  If the points on a scatter graph are very nearly along a straight line there is a high **correlation** between the variables.

16  A line that is drawn to pass as close as possible to all the plotted points on a scatter graph is called the **line of best fit**.

# Estimation and approximation

In this chapter you will round values and measurements to different degrees of accuracy and use approximations to calculate estimates.

## 11.1 Rounding to a number of decimal places

Sometimes you will be asked to round (or correct) a decimal number to a given number of decimal places. For example:

Asafa Powell ran 100 m in 9.771 seconds. Round his time to 1 decimal place (1 d.p.).

9.771 has 3 decimal places (digits after the decimal point).

To round to 1 decimal place, count 1 place from the decimal point and look at the next digit. If it is 5 or more you need to round up.

Asafa Powell, 100 m world record holder, 14 June 2005.

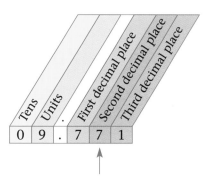

This digit is 7, so you need to round up

9.771 seconds to 1 decimal place (1 d.p.) is 9.8 seconds.

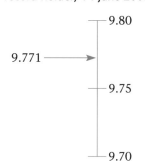

9.771 is closer to 9.8 than to 9.7

You can round (or correct) numbers to a given number of **decimal places (d.p.)**. The first decimal place is the first digit (zero or non-zero) after the decimal point.

Remember: In rounding, halves or 5s are usually rounded upwards.

___ **Example 1** _____

Round 46.382 to   (a) 1 decimal place      (b) 2 decimal places.

(a)   Rounding to 1 d.p. (1 digit after the decimal point):

46.382

The digit after the first decimal place is 8, so **round up**.

46.382 rounded to 1 d.p. is 46.4

**(b)** Rounding to 2 d.p.

46.382

The digit after the second decimal place is 2, so **round down**.

Notice that when you round down to 2 d.p. these two decimal places remain the same.

46.382 rounded to 2 d.p. is 46.38

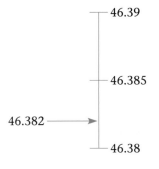

46.382 is closer to 46.38 than to 46.39

## Exercise 11A

**1** Copy this interval diagram.

**(a)** Mark the position of 46.3826 on the diagram.

**(b)** Write 46.382 67 rounded to 3 d.p.

**2** This table shows the times recorded for the first three athletes in an 800 m race:

| Name | Time |
|------|------|
| R. Grey | 1 min 45.4826 s |
| M. Hobson | 1 min 45.4768 s |
| T. Knight | 1 min 45.4817 s |

**(a)** Write these times correct to 2 d.p.

**(b)** Write the names of the athletes in the order in which they finished the race.

**3** Write these numbers correct to the number of decimal places given in brackets.

**(a)** 137.27 (1 d.p.)  **(b)** 0.673 81 (4 d.p.)

**(c)** 4.999 (1 d.p.)  **(d)** 8.999 (2 d.p.)

**(e)** 17.9939 (3 d.p.)  **(f)** 2.009 72 (4 d.p.)

**4** Carry out the following calculations and give your answers correct to the number of decimal places given in brackets.

**(a)** $24.56 \times 3.87$ (3 d.p.)  **(b)** $3.764 \times 2.593$ (3 d.p.)

**(c)** $2.888 \times 3.777$ (2 d.p.)  **(d)** $13.799 \times 12.752$ (1 d.p.)

# 11.2 Rounding to a number of significant figures

You will often be asked to round answers to '2 significant figures' (2 s.f.) or '3 significant figures' (3 s.f.). 'Significant' means 'important'.

When you are estimating the number of people at an open-air concert you don't need to say that there were exactly 8732 people there. You can give the number to two significant figures:

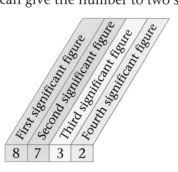

There were about 8700 people (to 2 s.f.).

This is called 'giving a value correct to two significant figures'.

Estimating the attendance as 8700 to 2 s.f. implies that the actual number is between 8650 and 8749 inclusive.

> You can round (or give) numbers to a given number of significant figures (s.f.). The first significant figure is the first non-zero digit in the number, counting from the left.

Rounding to a significant figure which is on the right of the decimal point is like the process used in rounding to decimal places. You look at the next digit after the significant figure:

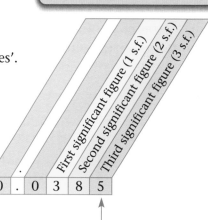

0.0385 correct to 2 s.f. is 0.039

The digit after the second significant figure is 5.

---

**Example 2**

Round 642.803

(a)   to 1 s.f.      (b)   to 2 s.f.      (c)   to 3 s.f.      (d)   to 4 s.f.      (e)   to 5 s.f.

You need the zeros to show the place value of the 6.

|     | 1 s.f. | 2 s.f. | 3 s.f. | . | 4 s.f. | 5 s.f. | 6 s.f. | = | | | . | | |         |
|-----|--------|--------|--------|---|--------|--------|--------|---|---|---|---|---|---|---------|
| (a) | 6 | 4 | 2 | . | 8 | 0 | 3 | = | 6 | 0 | 0 | | | (to 1 s.f.) |
| (b) | 6 | 4 | 2 | . | 8 | 0 | 3 | = | 6 | 4 | 0 | | | (to 2 s.f.) |
| (c) | 6 | 4 | 2 | . | 8 | 0 | 3 | = | 6 | 4 | 3 | | | (to 3 s.f.) |
| (d) | 6 | 4 | 2 | . | 8 | 0 | 3 | = | 6 | 4 | 2 | . | 8 | (to 4 s.f.) |
| (e) | 6 | 4 | 2 | . | 8 | 0 | 3 | = | 6 | 4 | 2 | . | 8 | 0 | (to 5 s.f.) |

You need the zero to show 5 significant figures.

## Exercise 11B

**1** Write these numbers correct to the number of significant figures given in brackets.

(a) 3.168 (3 s.f.)     (b) 964.8 (3 s.f.)

(c) 15.8 (2 s.f.)     (d) 9.9 (1 s.f.)

(e) 55.7639 (5 s.f.)     (f) 55.898 (4 s.f.)

**2** Using a calculator Samajit works out the answer to $113.12 \times 1.7341$ as 196.161 39

Write Samajit's answer correct to:

(a) 3 decimal places     (b) 3 significant figures

(c) 2 decimal places     (d) 2 significant figures

(e) the nearest whole number     (f) the nearest 10

(g) the nearest 100     (h) 7 significant figures.

**3** 43 672 spectators watched Draycott Town beat Borrowash Rovers in the Cup Final.
Write the number of spectators correct to:

(a) 4 s.f.     (b) 2 s.f.     (c) 1 s.f.

**4** Work out the following calculations and give your answers correct to the number of significant figures given in brackets.

(a) $54 \times 36$ (3 s.f.)     (b) $117 \times 38$ (3 s.f.)

(c) $148 \times 66$ (2 s.f.)     (d) $235 \times 364$ (2 s.f.)

(e) $65 \times 23$ (1 s.f.)     (f) $24 \times 42 \times 59$ (1 s.f.)

**5** Write these numbers correct to the number of significant figures given in brackets.

(a) 0.0032 (1 s.f.)     (b) 0.000 876 (2 s.f.)

(c) 0.008 97 (2 s.f.)     (d) 0.000 91 (1 s.f.)

(e) 0.0099 (1 s.f.)     (f) 0.0004 (1 s.f.)

**6** Carry out the following calculations and give your answers correct to the number of significant figures asked for.

(a) $0.3 \times 0.023$ (correct to 1 s.f.)

(b) $3.2 \div 48$ (correct to 4 s.f.)

(c) $0.007 \times 0.000\,41$ (correct to 2 s.f.)

**7** 1 inch is approximately equal to 2.54 cm. Write

(a) 1 cm in inches (correct to 2 s.f.)

(b) 1 mm in inches (correct to 2 s.f.)

(c) 1 metre in inches (correct to 3 s.f.)

(d) 1 km in inches (correct to 1 s.f.)

# 11.3 Checking and estimating

Get into the habit of checking the answers to your calculations. Sometimes a wrong answer is obvious: 0.42 cm for the average height of a woman in a survey or 2000 km for the distance travelled by a car on a motorway in an afternoon are clearly incorrect.

Once you notice that an answer is obviously wrong you can repeat the calculation to try and find the correct answer.

## Making an estimate

Another way of checking a calculation is to make an estimate.

> To estimate answers, round all the numbers to 1 significant figure and do the simpler calculation.

---

**Example 3**

Estimate the answer to

(a)   $5.12 \times 2.79$          (b)   $19.67 \div 2.8$          (c)   $\dfrac{2.75 \times 8.33}{5.23 + 2.74}$

(a)   Round all the numbers to 1 significant figure.
An estimate for $5.12 \times 2.79$ is $5 \times 3 = 15$
(Actual answer: 14.2848)

(b)   Round all the numbers to 1 significant figure:
$20 \div 3 = 6\frac{2}{3} = 7$ (to 1 significant figure).
(Actual answer: 7.025)

(c)   Round all the numbers to 1 significant figure:
$\dfrac{3 \times 8}{5 + 3} = \dfrac{24}{8} = 3$ as an estimate.
(Actual answer: $22.9075 \div 7.97 = 2.874...$)

---

**Worked examination question**

$$\dfrac{10.25 + 29.75}{0.2 \times 45}$$

Show how you would estimate the answer to this expression without using a calculator. Write down your estimate.

Round all the numbers to 1 s.f.:
$$\dfrac{10 + 30}{0.2 \times 50} = \dfrac{40}{10} = 4 \text{ as an estimate.}$$

## Exercise 11C

1. For each of parts **(a)** to **(f)**:
   - **(i)** Write down a calculation that could be used to estimate the answer.
   - **(ii)** Work out an estimated answer.
   - **(iii)** Use a calculator to work out the exact answer.
   - **(a)** $8.66 \times 9.56$
   - **(b)** $3.75 \times (2.36 - 0.39)$
   - **(c)** $37.12 \times 4.33$
   - **(d)** $(2095 \times 302) + 396$
   - **(e)** $\dfrac{187.3 \times 75.4}{47.9}$
   - **(f)** $\dfrac{0.634 \times 0.0176}{0.0425}$

2. Trevor's calculator is faulty. It doesn't show the decimal point so Trevor has answered the following questions by writing down the digits from the display. By estimating, find the correct answers including the decimal points.

| | |
|---|---|
| **(a)** $3.4 \times 2.5 = 85$ | **(b)** $5.6 \times 7.23 = 40488$ |
| **(c)** $2.42 \times 1.93 = 46706$ | **(d)** $10.63 \times 12.64 = 1343632$ |
| **(e)** $3.2 \times 5.1 \times 4.7 = 76704$ | **(f)** $2.9 \times 0.32 \times 8.7 = 80736$ |

3. Estimate the answer to each calculation, giving your answers to the nearest whole number:
   - **(a)** $36 \div 5$
   - **(b)** $47 \div 8$
   - **(c)** $103 \div 11$
   - **(d)** $148 \div 49$
   - **(e)** $239 \div 31$
   - **(f)** $197 \div 19$
   - **(g)** $281 \div 41$
   - **(h)** $796 \div 98$
   - **(i)** $352 \div 58$
   - **(j)** $\dfrac{53 \times 3}{49}$
   - **(k)** $\dfrac{38 \times 5}{19}$
   - **(l)** $\dfrac{24 \times 11}{59}$
   - **(m)** $\dfrac{41.2 \times 3.79}{3.17 \times 4}$
   - **(n)** $\dfrac{28.4 \times 70.17}{2.95 \times 4.21}$
   - **(o)** $\dfrac{61.8 \times 1.46}{39.2 - 18.8}$

## 11.4 Describing the accuracy of a measurement

Suppose you use a ruler marked in millimetres to measure a line as 237 mm, correct to the nearest millimetre.

The true length could be anywhere between 236.5 mm and 237.5 mm.

So the true length could be anywhere in a range between 0.5 mm below and 0.5 mm above the recorded value:

For any measurement you make:

> If you make a measurement correct to a given unit, the true value lies in a range that extends half a unit below and half a unit above the measurement.

## Exercise 11D

1   These lengths are all measured to the nearest millimetre.
    Write down the smallest and largest values of the possible range
    of each length.

(a)   3.9 cm          (b)   17.620 m          (c)   53.0 cm
(d)   1.030 m         (e)   29 mm

2   Copy and complete this table showing the attendances to the
    nearest hundred at these schools.

| School | Attendance to the nearest 100 | Lowest value of range | Greatest value of range |
|--------|-------------------------------|-----------------------|-------------------------|
| Southpark | 1400 | 1350 | 1450 |
| Westown | 400 | | |
| Eastgrove | 800 | | |
| Northbury | 1200 | | |
| Southone | 2100 | | |

The first one is done for you.

3   Kirsty ran a 1500 metre race. Her time to the nearest
    0.01 second was 4 minutes 7.56 seconds. Write down the range
    of times between which her time could lie.

4   The distance between two motorway junctions is given as
    17 miles to the nearest mile. Write down the range within which
    the true length could lie.

## 11.5  Upper and lower bounds

In the measuring example on page 219 the true length could be
anywhere between 236.5 mm and 237.5 mm.

−0.5 mm        +0.5 mm

236.5 mm                237.5 mm

237 mm

the smallest (or minimum)        the greatest (or maximum)
possible value is called the     possible value is called the
**lower bound**                  **upper bound**

The **lower bound** and the **upper bound** are the minimum and maximum possible values of a measurement or calculation.

> For more on upper and lower bounds see Chapter 23 (in Book 2).

---

**Example 4**

A rectangle has length 7.5 cm and width 4.3 cm, both measured to the nearest 0.1 cm.

Work out

(a) the lower bounds of the length and width

(b) the upper bounds of the length and width

(c) the maximum possible area (the upper bound of the area).

(a) The lower bound of the length is 7.45 cm.
   The lower bound of the width is 4.25 cm.

(b) The upper bound of the length is 7.55 cm.
   The upper bound of the width is 4.35 cm.

(c) The maximum possible area is:

$$\text{upper bound of length} \times \text{upper bound of width} = 7.55 \text{ cm} \times 4.35 \text{ cm}$$
$$= 32.8425 \text{ cm}^2$$

---

## Exercise 11E

**1** Each measurement is given correct to 3 decimal places. Write down
(i) the lower bound (ii) the upper bound.

  (a) 0.234 km      (b) 0.319 s      (c) 0.545 kg

  (d) 0.795 km      (e) 9.417 s      (f) 3.459 g

**2** (a) Jafar has a piece of wood of length 30 cm, correct to the nearest centimetre. Write down the minimum possible length of the piece of wood.

  (b) Fatima has a different piece of wood of length 18.4 cm, correct to the nearest millimetre. Write down the maximum and minimum lengths between which the length of her piece of wood must lie.

**3** The length of each side of a square, correct to 2 significant figures, is 3.7 cm.

  (a) Write down the least possible length of each side.

  (b) Calculate the greatest and least possible perimeters of this square.

  (c) When calculating the perimeter of the square, how many significant figures is it appropriate to give in the answer? Explain your answer.

  (d) If this question had referred to a regular octagon, instead of a square, would your answer to part (c) have been the same? Explain your answer.      [E]

**4** Stephanie ran 100 metres. The distance was correct to the nearest metre.

   **(a)** Write down the shortest distance Stephanie could have run.

Stephanie's time for the run was 14.8 seconds. Her time was correct to the nearest tenth of a second.

   **(b)** Write down
      **(i)** her shortest possible time for the run
      **(ii)** her longest possible time for the run.

   **(c)** Calculate **(i)** the lower bound **(ii)** the upper bound for her average speed. Write down all the figures on your calculator display.

   **(d)**   **(i)** Write down her average speed to an appropriate degree of accuracy.
      **(ii)** Explain how you arrived at your answer.    **[E]**

**5** The diagram represents a metal girder in the shape of a half cylinder. The radius of each semicircular end is 5.6 centimetres, correct to the nearest tenth of a centimetre.

   **(a)** Write down the upper and lower bounds of the radius.

The length of the girder is 1.20 metres, correct to the nearest centimetre.

   **(b)** Write down the upper and lower bounds of the length.

   **(c)** Calculate the upper and lower bounds of the volume of the girder. Give your answer in cubic centimetres ($cm^3$).

Diagram NOT accurately drawn

> For the formula for volume of a cylinder see Section 22.4 (in Book 2).

**6** Brazil has an area of $8\,500\,000\ km^2$ correct to the nearest $100\,000\ km^2$.

   **(a)** Write down the limits between which the area of Brazil must lie.

The population density of a country is the average number of people per $km^2$ of the country.

Brazil has a population of 184 million correct to the nearest million.

   **(b)** Calculate the maximum and minimum values of the population density of Brazil.    **[E]**

**7** The formula $S = \dfrac{F}{A}$ is used in engineering.

$F = 810$, correct to 2 significant figures.
$A = 2.93$, correct to 3 significant figures.

   **(a)** For the value of $F$, write down
      **(i)** the upper bound
      **(ii)** the lower bound.

(b) For the value of $A$, write down

    (i)   the upper bound     (ii)   the lower bound.

(c) Calculate (i) the upper bound and (ii) the lower bound for the value of $S$ for these values of $F$ and $A$. Write down all the figures on your calculator display.

(d) Write down this value of $S$ correct to an appropriate number of significant figures.    [E]

## Mixed exercise 11

1   Round these numbers to the number of decimal places given in brackets.

    (a)  9.4915  (1 d.p.)         (b)  0.0455  (3 d.p.)

    (c)  7.699    (2 d.p.)         (d)  7.4317  (2 d.p.)

2   Write these numbers to the number of significant figures given in brackets.

    (a)  423.58  (3 s.f.)        (b)  0.214 73  (4 s.f.)

    (c)  10 769  (2 s.f.)        (d)  90 873  (1 s.f.)

3   Write down a suitable estimation to check each answer:

    (a)  $56.25 \div 1.25 = 45$        (b)  $3.256 \times 1.5 = 4.884$

    (c)  $109.46 - 83.27 = 26.19$    (d)  $56.21 + 19.78 = 75.99$

    (e)  $\dfrac{20.47 + 3.82}{2.67 + 5.05} = 3.146$      (f)  $\dfrac{8.37 \times 3.81}{4.47 + 4.74} = 3.463$

4   A distance of 15.2 km has been rounded to 1 decimal place. Write down

    (a)  the largest value of the possible range

    (b)  the smallest value of the possible range.

5   To the nearest centimetre, $x = 4$ cm and $y = 6$ cm.

    (a)  Calculate the upper bound for the value of $xy$.

    (b)  Calculate the lower bound for the value of $\dfrac{x}{y}$.

        Give your answer correct to 3 significant figures.    [E]

6   The diagram represents two metal spheres of different sizes.
The radius of the smaller sphere is $r$ cm.
The radius of the larger sphere is $R$ cm.
$r = 1.7$ correct to 1 decimal place.
$R = 31.0$ correct to 3 significant figures.

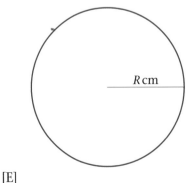

    (a)  Write down the upper and lower bounds of $r$ and $R$.

    (b)  Find the smallest possible value of $R - r$.    [E]

# Summary of key points

1 You can round (or give) numbers to a given number of **decimal places (d.p.)**.
The first decimal place is the first digit (zero or non-zero) after the decimal point.

2 You can round (or give) numbers to a given number of significant figures (s.f.).
The first significant figure is the first non-zero digit in the number, counting from the left.

3 To estimate answers, round all the numbers to 1 significant figure and do the simpler calculation.

4 If you make a measurement correct to a given unit, the true value lies in a range that extends half a unit below and half a unit above the measurement.

5 The **lower bound** and the **upper bound** are the minimum and maximum possible values of a measurement or calculation.

# 12 Sequences and formulae

In this chapter you will find formulae to describe sequences and use formulae from mathematics and other subjects.

## 12.1 Finding terms of a sequence

These diagrams show the triangular numbers:

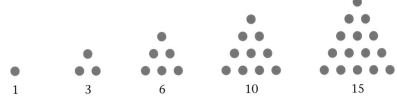

These numbers are a **sequence** – a succession of numbers formed according to a rule.

Each number in a sequence is called a **term**. 6 is the third term in the sequence of triangular numbers.

Sometimes you will be given an algebraic formula for the rule for the $n$th term of a sequence. You can use this to find any term in the sequence. The $n$th term is often written as $u_n$.

> The $n$th term is sometimes called the **general term**.

> When you know a formula for the $n$th term of a sequence, $u_n$, you can calculate any term in the sequence by substituting a value for $n$ in the formula. $n$ must be a positive integer ($n = 1, 2, 3 \ldots$).

### Example 1

The $n$th term of a sequence is given by $u_n = 2n - 1$. Find the first two terms of the sequence.

Substituting $n = 1$, the first term $u_1 = (2 \times 1) - 1 = 1$
Substituting $n = 2$, the second term $u_2 = (2 \times 2) - 1 = 3$

The first two terms are 1 and 3.

### Example 2

For a given sequence $u_n = 10 - 3n$. Find $u_2$.

Substituting $n = 2$, the second term $u_2 = 10 - (3 \times 2) = 4$

### Example 3

For a given sequence $u_n = 2n^2 + 3$. Find the fifth term of the sequence.

Substituting $n = 5$, the fifth term $u_5 = (2 \times 5^2) + 3 = 53$

## Exercise 12A

Find the first five terms of the sequences in questions **1–14**.

**1**  $u_n = 2n$            **2**  $u_n = n + 2$         **3**  $u_n = 3n + 7$

**4**  $u_n = 15 - 2n$      **5**  $u_n = n^2 + 5$       **6**  $u_n = 3n^2 - 1$

**7**  $u_n = (n + 1)^2$      **8**  $u_n = n^3$            **9**  $u_n = 2^n$

**10**  $u_n = (-2)^n$       **11**  $u_n = (\frac{1}{2})^n$        **12**  $u_n = \frac{1}{2}n(n + 1)$

**13**  $u_n = \dfrac{1}{n}$            **14**  $u_n = \dfrac{n}{n + 1}$

**15**  Find the sixth term of the sequence with $u_n = 4n - 7$.

## Finding which term has a given value

The number 105 is a term in the sequence given by the formula $u_n = 7(n + 4)$.

Which term in the sequence has this value?

You can find out by finding the value of $n$ when $u_n = 105$.
Substituting $u_n = 105$ in the formula gives the equation

$$7(n + 4) = 105$$
$$7n + 28 = 105$$
$$7n = 77$$
$$n = 11$$

> For more on manipulating formulae see Section 12.4.

So 105 is the 11th term of the sequence.

---

**Example 4**

A sequence is given by the formula $u_n = 2n^2 + 5$.
For which value of $n$ does $u_n = 103$?

Substituting $u_n = 103$ in the formula gives the equation:

$$2n^2 + 5 = 103$$
$$2n^2 = 98$$
$$n^2 = 49$$
$$\text{so} \quad n = 7$$

> Notice that $n = -7$ is also a solution of $n^2 = 49$, but for a sequence $n$ must be a positive integer. There is no $-7$th term in a sequence.

---

## Exercise 12B

Find the value of $n$ for which $u_n$ has the given value.

**1**  $u_n = 6n + 7, \quad u_n = 55$       **2**  $u_n = 7(n + 4), \quad u_n = 112$

**3**  $u_n = 7 - 3n, \quad u_n = -44$      **4**  $u_n = \dfrac{2n + 3}{3n + 1}, \quad u_n = \dfrac{17}{22}$

**5**  $u_n = n^2 + 5, \quad u_n = 149$       **6**  $u_n = 3n^2 - 8, \quad u_n = 235$

**7**  $u_n = (n - 8)^2, \quad u_n = 169$     **8**  $u_n = 2n^2 + 12, \quad u_n = 140$

**9**  $u_n = 3^n, \quad\quad u_n = 2187$       **10**  $u_n = n(n - 1), \quad u_n = 380$

## 12.2 Finding the formula for a sequence

### Arithmetic sequences

The first six terms of a sequence are

9,  14,  19,  24,  29,  34

By looking for a pattern in the sequence you can find a formula for the $n$th term $u_n$. This is sometimes called the **general term**.

A good way to start is to find the differences between successive terms:

> A sequence in which the differences between successive terms are equal is called an **arithmetic sequence**.

The terms go up in 5s, so the $n$th term will include $n$ lots of 5, or $5n$.

For the first term $n = 1$, so $5n = 5$. But the first term is 9, which is 4 more than $5n$. This suggests a formula of the form

$u_n = 5n + 4$

Trying a few values of $n$ gives

$u_1 = (5 \times 1) + 4 = 9$ ✓
$u_2 = (5 \times 2) + 4 = 14$ ✓
$u_3 = (5 \times 3) + 4 = 19$ ✓
$u_4 = (5 \times 4) + 4 = 24$ ✓

So the formula $u_n = 5n + 4$ does describe the sequence.

> The **general term** for an arithmetic sequence is of the form $u_n = an + b$. The value of $a$ is the difference between successive terms in the sequence.

**Example 5**

The first five terms of a sequence are

5,  3,  1,  −1,  −3

Find a formula for the $n$th number in the sequence, $u_n$.

As each term is 2 less than the previous one, the formula for $u_n$ will include $-2n$. But $u_n = -2n$ would give the sequence

−2,  −4,  −6,  −8,  ...

For the sequence to start at 5, add 7 to each term, giving

5,  3,  1,  −1,  −3,  ...

The formula that describes the sequence is $u_n = -2n + 7$

## Exercise 12C

Your answers to Exercise 12A may be helpful here.

Find formulae for $u_n$ to describe each of these sequences.

**1** 3, 4, 5, 6, 7, ...

**2** 5, 7, 9, 11, 13, ...

**3** 7, 11, 15, 19, 23, ...

**4** 9, 8, 7, 6, 5, ...

**5** 12, 10, 8, 6, 4, ...

**6** 7, 4, 1, −2, −5, ...

# 12.3 More about formulae

As well as describing sequences, formulae can also be used to describe other relationships between quantities.

An algebraic formula can be used to describe a relationship between two sets of values.

For example, the formula $C = \pi d$ describes the relationship between the diameter of a circle $d$ and its circumference $C$.

Notice the difference between a formula and an equation:

$C = \pi \times d$ is a **formula**.

If you substitute **any** value for $d$ the formula will give you a corresponding value for $C$.

Similarly if you substitute any value for $C$ it will give you a corresponding value for $d$.

$C = \pi \times 2.5$ is an **equation**.

The equation is only true for **one value** of $C$ ($C = 7.85$ to 2 d.p.).

You need to be able to evaluate formulae by substituting given values into them, including negative numbers and fractions.

## Example 6

The value of $s$ can be found from the formula $s = pt^2 + q$. Calculate the value of $s$ when

(a) $p = 1$, $q = 2$ and $t = \frac{1}{2}$

(b) $p = 5$, $q = -1$ and $t = -2$

(a) $s = 1 \times (\frac{1}{2})^2 + 2$

$= \frac{1}{4} + 2$

$= 2\frac{1}{4}$

(b) $s = 5 \times (-2)^2 - 1$

$= 5 \times 4 - 1$

$= 20 - 1$

$= 19$

**Worked examination question 1**

The diagram above is taken from a book about growing maize. The distance between the rows of plants is $d$ metres. The spacing between the plants in each row is $r$ metres.

The number, $P$, of plants per hectare is given by the formula

$$P = \frac{10\,000}{dr}$$

Given that $d = 0.8$ and $r = 0.45$, calculate the value of $P$. Give your answer correct to 2 significant figures.

$$P = \frac{10\,000}{0.8 \times 0.45}$$

$$= 27\,777.777$$

$$= 28\,000 \text{ (correct to 2 s.f.)}$$

## Exercise 12D

**1** $y = 2x - 5$     Calculate the value of $y$ when $x = -3$

**2** $A = lw$     Calculate the value of $A$ when $l = 8\frac{1}{2}$ and $w = 6\frac{1}{4}$

**3** $P = 2(l + w)$     Calculate the value of $P$ when $l = 8.3$ and $w = 6.8$

**4** $C = \pi d$     Calculate the value of $C$ correct to 3 s.f. when $d = 8.37$

**5** $y = 3x^2 + 2$     Calculate the value of $y$ when $x = -1$

**6** $A = \pi r^2$     Calculate the value of $A$ correct to 3 s.f. when $r = 3.9$

**7** $A = 2\pi r(r + h)$     Calculate the value of $A$ correct to 3 s.f. when $r = 3.7$ and $h = 5.9$

**8** $s = \frac{1}{2}gt^2$     Calculate the value of $s$ when $g = -10$ and $t = 3$

**9** $x = L(1 + at)$     Calculate the value of $x$ when $L = 100$, $a = 0.000\,019$ and $t = 80$

**10** $v = u + at$    Calculate the value of $v$ when $u = 5$, $a = -8$ and $t = 6$

**11** $V = \frac{1}{3}\pi r^2 h$    Calculate the value of $V$ correct to 3 s.f. when $r = 2.6$ and $h = 6.7$

**12** $I = \dfrac{PRT}{100}$    Calculate the value of $I$ when $P = 850$, $R = 5\frac{3}{4}$ and $T = 4$

**13** $s = ut + \frac{1}{2}at^2$    Calculate the value of $s$ when $u = -3$, $t = 5$ and $a = -4$

**14** $D = v + \dfrac{v^2}{20}$    Calculate the value of $D$ correct to 2 s.f. when $v = 31.6$

**15** $c = \sqrt{a^2 + b^2}$    Calculate the value of $c$ correct to 3 s.f. when $a = 3.7$ and $b = 8.3$

**16** $f = \dfrac{uv}{u + v}$    Calculate the value of $f$ when $u = 3.6$ and $v = -5.4$

**17** $r = \sqrt{\dfrac{A}{\pi}}$    Calculate the value of $r$ correct to 3 s.f. when $A = 37.2$

**18** $r = \sqrt{\dfrac{A}{4\pi}}$    Calculate the value of $r$ correct to 3 s.f. when $A = 21.3$

**19** $T = 2\pi\sqrt{\dfrac{L}{g}}$    Calculate the value of $T$ correct to 3 s.f. when $L = 23.4$ and $g = 9.8$

**20** $T = \dfrac{2Mmg}{M + m}$    Calculate the value of $T$ correct to 2 s.f. when $M = 3.8$, $m = 1.7$ and $g = 9.8$

## 12.4 Manipulating formulae

Sometimes when you substitute values into a formula you get an equation to solve.

---

**Example 7**

$C = \pi d$    Calculate the value of $d$ when $C = 23.2$, giving your answer correct to 3 s.f.

$$23.2 = \pi d$$

Dividing each side by $\pi$ gives

$$d = \frac{23.2}{\pi} = 7.38 \text{ (to 3 s.f.)}$$

---

Remember:
Whatever you do to one side of an equation, you must also do to the other side.

**Example 8**

$v = u + at$  Calculate the value of $t$ when $v = 39$, $u = 4$ and $a = 3$

$$39 = 4 + 3t$$

$$35 = 3t \text{ ——————————— Subtract 4 from both sides.}$$

$$t = 11\tfrac{2}{3} \text{ ——————————— Divide both sides by 3.}$$

**Worked examination question 2**

The air temperature $T$ °C outside an aircraft flying at a height of $h$ feet is given by the formula

$$T = 26 - \frac{h}{500}$$

The air temperature outside an aircraft is $-52$ °C. Calculate the height ($h$) of the aircraft.

$$-52 = 26 - \frac{h}{500}$$

$$\frac{h}{500} - 52 = 26 \text{ ——————— Add } \frac{h}{500} \text{ to both sides.}$$

$$\frac{h}{500} = 78 \text{ ——————— Add 52 to both sides.}$$

$$h = 39\,000 \text{ ——————— Multiply both sides by 500.}$$

The height of the aircraft is $39\,000$ feet.

## Exercise 12E

**1**  $C = \pi d$

Calculate the value of $d$ correct to 2 s.f. when $C = 56.8$

**2**  $A = lw$

Calculate the value of $l$ correct to 2 d.p. when $A = 32.94$ and $w = 6.1$

**3**  $C = 2\pi rh$

Calculate the value of $h$ correct to 2 s.f. when $C = 800$ and $r = 5.9$

**4**  $y = 5x + 7$

Calculate the value of $x$ when $y = 11$

**5**  $v = u + at$

Calculate the value of $a$ when $v = 17$, $u = -3$ and $t = 5$

**6**  $I = \dfrac{PRT}{100}$

Calculate the value of $R$ when $I = 45$, $P = 250$ and $T = 4$

$C = 2\pi rh$ is the formula for the area of the curved surface of a cylinder.

**7** $y = 8 + \frac{1}{4}x$    Calculate the value of $x$ when $y = 6$

**8** $y = 9 - 4x$    Calculate the value of $x$ when $y = 14$

**9** $y = 5 - \frac{1}{2}x$    Calculate the value of $x$ when $y = 2$

**10** $P = 2(l + w)$    Calculate the value of $w$ when $P = 42$ and $l = 13\frac{1}{2}$

**11** $S = \frac{1}{2}n(a + d)$    Calculate the value of $a$ when $S = 72$, $d = 3$ and $n = 18$

**12** $A = 2\pi r(r + h)$    Calculate the value of $h$ correct to 3 s.f. when $A = 540$ and $r = 4.9$

**13** $y = 2x^2$    Calculate the two possible values of $x$ when $y = 98$

**14** $A = \pi r^2$    Calculate the positive value of $r$ correct to 3 s.f. when $A = 50$

**15** $s = ut + \frac{1}{2}at^2$    Calculate the value of $u$ when $s = 121$, $t = 5$ and $a = 8$

**16** $c = \sqrt{a^2 + b^2}$    Calculate the positive value of $a$ when $c = 29.9$ and $b = 11.5$

**17** $r = \sqrt{\dfrac{A}{\pi}}$    Calculate the value of $A$ correct to 3 s.f. when $r = 8$

**18** $V = \frac{1}{3}\pi r^2 h$    Calculate the value of $h$ correct to 3 s.f. when $V = 100$ and $r = 2.5$

**19** $y = \dfrac{20}{x + 1}$    Calculate the value of $x$ when $y = 8$

**20** $f = \dfrac{uv}{u + v}$    Calculate the value of $v$ when $f = 12$ and $u = -8$

$y = 8 + \frac{1}{4}x$ is the formula – or equation – of a straight line with gradient $\frac{1}{4}$ and intercept on the $y$-axis of $(0, 8)$.

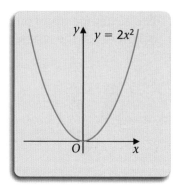

## 12.5 Changing the subject of a formula

$x$ is the **subject** of a formula when it appears on its own on one side of the formula and does not appear on the other side.

Sometimes you will need to rearrange a formula so that a letter such as $x$ is on one side of the equals sign with the rest of the formula on the other side. This is called **changing the subject** of the formula. You can use the same methods as you use to rearrange equations.

**Example 9**

Rearrange $ax + b = c$ to make $x$ the subject of the formula.

$ax = c - b$ ———— Subtract $b$ from both sides.

$x = \dfrac{c - b}{a}$ ———— Divide both sides by $a$.

**Example 10**

Make $x$ the subject of the formula $p - 5x = q$.

$p = 5x + q$ —— Add $5x$ to both sides.

$p - q = 5x$ ——— Subtract $q$ from both sides.

$\dfrac{p - q}{5} = x$ ——— Divide both sides by 5.

## Exercise 12F

In questions **1–14** make $x$ the subject of the formula.

**1**  $x + p = q$        **2**  $x + 7 = t$        **3**  $x - a = b$

**4**  $5x = w$        **5**  $nx = p$        **6**  $\frac{1}{3}x = f$

**7**  $\dfrac{x}{m} = d$        **8**  $\dfrac{ax}{b} = c$        **9**  $nx - p = q$

**10**  $5 - ax = b$        **11**  $c - dx = h$        **12**  $p - 2x = 3x + q$

**13**  $a - 4x = b - 7x$        **14**  $\dfrac{x}{m} + n = p$

**Worked examination question 3**

The formula below gives the Body Mass Index, $I$, of a person who is $h$ metres tall and weighs $W$ kg.

$$I = \dfrac{W}{h^2}$$

Make $h$ the subject of the formula.

$Ih^2 = W$ ———— Multiply both sides by $h^2$.

$h^2 = \dfrac{W}{I}$ ———— Divide both sides by $I$.

$h = \sqrt{\dfrac{W}{I}}$ ———— Take the square root of both sides.

$h$ is now on its own on one side – it is the subject of the formula.

**Worked examination question 4**

The approximate range, $R$ miles, of a radar mounted $x$ feet above sea level is given by the formula

$$R = \sqrt{2x}$$

Make $x$ the subject of the formula.

$R^2 = 2x$ ——— Square both sides.

$\frac{1}{2}R^2 = x$ ——— Divide both sides by 2.

$x$ is on its own on one side. The formula can be written as $x = \frac{1}{2}R^2$.

## Exercise 12G

In questions **1–30** make the letter in square brackets the subject of the formula.

**1**  $V = IR$               $[I]$

**2**  $A = lw$               $[l]$

**3**  $C = \pi d$             $[d]$

**4**  $V = lwh$              $[w]$

**5**  $v = u + at$           $[u]$

**6**  $v = u + at$           $[t]$

**7**  $C = 2\pi rh$          $[h]$

**8**  $I = \dfrac{PRT}{100}$   $[R]$

**9**  $P = 2(l + w)$         $[l]$

**10**  $A = 2\pi r(r + h)$   $[h]$

**11**  $\dfrac{y}{x} = 3$      $[x]$

**12**  $\dfrac{PV}{T} = k$     $[T]$

**13**  $y = 5x^2$            $[x]$

**14**  $E = kx^2$            $[x]$

**15**  $A = \pi r^2$          $[r]$

**16**  $S = \frac{1}{2}n(a + d)$   $[n]$

**17**  $S = \frac{1}{2}n(a + d)$   $[a]$

**18**  $y = kx^2$            $[x]$

**19**  $V = \frac{1}{3}\pi r^2 h$   $[h]$

**20**  $V = \frac{1}{3}\pi r^2 h$   $[r]$

**21**  $c = \sqrt{a^2 + b^2}$   $[a]$

**22**  $a = 2\sqrt{b^2 - 2}$   $[b]$

**23**  $t = \sqrt{\dfrac{2s}{g}}$   $[s]$

**24**  $T = 2\pi \sqrt{\dfrac{L}{g}}$   $[L]$

**25**  $x^2 + y^2 = 1$       $[y]$

**26**  $v^2 = u^2 + 2as$     $[u]$

**27**  $v = w\sqrt{a^2 - x^2}$   $[x]$

**28**  $y = 3\sqrt{1 - x^2}$   $[x]$

**29**  $y = \dfrac{5 + x}{1 - x}$   $[x]$

**30**  $f = \dfrac{uv}{u + v}$   $[u]$

# 12.6 Substituting one formula in another

You can sometimes eliminate one of the letters from a formula by substituting an expression from a second formula.

**Example 11**

Two formulae used when designing electrical circuits are $P = IV$ and $V = IR$.

Find a formula for $P$ in terms of $I$ and $R$.

In $P = IV$, replace $V$ by $IR$:

$$P = I \times IR$$
$$P = I^2R$$

**Example 12**

The length of a rectangle is $l$ and its area is $A$.
Find a formula for its perimeter, $P$, in terms of $l$ and $A$.

Let $w$ represent the width of the rectangle.

$$P = 2l + 2w \qquad (1)$$
$$A = lw \qquad (2)$$

Make $w$ the subject of formula (2):

$$w = \frac{A}{l}$$

In formula (1), replace $w$ by $\frac{A}{l}$:

$$P = 2l + \frac{2A}{l}$$

> Formula (1) gives $P$ in terms of $l$ and $w$. To find $P$ in terms of $l$ and $A$, you need to replace the term $2w$ with a term in $l$ and $A$.

## Exercise 12H

1   $P = IV$ and $V = IR$.
    Find a formula for $P$ in terms of $V$ and $R$.

2   $s = vt$ and $v = \frac{1}{2}gt$.
    Find a formula for $s$ in terms of $g$ and $t$.

3   $A = \pi r^2$ and $r = \dfrac{d}{2}$
    Find a formula for $A$ in terms of $d$.

4   $a = \dfrac{v^2}{r}$ and $v = rw$
    Find a formula for $a$ in terms of $r$ and $w$.

**5** The area of a square is $A$ and its perimeter is $P$.

(a) Find a formula for $A$ in terms of $P$.

(b) Find a formula for $P$ in terms of $A$.

Let $x$ represent the length of the square's sides and express $A$ and $P$ in terms of $x$.

**6** $x = at^2$ and $y = 2at$.
Find a formula for $x$ in terms of $a$ and $y$.

**7** $A = 2\pi r^2 + 2\pi rh$ and $V = \pi r^2 h$.
Find a formula for $A$ in terms of $r$ and $V$.

**8** A farmer encloses sheep in a rectangular pen using fencing for three sides and a long hedge for the other side. The length of the pen is $l$ and its width is $w$. The total length of fencing used is $F$ and the area enclosed is $A$. Find a formula for $F$ in terms of $A$ and $l$.

## Mixed exercise 12

**1** These are the first five numbers of a simple sequence:

$$3, \quad 12, \quad 27, \quad 48, \quad 75$$

(a) Write down the next two numbers of the sequence.

(b) Write down, in terms of $n$, an expression for the $n$th term of this sequence. [E]

**2** Write down the next two numbers for each sequence.

(a) 7, 11, 15, 19, 23, ...    (b) 30, 27, 24, 21, 18, ...

(c) 1, 2, 4, 8, 16, ...    (d) 3, 6, 10, 15, 21, ...

**3** Make $t$ the subject of $v = 7t + 30$ [E]

**4** Make $g$ the subject of $T = 2\pi\sqrt{\dfrac{a}{g}}$

**5** Make $r$ the subject of $A = 4\pi r^2$

**6** $y = 4t + 3$ and $x = 2t - 1$.
Find a formula for $y$ in terms of $x$.

**7** Make $v$ the subject of $f = \dfrac{uv}{u + v}$

**8** Make $u$ the subject of the formula $D = ut + kt^2$ [E]

**9** A formula used in science is $s = \frac{1}{2}gt^2$

Tracy has to work out the value of $s$ when $g = 9.81$ and $t = 23.67$

Before using her calculator to work out the value of $s$, Tracy decides to obtain an estimate for $s$.

(a) (i) Write down values for $g$ and $t$ which Tracy could use in her calculation for an estimate of $s$.

(ii) Calculate the estimate of $s$ that these values would give.

(b) Use your calculator to work out the actual value of $s$, giving your answer correct to two decimal places.

10 The formula for the volume $V$ of a cylinder with circular base of radius $r$ and vertical height $h$ is

$$V = \pi r^2 h$$

The radius of the base and the vertical height of a cylinder are measured to the nearest millimetre and quoted as $r = 7.4\,\text{cm}$ and $h = 10.8\,\text{cm}$, whilst $\pi = 3.1416$, correct to 4 decimal places.

(a) Without using a calculator and showing all your working, give sensible approximations for $\pi$, $r$ and $h$ and use these to find an estimate for the volume of the cylinder.

(b) Use your calculator and the quoted values of $\pi$, $r$ and $h$ to calculate the volume of the cylinder, giving your answer in cubic centimetres, correct to three significant figures.

(c) Using $\pi = 3.1416$, find the maximum possible volume of the cylinder, giving your answer correct to two decimal places.

11 In Florida the speed limit for motor vehicles is 55 miles per hour. The 'on the spot' fine for motorists caught exceeding this limit is 4 dollars for each mile per hour over 55 miles per hour.

(a) Write down a formula for $f$, the 'on the spot' fine in dollars, for a motorist caught travelling at $v$ miles per hour. You may assume that $v > 55$.

(b) Make $v$ the subject of the formula.  [E]

## Summary of key points

1 When you know a formula for the $n$th term of a sequence, $u_n$, you can calculate any term in the sequence by substituting a value for $n$ in the formula. $n$ must be a positive integer ($n = 1, 2, 3 \ldots$).

2 The **general term** for an arithmetic sequence is of the form $u_n = an + b$. The value of $a$ is the difference between successive terms in the sequence.

3 An algebraic formula can be used to describe a relationship between two sets of values.

4 $x$ is the **subject** of a formula when it appears on its own on one side of the formula and does not appear on the other side.

# 13 Measure and mensuration

This chapter is about measurement of lengths, areas and volumes – mainly of geometrical shapes.

In the GCSE exam you will need to be able to apply a number of formulae. *Some* of them will appear on the formula sheet, but you need to learn the formulae and understand how they are derived.

In this chapter you will also consider how the accuracy of measurement affects calculation of areas.

## 13.1 Continuous and discrete data

When someone says their age is 15 years, this is really an approximation. The age quoted is the number of complete years. You can quote the age more exactly as, say, 15 years and 200 days. But this is still only an approximation, to the nearest day. The age could be quoted even more accurately as, say 15 years, 200 days, 7 hours, 35 minutes and 10 seconds, but this is still only an approximation, now given to the nearest second.

Time passes in a **continuous** way, so if someone quotes his or her age, then they are a little older at the end of their statement than they were at the beginning. No matter how accurate the quote, it is never more than an approximation.

A similar argument is true for a measurement such as length. We might say that the length of a metal rod is 72 cm, but we are dependent on the accuracy of the measuring instrument.

For some data, these arguments do not apply. You might, for instance, be asked to quote the number of GCSE exams you are taking. This will be a whole number and you can quote it exactly. It is an example of **discrete** data.

The figure does not have to be a whole number. For instance, 10 students could take 76 GCSE exams between them. Then the mean number of GCSEs taken per person is 76 ÷ 10 = 7.6; this is still an exact number.

## 13.2 The measurement of continuous data

You will often see examples of continuous data. For instance, a road sign might read:

The distance is quoted to the nearest mile.
The actual distance could be anywhere between 75.5 and 76.5 miles.

---

**Example 1**

The dimensions of a rectangular lawn are given as

width = 5 m    length = 7 m

Each measurement is given correct to the nearest metre.

(a) Write the longest and shortest possible values for the width and the length of the rectangle.

(b) Calculate the largest and smallest possible values for the area of the lawn.

(a) For the width, the measurement of 5 m means that the true width can be anywhere between 4.5 m and 5.5 m.
The shortest possible width is 4.5 m and the longest possible width is 5.5 m.

For the length, the measurement of 7 m means that the true length can be anywhere between 6.5 m and 7.5 m.
The shortest possible length is 6.5 m and the longest possible length is 7.5 m.

(b) The area of a rectangle = width × length.
To find the smallest area we combine the shortest width with the shortest length. This gives a smallest possible area of $4.5 \times 6.5 = 29.25$ m$^2$.
The largest area is found by combining the longest width with the longest length. This gives a largest possible area of $5.5 \times 7.5 = 41.25$ m$^2$.

---

## Exercise 13A

1 A piece of carpet is rectangular. Its dimensions are quoted to the nearest 10 cm as

width = 3.4 m    length = 4.6 m

(a) Write the shortest and longest possible widths for the carpet.

(b) Write the shortest and longest possible lengths for the carpet.

(c) Calculate the smallest and largest possible areas for the carpet.

2 A car travels at a constant speed of 70 km per hour for a time of 2 hours and 45 minutes. Its speed is quoted to the nearest km/h and the time is quoted to the nearest minute. Calculate

(a) the maximum possible distance that the car could have travelled

(b) the minimum distance the car could have travelled.

# 13.3 Perimeter and area of triangles and quadrilaterals

You will need to know and apply the formulae for the perimeters and areas of many different shapes.

## Rectangle

Perimeter = $2(a + b)$

Area = $a \times b = ab$

## Triangle

Perimeter = $a + b + c$

Area = $\frac{1}{2} \times$ base $\times$ height

$\quad = \frac{1}{2}bh$

Area of triangle = $\frac{1}{2} \times$ area of rectangle

## Parallelogram

Perimeter = $2(a + b)$

Area = $bh$

## Trapezium

Perimeter = sum of the lengths of the four sides

Area = $\frac{1}{2}(a + b) \times h$ or $\frac{1}{2}(a + b)h$

---

**Example 2**

Work out the area of triangle $XYZ$.

If you take $YZ$ as the base, the height is $XW$.

The area of triangle $XYZ$ is $\frac{1}{2} \times$ base $\times$ height = $\frac{1}{2} \times 7 \times 5 = \dfrac{35}{2}$

The area of triangle $XYZ$ is $17.5\,\text{cm}^2$.

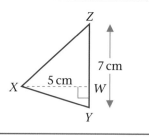

---

**Example 3**

Use the formula to calculate the area of the trapezium.

Area of trapezium = $\frac{1}{2}(a + b)h = \frac{1}{2}(3 + 10) \times 4$

$\qquad\qquad\qquad = \frac{1}{2} \times 13 \times 4 = 13 \times 2$

$\qquad\qquad\qquad = 26\,\text{cm}^2$

**Example 4**

Find the shaded area.

It is easiest to find the area of the larger rectangle and subtract the area of the smaller rectangle.

Large rectangle area: $12 \times 10 = 120 \text{ cm}^2$
Small rectangle area: $6 \times 4 = 24 \text{ cm}^2$
Area of shaded region: $120 - 24 = 96 \text{ cm}^2$

**Example 5**

$ABCD$ is a trapezium with $AB$ parallel to $DC$.
The lengths of $AB$ and $CD$ are in the ratio $1:2$.
The perpendicular distance between $AB$ and $CD = 12$ cm.
The area of $ABCD = 72 \text{ cm}^2$.

Calculate the length of $AB$.

The statement that the lengths of $AB$ and $CD$ are in the ratio $1:2$ means that $AB = \frac{1}{2} CD$.

Let the length of $AB = x$ cm, so the length of $CD = 2x$ cm.

$$\text{Area of } ABCD = \tfrac{1}{2}(AB + CD) \times h = \tfrac{1}{2}(x + 2x) \times 12$$
$$= \tfrac{1}{2}(3x) \times 12 = 18x$$

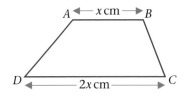

But the area $= 72 \text{ cm}^2$

so $\quad 18x = 72 \quad x = \dfrac{72}{18} = 4 \quad AB = 4 \text{ cm}$

## Exercise 13B

1   Work out the area and perimeters of these shapes:

(a)

(b)

2   (a)   Find, in its simplest form, an expression for the perimeter of this rectangle in terms of $x$.

(b)   Given that the perimeter is 50 cm, calculate the value of $x$.

(c)   Calculate the area of the rectangle.

**3** The area of a square in cm² is numerically equal to the perimeter of the square in cm.

(a) Calculate the length of a side of the square.

(b) Calculate the area of the square.

**4** A farmer uses exactly 1000 metres of fencing to fence off a square field. Calculate the area of the field.

**5** Calculate the area of each of these triangles:

(a)

8 cm   5 cm
12 cm

(b)

3 cm   5 cm
4 cm

(c)

6 cm
←15 cm→

**6** (a) Write down an expression for the perimeter of the triangle in terms of $x$.

(b) If the perimeter of the triangle is 29, calculate the value of $x$.

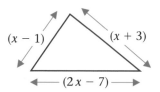

$(x - 1)$   $(x + 3)$

$(2x - 7)$

**7** Calculate the area of each parallelogram.

(a)

6 cm   5 cm
8 cm

(b)

3 cm   4 cm
12 cm

(c)

6 cm   5 cm
7 cm

**8** $ABCD$ is a parallelogram.

$$BC = AD = 14 \text{ cm} \qquad AB = DC = 8 \text{ cm}$$

The perpendicular distance between $AD$ and $BC$ is 5 cm.

(a) Calculate the area of the parallelogram.

(b) Calculate the perpendicular distance between $AB$ and $DC$.

*A*           *D*
8 cm   5 cm
*B*   14 cm   *C*

**9** The diagram shows a parallelogram and a square. These two shapes have equal areas.

Calculate the value of $x$ (the side of the square).

6 cm
15 cm

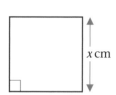
$x$ cm

**10** Find the shaded area in each diagram.

(a)

12 cm
5 cm
3 cm
10 cm

(b)
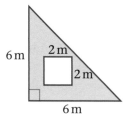
6 m   2 m
2 m
6 m

(c)
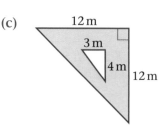
12 m
3 m
4 m
12 m

**11** *PQRS* is a trapezium with sides *PQ* and *SR* parallel. The perpendicular distance between *PQ* and *SR* = 8 cm. *PQ* = 6.4 cm and *SR* = 8.2 cm. Calculate the area of *PQRS*.

**12** *ABCD* is a trapezium with sides *AB* and *DC* parallel. The perpendicular distance between *AB* and *DC* = 18 cm. The lengths of *AB* and *DC* are in the ratio

$$AB : DC = 2 : 3$$

The area of *ABCD* = 54 cm². Calculate the length of *AB*.

# 13.4 Circumference and area of circles

Diameter = 2 × radius    or    $d = 2r$

Circumference = $2\pi r = \pi d$

Area = $\pi r^2 = \dfrac{\pi d^2}{4}$

---

**Worked examination question 1**

The diagram shows one face of a sheet of metal in the form of a rectangle with a semicircle cut out from one end.

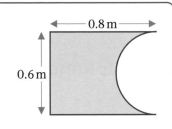

Calculate the area of the face of the sheet of metal.

Radius of semicircle = $\frac{1}{2} \times 0.6 = 0.3$ m

    Shaded area = area of rectangle − area of semicircle

           = $0.6 \times 0.8 - \frac{1}{2}\pi (0.3)^2$

           = $0.48 - \frac{1}{2}\pi \times 0.09$

           = $0.48 - 0.141$

           = $0.339$ m² (correct to 3 d.p.)

---

## Exercise 13C

**1** Calculate the circumference and area of each circle.

   (a)

   (b)

   (c)

2 Mrs de Silva lays out a circular flower bed of diameter 5 metres.

(a) Calculate the circumference of the flower bed.

(b) Calculate the area of the flower bed.

3 The circumference of a circle in centimetres is numerically equal to the area of the circle in square centimetres. Show that the radius of the circle must be 2 cm.

4 The circumference of a circle is 15 cm.

(a) Calculate the radius of the circle.

(b) Calculate the area of the circle.

5 The area of a circle is 114 cm². Calculate the circumference of the circle.

6 Calculate the area and perimeter of the semicircle

(a) giving your answer correct to 2 d.p.

(b) leaving your answer in terms of $\pi$.

7 The diagram represents a sheet of metal. It consists of a rectangle of length 60 cm and width 24 cm, and a semicircle. Calculate

(a) the perimeter of the sheet of metal

(b) the area of the sheet of metal.

# 13.5 Volume and surface area of 3-D shapes

## Cuboid

Total length around the edges = $4(a + b + c)$

Surface area = $2(ab + ac + bc)$

Volume = $abc$

In the special case when the cuboid is a cube, then

$a = b = c$

and

total distance around the edges = $12a$

surface area = $6a^2$

volume = $a^3$

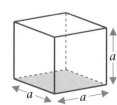

## Prisms

A cuboid is a special case of a prism. It is a rectangular prism.

For a general prism:

Surface area = 2 × area of base + total area of vertical faces

Volume = area of base × vertical height
= area of base × $h$

_____ **Example 6** _____

Calculate the height of a prism which has a base area of 25 cm² and a volume of 205 cm³.

$$\text{Volume} = \text{area of base} \times h$$
$$205 = 25 \times h$$
$$h = \frac{205}{25}$$

So $\qquad h = 8.2\text{ cm}$

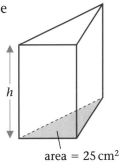

area = 25 cm²

_____ **Worked examination question 2 (Part question)** _____

$ABCDEF$ is a triangle-based prism.
The angle $A\hat{B}C = 90°$.

$AB = x$ cm, $\quad BC = (x + 3)$ cm $\quad$ and
$CD = 8$ cm.

8 cm

$x$ cm $\qquad (x + 3)$ cm

The volume of the prism = 40 cm³.
Show that $\quad x^2 + 3x - 10 = 0$

Volume of the prism = area of base × height
$$\text{Area of base} = \tfrac{1}{2} \times AB \times BC$$
$$= \tfrac{1}{2}x \times (x + 3) = \tfrac{1}{2}x(x + 3)$$
So the volume $= \tfrac{1}{2}x(x + 3) \times 8 = 4x(x + 3)$

But the volume = 40, so
$$4x(x + 3) = 40$$
$$x(x + 3) = 10 \qquad \text{(dividing through by 4)}$$
$$x^2 + 3x = 10$$

So, rearranging, or taking 10 from each side:
$$x^2 + 3x - 10 = 0 \qquad \text{(what you were asked to show)}$$

Note: a full question such as this in the exam would almost certainly go on to ask you to solve the equation
$$x^2 + 3x - 10 = 0$$
This is a quadratic equation. Solving quadratic equations is covered in Book 2, in Chapters 17 and 19.

**Worked examination question 3**

The diagram shows a solid door that is made from a rectangle with a semicircular top.

(a)   Work out the area of the cross-section of the door.

(b)   The door is made of metal and has a constant thickness of 5 cm.
      Work out the volume of the door.

(c)   The density of the metal is 7.8 grams per cm³.
      Work out the mass of the door.

(a)   The radius of the semicircle is half of the width of the door, so

$$\text{radius of semicircle} = \tfrac{1}{2} \times 1.4 = 0.7 \text{ metres}$$

$$\text{area of the semicircle} = \frac{\pi r^2}{2} = \frac{\pi \times 0.7^2}{2} = 0.769\,690\,2 \text{ m}^2$$

$$\text{area of rectangular part} = 1.4 \times 2.1 = 2.94 \text{ m}^2$$

So the total area of the cross-section of the door is

$$2.94 + 0.769\,690\,2 = 3.709\,690\,2 = 3.71 \text{ m}^2$$
(to 2 decimal places)

> To avoid rounding errors you should not round answers that precede the final answer.

(b)   The volume of the door can be found using the formula for the volume of a prism:

   volume = area of cross-section × depth (thickness)

The area of the door's cross-section is 3.709 690 2 m².

The thickness of the door is 5 cm.

Before applying any formula you need to make sure your units are consistent. It is meaningless to multiply 3.709 690 2 m² by 5 cm. You need to convert centimetres into metres:

   5 cm = 0.05 m

   Volume of door = 3.709 690 2 × 0.05
                  = 0.19 m³ (correct to 2 decimal places)

(c)   The relationship between mass, volume and density is

$$\text{density} = \frac{\text{mass}}{\text{volume}} \quad \text{or} \quad \text{mass} = \text{density} \times \text{volume}$$

Again you need to be consistent with the units.
The density is given as 7.8 grams per cm³.
The calculated volume is 0.19 m³.

1 m³

$$1\,m = 100\,cm$$
so $$1\,m^3 = 100 \times 100 \times 100 = 1\,000\,000\,cm^3$$

Hence the volume of the door $= 0.19 \times 1\,000\,000$
$$= 190\,000\,cm^3$$

The mass of the door $=$ density $\times$ volume
$$mass = 7.8 \times 190\,000$$
$$= 1\,500\,000\,grams$$
(correct to 2 significant figures)

It is sensible to give the most appropriate units.
You can change grams to kilograms by dividing by 1000.

So the mass of the door is $\dfrac{1\,500\,000}{1000} = 1500\,kg$

**Choosing the right degree of accuracy**

The density of the metal was given in the question to 2 significant figures. You should give your answer to the same degree of accuracy.

## Exercise 13D

**1**  Calculate the volume of a cube of side length
  (a)  5 cm          (b)  12 cm          (c)  3.8 cm

**2**  A cube has a volume of 1000 cm³. Calculate
  (a)  the length of a side of the cube
  (b)  the surface area of the cube.

**3**  Calculate the volume of a cuboid with sides of length
  (a)  5 cm, 6 cm and 6 cm          (b)  4.5 cm, 9.2 cm and 11.6 cm

**4**  The volume of the cuboid *ABCDEFGH* is 384 cm³.
  The edges *AB*, *BC* and *AF* are in the ratio
  $$AB : BC : AF = 1 : 2 : 3$$
  Calculate
  (a)  the length of *AB*
  (b)  the surface area of the cuboid.

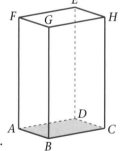

**5**  The diagrams show a prism and its base, which is a trapezium.

  (a)  Calculate the volume of the prism.
  (b)  Calculate the surface area of the prism.

**6** *ABCDEF* is a triangle-based prism.
Angle *ABC* = 90°, *AB* = 5 cm, *BC* = 8 cm and *CD* = 12 cm.
Calculate the volume of *ABCDEF*.

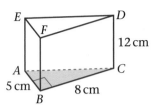

**7** *ABCDEF* is a wedge of volume 450 cm³.
Angle *ABC* = 90°, *AB* = 5 cm and *CD* = 15 cm.
Calculate the length of *BC*.

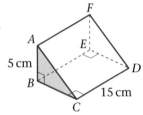

**8** This is the base of a prism of vertical height 24 cm.

Calculate the volume of the prism.

# 13.6 1-D, 2-D or 3-D?

The number line goes in one direction
(either horizontally or vertically).

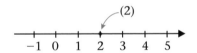

> The number line is **1-dimensional** or **1-D**.
> You can describe position on the number line using
> one number or coordinate, for example (2).

Coordinate grids and flat shapes go in two directions.

> Flat shapes are **2-dimensional** or **2-D**.
> You can describe position on a flat shape using two
> numbers or coordinates, for example (2, 1).

Solid shapes go in three directions.

> Solid shapes are **3-dimensional** or **3-D**.
> You can describe position in a solid shape
> using three numbers or coordinates,
> for example (4, 1, 2).

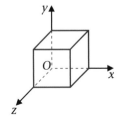

This diagram shows a 3-D grid. The *x*-, *y*- and *z*-axes are all at right angles to each other. The lengths of the edges of the cuboid are 2, 2 and 1 units.

To get to point *P* from *O*, you go 3 units along the *x*-axis, then 1 unit parallel to the *y*-axis, then 2 units parallel to the *z*-axis.

The coordinates of point *P* are (3, 1, 2).

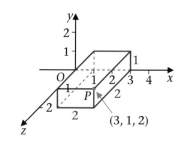

### Example 7

The diagram represents a cuboid on a 3-D grid.
*OR* = 2 units, *OP* = 4 units and *OS* = 3 units.
Find the coordinates of
(a) *S*  (b) *P*  (c) *R*  (d) *V*  (e) *U*  (f) *O*
(g) Find the mid-point of *PV*.

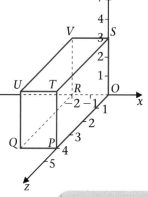

(a) To get to *S* from *O* you go 0 along the *x*-axis,
    3 units up the *y*-axis and 0 units parallel
    to the *z*-axis.
    So *S* = (0, 3, 0)
(b) Similarly *P* = (0, 0, 4)
(c) *R* = (−2, 0, 0)
(d) *V* = (−2, 3, 0)
(e) To get to *U* from *O* you go −2 units along the *x*-axis,
    3 units parallel to the *y*-axis and 4 units parallel
    to the *z*-axis.
    So *U* = (−2, 3, 4)
(f) *O* = (0, 0, 0)
(g) Mid-point of *PV* = $\left(\dfrac{0 + -2}{2}, \dfrac{0 + 3}{2}, \dfrac{4 + 0}{2}\right)$

$= (-1, 1\frac{1}{2}, 2)$

> Remember to give the coordinates in the order (*x*, *y*, *z*).

> *A* (*x*, *y*) *B* (*p*, *q*)
> Mid-point of *AB*
> $= \dfrac{x + p}{2}, \dfrac{y + q}{2}$

### Exercise 13E

**1** Say whether each shape is 1-D, 2-D or 3-D.
(a) pentagon  (b) pyramid  (c) rectangle  (d) cone

**2** Write down all the 3-dimensional coordinates from this list:
(4)       (2, 1, 3)    (6, 5)    (4, 3, 1)    (6)
(10, 7)   (5, 2, 12)   (8, 2)    (27, 3, 11)  (245)

**3** Write down the coordinates of each vertex of this cuboid:

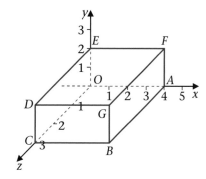

**4** (a) Write down the coordinates of each vertex of this cuboid.

(b) Write down the mid-points of

(i) *DG*

(ii) *EB*

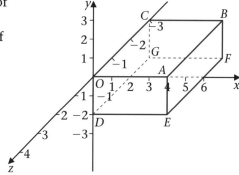

# 13.7 Dimension theory

It can be easy to forget the formulae for perimeters, areas and volumes or to confuse them.

For instance, the formulae for the circumference and the area of a circle are

$$C = 2\pi r \qquad A = \pi r^2$$

which are somewhat similar. You could easily confuse one with the other.

In the formula for the circumference, *r* represents the radius of the circle. It has units of length. You say that *r* has **dimension** = 1

In the formula for the circumference, $\pi$ is just a number (about equal to 3.14).
It is dimensionless. You say it has dimension = 0.
The 2 in the formula is also just a number.
So the 2 is also dimensionless (dimension = 0).

The formula for the area of a circle is:

$$A = \pi r^2$$

Here $\pi$ is again dimensionless.

The $r^2$ part is length $\times$ length (it has units of area).
So $r^2$ has dimension = 2.

---

**Example 8**

Check the dimensions of $V = abc$ for the volume of a cuboid.

*a*, *b* and *c* each have dimension = 1

So *abc* has dimension = 3, which is correct for a volume.

> An incorrect formula may be dimensionally correct. Dimension theory only helps you rule out *some* incorrect formulae!

All expressions for length or distance have dimension = 1.
All expressions for area have dimension = 2.
All expressions for volume have dimension = 3.
Numbers (like $\pi$ and 2) are dimensionless.

This is called **dimension theory**. It gives a simple method for
checking that you may have the correct formula for a given situation,
since a correct formula will have the same dimensions on both sides.

---

**Example 9**

Yvonne is using a formula sheet to work out the volume and the area of the curved surface
of a cylinder. Unfortunately a blot on the sheet covers up part of the information.

Her sheet looks like this:

$$= \pi r^2 h$$
$$= 2\pi r h$$

Yvonne knows that one of these gives the volume and the other the area of the curved surface.

How could she tell which formula is which?

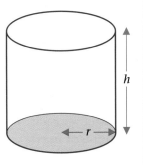

Volume has dimension = 3.
In the expression $\pi r^2 h$, $\pi$ is a number, $r$ is a length and $h$ is a length.
$\pi$ is dimensionless. $r^2$ has dimension = 2. $h$ has dimension = 1.
So $\pi r^2 h$ has dimension = 3.
So this is a formula for a volume.

In the expression $2\pi r h$,
2 and $\pi$ are dimensionless whilst $r$ and $h$ each have dimension = 1.
So $2\pi r h$ has dimension = 2 and is an expression for an area.

---

You should be able to use **dimension theory** to confirm whether
formulae are for length, area or volume:

● length has dimension = 1
● area has dimension = 2
● volume has dimension = 3

## Exercise 13F

**1**   Here are two expressions related to a sphere of radius $r$:

$$4\pi r^2 \quad \text{and} \quad \frac{4\pi r^3}{3}$$

One of these gives the volume of a sphere and the other the
surface area of the sphere. State, with an explanation, which
formula gives the surface area of a sphere.

**2** The volume of a solid is given by $V = \lambda a^n b^m$, where $\lambda$ is dimensionless, $a$ and $b$ have dimensions of length and $n$ and $m$ are non-negative integers. State the possible values of $n$ and $m$.

**3** The table below shows some expressions.
The letters $x$, $y$ and $z$ represent lengths.

Copy the table. Place a tick in the appropriate column for each expression to show whether the expression can be used to represent a length, an area, a volume or none of these.

| Expression | Length | Area | Volume | None of these |
|---|---|---|---|---|
| $x + y + z$ | | | | |
| $xyz$ | | | | |
| $xy + yz + xz$ | | | | |

**4** Here are three expressions.

| Expression | Length | Area | Volume | None of these |
|---|---|---|---|---|
| $\pi a^2 b$ | | | | |
| $\pi b^2 + 2h$ | | | | |
| $2ah$ | | | | |

$a$, $b$ and $h$ are lengths. $\pi$ and 2 are numbers and have no dimensions.

Copy the table and place a tick in the correct column to show whether each expression can be used for length, area, volume or none of these.

## Mixed exercise 13

**1** The area of a pane of glass is $12\,000 \text{ cm}^2$.
Work out the area of this pane of glass in $\text{m}^2$.

**2** The volume of a large packing case is $3.4 \text{ m}^3$.
Work out the volume of this packing case in $\text{cm}^3$.

**3** Here is a cuboid. The rectangular base has width 4 m and length 5 m. The height is 300 cm. The dimensions are all quoted correct to the nearest metre.

(a) Calculate the maximum possible volume of the cuboid.

(b) Calculate the maximum possible total surface area.

**4** The diagram represents the plan of a sports field.
The field is in the form of a rectangle with semicircular pieces at each end.

Calculate

(a) the perimeter of the field    (b) the area of the field.

**5** Calculate the area of the trapezium *ABCD*.

**6** The circumference of a circle is 44 cm.
Calculate the area of the circle.

**7** Calculate the volume and surface
area of the wedge *ABCDEF*
in which

Angle $A\hat{B}C = 90°$

$AB = 5$ cm,   $AC = 13$ cm,
$BC = 12$ cm   and   $CD = 20$ cm

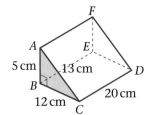

**8** The cuboid has a square base of side length *x* cm.
The height of the cuboid is *h* cm.
The volume of the cuboid is 50 cm³.

(a)  Show that $x = \sqrt{\dfrac{50}{h}}$.

(b)  Calculate the value of *x* when *h* = 4.

(c)  Calculate the value of *h* when *x* = 5.

**9** (a)  List the coordinates of all the
vertices of the cuboid.

(b)  Write down the coordinates
of the mid-point of

(i)  *AD*
(ii)  *FC*

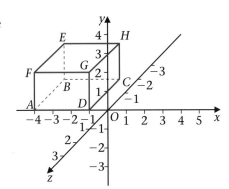

**10** In the expression $\mu a^2 h$, $\mu$ is dimensionless and *a* and *h* have
dimensions of length.
Explain whether the expression represents a length, an area or
a volume.

**11** An estate agent quotes the dimensions of a rectangular floor of a
room as 4.3 metres by 3.7 metres, both correct to 10 cm.
(a)  Write down the maximum and minimum possible values
for each of these dimensions.
(b)  Calculate the maximum and minimum possible values for
the area of the floor, giving your answers correct to three
significant figures in each case.

# Summary of key points

**1** Perimeter of a rectangle = $2(a + b)$
Area of a rectangle = $a \times b = ab$

**2** Perimeter of a triangle = $a + b + c$
Area of a triangle = $\frac{1}{2} \times$ base $\times$ height
$= \frac{1}{2}bh$

**3** Perimeter of a parallelogram = $2(a + b)$
Area of a parallelogram = $bh$

**4** Perimeter of a trapezium = sum of the lengths of the four sides
Area of a trapezium = $\frac{1}{2}(a + b)h$

**5** Diameter of a circle = $d = 2 \times$ radius = $2r$
Circumference = $2\pi r = \pi d$
Area of a circle = $\pi r^2 = \dfrac{\pi d^2}{4}$

**6** Total length around the edges of a cuboid = $4(a + b + c)$
Surface area of a cuboid = $2(ab + ac + bc)$
Volume of a cuboid = $abc$

**7** Surface area of a prism = $2 \times$ area of base + total area of vertical faces
Volume of a prism = area of base $\times h$

**8** You should be able to use **dimension theory** to confirm whether formulae are for length, area or volume:
- length has dimension = 1
- area has dimension = 2
- volume has dimension = 3

# 14 Simplifying algebraic expressions

In this chapter you will extend your skills in simplifying algebraic expressions, including dealing with indices and algebraic fractions.

## 14.1 Index notation

$x \times x$ is usually written as $x^2$ and is read as '$x$ squared'.

$x \times x \times x$ is usually written as $x^3$ and is read as '$x$ cubed'.

When $x$ is multiplied by itself any number of times, you say it is raised to a 'power' or 'index'. For example, $x \times x \times x \times x \times x$ is usually written as $x^5$ and is read as '$x$ to the power of five' or '$x$ to the fifth'.

> In the expression $x^n$ the number $x$ is called the **base** and the number $n$ is called the **index** or power.

$x^1$, read as '$x$ to the power of one', is usually written just as $x$.

> $x^1 = x$

The mathematical plural of index is **indices**.

## 14.2 Multiplying expressions involving indices

### Multiplying $x^m \times x^n$

In number:

$$4^2 \times 4^3 = 4^{2+3} = 4^5$$

For more on this, see Chapter 1.

In algebra:

$$x^2 \times x^3 = (x \times x) \times (x \times x \times x)$$
$$= x^5$$

So $\quad x^2 \times x^3 = x^{2+3} = x^5$

For more on this, see Chapter 2.

In general, the rule for multiplying algebraic expressions involving powers is

> $x^m \times x^n = x^{m+n}$

You may find it easier to remember this rule as: 'To multiply numbers which have the same base, add the indices'.

---

**Example 1**

Simplify $2x^3 \times 5x^4$.

$$2x^3 \times 5x^4 = 2 \times x^3 \times 5 \times x^4$$
$$= 2 \times 5 \times x^3 \times x^4$$
$$= 10 \times x^{3+4}$$
$$= 10x^7$$

> A common error is to forget that the numbers must have the same base. For example:
> $$2^3 \times 3^2 \neq 6^5$$
> ($\neq$ means 'is **not equal** to').

---

The rule for multiplying algebraic expressions involving powers can also be used with more complicated expressions like this:

**Example 2**

Simplify $4a^2b^3 \times 3ab^2 \times 2b$.

$$4a^2b^3 \times 3ab^2 \times 2b = 4 \times a^2 \times b^3 \times 3 \times a^1 \times b^2 \times 2 \times b^1$$
$$= 4 \times 3 \times 2 \times a^2 \times a^1 \times b^3 \times b^2 \times b^1$$
$$= 24 \times a^{2+1} \times b^{3+2+1}$$
$$= 24a^3b^6$$

---

## Multiplying out $(x^m)^n$

$(x^2)^3$ means $(x^2) \times (x^2) \times (x^2)$  or  $x^2 \times x^2 \times x^2$

so  $(x^2)^3 = x^{2+2+2} = x^6 = x^{2 \times 3}$

Similarly $(x^3)^4$ means $x^3 \times x^3 \times x^3 \times x^3 = x^{3+3+3+3} = x^{12} = x^{3 \times 4}$

In general, the rule for multiplying algebraic expressions involving powers is

$$(x^m)^n = x^{m \times n} = x^{mn}$$

---

**Example 3**

Simplify  (a) $(x^2)^6$    (b) $(xy^2)^3$    (c) $(2x^3)^5$

(a)  $(x^2)^6 = x^{2 \times 6} = x^{12}$

(b)  $(xy^2)^3 = (x)^3 \times (y^2)^3 = x^3 \times y^{2 \times 3} = x^3 \times y^6 = x^3y^6$

(c)  $(2x^3)^5 = (2)^5 \times (x^3)^5 = 32 \times x^{3 \times 5} = 32 \times x^{15} = 32x^{15}$

---

## Exercise 14A

> Simplify $x + 2x + 3x$ first.

Simplify these expressions.

| | | | |
|---|---|---|---|
| **1** $x^3 \times x^5$ | **2** $y^4 \times y^4$ | **3** $6x \times x^6$ | **4** $a^3 \times 5a$ |
| **5** $2a^2 \times 3a \times 4a^3$ | **6** $2y^3 \times 4y^2 \times 6$ | **7** $2x^2 \times 5x^3y^2$ | **8** $3a^2b^3 \times 2a^3 \times 4b^2$ |
| **9** $ab \times abc^2$ | **10** $2a^2b \times 3b^2c^3 \times 3c^2$ | **11** $2x^2 \times 3y^3$ | **12** $(x^2)^4$ |
| **13** $(3a^2)^2$ | **14** $(2x^2)^3$ | **15** $2(a^4)^5$ | **16** $2(xy^2)^3 \times x$ |
| **17** $(3x^4)^2 \times 7$ | **18** $7(a^2)^3 \times 2a^3b^2 \times (ab)^4$ | **19** $(x + 2x + 3x)^2$ | **20** $(x \times x + 2x^2)^3$ |

## 14.3 Dividing expressions involving indices

Chapter 1 shows you how to divide numbers in index form. For example

$$5^6 \div 5^4 = 5^2$$

In the same way:

$$x^6 \div x^4 = \frac{\cancel{x} \times \cancel{x} \times \cancel{x} \times \cancel{x} \times x \times x}{\cancel{x} \times \cancel{x} \times \cancel{x} \times \cancel{x}}$$

$$= x^2$$

In general:　　$x^m \div x^n = x^{m-n}$

You may find it easier to remember this rule as 'To divide numbers which have the same base, subtract the indices'.

---

**Example 4**

Simplify　(a) $x^6 \div x^2$　　(b) $8a^5 \div 4a^3$　　(c) $15x^4y^3 \div 3xy^2$

(a)　$x^6 \div x^2 = x^{6-2} = x^4$　　　　(b)　$8a^5 \div 4a^3 = \frac{8}{4}a^{5-3} = 2a^2$

(c)　$15x^4y^3 \div 3xy^2 = 15x^4y^3 \div 3x^1y^2 = \frac{15}{3}x^{4-1}y^{3-2} = 5x^3y^1 = 5x^3y$

---

### Exercise 14B

Simplify these expressions.

| | | | | | | | |
|---|---|---|---|---|---|---|---|
| **1** | $x^7 \div x^4$ | **2** | $6a^5 \div 2a^2$ | **3** | $18x^4y^3 \div 3x^3$ | **4** | $x^2 \div x^4$ |
| **5** | $a^7 \div a$ | **6** | $6a^5 \div 4xa^2$ | **7** | $12x^4 \div 3x^4$ | **8** | $x^4 \div x^2$ |
| **9** | $15q^5 \div 3q^3$ | **10** | $6r^5 \div 3r$ | **11** | $8e^8 \div 4e^4$ | **12** | $12p^8 \div 4p^3$ |

## 14.4 Zero, negative and fractional indices

### The zero index

Here is how to find the value of an expression to the power zero.
$2^0$ can be written as:

$$2^3 \div 2^3 = 2^{3-3} = 2^0$$

But　　$2^3 \div 2^3 = \frac{2^3}{2^3} = 1$

so　　　　　$2^0 = 1$

Putting $n = m$ in the rule for dividing algebraic expressions involving powers gives

$$x^m \div x^m = x^{m-m}$$

So　　　$\frac{x^m}{x^m} = x^0$

$$1 = x^0$$

$x^0 = 1$ for all non-zero values of $x$.

gives 'Error' on most calculators.

What does your calculator display if you input

(a) a small negative number instead of the first 0

(b) a small positive decimal number instead of the second 0?

# Negative indices

You can also find the value of an expression to a negative power.
For example, $6^{-2}$ can be written as

$$6^3 \div 6^5 = 6^{3-5} = 6^{-2}$$

So

$$\frac{\cancel{6} \times \cancel{6} \times \cancel{6}}{\cancel{6} \times \cancel{6} \times \cancel{6} \times 6 \times 6} = 6^{-2}$$

or

$$\frac{1}{6^2} = 6^{-2}$$

Putting $m = 0$ in the rule for dividing algebraic expressions involving powers gives

$$x^0 \div x^n = x^{0-n}$$

So

$$\frac{x^0}{x^n} = x^{-n}$$

which gives

$$\frac{1}{x^n} = x^{-n}$$

$$x^{-n} = \frac{1}{x^n}$$

> **Remember:**
> $$x^0 = 1$$
> so $$\frac{x^0}{x^n} = \frac{1}{x^n}$$

> The reciprocal of
> $$x^n = 1 \div x^n = \frac{1}{x^n}$$

This result can be written in words as: $x^{-n}$ means the **reciprocal** of $x^n$.

# Fractional indices

To see what a fractional power means, compare these expressions involving square roots.

$$\sqrt{25} \times \sqrt{25} = 25$$

$$\sqrt{x} \times \sqrt{x} = x = x^1$$

and

$$x^{\frac{1}{2}} \times x^{\frac{1}{2}} = x^{\frac{1}{2} + \frac{1}{2}} = x^1$$

So

$$x^{\frac{1}{2}} = \sqrt{x}$$

Similarly

$$\sqrt[3]{x} \times \sqrt[3]{x} \times \sqrt[3]{x} = x$$

and

$$x^{\frac{1}{3}} \times x^{\frac{1}{3}} \times x^{\frac{1}{3}} = x$$

So

$$x^{\frac{1}{3}} = \sqrt[3]{x}$$

> **Remember:**
> $\sqrt[3]{\phantom{x}}$ means 'cube root'.

In general:

$$x^{\frac{1}{n}} = \sqrt[n]{x}$$

---

**Example 5**

Find the value of $8^{-\frac{1}{3}}$

$$8^{-\frac{1}{3}} = \frac{1}{8^{\frac{1}{3}}} = \frac{1}{\sqrt[3]{8}} = \frac{1}{2}$$

## Exercise 14C

Find the value of these expressions.

**1** $25^{\frac{1}{2}}$     **2** $16^{\frac{1}{4}}$     **3** $64^{\frac{1}{3}}$     **4** $49^{-\frac{1}{2}}$     **5** $81^{-\frac{1}{4}}$

**6** $216^{\frac{1}{3}}$     **7** $125^{-\frac{1}{3}}$     **8** $100^{-\frac{1}{2}}$     **9** $(\frac{1}{4})^{\frac{1}{2}}$     **10** $(0.064)^{\frac{1}{3}}$

## 14.5 Combining indices

You can use the rule for multiplying algebraic expressions involving indices to show that

$$(\sqrt[n]{x})^m = (x^{\frac{1}{n}})^m = x^{\frac{1}{n} \times m} = x^{\frac{m}{n}}$$

and that     $\sqrt[n]{x^m} = (x^m)^{\frac{1}{n}} = x^{m \times \frac{1}{n}} = x^{\frac{m}{n}}$

$$\boxed{\frac{1}{n} \times m = \frac{m}{n}}$$

$$\boxed{x^{\frac{m}{n}} = (\sqrt[n]{x})^m \quad \text{or} \quad x^{\frac{m}{n}} = \sqrt[n]{x^m}}$$

**Example 6**

Find the value of $81^{\frac{3}{4}}$

Here $m = 3$ and $n = 4$. Substituting in the rule above gives

$$81^{\frac{3}{4}} = (\sqrt[4]{81})^3 = (3)^3 = 27$$

**Example 7**

Simplify    **(a)** $(25x^2)^{\frac{1}{2}}$     **(b)** $(8x^6)^{-\frac{1}{3}}$

**(a)** $(25x^2)^{\frac{1}{2}} = (25)^{\frac{1}{2}}(x^2)^{\frac{1}{2}}$

$\qquad = \sqrt{25}(x^{2 \times \frac{1}{2}})$

$\qquad = 5x^1$

$\qquad = 5x$

**(b)** $(8x^6)^{-\frac{1}{3}} = (8)^{-\frac{1}{3}}(x^6)^{-\frac{1}{3}}$

$\qquad = \dfrac{1}{\sqrt[3]{8}}(x^{6 \times (-\frac{1}{3})})$

$\qquad = \dfrac{1}{2}x^{-2}$  or  $\dfrac{1}{2x^2}$

## Exercise 14D

**1** Find the value of

(a) $8^{\frac{1}{3}}$   (b) $1000^{-\frac{2}{3}}$   (c) $32^{\frac{2}{5}}$   (d) $(0.25)^{-\frac{5}{2}}$   (e) $27^{\frac{4}{3}}$

**2** Find the value of

(a) $25^{\frac{3}{2}}$     (b) $16^{\frac{5}{4}}$     (c) $4^{\frac{5}{2}}$     (d) $8^{-\frac{2}{3}}$

(e) $(0.125)^{-\frac{5}{3}}$   (f) $125^{\frac{2}{3}}$     (g) $(\frac{1}{8})^{\frac{2}{3}}$     (h) $64^{-\frac{5}{6}}$

(i) $1296^{\frac{1}{4}}$     (j) $(\frac{27}{8})^{\frac{2}{3}}$     (k) $(\frac{343}{512})^{-\frac{2}{3}}$     (l) $25^{-\frac{3}{2}}$

3   Simplify

(a)  $(3x^0)^2$          (b)  $a^{-2} \div \dfrac{1}{a^4}$          (c)  $(\sqrt{xy})^3 \times y$

(d)  $(9x^2)^{\frac{1}{2}}$          (e)  $(8x^{-3})^{\frac{1}{3}}$          (f)  $(25a^{-4})^{-\frac{1}{2}}$

(g)  $(81x^2)^{\frac{3}{2}}$          (h)  $32\sqrt{x} \times (16x^2)^{-\frac{1}{4}}$          (i)  $4^{\frac{3}{2}} \times (9y^4)^{\frac{1}{2}}$

# 14.6 Equations involving indices

**Example 8**

Find the value of $k$ in

(a)  $x^k = \dfrac{1}{x^{-2}}$          (b)  $x^k = \sqrt{x} \div \dfrac{1}{x^3}$          (c)  $x^k = \dfrac{x \times \sqrt[3]{x^4}}{(\sqrt[4]{x})^2}$          (d)  $4^{k+1} = 8$

(a)          $x^k = \dfrac{1}{x^{-2}}$

  $= (x^{-2})^{-1}$

Using the rule for multiplying out $(x^m)^n$ gives

  $x^k = x^2$

So          $k = 2$  ———— Comparing indices.

(b)          $x^k = \sqrt{x} \div \dfrac{1}{x^3}$

  $= x^{\frac{1}{2}} \div x^{-3}$

  $= x^{\frac{1}{2} - (-3)}$

  $= x^{\frac{1}{2} + 3} = x^{3\frac{1}{2}}$

So          $k = 3\frac{1}{2}$

(c)          $x^k = \dfrac{x \times \sqrt[3]{x^4}}{(\sqrt[4]{x})^2}$

  $= \dfrac{x^1 \times x^{\frac{4}{3}}}{x^{\frac{2}{4}}}$

  $= \dfrac{x^{1 + \frac{4}{3}}}{x^{\frac{1}{2}}}$

  $= \dfrac{x^{\frac{7}{3}}}{x^{\frac{1}{2}}}$

  $= x^{\frac{7}{3} - \frac{1}{2}}$

  $= x^{\frac{11}{6}}$

So          $k = \dfrac{11}{6}$

(d)          $4^{k+1} = 8$

  $= 4 \times 2$

  $= 4 \times \sqrt{4}$

  $= 4^1 \times 4^{\frac{1}{2}}$

  $= 4^{1\frac{1}{2}}$

So   $k + 1 = 1\frac{1}{2}$

  $k = \frac{1}{2}$

**Alternative method:**
Because 4 and 8 are multiples of 2, you can also answer part **(d)** like this:

  $4^{k+1} = 8$

  $(2^2)^{k+1} = (2)^3$

  $2^{2k+2} = 2^3$

  $2k + 2 = 3$

  $2k = 1$

  $k = \frac{1}{2}$

## Exercise 14E

1   Find the value of $k$ in

(a)  $x^k = \sqrt{x}$          (b)  $y^k = 1$          (c)  $a^k = 1 \div a^3$

(d)  $x^k = \sqrt[3]{x^2}$          (e)  $y^k = y^2\sqrt{y^3}$          (f)  $a^k = \sqrt{a} \div \dfrac{1}{a^4}$

(g)  $x^{k+1} = (x^{-2})^{-3}$          (h)  $2^k = 16$          (i)  $3^k = 27$

(j)  $25^k = 5$          (k)  $9^k = 27$          (l)  $4^{\frac{k}{2}} = 8$

## 14.7 Algebraic fractions

$\dfrac{9x^4}{6x}$ and $\dfrac{3(x+8)}{3x}$ are examples of **algebraic fractions**.

Fractions can be simplified by cancelling *only* if the numerator and the denominator have a common factor.

---

**Example 9**

Simplify:

(a) $\dfrac{9x^4}{6x}$

(b) $\dfrac{3(x+8)}{3x}$

(a) $\dfrac{9x^4}{6x} = \dfrac{3 \times \cancel{3} \times \cancel{x} \times x^3}{2 \times \cancel{3} \times \cancel{x}} = \dfrac{3x^3}{2}$

(b) $\dfrac{3(x+8)}{3x} = \dfrac{\cancel{3} \times (x+8)}{\cancel{3} \times x} = \dfrac{x+8}{x}$

> Check this answer using the rule for dividing indices.

> You can't cancel the $x$'s here as $x$ isn't a common factor of $x$ and $(x+8)$.

---

## Multiplying and dividing algebraic fractions

When you multiply algebraic fractions, you should cancel any factor which is common to both numerator and denominator. When no further cancelling is possible you can then multiply the remaining numerators and denominators.

---

**Example 10**

Simplify $\dfrac{x^4}{y} \times \dfrac{xy}{z} \times \dfrac{z}{x^3}$

$\dfrac{x^4}{y} \times \dfrac{xy}{z} \times \dfrac{z}{x^3} = \dfrac{x \times \cancel{x^3}}{\cancel{y}} \times \dfrac{x \times \cancel{y}}{\cancel{z}} \times \dfrac{\cancel{z}}{\cancel{x^3}}$  ———— Cancel by $x^3$, then by $y$, then by $z$.

$= \dfrac{x}{1} \times \dfrac{x}{1} \times \dfrac{1}{1} = \dfrac{x \times x \times 1}{1 \times 1 \times 1} = \dfrac{x^2}{1} = x^2$

---

> Dividing by an algebraic fraction is equivalent to multiplying by its reciprocal.
> For example, to divide by $\dfrac{a}{b}$ you can multiply by $\dfrac{b}{a}$.

To see why this works, notice that

$$1 = \frac{a}{b} \times \frac{b}{a}$$

Dividing both sides by $\dfrac{a}{b}$ gives

$$1 \div \frac{a}{b} = 1 \times \frac{b}{a}$$

So dividing 1 by $\dfrac{a}{b}$ is the same as multiplying 1 by the reciprocal of $\dfrac{a}{b}$.

> The reciprocal of $\dfrac{a}{b}$ is $\dfrac{b}{a}$.

**Example 11**

Simplify $3x \div \dfrac{a}{b}$

$$3x \div \dfrac{a}{b} = \dfrac{3x}{1} \times \dfrac{b}{a} = \dfrac{3xb}{a}$$

**Example 12**

Simplify $\dfrac{x^2(x + 2)}{y^2} \div \dfrac{x(x + 4)}{y^3}$

$$\dfrac{x^2(x + 2)}{y^2} \div \dfrac{x(x + 4)}{y^3} = \dfrac{x^2(x + 2)}{y^2} \times \dfrac{y^3}{x(x + 4)}$$ ————— Multiply by the reciprocal.

$$= \dfrac{\cancel{x} \times x \times (x + 2)}{y^2} \times \dfrac{y^2 \times y}{\cancel{x} \times (x + 4)}$$ ————— Cancel by $x$ and then by $y^2$.

$$= \dfrac{x(x + 2)}{1} \times \dfrac{y}{x + 4} = \dfrac{xy(x + 2)}{x + 4}$$ ————— No further cancelling is possible here.

## Exercise 14F

Simplify these expressions.

**1** $\dfrac{xy}{4y}$

**2** $\dfrac{abc}{acd}$

**3** $\dfrac{24x^2}{6x}$

**4** $\dfrac{8st}{6sr}$

**5** $\dfrac{12a^2}{b^3} \times \dfrac{b^4}{4a}$

**6** $\dfrac{4(x - 2)}{2(x - 2)}$

**7** $\dfrac{2(x + 2)}{4x}$

**8** $\dfrac{9(x + 4)}{3(x + 4)(x - 4)}$

**9** $\dfrac{y^3(y - 2)}{x^2} \div \dfrac{y(y - 6)}{x^5}$

# 14.8 Adding and subtracting algebraic fractions

To add or subtract algebraic fractions you can use the same methods as for ordinary numerical fractions.

> For more on this, see Chapter 4.

Both fractions must have the same denominator. If they do not, find their lowest common multiple (LCM) and change each fraction to an equivalent fraction with this denominator.

Here is a numerical example as a reminder.

To add $\frac{1}{3}$ and $\frac{1}{5}$ find the lowest common multiple of 3 and 5.
The LCM is 15.

Change each fraction to an equivalent fraction with this denominator:

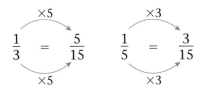

So $\frac{1}{3} + \frac{1}{5}$ is equivalent to

$$\frac{5}{15} + \frac{3}{15} = \frac{8}{15}$$

In general, to add two fractions $\dfrac{1}{n} + \dfrac{1}{m}$ you can change them to equivalent fractions with denominator $m \times n$.

$$\frac{1}{n} + \frac{1}{m} = \frac{m+n}{mn}$$

The following examples show you how to add two algebraic fractions, but a similar process can be used to subtract or add three or more fractions.

---

**Example 13**

Write as a single fraction in its lowest terms:

(a) $\quad \dfrac{2}{3} + \dfrac{1}{4}$       (b) $\quad \dfrac{2}{y} + \dfrac{1}{z}$       (c) $\quad \dfrac{2}{(x+1)} + \dfrac{1}{(x+2)}$

(a) $\quad \dfrac{2}{3} + \dfrac{1}{4}$

$$= \frac{2 \times 4}{3 \times 4} + \frac{1 \times 3}{4 \times 3}$$

$$= \frac{8}{12} + \frac{3}{12}$$

$$= \frac{8+3}{12}$$

$$= \frac{11}{12}$$

(b) $\quad \dfrac{2}{y} + \dfrac{1}{z}$

$$= \frac{2 \times z}{y \times z} + \frac{1 \times y}{z \times y}$$

$$= \frac{2z}{yz} + \frac{y}{zy}$$

$$= \frac{2z+y}{yz}$$

(c) $\quad \dfrac{2}{(x+1)} + \dfrac{1}{(x+2)}$

$$= \frac{2(x+2)}{(x+1)(x+2)} + \frac{1(x+1)}{(x+2)(x+1)}$$

$$= \frac{2x+4}{(x+1)(x+2)} + \frac{x+1}{(x+2)(x+1)}$$

$$= \frac{2x+4+x+1}{(x+1)(x+2)}$$

$$= \frac{3x+5}{(x+1)(x+2)}$$

---

When the denominators have no common factor, the LCM is the product of all the denominators.

The next example shows you how to find the LCM when the denominators have a common factor, by writing the denominators in terms of their prime factors.

> For more on prime factors see Section 1.1.

**Example 14**

Write as a single fraction:

(a) $\dfrac{5}{12} - \dfrac{2}{9}$

(b) $\dfrac{5}{x(x+1)} - \dfrac{2}{x^2}$

In both examples, the denominators have a common factor.

To find the LCM first split each denominator into its prime factors.

Then write the denominator of the first fraction and multiply it by the 'remaining' factors of the other denominators.

(a) $\dfrac{5}{12} - \dfrac{2}{9}$

$12 = 2 \times 2 \times 3$ and $9 = 3 \times 3$
The LCM is $2 \times 2 \times 3 \times 3 = 36$

$= \dfrac{5 \times 3}{12 \times 3} - \dfrac{2 \times 4}{9 \times 4}$

$= \dfrac{15}{36} - \dfrac{8}{36}$

$= \dfrac{15 - 8}{36}$

$= \dfrac{7}{36}$

(b) $\dfrac{5}{x(x+1)} - \dfrac{2}{x^2}$

$x(x+1) = x \times (x+1)$ and $x^2 = x \times x$
The LCM is $x \times (x+1) \times x = x^2(x+1)$

$= \dfrac{5 \times x}{x(x+1) \times x} - \dfrac{2(x+1)}{x^2(x+1)}$

$= \dfrac{5x}{x^2(x+1)} - \dfrac{2(x+1)}{x^2(x+1)}$

$= \dfrac{5x - 2(x+1)}{x^2(x+1)}$

$= \dfrac{5x - 2x - 2}{x^2(x+1)}$

$= \dfrac{3x - 2}{x^2(x+1)}$

## Checking your solutions

In the GCSE exam you should check your algebra solutions by choosing suitable numbers for the unknown (usually $x$). When checking work on algebraic fractions, do not choose a value of $x$ which makes a denominator zero.

For example, in part (b) of Example 14 you could choose $x = 1$ to check.

This makes the expression in the question $\dfrac{5}{2} - 2 = \dfrac{1}{2}$ which checks

with the expression in the answer $\dfrac{3 - 2}{1^2(1 + 1)} = \dfrac{1}{2}$.

## Exercise 14G

1 Write each expression as a single fraction in its lowest terms.

(a) $\dfrac{x}{5} + \dfrac{2x}{5}$      (b) $\dfrac{1}{x} + \dfrac{1}{y}$      (c) $\dfrac{2}{x} + \dfrac{3}{5x}$

(d) $\dfrac{2x}{3} + \dfrac{x}{4}$      (e) $\dfrac{a-1}{3} + \dfrac{a+2}{4}$      (f) $\dfrac{x+3}{2} - \dfrac{2x-1}{5}$

(g) $\dfrac{2}{x+1} - \dfrac{1}{x+2}$      (h) $\dfrac{1}{x} + \dfrac{1}{2-x}$      (i) $\dfrac{1}{2} + \dfrac{2}{y-5}$

2 Find the LCM for the denominators

(a) 6 and 9                  (b) $x^2$ and $x(x-1)$

(c) $4(x-1)(x+1)$ and $6(x+1)$      (d) $x^3(1-x)$ and $x^2(1+x)$

3 Write each expression as a single fraction in its lowest terms.

(a) $\dfrac{a}{6} + \dfrac{a}{9}$            (b) $\dfrac{2}{x^2} - \dfrac{1}{x(x-1)}$

(c) $\dfrac{x}{4(x-1)(x+1)} - \dfrac{1}{6(x+1)}$    (d) $\dfrac{2}{x^3(1-x)} - \dfrac{1}{x^2(1+x)}$

4 Winston was asked to write

$$\dfrac{6}{(x-2)} - \dfrac{4}{(x+2)}$$

as a single fraction in its lowest terms. In his solution he has made two mistakes.

Find where these errors occur and write a correct solution.

$$\dfrac{6}{(x-2)} - \dfrac{4}{(x+2)} \qquad LCM = (x-2)(x+2)$$

$$= \dfrac{6(x+2)}{(x-2)(x+2)} - \dfrac{4(x-2)}{(x+2)(x-2)} = \dfrac{6(x+2) - 4(x-2)}{(x-2)(x+2)}$$

$$= \dfrac{6x+12-4x-8}{(x-2)(x+2)} = \dfrac{2x+4}{(x-2)(x+2)} = \dfrac{2(\cancel{x+2})}{(x-2)(\cancel{x+2})}$$

$$= \dfrac{\overset{1}{\cancel{2}}}{x - \underset{1}{\cancel{2}}} = \dfrac{1}{x-1}$$

## 14.9 Factorising

Chapter 2 introduces factorisation as the opposite of expanding brackets. For example, here is how to factorise $2a^2 + 6a$:

$$2a^2 + 6a = 2 \times a \times a + 2 \times 3 \times a$$

The highest common factor (HCF) of the two terms is $2 \times a$, so $2a$ will go outside the brackets:

$$2a^2 + 6a = 2a(a+3)$$

This section shows you how to factorise more complicated algebraic expressions. In each case the first step is to 'take out' the HCF.

Another way of thinking about this is to see the factors as the lengths of the sides of rectangles. Products such as $2a^2$ are the areas of rectangles.

For a reminder on how to find the HCF see Section 1.1.

---

**Example 15**

Factorise the expression $14ax^3 + 7x^2$.

$14ax^3 + 7x^2$ ———————— Look for common factors of the terms $14ax^3$ and $7x^2$.

$= 7x^2(2ax + 1)$ ———————— $7x^2$ is a common factor so it can be taken outside the bracket.

---

**Example 16**

Factorise the expression $cd^2 + 5c$.

$cd^2 + 5c$ ———————— Look for common factors of the terms $cd^2$ and $5c$.

$= c(d^2 + 5)$ ———————— $c$ is a common factor so it can be taken outside the bracket.

---

## Exercise 14H

Factorise each of these expressions.

1  (a)  $8x^2 + 4x$        (b)  $6p^2 + 3p$        (c)  $6x^2 - 3x$

   (d)  $3b^2 - 9b$        (e)  $12a + 3a^2$        (f)  $15c - 10c^2$

   (g)  $21x^4 + 14x^3$     (h)  $16y^3 - 12y^2$     (i)  $6d^4 - 4d^2$

2  (a)  $ax^2 + ax$        (b)  $pr^2 - pr$        (c)  $ab^2 - ab$

   (d)  $qr^2 - q^2$        (e)  $a^2x + ax^2$        (f)  $b^2y - by^2$

   (g)  $6a^3 - 9a^2$        (h)  $8x^3 - 4x^4$        (i)  $18x^3 + 12x^5$

3  (a)  $12a^2b + 18ab^2$        (b)  $4x^2y - 2xy^2$

   (c)  $4a^2b + 8ab^2 + 12ab$        (d)  $4x^2y + 6xy^2 - 2xy$

   (e)  $12ax^2 + 6a^2x - 3ax$        (f)  $a^2bc + ab^2c + abc^2$

Don't forget to check your solutions.

# 14.10 Factorising by pairing

An expression such as $ab + cd + bc + ad$ can be factorised by pairing terms that have common factors:

$ab + cd + bc + ad = ab + bc + ad + cd$ ———————— Put terms in pairs that have common factors.

$= b(a + c) + d(a + c)$ ———————— Bracket term must be a factor of both pairs.

$= (a + c)(b + d)$ ———————— $(a + c)$ is a facor of both pairs.
$(a + c)(b + d)$ is the same as $(b + d)(a + c)$.

---

**Example 17**

Factorise $5a(x - y) + (y - x)$ completely.

$5a(x - y) + (y - x) = 5a(x - y) - 1(x - y)$ ———————— $(y - x) = -1(x - y)$

$= (x - y)(5a - 1)$ ———————— $(x - y)$ is a common factor.

**Example 18**

Factorise $2ab - 12cd + 6ac - 4bd$ completely.

$2ab - 12cd + 6ac - 4bd$

$\quad = 2[ab - 6cd + 3ac - 2bd]$ —————— 2 is the HCF.

$\quad = 2[ab + 3ac - 2bd - 6cd]$ —————— Group in pairs that have a common factor.

$\quad = 2[a(b + 3c) - 2d(b + 3c)]$ —————— Factorise in pairs to get $(b + 3c)$ as a common factor.

$\quad = 2(b + 3c)(a - 2d)$

> Before factorising the second pair, leave a space then write in the bracket term like this:
>
> $\quad 2[a(b + 3c) \; ? \; ? \; (b + 3c)]$
>
> That should help you find the correct common factor and correct sign.

## Exercise 14I

Factorise each expression completely.

| | | | |
|---|---|---|---|
| **1** | $x(p + q) + y(p + q)$ | **2** | $3(x + y) - z(x + y)$ |
| **3** | $5(x - y) + x(y - x)$ | **4** | $10(a - b) - 2x(b - a)$ |
| **5** | $xy + 2x + zy + 2z$ | **6** | $ay + 2b + 2ab + y$ |
| **7** | $x - b - x^2 + bx$ | **8** | $x^2 + yz - xy - zx$ |
| **9** | $2ab - 10 + 2a - 10b$ | **10** | $3a - 3ab + 6bc - 6c$ |

# 14.11 Factorising quadratic expressions

$2x^2 - 5x + 4$, $3x^2 - 27$, $y^2 + 20y$ and $t^2$ are all examples of quadratic expressions.

> An expression of the form $ax^2 + bx + c$, with $a \neq 0$, is called a **quadratic expression** in $x$.

The expression $3y^2 - 20y$ is a quadratic expression in $y$.

> In the expression $ax^2 + bx + c$
> - the coefficient of $x^2$ is $a$
> - the coefficient of $x$ is $b$
> - the constant term is $c$.

> $c$ is a number.

**Example 19**

Write the quadratic expression in $x$ in which the coefficient of $x^2$ is 1, the coefficient of $x$ is $-2$ and the constant term is $-3$.

$\quad 1x^2 + (-2)x + (-3) = x^2 - 2x - 3$

To factorise quadratic expressions of the form $ax^2 + bx$, take out the HCF.

For example $3x^2 + 18x = 3x(x + 6)$.

Chapter 2 shows you how to expand expressions such as $(x - 3)(2x + 5)$ to get $2x^2 - x - 15$. You can reverse this process to factorise a quadratic expression.

## Factorising quadratic expressions of the form $ax^2 + bx + c$

### Example 20

Factorise $x^2 - 8x + 15$.

**Step 1**    Check the equation is in the form $ax^2 + bx + c$.

**Step 2**    Multiply the coefficient of $x^2$ by the constant term:

$$a \times c = 15$$

**Step 3**    Find the two factors of this product which add to give the coefficient of $x$.

Here the factors are $-3$ and $-5$.

> Factors of 15 are:
> 1 and 15    ✗
> 3 and 5    ✗
> −1 and −15  ✗
> −3 and −5  ✓

**Step 4**    Rewrite the $bx$ term using these two factors:

$$-3x - 5x$$

**Step 5**    Proceed as for factorising by pairing:

$$x^2 - 3x - 5x + 15 = x(x - 3) - 5(x - 3) = (x - 5)(x - 3)$$

To factorise $ax^2 + bx + c$, start by looking for two numbers whose product is $ac$ and whose sum is $b$.

### Example 21

Factorise $6x^2 - 45 - 3x$.

**Step 1**    Take out any HCF and apply the remaining steps to the other factor

$$3[2x^2 - 15 - x]$$

> The other factor is $2x^2 - 15 - x$

**Step 2**    Rearrange into the form $ax^2 + bx + c$

$$3[2x^2 - x - 15]$$

**Step 3**    Multiply the coefficient of $x^2$ by the **constant term**. Find the two factors of this product which add to give the **coefficient of $x$**

$$2 \times (-15) = -30$$

> The other factor is $2x^2 - 15 - x$
> Try:
> −30 and 1 ✗
> −15 and 2 ✗
> −10 and 3 ✗
> −6 and 5 ✓

**Step 4**    Rewrite the $bx$ term using these two factors:

$$3[2x^2 - 6x + 5x - 15]$$

**Step 5**    Proceed as for factorising by pairing:

$$3[2x(x - 3) + 5(x - 3)]$$
$$= 3[(x - 3)(2x + 5)]$$

---

**Example 22**

Factorise $14x - 6 - 4x^2$.

**Step 1**　$14x - 6 - 4x^2 = 2[7x - 3 - 2x^2]$ ——————— 2 is the HCF.

**Step 2**　　　　　　　　$= 2[-2x^2 + 7x - 3]$ ——————— Rearrange

**Step 3**　$(-2) \times (-3) = (+6)$

　　　　You need factors of $+6$ which add to $+7$.

　　　　　　　$(+2) + (+3) = 5$ ✘
　　　　　　　$(+6) + (+1) = +7$ ✔

　　　　$14x - 6 - 4x^2 = 2[-2x^2 + 7x - 3]$

**Step 4**　　　　　　　　$= 2[-2x^2 + 6x + 1x - 3]$

**Step 5**　　　　　　　　$= 2[-2x(x - 3) + 1(x - 3)]$

　　　　　　　　　　　$= 2[(x - 3)(-2x + 1)]$ •——

> This can also be expressed as:
> $2[(x - 3)(1 - 2x)]$　or
> $-2(x - 3)(2x - 1)$

---

**Example 23**

Find two numbers whose product $P$ is $-60$ and whose sum $S$ is $-7$.

The product is negative, so the two numbers must have different signs (and therefore one number must be odd and the other even).

The greater number must have the negative sign because the sum is negative.

Try:　$+1, -60$ ✘　　$+3, -20$ ✘
　　　　$+4, -15$ ✘　　$+5, -12$ ✔

---

## Exercise 14J

**1**　Factorise

　(a)　$x^2 + 3x$

　(b)　$8x + 24$

　(c)　$x^2 + 3x + 8x + 24$

　(d)　$x^2 + 6x$

　(e)　$2x + 12$

　(f)　$x^2 + 6x + 2x + 12$

　(g)　$x^2 - 5x$

　(h)　$8x - 40$

　(i)　$x^2 - 5x + 8x - 40$

　(j)　$x^2 + 5x + 3x + 15$

　(k)　$x^2 + 4x - 8x - 32$

　(l)　$x^2 - 6x - 2x + 12$

　(m)　$x^2 + 4x - 3x - 12$

　(n)　$x^2 + 15 + 3x + 5x$

　(o)　$x^2 + 63 - 7x - 9x$

> Your first step must be to look for the HCF.

**2**　Write the quadratic expression in $x$ in which the coefficient of $x^2$ is 1, the coefficient of $x$ is $-5$ and the constant term is $-6$.

**3** In each of the following, find two numbers whose product is $P$ and whose sum is $S$.

(a) $P = 6$, $S = -5$      (b) $P = 6$, $S = 7$

(c) $P = 12$, $S = -8$      (d) $P = 60$, $S = 19$

(e) $P = -24$, $S = -2$      (f) $P = -24$, $S = 10$

(g) $P = -48$, $S = -13$      (h) $P = -48$, $S = 8$

**4** Factorise

(a) $x^2 - 5x + 4$      (b) $x^2 + 7x + 10$

(c) $x^2 - 2x - 15$      (d) $5x + 6 + x^2$

(e) $10 - 11x + x^2$      (f) $y^2 - y - 12$

**5** Factorise each expression completely.

(a) $2x^2 - 5x + 3$      (b) $6x^2 + 42x + 60$

(c) $2y^2 - y - 10$      (d) $6a^2 + 10a + 4$

(e) $4x^2 - 5x - 6$      (f) $75 + 35x - 20x^2$

(g) $5x^2 + 3 - 16x$      (h) $x^4 + 5x^2 + 6$ ⟵ Let $x^2 = y$.

(i) $2x^4 + 14x^2 + 24$

**6** Factorise $x^{2n} + 9x^n + 8$. ⟵ Let $x^n = y$.

**7** Factorise $x^{4n+1} + 6x^{2n+1} + 8x$ completely. ⟵ Question 7 is harder than the others. Only attempt it if you are confident with factorising expressions.

After further practice, you may be able to factorise some of the quadratics more directly. Diagrams can help, as shown in the next example.

---

**Example 24**

Factorise $2x^2 + 7x - 15$.

You need to find factors of $-30$ whose sum is $+7$.

These are $+10$ and $-3$

$2x^2 + 7x - 15 = (2x\ \underline{?}\ \ \underline{?}\ )(x\ \underline{?}\ \ \underline{?}\ )$

$= (2x\ \underline{?}\ 3)(x\ \underline{?}\ 5)$

$= (2x - 3)(x + 5)$

| | $2x$ | |
|---|---|---|
| $x$ | $2x^2$ | |
| | | |

| | $2x$ | $-3$ |
|---|---|---|
| $x$ | $2x^2$ | $-3x$ |
| $5$ | $+10x$ | |

| | $2x$ | $-3$ |
|---|---|---|
| $x$ | $2x^2$ | $-3x$ |
| $5$ | $+10x$ | $-15$ |

## 14.12 The difference of two squares

The expression $x^2 - y^2$ is called a difference of two squares.
There is an easy way to factorise an expression like this.

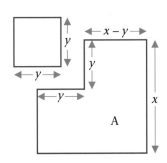

Here is a square of side $x$ with a square of side $y$ cut out of the top left corner. The part A which is left has an area $x^2 - y^2$.

Imagine cutting along the dotted line and moving the shaded piece B around to the bottom end of C.

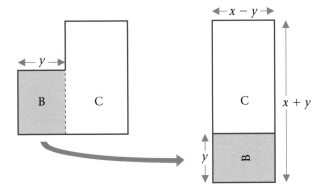

From the diagram you can see that

$$\text{area A} = \text{area B} + \text{area C}$$
$$= \text{area (B + C)}$$

and $\quad x^2 - y^2 = (x - y)(x + y)$

So to factorise the difference of two squares you can use

$$x^2 - y^2 = (x - y)(x + y)$$

**Example 25**

Factorise completely:

(a) $x^2 - 16$      (b) $3x^2 - 27$      (c) $18x^2 - 2(x + 5)^2$

(a) $x^2 - 16$
$$= x^2 - 4^2$$
$$= (x - 4)(x + 4)$$

(b) $3x^2 - 27$
$$= 3[x^2 - 9]$$
$$= 3[x^2 - 3^2]$$
$$= 3(x - 3)(x + 3)$$

(c) $18x^2 - 2(x + 5)^2$
$$= 2[9x^2 - (x + 5)^2]$$
$$= 2[(3x)^2 - (x + 5)^2]$$
$$= 2[3x - (x + 5)][3x + (x + 5)]$$
$$= 2(2x - 5)(4x + 5)$$

Two other results which you should memorise are:

$$x^2 + 2ax + a^2 = (x + a)^2$$

$$x^2 - 2ax + a^2 = (x - a)^2$$

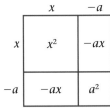

So, for example, putting $a = 6$ in $x^2 + 2ax + a^2 = (x + a)^2$ you get

$$x^2 + 12x + 36 = (x + 6)^2$$

## Exercise 14K

**1** Factorise each expression completely.

(a) $x^2 - 1$      (b) $x^2 - 25$      (c) $4x^2 - 9$

(d) $9x^2 - (x-3)^2$      (e) $2p^2 - 98$      (f) $2x^2 - 8y^2$

(g) $x^2 + 4x + 4$      (h) $x^2 - 6x + 9$      (i) $2x^2 + 28x + 98$

**2** Factorise each expression completely.

(a) $x^2 - 4$      (b) $x^2 - 3x$      (c) $x^2 - 3x - 4$

(d) $4x^2 - 36$      (e) $4x^2 - 70x$      (f) $4x^2 - 70x - 36$

(g) $x^2 + 2x + 1$      (h) $x^2 + 2x$      (i) $2x - 28 + 8x^2$

**3** Factorise these expressions in as straightforward a way as you can. Copy (a)–(f) which have been partly done for you and complete the blanks. Check your factors by mentally expanding your answers.

> For a reminder on expanding expressions involving brackets see Section 2.7.

(a) $x^2 - 5x + 4$ •————— $x^2 + 5x + 4 + (x - 4)(x \_\_\_\_)$

(b) $x^2 + 9x - 36$ •————— $x^2 + 9x - 36 = (x + 12)(\_\_\_\_)$

(c) $x^2 + 4x - 32$ •————— $x^2 + 4x - 32 = (x + 8)(\_\_\_\_)$

(d) $2x^2 - 7x + 5$ •————— $2x^2 - 7x + 5 = (x - 1)(\_\_\_\_)$

(e) $4x^2 - 3x - 7$ •————— $4x^2 - 3x - 7 = (\_\_\_\_ - 7)(\_\_\_\_ + 1)$

(f) $5x^2 - 7x - 6$ •————— $5x^2 - 7x - 6 = (5x \_\_\_\_)(\_\_\_\_)$

(g) $x^2 - 4x + 3$      (h) $y^2 + 7y + 10$      (i) $x^2 + 2x - 15$

(j) $x^2 - 4x - 21$      (k) $y^2 + 8y + 16$      (l) $4x^2 - 20x + 25$

(m) $5x^2 - 13x + 6$      (n) $4x^2 + x - 5$      (o) $5x^2 + 7x - 6$

# 14.13 Further fractional algebraic expressions

This section shows you how to combine the skills developed in the previous two sections to simplify expressions which contain more difficult algebraic fractions.

The steps to be taken to do this are:

**Step 1** Factorise all expressions completely.

**Step 2** Cancel fully.

**Step 3** Complete the fraction calculation.

**Example 26**

Simplify $\dfrac{2x-4}{x^2-5x+6} \div \dfrac{3x^2+9x}{x^2-9}$

$$\dfrac{2x-4}{x^2-5x+6} \div \dfrac{3x^2+9x}{x^2-9} = \dfrac{2(x-2)}{(x-3)(x-2)} \div \dfrac{3x(x+3)}{(x-3)(x+3)} \qquad \text{Step 1}$$

$$= \dfrac{2}{(x-3)} \div \dfrac{3x}{(x-3)} \qquad\qquad \text{Step 2}$$

$$= \dfrac{2}{(x-3)} \times \dfrac{(x-3)}{3x} \qquad\qquad \text{Multiply by the reciprocal.}$$

$$= \dfrac{2}{(x-3)} \times \dfrac{(x-3)}{3x} \qquad\qquad \text{Cancel by } (x-3).$$

$$= \dfrac{2}{3x}$$

**Example 27**

Write $\dfrac{6x-30}{2x^2-50} + \dfrac{21}{x^2+3x-10}$ as a single fraction.

$$\dfrac{6x-30}{2x^2-50} + \dfrac{21}{x^2+3x-10} = \dfrac{{}^{3}6(x-5)}{2(x-5)(x+5)} + \dfrac{21}{(x+5)(x-2)} \qquad \text{Factorise fully.}$$

$$= \dfrac{3}{(x+5)} + \dfrac{21}{(x+5)(x-2)} \qquad\qquad \text{Cancel by } 2(x-5).$$

$$= \dfrac{3(x-2)}{(x+5)(x-2)} + \dfrac{21}{(x+5)(x-2)} \qquad\qquad \text{LCM is } (x+5)(x-2).$$

$$= \dfrac{3(x-2)+21}{(x+5)(x-2)}$$

$$= \dfrac{3x+15}{(x+5)(x-2)}$$

$$= \dfrac{3(x+5)}{(x+5)(x-2)} \qquad\qquad\qquad \text{Factorise } 3x+15.$$

$$= \dfrac{3}{x-2}$$

> Take out the HCF, giving
> $2x^2-50 = 2(x^2-25)$
> Then use the difference of two squares for $x^2-25$

## Exercise 14L

Simplify each expression as fully as possible.

**1** $\dfrac{x^2-4}{2x-4}$

**2** $\dfrac{x^2-5x+4}{x^2-16}$

**3** $\dfrac{4x+8}{4x^2-8x} \div \dfrac{x^2-4}{x^2+2x}$

**4** $\dfrac{x^2+11x+18}{x^2+3x+2}$

**5** $\dfrac{x^2+6x+8}{x^2+4x}$

**6** $\dfrac{1}{x+1} - \dfrac{x-2}{x^2+3x+2}$

**7** $\dfrac{x^2-5x+4}{x^2-16} + \dfrac{x^2+11x+18}{x^2+6x+8}$

## Mixed exercise 14

**1** Simplify (a) $\dfrac{x^6}{x^2}$  (b) $(y^4)^3$  (c) $(m^{-4})^{-2}$  (d) $2t^2 \times 3r^3t^4$    [E]

**2** Factorise each expression fully.
  (a) $2p^2 - 4pq$   (b) $(p + q)^2 + 5(p + q)$   (c) $x^2 + 7x + 6$

**3** Factorise (a) $3x^2 + 6xy$   (b) $2(x - 5)^2 + 3(x - 5)$

**4** Simplify (a) $\dfrac{3(y + 2)}{(y + 2)^2}$  (b) $\dfrac{3x - 3}{x^2 - 1}$

**5** Simplify $\dfrac{4x^2 - 9}{2x^2 - 5x + 3}$

**6** Simplify $\dfrac{2}{x + 1} + \dfrac{3}{x - 1} - \dfrac{5}{x^2 - 1}$

**7** Simplify (a) $p^2 \times p^7$   (b) $x^8 \div x^3$   (c) $\dfrac{y^4 \times y^3}{y^5}$    [E]

**8** Evaluate (a) $3^{-2}$   (b) $36^{\frac{1}{2}}$   (c) $27^{\frac{2}{3}}$   (d) $\left(\dfrac{16}{81}\right)^{-\frac{3}{4}}$    [E]

**9** (a) Factorise $9x^2 - 6x + 1$

  (b) Simplify $\dfrac{6x^2 + 7x - 3}{9x^2 - 6x + 1}$    [E]

**10** Simplify $\dfrac{5}{x - 1} - \dfrac{5}{x^2 - 3x + 2}$

**11** Simplify $\dfrac{4x^2 - 25}{4x^2 + 8x - 5}$

**12** For the identity $(px + 3)^2 - 2x^2 + qx = 7x^2 + 12x + r$ find the values of $p$, $q$ and $r$.

**13** $p$ is a prime number not equal to 7.
  (a) Write down the HCF of $49p$ and $7p^2$.
  (b) $x$ and $y$ are different prime numbers
    (i) Write down the HCF of the two expressions $x^2y$ and $xy^2$.
    (ii) Write down the LCM of the two expressions $x^2y$ and $xy^2$.
    [E]

**14** Find the value of $k$ in
  (a) $4^k = 64$   (b) $x^k = x^2 \div \dfrac{1}{x^5}$   (c) $\dfrac{1}{9} = 3^k$

# Summary of key points

1  In the expression $x^n$, the number $x$ is called the **base** and the number $n$ is called the **index** or power.

2  $x^1 = x$

3  $x^m \times x^n = x^{m+n}$

4  $(x^m)^n = x^{m \times n} = x^{mn}$

5  $x^m \div x^n = x^{m-n}$

6  $x^0 = 1$ for all non-zero values of $x$.

7  $x^{-n} = \dfrac{1}{x^n}$

8  $x^{\frac{1}{n}} = \sqrt[n]{x}$

9  $x^{\frac{m}{n}} = (\sqrt[n]{x})^m$   or   $x^{\frac{m}{n}} = \sqrt[n]{x^m}$

10  Dividing by an algebraic fraction is equivalent to multiplying by its reciprocal.
For example, to divide by $\dfrac{a}{b}$ you can multiply by $\dfrac{b}{a}$.

11  $\dfrac{1}{n} + \dfrac{1}{m} = \dfrac{m+n}{mn}$

12  An expression of the form $ax^2 + bx + c$, with $a \neq 0$, is called a **quadratic expression** in $x$.

13  In the expression $ax^2 + bx + c$
   - the coefficient of $x^2$ is $a$
   - the coefficient of $x$ is $b$
   - the constant term is $c$.

14  To factorise $ax^2 + bx$, take out the highest common factor (HCF).

15  To factorise $ax^2 + bx + c$, start by looking for two numbers whose product is $ac$ and whose sum is $b$.

16  $x^2 - y^2 = (x - y)(x + y)$ is called the **difference of two squares**.

17  $x^2 + 2ax + a^2 = (x + a)^2$

18  $x^2 - 2ax + a^2 = (x - a)^2$

# 15 Pythagoras' theorem

Pythagoras was a Greek mathematician and philosopher who lived during the sixth century BC. The theorem that carries his name, **Pythagoras' theorem**, is perhaps the best known theorem in the whole of mathematics. It is also extremely useful, very important and a regular feature in GCSE exam papers.

In this chapter you will use Pythagoras' theorem to find the lengths of sides in right-angled triangles.

## 15.1 Pythagoras' theorem

Pythagoras' theorem states that:

> For any **right-angled triangle**, the area of the square formed on the hypotenuse is equal to the sum of the areas of the squares formed on the other two sides.

In symbols:

$$c^2 = a^2 + b^2$$

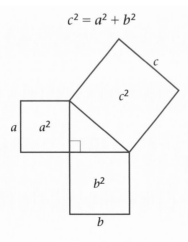

## Confirming the theorem

The area of the small square is 9 square units.

The area of the middle square is 16 square units.

The area of the large square is 25 square units.

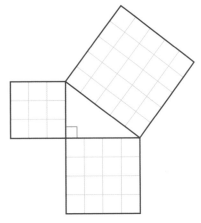

Area of small square + area of middle square = area of large square

$$9 \quad + \quad 16 \quad = \quad 25$$

## Exercise 15A

**1** On squared paper draw a right-angled triangle $PQR$ with the 90° angle at $Q$. Make $PQ = 4.5$ units and $QR = 6$ units.

Draw squares on the three sides of the triangle.

Confirm, by counting squares, that the area of the square drawn on the hypotenuse $PR$, that is the largest square, is

$$4.5^2 + 6^2 = 20.25 + 36 = 56.25 \text{ squares}$$

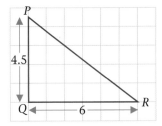

**2 (a)** Draw squares of side 5 cm, 12 cm and 13 cm on squared paper and cut them out.

**(b)** Draw triangle $PQR$ on squared paper, with $PQ = 5$ cm, $QR = 12$ cm and a right angle at $Q$.

**(c)** Use your cut-out squares to confirm that

$$\frac{\text{area of square}}{\text{on } PQ} + \frac{\text{area of square}}{\text{on } QR} = \frac{\text{area of square}}{\text{on } PR}$$

# 15.2 Finding lengths using Pythagoras' theorem

Pythagoras' theorem is used to find the length of one side of a right-angled triangle, when the other two lengths are known, using the formula $c^2 = a^2 + b^2$.

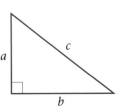

**Example 1**

Calculate the length of the side marked $x$.

$$x^2 = 24^2 + 7^2$$
$$= 576 + 49$$
$$= 625$$
$$x = \sqrt{625}$$
$$= 25 \text{ cm}$$

**Example 2**

In triangle $LMN$, angle $N = 90°$, $LN = 13$ cm and $MN = 7$ cm.

Calculate $LM$ correct to one decimal place.

First make a sketch.

$$c^2 = a^2 + b^2$$
$$LM^2 = NM^2 + NL^2$$
$$= 7^2 + 13^2$$
$$= 49 + 169$$
$$= 218$$

So $\quad LM = \sqrt{218}$
$$= 14.8 \text{ cm (to 1 d.p.)}$$

> The side opposite the right angle is the **hypotenuse**.

$\sqrt{218}$ is not a square number, so $\sqrt{218}$ cannot be worked out exactly as an ordinary number. It is a non-terminating decimal number.

However $\sqrt{218}$ is an exact value. A number written like this (the square root of an integer) is called a **surd**. A surd is always the positive square root.

> For more on surds see Chapter 23 (in Book 2).

If you were not allowed to use a calculator, you could leave your answer in surd notation as $\sqrt{218}$ cm.

## Exercise 15B

1 Calculate the lengths marked with letters in these triangles:

(a)

(b)

(c)

(d)

2 Give your answers correct to one decimal place.

(a) Find $YZ$.

(b) Find $SU$.

**(c)** Find *JL*.

**(d)** Find *AC*.

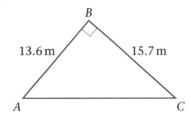

**3** A rectangle measures 10 cm by 24 cm.
Calculate the length of a diagonal.

**4** The diagonal of a square has a length
of 20 cm.
Calculate the length of a side of the square.

## 15.3 Using Pythagoras' theorem to find one of the shorter sides of a triangle

You can use the formula $a^2 + b^2 = c^2$ to calculate the longest side $c$
of a right-angled triangle. If you need to find one of the shorter sides
($a$, for example) it is easier to change the formula so that $a^2$ is on its
own on one side.

Pythagoras' theorem states that

$$a^2 + b^2 = c^2$$

Subtract $b^2$ from both sides:

$$a^2 + b^2 - b^2 = c^2 - b^2$$
$$a^2 = c^2 - b^2$$

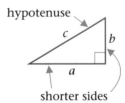

---

**Example 3**

In triangle *DEF*, angle *F* is a right angle, *DF* = 5 cm and *DE* = 7 cm.
Calculate the length of *EF*.

$$a^2 = c^2 - b^2$$
$$EF^2 = 7^2 - 5^2$$
$$= 49 - 25$$
$$= 24$$

So    $EF = \sqrt{24}$

$$= 4.898... = 4.9 \text{ cm (correct to 1 d.p.)}$$

> Always check that the
> hypotenuse is still the
> longest side. If not, look
> for your mistake.

## Exercise 15C

**1** Calculate the lengths marked with letters in these triangles.

(a)

(b)

(c)

(d)

**2** Give your answers correct to one decimal place.

(a) Find *OP*.

(b) Find *RS*.

(c) Find *TV*.

(d) Find *XY*.

**3** An isosceles triangle *XYZ* has *XY* = 26 cm, *ZX* = 26 cm and *ZY* = 18 cm.

Calculate the height of triangle *XYZ*.

**4**

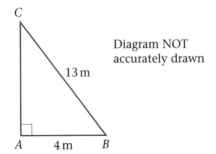

Diagram NOT accurately drawn

*ABC* is a right-angled triangle. *AB* is of length 4 m and *BC* is of length 13 m.

Calculate the length of *AC*. [E]

**5** A ladder extends to 10 metres in length and is placed 2 metres from a vertical wall on horizontal ground. How high up the wall will the ladder reach, to the nearest centimetre?

10 m

2 m

**6** A yacht leaves a port, $P$, and travels 43 km due South to a buoy, $B$.

At $B$ the yacht turns due East and travels to a lighthouse, $L$.

At $L$, the yacht turns again and travels in a straight line back to $P$.

The straight line distance from $L$ to $P$ is 54 km.

Calculate the total distance travelled by the yacht.

## 15.4 Pythagoras' theorem applied twice

Sometimes you need to find the length of one side before you can find the length of another side. You may need to apply Pythagoras' theorem twice.

---

**Example 4**

Calculate the lengths marked $x$ and $y$.

First   $x^2 = 3^2 + 4^2$
         $= 9 + 16$
         $x = \sqrt{25}$
         $= 5$ cm

Then   $y^2 + x^2 = 13^2$
        $y^2 + 5^2 = 13^2$
        $y^2 + 25 = 169$
        $\quad y^2 = 169 - 25$
        $\quad y = \sqrt{144}$
        $\quad\quad = 12$ cm

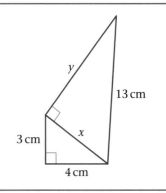

13 cm

3 cm

4 cm

---

### Exercise 15D

**1** Calculate each of the lengths marked with a letter.

**(a)**

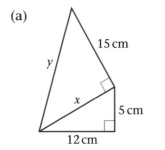

15 cm

$y$

$x$

5 cm

12 cm

**(b)**

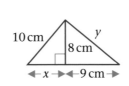

10 cm

8 cm

$y$

$x$   9 cm

**(c)**

41 cm

$x$

$y$

40 cm   50 cm

# 15.5 The distance between two points

**Example 5**

*A* is the point with coordinates (2, 1).
*B* is the point with coordinates (8, 9).

Find the straight line distance from *A* to *B*.

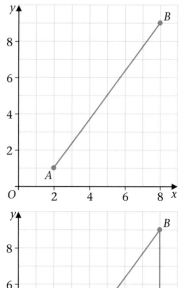

This can be done using Pythagoras' theorem.
First we make a triangle *ABM*, where the angle at
*M* is 90°, *M* is horizontally across from *A* and
vertically below *B*.

$AM = 6$ units    $BM = 8$ units

Using Pythagoras' theorem:   $AB^2 = AM^2 + BM^2$

$$= 6^2 + 8^2$$
$$= 36 + 64$$
$$= 100$$
$$AB = 10 \text{ units}$$

The distance between two points on a
coordinate grid is

$$d = \sqrt{(x_2 - x_1)^2 + (y_2 - y_1)^2}$$

# Exercise 15E

1   Work out the distance between the
    points *P* and *Q*.

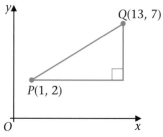

2   Calculate the distance between the points in each pair.

   (a)   (1, 2) and (5, 5)      (b)   (3, 5) and (5, 9)

   (c)   (−1, 4) and (7, 12)   (d)   (−2, 6) and (9, −4)

   (e)   (8, −3) and (12, −6)  (f)   (−2, −3) and (−7, 8)

> You may find it helpful to
> make a sketch first.

**3** Calculate the distance *PQ*.

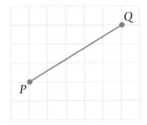

> Each square of the grid is
> 1 unit by 1 unit.

## 15.6 Non right-angled triangles

### When all angles are acute

The labels *L*, *M* and *S* are used to indicate
the lengths of the longest side, the middle
side and the shortest side, respectively.

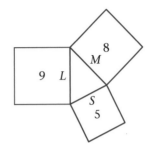

The area of the largest square is
9 square units.
The area of the middle square is
8 square units.
The area of the smallest square is
5 square units.

> In a triangle with sides of length *L* (longest), *M* (middle) and
> *S* (shortest), if $L^2 < M^2 + S^2$ then the angles are all acute.

### When one angle is obtuse

In this diagram one angle is obtuse, and *L*, the longest side, is
opposite this angle.

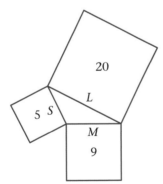

The area of the largest square is 20 square units.
The area of the middle square is 9 square units.
The area of the smallest square is 5 square units.

> In a triangle with sides of length *L* (longest), *M* (middle) and
> *S* (shortest), if $L^2 > M^2 + S^2$ then one angle is obtuse.

___ **Example 6** ___

The lengths of the sides of a triangle are 3 cm, 5 cm and 6 cm.

Work out whether the angles of this triangle are all acute, whether one is obtuse or whether one is a right angle.

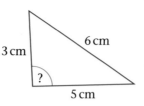

The longest side, $L = 6$ cm

The middle side, $M = 5$ cm

The shortest side, $S = 3$ cm

$$L^2 = 6^2 = 36 \qquad M^2 = 5^2 = 25 \qquad S^2 = 3^2 = 9$$

$$M^2 + S^2 = 25 + 9 = 34$$

so $\quad L^2 > M^2 + S^2$

So one of the angles is obtuse.

## Exercise 15F

**1** You will need some squared paper. On it draw

    **(a)** a triangle where all angles are acute

    **(b)** a triangle where one angle is obtuse.

Using the symbols $L$, $M$ and $S$ for the longest, middle and shortest sides respectively, convince yourself that in case (a) $L^2 < M^2 + S^2$ and in case (b) $L^2 > M^2 + S^2$.

**2** The numbers in the brackets are the lengths in centimetres of the sides of triangles.

In each case, work out whether the angles of the triangle are all acute, whether one angle is obtuse or whether the triangle is right-angled.

> When
> $L^2 = M^2 + S^2$
> the triangle is **right-angled**.

    **(a)** (4, 7, 9)      **(b)** (5, 11, 12)      **(c)** (3, 14, 15)

    **(d)** (9, 41, 40)      **(e)** (17, 10, 13)      **(f)** (8, 8, 12)

## 15.7 Pythagorean triples

Any set of three numbers, usually positive whole numbers $(a, b, c)$, which satisfy (fit into) the relationship

$$c^2 = a^2 + b^2 \text{ (assuming } c \text{ to be the largest)}$$

is known as a **Pythagorean triple**.

The two most famous Pythagorean triples are

    (3, 4, 5)    and    (5, 12, 13)

They are worth remembering.

## Exercise 15G

1   Check that (3, 4, 5) and (5, 12, 13) are Pythagorean triples.

2   Which of the following are Pythagorean triples?
    Show all your working.

   (a)   (6, 8, 10)    (b)   (7, 24, 25)    (c)   (9, 40, 41)

   (d)   (8, 23, 30)    (e)   (11, 60, 61)    (f)   (1, 1, 2)

# 15.8 Pythagoras' theorem in three dimensions

You can use Pythagoras' theorem in three dimensions to find the length of the longest diagonal of a cuboid.

> The longest diagonal is often called a **space diagonal**.

### Example 7

A cuboid measures 4 cm by 5 cm by 8 cm.
Work out the length of the longest diagonal of this cuboid.

One of the longest diagonals is *HB*.

By Pythagoras' theorem:

$$HB^2 = HD^2 + DB^2$$

$HD = 8$

> The four diagonals *HB*, *GA*, *EC* and *FD* are all equal. You can find the length of any one.

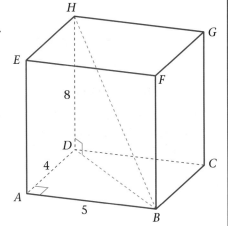

To find the length of *DB*, look at the base *ABCD*.

Using Pythagoras' theorem:   $DB^2 = AB^2 + AD^2$
$$= 5^2 + 4^2$$
$$= 25 + 16$$
$$DB^2 = 41$$

*HB* can now be found:   $HB^2 = HD^2 + DB^2$
$$= 8^2 + 41$$
$$= 64 + 41$$
$$= 105$$
$$= \sqrt{105}$$
$$= 10.25 \text{ cm (to 2 d.p.)}$$

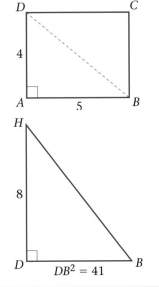

The length of the longest diagonal of a cuboid with dimensions $a$, $b$, $c$ is

$$d = \sqrt{a^2 + b^2 + c^2}$$

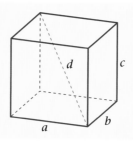

## Exercise 15H

1  Calculate the length of the longest diagonal of a cuboid which has sides of length 5 cm, 8 cm and 12 cm.

2  Calculate the length of the longest diagonal of a cuboid which has sides of length 6.2 mm, 8.3 mm and 15.1 mm.

3  $VABC$ is a triangle-based pyramid.

   The base $ABC$ is a triangle, right-angled at $A$. The vertex $V$ is vertically above $A$. $AB = 5$ cm, $AC = 12$ cm and $VA = 17$ cm.

   **(a)**  Calculate the lengths of    **(i)** $BC$    **(ii)** $VB$    **(iii)** $VC$.

   **(b)**  Work out whether the angle $BVC$ is acute, obtuse or a right angle.

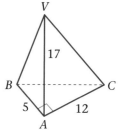

# 15.9 The equation of a circle

___ Example 8 ___

Find the equation of the circle with centre at the origin (0, 0) and radius 3 units.

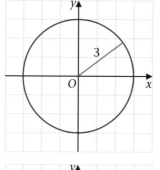

Mark any general point, $P$, on the circle, with coordinates $(x, y)$.

Using Pythagoras' theorem:

$$x^2 + y^2 = 3^2 \ (= 9)$$

The result will be true for *every* point on the circle.

The *equation* of this circle is

$$x^2 + y^2 = 3^2 \quad \text{or} \quad x^2 + y^2 = 9$$

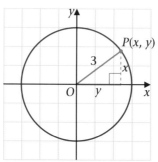

The equation of any circle, centre the origin and radius $r$ units is

$$x^2 + y^2 = r^2$$

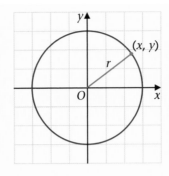

## Exercise 15I

**1** Write down the equation of each circle.

(a)

(b)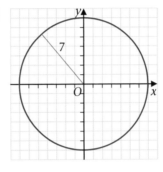

**2** Find the equation of the circle
  (a)  radius 5 units, centre the origin
  (b)  radius 12 units, centre the origin
  (c)  radius 15 units, centre the origin.

**3** A circle has its centre at the origin and passes through the point (5, 12).
    Find the equation of this circle.

**4** A circle of radius 5 units is drawn with its centre at the origin.
    Find the coordinates of 8 points which lie on the circle and have integer values for their coordinates.

## Mixed exercise 15

**1** Calculate the length $PQ$.

**2** The diagram shows a ladder of length 8 metres resting between horizontal ground and a vertical wall.

The distance from the base of the wall to the bottom of the ladder is 5 metres.

Calculate the height of the top of the ladder above the ground.

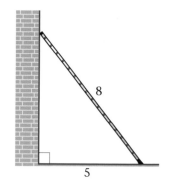

**3** A yacht leaves a harbour, *H*, and travels due North for an unknown distance until it reaches a marker buoy, *B*.

At *B* the yacht turns due East and travels for 30 km to a lighthouse, *L*.

At *L* the yacht turns again and travels in a straight line back to *H*. The distance from *L* to *H* is recorded as 43 km.

Calculate the distance from *H* to *B*.

**4** Calculate the lengths marked *x* and *y*.

**5** Points *A* and *B* have coordinates $(-3, 7)$ and $(5, -4)$, respectively. Calculate the distance *AB*.

**6** *ABC* is a triangle.
$AB = 7$ cm      $AC = 8$ cm      and      $BC = 11$ cm
Work out whether the angles of *ABC* are all acute, whether one is obtuse or whether the triangle is right-angled.

**7** Showing all your working, explain which of these sets are Pythagorean triples:
   (a)   (4, 6, 8)
   (b)   (10, 24, 26)
   (c)   (1, 2, 3)

**8** A cuboid measures 8 cm by 12 cm by 15 cm.
Calculate the length of the longest diagonal of the cuboid.

9    *ABCDEF* is a prism.

The horizontal base *ABCD* is a rectangle with *AB* = 12 cm and *BC* = 20 cm.
The vertical face *ADEF* is also a rectangle with *AF* = 5 cm.
Angles *FAB* and *EDC* are right angles.
Calculate the lengths

(a)   *FB*          (b)   *BD*          (c)   *FC*.

10   Calculate the value of *x*.

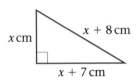

11   Find the equation of the circle with radius 4 units, centre the origin.

12   A circle has its centre at the origin and passes through the point (8, 15). Write down the equation of this circle.

13   **A special challenge**
Pythagoras' theorem states that for squares *A*, *B* and *C*,

area of *C* = area of *A* + area of *B*

But do the shapes drawn on the sides of the right-angled triangle have to be squares? Justify your answer.

This challenge question is outside the GCSE specification for Pythagoras' theorem. You can try it if you have completed all the other work on Pythagoras.

# Summary of key points

1   For any **right-angled triangle**, the area of the square formed on the hypotenuse is equal to the sum of the areas of the squares formed on the other two sides:

$$c^2 = a^2 + b^2$$

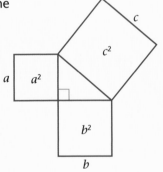

2   The distance between two points on a coordinate grid is

$$d = \sqrt{(x_2 - x_1)^2 + (y_2 - y_1)^2}$$

3   In a triangle with sides of length *L* (longest), *M* (middle) and *S* (shortest):
   • if   $L^2 < M^2 + S^2$     the angles are acute
   • if   $L^2 > M^2 + S^2$     the angle is obtuse
   • if   $L^2 = M^2 + S^2$     one angle is a right angle.

**4** Some well-known Pythagorean triples are

$$(3, 4, 5) \quad (5, 12, 13) \quad (6, 8, 10) \quad (7, 24, 25)$$

**5** The length of the longest diagonal of a cuboid with dimensions $a$, $b$, $c$  is

$$d = \sqrt{a^2 + b^2 + c^2}$$

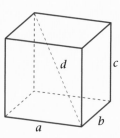

**6** The equation of any circle, centre the origin and radius $r$ units is

$$x^2 + y^2 = r^2$$

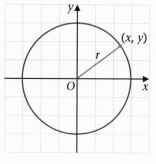

# Answers

## Chapter 1 Exploring numbers 1

### Exercise 1A

1. (a) 1, 2, 3, 4, 6, 8, 12, 24
   (b) 1, 2, 3, 4, 6, 9, 12, 18, 36
   (c) 1, 2, 4, 7, 11, 14, 22, 28, 44, 77, 154, 308
   (d) 1, 7, 11, 13, 77, 91, 143, 1001
   (e) 1, 2, 4, 5, 7, 8, 10, 14, 20, 25, 28, 35, 40, 50, 56, 70, 100, 140, 175, 200, 280, 350, 700, 1400
   (f) 1, 53
2. 2, 3, 5, 7, 11, 13, 17, 19, 23, 29, 31, 37, 41, 43, 47, 53, 59, 61, 67, 71, 73, 79, 83, 89, 97
3. Yes $2 + 3 = 5$, $2 + 5 = 7$, $2 + 11 = 13$ etc.
   One of the primes *must* be 2.
4. (a) $2^3 \times 3$ (b) $2^5$  (c) $2 \times 3^2$ (d) 13
   (e) $2^3 \times 3^2$ (f) $2 \times 5^2$ (g) $3^2 \times 11$ (h) $2^3 \times 3 \times 5$
5. (a) 4  (b) 3  (c) 6  (d) 12  (e) 36  (f) 28
6. (a) 12  (b) 12  (c) 14  (d) 30  (e) 144  (f) 850
7. Every 120 seconds (2 minutes)
8. (a) (i) 60  (ii) 124  (iii) 217  (iv) 511  (v) 63
   (b) $p + 1$

   (d) $1 + p + p^2 + \ldots + p^n = \left(\dfrac{p^{n+1} - 1}{p - 1}\right)$

### Exercise 1B

1. (a) 64  (b) 343  (c) 144  (d) 1000
   (e) 1, 4, 9, 16, 25, 36, 49, 64, 81, 100, 121, 144
   (f) 1, 8, 27, 64, 125, 216, 343, 512
2. (a) (i) 1, 9, 49, 64  (ii) 1, 8, 64
   (b) (i) 4, 16  (ii) 27, 125
   (c) (i) 64, 81, 144  (ii) 64, 125
   (d) (i) 81, 100, 169  (ii) 125, 216

### Exercise 1C

1. (a) 169  (b) 12.25  (c) 1600  (d) 75.69
   (e) 384.16  (f) 3294.76
2. (a) 216  (b) 13.824  (c) 8000  (d) $-2.197$
   (e) 2406.104  (f) 47 437.928
3. (a) 11  (b) 15  (c) 130  (d) 1.7
   (e) 0.7  (f) 5.8
4. (a) 15.91  (b) 48.38  (c) 4.29  (d) 92.07
   (e) 5.43  (f) 1351.28
5. (a) 4.08  (b) 15.4  (c) 2.98  (d) $-2.10$
   (e) 9.59  (f) 187

### Exercise 1D

1. (a) 64  (b) 100 000  (c) 625  (d) 343
   (e) 20 736 (f) 0.590 49
2. (a) $10^3$  (b) $5^3$  (c) $2^9$  (d) $7^4$
   (e) $5^4$  (f) $3^9$
3. $64 = 2 \times 2 \times 2 \times 2 \times 2 \times 2 = 2^6 = 4 \times 4 \times 4 = 4^3$
4. $2^5$, by 7

### Exercise 1E

1. (a) $5^6 = 15\,625$  (b) $5^8 = 390\,625$  (c) $10^2 = 100$
   (d) $12^3 = 1728$  (e) $3^7 = 2187$  (f) 1
   (g) 1  (h) $5^{-2} = 0.04$  (i) 6
   (j) 150  (k) 14  (l) $4^6 = 2^{12} = 4096$
   (m) $5^9 = 1\,953\,125$  (n) $2^{10} = 1024$  (o) $3^{-4} = \frac{1}{81}$
   (p) $4^5 = 1024$  (q) $6^{-1} = \frac{1}{6}$  (r) $5^5 = 3125$

(s) $2^2 = 4$  (t) 4  (u) $5^{-6} = \frac{1}{15\,625}$
(v) $3^{-4} = \frac{1}{81}$  (w) $2^{-4} = \frac{1}{16}$  (x) $3^2 = 9$
2. $2^4 = 4^2$

### Exercise 1F

1. (a) 2  (b) $\frac{1}{2}$  (c) 8  (d) $\frac{1}{5}$  (e) 2  (f) $\frac{1}{2}$
   (g) $\frac{1}{8}$  (h) $\frac{1}{5}$  (i) $\frac{1}{10}$  (j) 10  (k) 125  (l) $\frac{1}{4}$
2. (a) $2^{10} = 1024$  (b) $3^2 = 9$  (c) 1
   (d) $5^0 = 1$  (e) 40  (f) $4^{-6} = \frac{1}{4096}$
   (g) $10^{-2} = \frac{1}{100}$  (h) $5^4 = 625$
3. (a) 3  (b) 5  (c) $\frac{1}{7}$  (d) 4  (e) 8  (f) $\frac{1}{100}$

### Exercise 1G

1. (a) 8  (b) $\frac{1}{4}$  (c) 0.0001  (d) 10 000 000 000
   (e) 800 000  (f) 400  (g) 0.008  (h) 3 200 000
   (i) 0.000 001  (j) $\frac{1}{256}$
2. 1000
3.

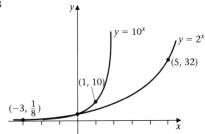

4. (a) $\frac{4}{5}$  (b) 1  (c) $-4$
5. $2^{n+1} - 1$

### Mixed exercise 1

1. $2^2 \times 3 \times 13$
2. (a) 6, 12  (b) 6, 90
3. (a) $2^3$  (b) $5^{-6}$
4. (a) 9  (b) 6  (c) $\frac{1}{6}$
5. (b) $n + 1$  (c) $\tau(n \times m) = \tau(n) \times t(m)$ if $n$, $m$ have no common factors except 1.
6. $n$th term $= (n - 1)$th term $+ (n - 3)$rd term
7. $1^3 + 2^3 + 3^3 + \ldots + n^3 = (1 + 2 + \ldots + n)^2$
8. (a) LD(square number) = 0, 1, 4, 5, 6, 9 only
   (b) LD$(n \times m) =$ LD [LD$(n) \times$ LD$(m)$]
   (c) Cannot because $10n + 7$ has LD = 7
9. (a) $\frac{12}{5}$  (b) $-\frac{4}{3}$  (c) $-\frac{5}{2}$  10. $\dfrac{5^{n+1} - 1}{4}$

## Chapter 2 Essential algebra

### Exercise 2A

1. (a) 13  (b) 17  (c) $-1$  (d) 2.5
   (e) 4  (f) 14  (g) $3\frac{2}{5}$  (h) 1.5
2. (a) 16  (b) 15  (c) 32
   (d) 9  (e) 15  (f) 14
3. (a) 35  (b) 8  (c) 6
   (d) 10  (e) 4  (f) $-5$
4. (a) 3  (b) 4  (c) 6  (d) 3  (e) 5

### Exercise 2B

1. (a) 101  (b) 47 (c) 14  (d) 147 (e) 23  (f) 6
2. (a) 19  (b) 33 (c) 27  (d) 20 (e) 16  (f) 7
3. (a) 44  (b) 10 (c) 16  (d) 20 (e) 30  (f) 3

## Exercise 2C

1 (a) $a^4$    (b) $b^5$    (c) $c^6$    (d) $y^4$
2 (a) $6a^2b^4$    (b) $10p^6q^4$    (c) $9x^4y^4$    (d) $3s^2t^5$

## Exercise 2D

1 (a) $2n + 6$    (b) $12p + 8$    (c) $2y^2 + 3y$
  (d) $2x^2 + 10x$    (e) $3n - 6$    (f) $2p - 3$
2 (a) $4n + 12$    (b) $2p - 8$    (c) $5a + 5$
  (d) $6x - 2$    (e) $20q - 12$    (f) $6r + 3s$
  (g) $ab + 2a$    (h) $p^2 + pq$    (i) $2p^2 - p$
3 (a) $3x + 18$    (b) $4y - 8$    (c) $7t + 7$
  (d) $12x + 8$    (e) $15y - 20$    (f) $6p + 2q$
  (g) $x^2 + 3x$    (h) $x^2 + xy$    (i) $3y^2 - 2y$
4 (a) $2m + 10$    (b) $9n - 36$    (c) $8u - 8$
  (d) $35x + 15$    (e) $4y^2 - 24y$    (f) $6x^4 + 15x^2$
  (g) $20t^5 - 12t^3$    (h) $12x^5 + 28x^2y$    (i) $15y^4 - 20yx^2$

## Exercise 2E

1 (a) $8r + 2$    (b) $2p - 6$    (c) $10x + y$    (d) $5m$
2 (a) $14a + 2b$    (b) $5p + q$    (c) $10r - 2s$    (d) $9p$
3 (a) $7x - y$    (b) $10m - 7n$    (c) $4p - 4q$    (d) $6p$
4 (a) $3a - 3b$    (b) $r^2 + r$    (c) $2mn$    (d) $3m + n$
5 (a) $3n + 2$    (b) $3n - 2$    (c) $2n - 4$
  (d) $3p + 5r$    (e) $r - 2q$    (f) $2r - s$

## Exercise 2F

1 (a) $a + 3b$    (b) $p + 5q$    (c) $2n - 1$
  (d) $4s - 4r$    (e) $6y$    (f) $rs - 3r$
2 (a) $x - 2y$    (b) $11x - 3y$    (c) $2x^2 - x$
  (d) $20y^2 - 23y + 6$    (e) $2x^2 - 9x + 10$    (f) $16y^4 + 9y^3$

## Exercise 2G

1   $5(x - 4)$     2   $8(x + 3)$     3   $6(2x + 3)$
4   $5(4x - 5)$     5   $8(x^2 - 3)$     6   $9(x^2 + 4)$
7   $5(2x^2 - 3)$     8   $x(x + 6)$     9   $x(x - 1)$
10   $p(x - 3)$     11   $q(x + q)$     12   $5x(x - 3)$
13   $3x(2x + 3)$     14   $5x(3x - 7)$     15   $4x(2 - 3x)$
16   $ax(x + 1)$     17   $2a(2x - 3)$     18   $3ax(2x + 5)$

## Exercise 2H

1 (a) $x^2 + 3x + 2$

   (b) $x^2 + 10x + 16$

   (c) $x^2 + 6x + 9$

   (d) $x^2 + ax + bx + ab$

2 (a) $ab + 3a + 4b + 12$    (b) $cd + 4c + 5d + 20$
  (c) $xy + 6x + 3y + 18$    (d) $a^2 + 11a + 24$
  (e) $b^2 + 11b + 28$    (f) $x^2 + 8x + 12$

3 (a) $2ab + 8a + 3b + 12$    (b) $3bc + 9b + 2c + 6$
  (c) $4cd + 24c + 3d + 18$    (d) $2a^2 + 11a + 15$
  (e) $3b^2 + 10b + 8$    (f) $4c^2 + 13c + 10$
4 (a) $ab - 3a - 4b + 12$    (b) $cd - 4c - 5d + 20$
  (c) $xy - 6x - 3y + 18$    (d) $a^2 - 11a + 24$
  (e) $b^2 - 11b + 28$    (f) $x^2 - 8x + 12$
5 (a) $ab + 3a - 4b - 12$    (b) $cd - 4c + 5d - 20$
  (c) $xy + 6x - 3y - 18$    (d) $a^2 + 5a - 24$
  (e) $b^2 - 3b - 28$    (f) $x^2 + 4x - 12$
6 (a) $2ab + 10a - 5b - 25$    (b) $3b^2 - 14b - 24$
  (c) $3c^2 - 11c + 6$    (d) $3a^2 - 19a + 20$
  (e) $3x^2 + 11x - 20$    (f) $2a^2 - 9a - 18$
7 (a) $2x^2 + 5xy + 3y^2$    (b) $3x^2 - xy - 4y^2$
  (c) $5x^2 - 8xy + 3y^2$    (d) $6x^2 + 23xy + 20y^2$
  (e) $6x^2 - 5xy - 25y^2$    (f) $12x^2 - 28xy + 15y^2$
8 (a) $x^2 + 6x + 9$    (b) $y^2 - 10y + 25$
  (c) $4x^2 + 4x + 1$    (d) $9y^2 - 24y + 16$
  (e) $9x^2 + 30xy + 25y^2$    (f) $36x^2 - 84xy + 49y^2$
9 (a) $3a^2 - 5a - 2$    (b) $12p^2 + 5p - 2$
  (c) $3a^2 + 5a + 2$    (d) $12p^2 + 14p + 4$
  (e) $2b^2 - 5b + 3$    (f) $8b^2 + 2b - 1$
10 (a) $2a + b + 2$    (b) $pq - p + q - 2$
  (c) $3r^2 - 5r - sr + 2s$    (d) $4p^2$
11 (a) $9x^2 - 1$    (b) $1 - 16x^2$
  (c) $4x^2 - 25$    (d) $49x^2 - 4$
12 (a) $5x^2 - 20x - 60$    (b) $4x^2 - 4$
  (c) $30x^2 + 4x - 2$    (d) $36x^2 - 3x - 18$

## Exercise 2I

1 $x^2 + 10x + 25$     2 $x^2 - 6x + 9$     3 $x^2 + 18x + 81$
4 $x^2 - 4x + 4$     5 $p^2 + 2pq + q^2$     6 $p^2 - 2pq + q^2$
7 $x^2 + 6x + 9$     8 $x^2 - 14x + 49$     9 $x^2 - 2ax + a^2$
10 (a) $(x + 4)^2 = x^2 + 8x + 16$
   (b) $(x - 10)^2 = x^2 - 20x + 100$
   (c) $(x + 1)^2 = x^2 + 2x + 1$
   (d) $(x - 12)^2 = x^2 - 24x + 144$

## Exercise 2J

1   $5$     2   $4$     3   $2\frac{1}{2}$     4   $2\frac{3}{5}$     5   $\frac{3}{7}$
6   $0$     7   $\frac{5}{6}$     8   $\frac{7}{9}$     9   $-3$     10   $-2$
11   $-2\frac{1}{2}$     12   $-2\frac{2}{5}$     13   $-\frac{5}{8}$     14   $-\frac{1}{2}$     15   $-\frac{2}{5}$
16   $1$     17   $-2$     18   $2$     19   $-4$     20   $-6$
21   $-2\frac{3}{5}$     22   $1\frac{1}{2}$     23   $\frac{1}{6}$     24   $-\frac{1}{4}$     25   $-1\frac{4}{5}$

## Mixed exercise 2

1 (a) $19$    (b) $9$    (c) $54$    (d) $90$    (e) $100$
  (f) $243$    (g) $6$    (h) $154$    (i) $4$    (j) $4\frac{1}{2}$
2 (a) $9a + 3b$    (b) $5ab$    (c) $4a - 3a^2$
  (d) $5p - 5q$    (e) $4d - c$
3 (a) $5p + 16$    (b) $12p + 5$    (c) $7a - 7b$    (d) $-11$
4   $pq - p^3$
5 (a) $y^2 + 2y - 15$       (b) $12x^2 + 11x + 2$
  (c) $25y^2 - 30y + 9$     (d) $9a^2 - 12ab + 4b^2$
6 (a) $24$   (b) $4$    (c) $12$   (d) $\frac{3}{5}$    (e) $-5$    (f) $5$
7 (a) $2(2p - 3)$    (b) $3(3q + 1)$    (c) $2(3a + 2b)$
  (d) $a(b + a)$    (e) $2a(b + c)$    (f) $2a(4a - 3)$

# Chapter 3 Shapes

## Exercise 3A

1 (a) $a = 48°$    (b) $b = 106°$,   $c = 74°$,   $d = 74°$
  (c) $e = 111°$    (d) $f = 60°$,   $g = 120°$    (e) $h = 51\frac{3}{7}°$
2 (a) $a = 35°$,   $b = 50°$,   $c = 50°$,   $d = 95°$
  (b) $e = 68°$,   $f = 68°$    (c) $g = 149°$,   $h = 125°$   $i = 55°$

## Exercise 3B

1 $a = 35°$ (interior angles of a triangle)
2 $b = 35°$ (interior angles of a triangle)
3 $c = 70°$ (interior angles of a triangle)
  $d = 110°$ (angles on a straight line)
4 $e = 52°$ (angles on a straight line)
  $f = 85°$ (interior angles of a triangle)
5 $g = 47°$ (corresponding angles)
  $h = 101°$ (interior angles of a triangle)
  $i = 101°$ (corresponding angles)

## Exercise 3C

1 (a) isosceles triangle    (b) parallelogram
  (c) parallelogram         (d) square
2 (a) $1440°$               (b) $144°$

## Exercise 3D

$a + b + c = d + e + f = 180°$
$a + b + c + d + e + f = 360°$

## Exercise 3E

1

2     3

4 (a)    plan    front    side    (b)    plan    front    side

5 (a)     (b)    (c)

6

7 (a)     (b)

Side
elevation

8

Plan

Scale 1 cm : 2 cm

Front
elevation

Side
elevation

## Exercise 3F

1 (a) No. Only the angles are equal. The corresponding sides
      may not be the same length.
  (b) Yes. $PQRS = TUVW$
      Corresponding angles and sides are equal.
  (c) Yes. $XYZ = NLM$ (RHS)
2 (a) $ABC, YZX$ (SAS)        (b)  $ABC, EFD$ (AAS)
  (c) $XYZ, QRP$ (RHS)
3 $AB = CD$ (opposite sides of a parallelogram)
  $AD = BC$ (opposite sides of a parallelogram)
  $BD = BD$ (common)
  Triangles $ABD, CDB$ are congruent (SSS)
4 $BC = BD - CD$
  $DE = CE - CD$
  But $BD = CE$ (given)
  $\therefore BC = DE$
  $CA = AD$ (given)
  $\angle BCA = 180° - \angle ACD$
  $\angle ADE = 180° - \angle ADC$
  But $\angle ACD = \angle ADC$ (base angles of an isosceles $\triangle$)
  $\therefore \angle BCA = \angle ADE$
  Triangles $ABC, ADE$ are congruent (SAS)
5 $\angle ABC = \angle ACB$ (base angles of isosceles $\triangle$)
  $\angle ABC = \angle ADE$ (corresponding angles)
  $\angle ACB = \angle AED$
  $\angle ADE = \angle AED$ and $ADE$ is isosceles
  $\angle AD = \angle AE$
  Triangles $ACD$ and $ABE$ are congruent (SAS)
6 $\angle ABE = 180° - 2 \times \angle AEB$ (3rd angle in an isosceles $\triangle$)
  $\angle DBC = 180° - 2 \times \angle BDC$
  But $\angle AEB = \angle BDC$
  $\therefore \angle ABE = \angle DBC$
  $\angle ABD = \angle ABE + \angle EBD$
  $\angle EBC = \angle DBC + \angle EBD$
  Therefore $\angle ABD = \angle EBC$
           $AB = EB$ (given)
           $BD = BC$ (given)
  Triangles $ABD, EBC$ are congruent (SAS)
7 Yes, $ABC = FED$ (RHS)
  $AB = 4$ cm (Pythagoras' theorem)

**Activity**
For example:

## Exercise 3G

1 (a) 4 (b) 2.34 (c) 19.8 (d) $d = 6.72$, $e = 4.8$
2 (a) $x = 1.5$, $y = 3$ (b) 12.8
(c) $x = 3.75$, $y = 5.25$, $z = 6.75$
3 A and C   B and E   D and F
4 squares   circles   equilateral triangles   regular hexagons
5 cubes   spheres   tetrahedrons   octahedrons
6 (a) (ii) (b) (iii) (c) (iii)
7 (a) Two pairs of sides in same ratio, included angle equal.
  $x = 4.72$
(b) All corresponding angles equal.
  $y = 1.8$
(c) All corresponding angles equal.
  $a = 7.68$, $b = 9.6$
8 (a) All corresponding angles equal.
(b) $x = 3.2$, $y = 2.625$

## Exercise 3H

1 (a) 4 (b) 9 (c) infinite
2

3 (a)

(b) 3 planes of this type:       6 planes of this type:

The cube and regular octahedron both have 9 planes of symmetry.

## Mixed exercise 3

1 (a) (i) 29°  (ii) 122°
  (b) (i) 30°  (ii) 75°  (iii) 75°  (iv) 150°
2 (a)

| Cuboid | 8 | 6 | 12 |
|---|---|---|---|
| Triangular prism | 6 | 5 | 9 |
| Hexagonal prism | 12 | 8 | 18 |
| Octagonal prism | 16 | 10 | 24 |
| Triangle-based pyramid | 4 | 4 | 6 |
| Square-based pyramid | 5 | 5 | 8 |

(b) $V + F = E + 2$

3 (a)

| Tetrahedron | 4 | 4 | 6 |
|---|---|---|---|
| Cube | 8 | 6 | 12 |
| Octahedron | 6 | 8 | 12 |
| Dodecahedron | 20 | 12 | 30 |
| Icosahedron | 12 | 20 | 30 |

(b) 3, 4, 5
(c) Six regular triangular faces meeting at a vertex have a total of 360°, which creates a surface not a vertex.
(d) Regular polyhedra require 3 or more faces to create a vertex. 3 interior angles of regular hexagons = $3 \times 120°$ = 360°, creating a surface not a vertex.
4 $A$ and $F$   $B$ and $D$   $C$ and $H$   $E$ and $G$
5 (a) $y = 2.7$
(b) $q = 4.2$, $r = 5.88$ (c) $x = 6$ (d) $p = 25.2$
6 (a) Alternate angles and vertically opposite angles are equal so interior angles all match.
(b) $x = 1.6$, $y = 4.48$
7 (a) $AXY$ and $ABC$
(b) One interior angle is shared, the other two are corresponding angles.
(c) 1.9125
(d) 1.788
8 $PQ = QR$ (equal sides of a kite)
$PS = RS$ (equal sides of a kite)
$QS$ is common to both. Therefore the two triangles are congruent. (SSS)
9 Area of triangle $= \frac{1}{2} \times$ base $\times$ height

Area $ABC = \frac{1}{2} \times BC \times h$

Area $ACD = \frac{1}{2} \times CD \times h$

$\dfrac{\text{Area } ABC}{\text{Area } ACD} = \dfrac{BC}{CD}$

10 $\dfrac{\text{Area } YXW}{\text{Area } WXZ} = \dfrac{YW}{WZ}$   (from 9)

$Y\hat{X}W = W\hat{X}Z$.   Label these angles $\alpha$

$\dfrac{\text{Area } YXW}{\text{Area } WXZ} = \dfrac{\frac{1}{2}XY \times XW \sin \alpha}{\frac{1}{2}XW \times XZ \sin \alpha} = \dfrac{XY}{XZ}$

$\therefore \quad \dfrac{XY}{XZ} = \dfrac{YW}{WZ}$

# Chapter 4 Fractions and decimals

## Exercise 4A

1 (a) $\frac{3}{4} = \frac{6}{8} = \frac{9}{12} = \frac{12}{16} = \frac{15}{20} = \frac{18}{24}$  (b) $\frac{2}{7} = \frac{4}{14} = \frac{6}{21} = \frac{8}{28} = \frac{10}{35} = \frac{12}{42}$
  (c) $\frac{4}{5} = \frac{8}{10} = \frac{12}{15} = \frac{16}{20} = \frac{20}{25} = \frac{24}{30}$  (d) $\frac{3}{9} = \frac{6}{18} = \frac{9}{27} = \frac{12}{36} = \frac{15}{45} = \frac{18}{54}$
2 (a) $\frac{1}{6} = \frac{3}{18}$ (b) $\frac{3}{7} = \frac{6}{14}$ (c) $\frac{3}{8} = \frac{18}{48}$ (d) $\frac{4}{7} = \frac{12}{21}$
  (e) $\frac{5}{6} = \frac{30}{36}$ (f) $\frac{2}{3} = \frac{6}{9}$ (g) $\frac{4}{9} = \frac{24}{54}$ (h) $\frac{5}{7} = \frac{40}{56}$
3 (a) $\frac{9}{10} = \frac{90}{100}$ (b) $\frac{3}{5} = \frac{9}{15}$ (c) $\frac{2}{5} = \frac{8}{20}$ (d) $\frac{5}{8} = \frac{25}{40}$
  (e) $\frac{8}{9} = \frac{40}{45}$ (f) $\frac{7}{12} = \frac{84}{144}$ (g) $\frac{7}{8} = \frac{49}{56}$ (h) $\frac{2}{9} = \frac{18}{81}$

## Exercise 4B

1 $\frac{5}{12}, \frac{1}{2}, \frac{2}{3}$
2 $\frac{2}{5}, \frac{3}{7}, \frac{5}{8}$
3 $\frac{8}{12}, \frac{3}{4}, \frac{7}{8}$
4 $\frac{2}{15}, \frac{1}{5}, \frac{1}{3}$
5 $\frac{13}{16}, \frac{5}{6}, \frac{7}{8}$

## Exercise 4C

**1**

| | Tens | Units | . | tenths | hundredths | thousandths | ten thousandths | hundred thousandths |
|---|---|---|---|---|---|---|---|---|
| (a) | | 0 | . | 2 | 6 | | | |
| (b) | | 1 | . | 7 | 9 | | | |
| (c) | 3 | 8 | . | 2 | 4 | | | |
| (d) | 1 | 4 | . | 8 | | | | |
| (e) | | 0 | . | 0 | 1 | 0 | 1 | |
| (f) | | 0 | . | 0 | 3 | 3 | | |
| (g) | | 2 | . | 6 | 4 | 5 | | |
| (h) | 8 | 0 | . | 9 | 3 | 4 | | |
| (i) | | 4 | . | 3 | 9 | 8 | 5 | 2 |
| (j) | | 0 | . | 0 | 0 | 1 | 1 | |
| (k) | | 5 | . | 1 | 0 | 7 | | |
| (l) | | 9 | . | 8 | 3 | 0 | 2 | |
| (m) | | 7 | . | 4 | 5 | 7 | | |
| (n) | 1 | 3 | . | 0 | 3 | 0 | 6 | |
| (o) | 5 | 4 | . | 7 | 0 | 5 | | |
| (p) | 1 | 0 | . | 5 | 0 | 3 | 0 | 1 |

**2** (a) 4.101 m, 4.009 m, 4.0059 m
(b) 1.25 kg, 0.55 kg, 0.525 kg, $\frac{1}{8}$ kg
(c) 5.306 km, 5.305 km, 5.204 km, 5.202 km
(d) 9.99 t, 9.904 t, $9\frac{9}{10}$ t, 9.804 t
(e) 6.556 s, 6.554 s, $5\frac{3}{4}$ s, 5.623 s
(f) 2.02 cl, 2.0 cl, $\frac{1}{5}$ cl, 0.022 cl
(g) 6.306 km, 6.305 km, 6.204 km, 6.202 km
(h) 6.643 t, 6.448 t, 6.443 t, 4.512 t
(i) $10\frac{4}{5}$ cm, 9.8 cm, 9.08 cm, 1.08 cm
(j) 8.88 m, 8.801 m, 8.8 m, 8.701 m

## Exercise 4D

**1** 13.1   **2** 27.9   **3** 1.7   **4** 28.8   **5** 4.9   **6** 6.4
**7** 10.6   **8** 27.6   **9** 1.2   **10** 1.3   **11** 6.3   **12** 5.1
**13** (a) 11.242   (b) 154 000

## Exercise 4E

**1** (a) 8   (b) 40   (c) 2.4
**2** (a) 17.1   (b) 29.2   (c) 26
**3** (a) 26   (b) 14.5   (c) 415
  (d) 4520   (e) 521   (f) 56.2

## Exercise 4F

**1** (a) 0.8   (b) 0.25   (c) 1.125   (d) 0.19
  (e) 3.6   (f) 0.52   (g) 0.625   (h) 3.425
**2** (a) 0.14   (b) 4.1875   (c) 3.15   (d) 4.3125
  (e) 0.007   (f) 1.28   (g) 15.9375   (h) 2.35

## Exercise 4G

**1** (a) $\frac{12}{25}$   (b) $\frac{1}{4}$   (c) $1\frac{7}{10}$   (d) $3\frac{203}{500}$   (e) $4\frac{3}{1000}$
**2** (a) $2\frac{1}{40}$   (b) $\frac{49}{1000}$   (c) $4\frac{7}{8}$   (d) $3\frac{3}{4}$   (e) $10\frac{101}{1000}$
**3** (a) $\frac{5}{8}$   (b) $2\frac{64}{125}$   (c) $\frac{13}{16}$   (d) $14\frac{7}{50}$   (e) $9\frac{3}{16}$

## Exercise 4H

**1** (i) 0.833333   (ii) $0.8\dot{3}$   **2** (i) 1.222222   (ii) $1.\dot{2}$
**3** (i) 3.166666   (ii) $3.1\dot{6}$   **4** (i) 0.916666   (ii) $0.91\dot{6}$
**5** (i) 5.555555   (ii) $5.\dot{5}$   **6** (i) 4.818181   (ii) $4.\dot{8}\dot{1}$
**7** (i) 0.068181   (ii) $0.6\dot{8}\dot{1}$   **8** (i) 2.636363   (ii) $2.\dot{6}\dot{3}$
**9** (i) 9.954545   (ii) $9.9\dot{5}\dot{4}$   **10** (i) 0.833333   (ii) $0.8\dot{3}$

## Exercise 4I

**1** (a) $\frac{1}{2}$   (b) $\frac{6}{7}$   (c) $1\frac{1}{5}$   (d) $1\frac{3}{5}$
  (e) $3\frac{2}{9}$   (f) $2\frac{2}{3}$   (g) $1\frac{3}{4}$   (h) $1\frac{7}{8}$
**2** (a) $\frac{7}{8}$   (b) $3\frac{3}{8}$   (c) $1\frac{3}{8}$   (d) $6\frac{5}{8}$
  (e) $4\frac{1}{16}$   (f) $4\frac{3}{8}$   (g) $1\frac{1}{16}$   (h) $4\frac{3}{16}$
**3** (a) $\frac{23}{40}$   (b) $\frac{11}{30}$   (c) $2\frac{29}{30}$   (d) $\frac{20}{21}$
  (e) $3\frac{19}{42}$   (f) $3\frac{41}{42}$   (g) $5\frac{13}{15}$   (h) $2\frac{8}{9}$
**4** $7\frac{1}{12}$ miles   **5** $17\frac{1}{2}$ in   **6** $3\frac{11}{16}$ in   **7** $\frac{17}{30}$   **8** $1\frac{22}{35}$ lb

## Exercise 4J

**1** (a) $\frac{1}{2}$   (b) $\frac{1}{4}$   (c) $\frac{1}{2}$   (d) $\frac{3}{7}$
**2** (a) $\frac{1}{8}$   (b) $\frac{3}{8}$   (c) $\frac{1}{8}$   (d) $2\frac{3}{8}$
**3** (a) $2\frac{3}{20}$   (b) $2\frac{18}{35}$   (c) $5\frac{4}{15}$   (d) $3\frac{29}{72}$
**4** (a) $3\frac{5}{24}$   (b) $2\frac{4}{9}$   (c) $3\frac{17}{40}$   (d) $3\frac{6}{35}$
**5** $4\frac{5}{8}$ kg   **6** $3\frac{1}{8}$ pints   **7** $2\frac{1}{8}$ ft   **8** $\frac{1}{12}$   **9** $2\frac{1}{8}$ km

## Exercise 4K

**1** (a) 9   (b) 30   (c) 28 litres   (d) 21 pints
**2** (a) £15   (b) 3.704 kg   (c) £2.64   (d) 62.05 litres
**3** (a) 27 kg   (b) £2.22   (c) 654.5 km   (d) 280 people
**4** (a) £17.00   (b) 168 toys   (c) 720 cars   (d) £37.15
**5** 140 days   **6** 21
**7** (a) $\frac{3}{16}$   (b) $\frac{8}{15}$   (c) $\frac{4}{21}$   (d) $\frac{4}{15}$
  (e) $\frac{2}{35}$   (f) $\frac{10}{21}$   (g) $\frac{3}{8}$   (h) $\frac{1}{5}$
**8** (a) $\frac{2}{7}$   (b) $\frac{5}{14}$   (c) $\frac{2}{5}$   (d) $\frac{1}{6}$
  (e) $\frac{1}{7}$   (f) $\frac{2}{5}$   (g) $3\frac{1}{2}$   (h) $\frac{13}{20}$
**9** (a) $\frac{8}{9}$   (b) $\frac{14}{15}$   (c) $\frac{3}{8}$   (d) $3\frac{3}{4}$
  (e) $\frac{5}{8}$   (f) $1\frac{13}{15}$   (g) 16   (h) 3
**10** £32.65   **11** £1.08   **12** $20\frac{5}{8}$ lb   **13** $14\frac{5}{8}$ min
**14** $24\frac{1}{6}$ m²

## Exercise 4L

**1** (a) $\frac{4}{9}$   (b) $\frac{8}{15}$   (c) $\frac{9}{16}$   (d) 2
**2** (a) $\frac{2}{9}$   (b) $\frac{1}{9}$   (c) $1\frac{1}{6}$   (d) $1\frac{3}{4}$
**3** (a) $\frac{8}{9}$   (b) $7\frac{1}{2}$   (c) $6\frac{9}{10}$   (d) $1\frac{13}{20}$
  (e) $\frac{3}{5}$   (f) $1\frac{1}{9}$   (g) $\frac{4}{9}$   (h) $\frac{9}{10}$
**4** 16   **5** 36   **6** $11\frac{2}{11}$ days

## Exercise 4M

**1** 4.95 t   **2** 289 cars   **3** $\frac{2}{9}$   **4** $\frac{17}{45}$
**5** $1\frac{3}{5}$ miles   **6** 605   **7** $\frac{9}{16}$   **8** $\frac{27}{55}$

## Mixed exercise 4

**1** (a) $\frac{5}{9} = \frac{10}{18} = \frac{15}{27} = \frac{20}{36} = \frac{25}{45}$   (b) $\frac{2}{5} = \frac{4}{10}$
  (c) $\frac{3}{8} = \frac{24}{64}$   (d) $\frac{8}{7} = \frac{40}{35}$
**2** $\frac{2}{5}, \frac{7}{10}, \frac{3}{4}, \frac{7}{8}$
**3** (a) 0.875   (b) 2.75   (c) 4.36   (d) $0.\dot{7}$   (e) $2.8\dot{3}$
**4** (a) $\frac{1}{25}$   (b) $2\frac{29}{40}$   (c) $5\frac{17}{25}$   (d) $\frac{3}{10}$   (e) $\frac{9}{20}$
**5** $\frac{4}{5}$ kg
**6** $8\frac{3}{8}$ ft
**7** (a) 85.1   (b) 24.5   (c) 5.7   (d) 1.2
  (e) 75   (f) 712
**8** $4\frac{11}{16}$ ft
**9** 16 bags
**10** $\frac{8}{9}$
**11** $4\frac{11}{12}$ in
**12** $\frac{1}{8}$
**13** £18
**14** 3.91 km, 3.9 km, 3.671 km, 3.506 km, 3.451 km, 3.008 km

# Chapter 5 Collecting and recording data

## Exercise 5A

Qualitative: (b), (g), (h).
Quantitative, discrete: (e), (i), (j).
Quantitative, continuous: (a), (c), (d), (f), (k).
(f) and (k) are continuous variables but they are usually treated as if they were discrete.

## Exercise 5B

1 (a) random    (b) biased    (c) random
   (d) random    (e) random
2 (a) (i) 25    (ii) 8.5
   (b) She can't sample 0.5. She can double the sample size or decide, by tossing a coin, to sample 8 or 9.
   (c) 7.25
   (d) She can't sample fractions of a student, so she will need to round to the nearest whole numbers.
3 (a) 800    (b) 1020    (c) 567
4 Every 50th person in the directory starting at a random name from first to fiftieth.

## Exercise 5C

1 (a) $X$    (b) $Y$    (c) $Y$    (d) $X$
   (e) $Y$    (f) $X$    (g) $X$    (h) $X$
2 (a) The question is biased.

(b) 'Terrible', 'quite good' and 'OK' mean different things to different people.
(c) The question is biased.
(d) The question cannot be answered if you have never played football.
(e) The question does not specify a period (e.g. each day/week).
(f) Everyone may not have the same local library.
3 (a) less than £5,    £5 to £9.99,
   £10 to £14.99,    £15 to £19.99
   (Other answers are possible.)

## Exercise 5E

1 (a) secondary    (b) secondary    (c) primary
   (d) primary    (e) secondary

## Exercise 5F

1 1–10 4;   11–20 5;   21–30 5;   31–40 8
2 (a) 1–5 2;   6–10 5;   11–15 7;   16–20 8;   21–25 13;   26–30 5
   (b) 1–3 1;   4–6 1;   7–9 4;   10–12 4;   13–15 4;   16–18 4;   19–21 6;   22–24 5;   25–27 10;   28–30 1
   (c) Six intervals are best. There is no useful extra information from the ten intervals.
3 61.0–61.9 6;   62.0–62.9 9;   63.0–63.9 8;   64.0–64.9 5;   65.0–65.9 6;   66.0 and over 2

## Exercise 5G

**1**

| Waist (cm) | Height (cm) | | | |
|---|---|---|---|---|
| | $160 \leqslant h < 170$ | $170 \leqslant h < 180$ | $180 \leqslant h < 190$ | $190 \leqslant h < 200$ |
| $65 \leqslant x < 70$ | | | | |
| $70 \leqslant x < 75$ | | | | |
| $75 \leqslant x < 80$ | | | | |
| $80 \leqslant x < 85$ | | | | |
| $85 \leqslant x < 90$ | | | | |
| $90 \leqslant x < 95$ | | | | |
| $95 \leqslant x < 100$ | | | | |

**2**

| Length of journey (km) | Average speed of journey (km/h) | | | | | |
|---|---|---|---|---|---|---|
| | $30 \leqslant s < 35$ | $35 \leqslant s < 40$ | $40 \leqslant s < 45$ | $45 \leqslant s < 50$ | $50 \leqslant s < 55$ | $55 \leqslant s < 60$ |
| $10 \leqslant x < 20$ | | | | | | |
| $20 \leqslant x < 30$ | | | | | | |
| $30 \leqslant x < 40$ | | | | | | |
| $40 \leqslant x < 50$ | | | | | | |
| $50 \leqslant x < 60$ | | | | | | |
| $60 \leqslant x < 70$ | | | | | | |
| $70 \leqslant x < 80$ | | | | | | |
| $80 \leqslant x < 90$ | | | | | | |
| $95 \leqslant x < 100$ | | | | | | |

**3**

| No. of eggs | Height of nest (cm) | | | |
|---|---|---|---|---|
| | $0 \leqslant h < 100$ | $100 \leqslant h < 200$ | $200 \leqslant h < 300$ | $300 \leqslant h < 400$ |
| 1 | | | | |
| 2 | | | | |
| 3 | | | | |
| 4 | | | | |
| 5 | | | | |
| 6 | | | | |
| 7 | | | | |

**4 (a)**

| | Sd | S | O | Total |
|---|---|---|---|---|
| Boys | 12 | 3 | 1 | 16 |
| Girls | 8 | 4 | 2 | 14 |
| Total | 20 | 7 | 3 | 30 |

**(b)** 4

## Exercise 5H

**1** (a)

| Length (cm) | | Frequency |
|---|---|---|
| 1 up to but not including 2 | | 0 |
| 2 | 3 | 2 |
| 3 | 4 | 6 |
| 4 | 5 | 8 |
| 5 | 6 | 8 |
| 6 | 7 | 4 |
| 7 | 8 | 2 |

(b)

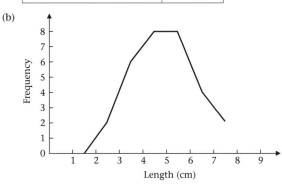

**2** (a) You can't tell at what point the two boys gave up – it could have been quite quickly. You cannot 'make up' data for them so in this case it is best to ignore the two stars and consider the data for the 23 boys who completed the task.

(b)

| Time (s) | | Frequency |
|---|---|---|
| 10 up to but not including 20 | | 0 |
| 20 | 30 | 3 |
| 30 | 40 | 3 |
| 40 | 50 | 7 |
| 50 | 60 | 4 |
| 60 | 70 | 3 |
| 70 | 80 | 2 |
| 80 | 90 | 1 |

(c) The peak of the boys' frequency polygon is in the same interval as the girls' one. However, the boys' frequency polygon is extended towards longer times – especially if the two who gave up are included.

## Mixed exercise 5

**1** Make the question specific and comparative, e.g. 'Which food do you eat most often in the school canteen?'

**2** Give a time frame and a numerical quantifier, e.g. 'How many hours of television did you watch last Saturday?'

**3** For example:

| | Tally |
|---|---|
| Comedy | |
| Horror | |
| Drama | |
| Fantasy | |
| Documentary | |
| Romance | |

**4** For example:

| | Hot sweet | Cold sweet | Hot drink | Cold drink |
|---|---|---|---|---|
| Salad | | | | |
| Sandwiches | | | | |
| Hot meal | | | | |

**5** Number each student from 0–999. Select students using random numbers.

**6** (a) Not random, but unlikely to be biased.
(b) Random (unless the survey concerns possible effects of season of birth).
(c) Biased.
(d) Random (as long as the survey is not concerned with sport).

**7** (a) His friends may have similar interests.
(b) Take a random sample from the school.
A bigger sample (30 or more).

**8** (i) **Random sample**: Number each student in the school and use random numbers to select the 60 students.
(ii) **Systematic sample**: From a list of the students, use random numbers to select a student from the first 20 students. Start from this student and select every 20th student from the list.
(iii) **Stratified sample**: Stratify the school according to Upper school and Lower school – 400 and 800 students (say). Use random numbers to select 20 students from Upper school and 40 students from Lower school.

**9** 7 students

**10**

| | Tea bags | Packet tea | Instant tea | Total |
|---|---|---|---|---|
| 50 g | 2 | 0 | 5 | 7 |
| 100 g | 35 | 20 | 5 | 60 |
| 200 g | 15 | 5 | 13 | 33 |
| Total | 52 | 25 | 23 | 100 |

**11** (a)

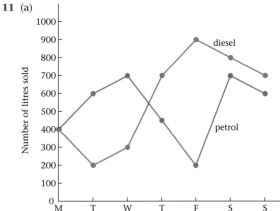

(b) Large sales of petrol correspond to smaller sales of diesel, and vice versa. Total sales were largest on Saturday and Sunday.

12

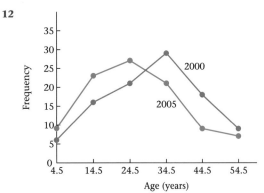

Generally there was a greater number of older members (and smaller number of younger members) in 2000.

# Chapter 6 Solving equations and inequalities

## Exercise 6A

1 $x = -5$  2 $x = -2$  3 $x = 2\frac{1}{2}$  4 $x = -5\frac{1}{2}$
5 $a = -3$  6 $b = 1.6$  7 $c = -3\frac{1}{2}$  8 $p = 3$
9 $q = 4$  10 $s = -4$

## Exercise 6B

1 18  2 $-6$  3 24  4 $9\frac{1}{3}$  5 $4\frac{1}{2}$
6 14  7 $-6$  8 $-12$  9 6  10 $-6\frac{2}{3}$

## Exercise 6C

1 4  2 3  3 $\frac{1}{2}$  4 $\frac{4}{5}$  5 $-2$
6 $-1$  7 $1\frac{1}{2}$  8 $3\frac{2}{3}$  9 $-1\frac{1}{3}$  10 $-2\frac{1}{5}$

## Exercise 6D

1 1  2 $\frac{1}{2}$  3 $-1\frac{1}{2}$  4 $-3$  5 $\frac{3}{5}$
6 $-\frac{3}{4}$  7 $1\frac{1}{5}$  8 1  9 0  10 $-2\frac{1}{3}$

## Exercise 6E

1 4  2 $-3$  3 $2\frac{1}{6}$  4 $3\frac{1}{3}$  5 $\frac{4}{5}$
6 $6\frac{1}{2}$  7 $-1$  8 1  9 $1\frac{1}{2}$  10 2
11 $-3$  12 $-2\frac{1}{2}$  13 2  14 $-2$  15 2
16 4  17 $\frac{1}{2}$  18 15  19 $-14$  20 0
21 $\frac{1}{2}$

## Exercise 6F

1 60  2 60  3 28  4 12  5 8
6 15  7 24  8 $6\frac{5}{8}$  9 33  10 $3\frac{1}{9}$

## Exercise 6G

1 18
2 7
3 (a) $8 + 2p = 28 - 6p$  (b) $p = 2\frac{1}{2}$  (c) 13
4 (a) $30 + x = 45 - 2x$  (b) $x = 5$  (c) 35
5 (a) $15 - 3c = 12 - 2c$  (b) £3
6 (a) $70 - 60g = 60 - 20g$  (b) $\frac{1}{4}$ litre

## Exercise 6H

1 $x > 1$  2 $x \leqslant -2$  3 $-3 \leqslant x < 2$  4 $0 \leqslant x < 3$
5 ![number line 0 1 2 3 4 5]  6 ![number line -2 -1 0 1 2 3]  7 ![number line -5 -4 -3 -2 -1 0]
8 ![number line 1 2 3 4 5 6]  9 ![number line -3 -2 -1 0 1 2]  10 ![number line -3 -2 -1 0 1 2]

## Exercise 6I

1 $x \leqslant 3$  2 $x > \frac{2}{5}$  3 $x \leqslant 1\frac{2}{3}$  4 $x < -3$
5 $a \geqslant 1$  6 $b < -1$  7 $c > -4$  8 $d \leqslant 1\frac{1}{2}$
9 $e \leqslant -4$  10 $f < -28$  11 $g \leqslant 2$  12 $h \geqslant \frac{1}{2}$
13 $j > -1$  14 $k \leqslant 1\frac{2}{3}$  15 $m \geqslant -3\frac{1}{2}$  16 $n > -1\frac{1}{2}$

## Exercise 6J

1 $1 < p \leqslant 6$  2 $5 < q < 7\frac{1}{2}$
3 $-1 \leqslant r \leqslant 2$  4 $-6 < s < 4$

## Exercise 6K

1 (a) $-2, -1, 0, 1$  (b) 1, 2, 3, 4
  (c) $-3, -2, -1$  (d) 0, 1, 2, 3
2 (a) e.g. $2 \leqslant x \leqslant 5$  (b) e.g. $0 \leqslant x \leqslant 3$
  (c) e.g. $-3 \leqslant x \leqslant -1$  (d) e.g. $-2 \leqslant x \leqslant 2$
3 (a) 2  (b) 1  (c) $-1$  (d) $-3$
4 (a) $-1$  (b) 2  (c) 0  (d) 2
5 (a) 2, 3  (b) 2, 3
  (c) $-2, -1, 0, 1, 2$  (d) 0, 1

## Exercise 6L

1 $x > 11\frac{2}{3}$  2 $x > 4$  3 $x \leqslant -3\frac{1}{2}$  4 $x \geqslant 2$
5 $x > -\frac{1}{2}$  6 $x \leqslant -1$  7 $x > 2\frac{1}{2}$  8 $x < -1$
9 $x \leqslant 3\frac{1}{5}$  10 $x < 0$  11 $x < -1\frac{1}{3}$  12 $x \geqslant -\frac{1}{2}$
13 $x < -8$  14 $x < -2$

## Mixed exercise 6

1 3  2 $1\frac{2}{5}$  3 $-1$  4 4
5 $-6$  6 $\frac{2}{3}$  7 $-2$  8 $-2\frac{1}{2}$
9 $\frac{3}{5}$  10 8  11 $-8$  12 6
13 2  14 $2\frac{1}{2}$  15 7  16 27p
17 (a) 5 cm
   (b) 2 cm
18 (a) ![number line 5 6 7 8 9]  (b) ![number line -7 -6 -5 -4 -3]

   (c) ![number line 3 4 5 6 7]  (d) ![number line -4 -3 -2 -1 0]
19 (a) $x < 2$  (b) $x \leqslant -2$  (c) $x < 1\frac{1}{3}$
20 (a) (i) 3  (ii) 3
   (b) (i) 3  (ii) 0
21 $P = 53$
22 $x \leqslant 3\frac{2}{5}$
23 $y = 1\frac{6}{7}$

# Chapter 7 Transformations, loci and constructions

## Exercise 7A

**1** (a) $\begin{pmatrix} 2 \\ -2 \end{pmatrix}$

(b) $\begin{pmatrix} -2 \\ 2 \end{pmatrix}$

(c) $\begin{pmatrix} 5 \\ 0 \end{pmatrix}$

(d) $\begin{pmatrix} -7 \\ 2 \end{pmatrix}$

(e) $\begin{pmatrix} -6 \\ -3 \end{pmatrix}$

**2** (a)

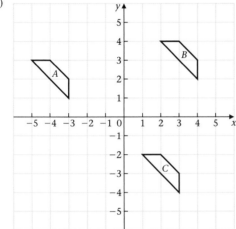

(c) $\begin{pmatrix} 6 \\ -5 \end{pmatrix}$    (d) $\begin{pmatrix} -6 \\ 5 \end{pmatrix}$

**3**

(a) $A$ (3, 3), $B$ (6, 4)     (b) $A$ (6, 5), $B$ (9, 6)

(c) $\begin{pmatrix} 6 \\ 4 \end{pmatrix}$     (d) $A$ (1, 4), $B$ (4, 5)

(e) $A$ (1, 4), $B$ (4, 5)     (f) They are the same.

## Exercise 7B

**1**

**2** A reflection in the line $x = 2$

**3**

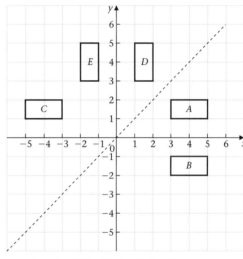

(a) (ii) (3, −1) (3, −2) (5, −2) (5, −1)
    (iii) $x$ coordinate remained the same
        $y$ coordinate changed sign

(b) (ii) (−3, 1) (−3, 2) (−5, 2) (−5, 1)
    (iii) $x$ coordinate changed sign
        $y$ coordinate remained the same

(e) Reflection in line $y = -x$

**4**

## Exercise 7C

**1**

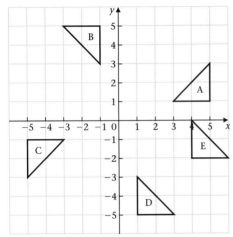

(a) (−1, 3) (−1, 5) (−3, 5)
(b) (−3, −1) (−5, −1) (−5, −3)
(c) Rotate 180° about the origin
(d) (1, −3) (1, −5) (3, −5)
(e) Rotate 180° about the origin

**2** A rotation through 180° about the point (0, 0). (A half turn about (0, 0).)

## Exercise 7D

**1 (a)**

**(b)**

**(c)**

**(d)**

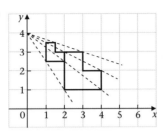

**2** Enlargement, scale factor $\frac{1}{2}$, centre (7, 1)

**3**

**4**

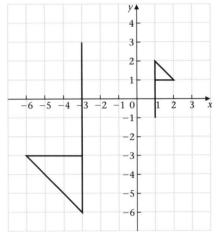

**5** (a) (1, 1) scale factor 2
(b) (3, 3) scale factor 3
(c) (3, 3) scale factor $\frac{1}{3}$
(d) (2, 0) scale factor −1

**6** repeat 4 [fd 45 rt 90]

**7** (a) Scale factor $\frac{3}{2}$, centre (−1, −1)
(b) Scale factor $\frac{2}{3}$, centre (−1, −1)
(c) Each is the inverse of the other.

**8**

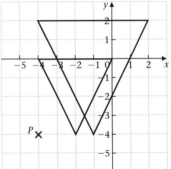

**9** Enlargement, scale factor $-1\frac{1}{2}$, centre (1, 1)

## Exercise 7E

**1**

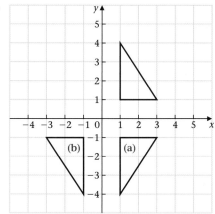

(c) Rotation 180° about origin.

**2**

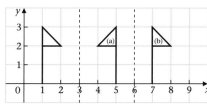

(c) Translation $\begin{pmatrix} 6 \\ 0 \end{pmatrix}$

**3**

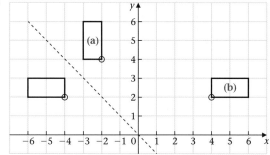

(c) Reflection in $x = 0$ ($y$-axis)

**4**

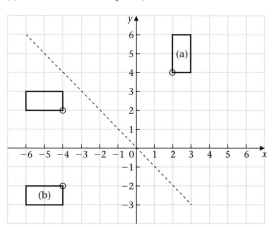

(c) Reflection in $y = 0$ ($x$-axis)

**5**

(b) Rotation 180° about point (2, 1)

**6**

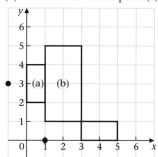

**7** (a) Enlargement, scale factor 2, centre (0, 0)
(b)

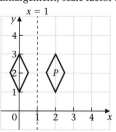

## Exercise 7F

**1** (a) 7.6 m (b) 4.3 m
**2** (a) 80 m (b) 1.5 m
**3** (a) 14 km (b) 31 km (c) 2.7 cm
**4** (a) 1:200
(b) 3 cm by 2 cm
(c) 6 m by 4 m
(d) 2 m
**5** The scale drawing should have the marked dimensions.

8 cm, 3 cm, 2 cm, 6 cm, 6 cm, 5 cm, 3 cm, 5 cm, Scale 1:50

## Exercise 7G

**6** 60°
**8** (a) $x = 120°$ (b) $y = 30°$
**10** (b) 8.77 cm

## Exercise 7H

1 Pupils should draw the perpendicular bisector of *AB*.

2

2.5 cm

4 cm

2.5 cm

3 The locus will consist of 4 quarter circles with centres on a straight line. The radii depend on the size of the box and position of the point. If the point is on one of the edges the box is tipped about, there will be only 3 quarter circles.)

4 (a)

22.3 m

150 m

(b) 440 m to 3 s.f.

5 (a) 15 cm

(b)

75 cm

75 cm

15 cm

283 cm

6

1.8 m

0.3 m

1.2 m

0.8 m

1.4 m

7 Daniel could attend Ayleton or Bankbury

8 Students should draw the bisector of the angle at the gate.

9

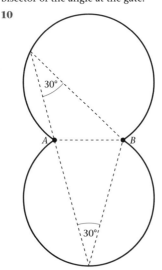

10

*P*

45°

*A*          *B*

45°

*P*

30°

*A*          *B*

30°

## Exercise 7I

1 (a)          (b)    (c)          (d)          (e)

16°

200°          325°          168°

9°

2 (a) 063°          (b) 170°          (c) 332°
3 (a) 235°          (b) 115°          (c) 295°
4 240°
5 325°
6 (a) 180° + bearing of *B* from *A*
   (b) bearing of *B* from *A* − 180°

## Mixed exercise 7

1 (a)

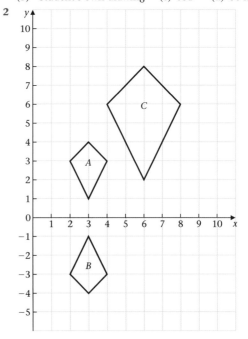

30 km          L

B    75°

40 km

H

(b) Student's own drawing    (c) 031°    (d) 56 km

2

*y*

10
9
8
7
6          C
5
4
3    A
2
1

0    1   2   3   4   5   6   7   8   9   10   *x*

−1
−2
−3    B
−4
−5

**3** (a)

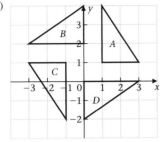

(b) Rotation, 180° about (0, 1)

**4**

**5** (a)

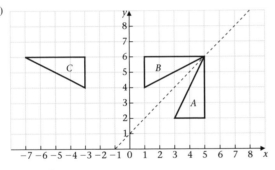

(b) $y = x + 1$
(c) 90° anticlockwise rotation around $(-1, 0)$

**6** (a) 3 km
(b)

**7**

**8**

**9**

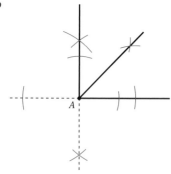

**11** 081°

# Chapter 8 Using basic number skills

## Exercise 8A

**1** (a) 112%    (b) 117%    (c) 130%
    (d) 111%    (e) 108.5%
**2** (a) 1.24    (b) £13 454
**3** (a) 1.4    (b) £21.56
**4** £1525.15
**5** 1.04
**6** (a) £144    (b) 70 kg    (c) 2.784 m
    (d) £1370.20    (e) 128.52 cm

## Exercise 8B

**1** (a) 84%      (b) 89%
    (c) 95%      (d) 78%
**2** (a) 0.66      (b) £3.47 to 2 d.p.
**3** 77.9 kg
**4** (a) £96    (b) 42 kg    (c) 2.016 m
    (d) £1109.80    (e) 123.48 cm
**5** (a) 1.06    (b) £106    (c)

| Date | Amount |
|------|--------|
| 1/1/99 | £100 |
| 1/1/00 | £106 |
| 1/1/01 | £112 |
| 1/1/02 | £119 |
| 1/1/03 | £126 |

**6** (a) £12 320    (b)

| New price | £14 000 |
|-----------|---------|
| Value after 1 year | £12 320 |
| Value after 2 years | £10 102 |
| Value after 3 years | £9597 |
| Value after 4 years | £9117 |
| Value after 5 years | £8662 |

**7** (a) 1.1    (b) 1.188

## Exercise 8C

**1** (a) $\frac{7}{9}$    (b) 1    (c) 77.$\dot{7}$%    (d) 100%
**2** (a) 50%    (b) 60%    (c) 16.73%    (d) 20%
**3** (a) 8 km    (b) 10.6 km    (c) 32.5%
**4** (a) £5460    (b) 58%
**5** (a) 7.5 litres    (b) 25%

## Exercise 8D

**1** (a) £260    (b) 32.5%    (c) 20.6% to nearest 0.1%
**2** (a) 33%    (b) 27%    (c) 12%    (d) 8%    (e) 55%
**3** (a) 20%, 31.2%, 40%, 47.2%    (b) 12.8%

## Exercise 8E

**1** £428.40     **2** £54 538     **3** 13.04
**4** (a) 42.86%    (b) 33.3%    (c) 4.76% decrease

## Exercise 8F

**1** (a) 90%    (b) pre-sale price $\xrightarrow{\times 0.9}$ £540    (c) £600
**2** £2.78
**3** £104.11
**4** (a) 117.5%    (b) pre-VAT price $\xrightarrow{\times 1.175}$ £320    (c) £272.34
**5** (a) 175    (b) 14
**6** (a) £13 333.33
    (b) £14 814.82

## Exercise 8G

**1** (a) £14.63    (b) 5.852%
**2**

| Year | Amount at start of year | Interest | Total amount at year end |
|------|-------------------------|----------|--------------------------|
| 6 | £334.56 | £334.56 × 0.06 | £354.63 |
| 7 | £354.63 | £354.63 × 0.06 | £375.91 |
| 8 | £375.91 | £375.91 × 0.06 | £398.46 |
| 9 | £398.46 | £398.46 × 0.06 | £422.37 |
| 10 | £422.37 | £422.37 × 0.06 | £447.71 |

**3** (a) £47.71    (b) 19.1%    (c) 7.9%
**4** (a) approx 12 years    (b) 16 years 8 months
**5** (a) £1082    (b) £1370.59    (c) £1878.53
**6** If an annual interest rate of 50% is paid, then after the first year the value of the investment increases to 150% of its original value, and during the second year the value of the investment increases by 50% of its value *at the end of the first year*, giving an overall increase of 125%.
**7** (a) £7440    (b) £24.80 per month
    (c) £644.80    (d) £754.32
**8** (a) £10 800    (b) £9720    (c) £7085.88
    (d) 6 years 7 months approx
**9** (a) 1.602    (b) 2.027    (c) 3.247
**10** (a) £550.16    (b) £1755.16    (c) £973.36

## Exercise 8H

**1** (a) 87.17 km/h    (b) 54 mph
**2** 25.71 mph
**3** (a) 1.25 h    (b) 0.4 h    (c) 0.1 h    (d) 0.42 h
    (e) 0.75 h    (f) 0.17 h
**4** (a) 162 min    (b) 2.7 h    (c) 18.52 km/h
**5** (a) Shannon by 4 minutes    (b) 1.63 h or 1 h 38 min
**6** (a) 24 min    (b) 5 h 18 min    (c) 3 h 15 min
    (d) 6 h 17.4 min    (e) 3 h 54 min    (f) 9 h 52.8 min
**7** (a) 5 hours    (b) 5 km/h
**8** (a) 456 km    (b) 6.85 h    (c) 66.57 km/h

## Exercise 8I

**1** 14.5 km/l
**2** (a) (i) 42 litres    (ii) 14 km/litre
    (b) 84 km
**3** (a) (i) regular 0.8125 p/h    longlife 0.78 p/h
       (ii) regular 123 h/£    longlife 128 h/£
    (b) Longlife cheaper per hour or more hours/£
**4** (a) 1.424 francs/dollar    (b) 0.702 dollars/franc
**5** (a) Cold 184 litres/min    Hot 115 litres/min
    (b) 3 min 4.6 sec
**6** (a) (i) 0.16 litres/km    (ii) 6.4 litres/hour
    (b) (i) 10 km    (ii) 1.6 litres

## Exercise 8J

**1** 100 hours
**2** (a) (i) 0.00026 m³/sec (ii) 15.6 litres/min
  (b) 1 hr 4 min 6 sec
  (c) 51 min 17 sec

## Exercise 8K

**1** (a) 32000 cm³ (b) 32 m
**2** (a) 2800 cm³ (b) 75 g/cm³
**3** (a) 6475 kg (b) 0.463 m³
**4** (a) 546 cm³ (b) 6.41 g/cm³

## Exercise 8L

**1** (a) (i) $\frac{2}{}$ (ii) $\frac{4}{}$ (iii) $\frac{6}{}$
  (b) (i) $\frac{1}{6}$ (ii) $\frac{1}{3}$ (iii) $\frac{1}{2}$
**2** (a) Sally $\frac{1}{5}$ Brian $\frac{3}{10}$ Mark $\frac{1}{2}$
  (b) Sally £8 Brian £12 Mark £20
**3** (a) 8 parts (b) $\frac{3}{8}$ (c) £101.25 (d) $\frac{5}{8}$
  (e) £168.75
**4** (a) 5:2 (b) Danny $\frac{5}{7}$ (Melissa $\frac{2}{7}$) (c) £19
  (d) £60 (e) £10
**5** (a) 4:1 (b) 18 marks
**6** (a) $\frac{2}{7}$ (b) 68 boxes (c) £32.64
**7** (a) £120 (b) 2:1 (c) £282
**8** (a) 540 (b) 180 (c) 324 (d) 216
**9** (a) 86 (b) 86:5 (c) 86 (d) 80

## Exercise 8M

**1** (a) $\frac{5}{13}$ (b) $\frac{8}{13}$ (c) 60 (d) 195
**2** 9.37 km/litre
**3** (a) 5:8 (b) No, 56 km/h (c) 112 km/h
**4** (a) 50 (b) 37.5 (c) 1:1.75
**5** (a) 27 days (b) 21 days (c) 6 days (d) 75 days
**6** (a) 6:3:1 (b) 81 goals (c) 135 goals
**7** 60 years, 30 years, 20 years, 12 years

## Exercise 8N

**1** (a) $10^2$ (b) $10^3$ (c) $10^6$ (d) $10^{10}$
**2** (a) 6 million (b) 3.4 million (c) 7.8 million
  (d) 5.5 million (e) 2.65 million (f) 7.642 million
**3** (a) $3.1 \times 10^6$ (b) $4.3 \times 10^6$ (c) $5 \times 10^5$
  (d) $2.4 \times 10^6$ (e) $7.8 \times 10^6$ (f) $8.6 \times 10^6$
  (g) $4 \times 10^6$ (h) $9 \times 10^6$ (i) $4 \times 10^5$
**4** (a) $10^3$ (b) $10^4$ (c) $10^1$ (d) $10^6$ (e) $10^5$ (f) $10^3$
**5**

| | Standard form |
|---|---|
| (a) | $7.4 \times 10^4$ |
| (b) | $2.6 \times 10^2$ |
| (c) | $6.8 \times 10^5$ |
| (d) | $4.5 \times 10^1$ |
| (e) | $9.9 \times 10^6$ |
| (f) | $6.2 \times 10^1$ |
| (g) | $8 \times 10^0$ |

**6** (a) $1.6 \times 10$ (b) $4.3 \times 10^3$
  (c) $6.5 \times 10^5$ (d) $8.7 \times 10^7$
  (e) $6.7 \times 10^2$ (f) $8.65 \times 10^2$
  (g) $9.87 \times 10^6$ (h) $9.85 \times 10^4$
  (i) $8.05 \times 10^{11}$

## Exercise 8O

**1** (a) 420 (b) 67000 (c) 5500 (d) 7500000
  (e) 620000 (f) 73000 (g) 24000000 (h) 11
  (i) 7.25
**2** (a) $9 \times 10^2$ (b) $9.6 \times 10^3$ (c) $4.05 \times 10^4$
  (d) $3.91 \times 10^5$ (to 2 d.p.)

## Exercise 8P

**1**

| | Standard form |
|---|---|
| (a) | $2.4 \times 10^{-3}$ |
| (b) | $2 \times 10^{-1}$ |
| (c) | $6 \times 10^{-5}$ |
| (d) | $1.5 \times 10^{-1}$ |
| (e) | $7 \times 10^{-3}$ |
| (f) | $4.5 \times 10^{-4}$ |
| (g) | $3.46 \times 10^{-2}$ |
| (h) | $1.25 \times 10^{-3}$ |

**2** (a) $2 \times 10^{-3}$ (b) $1.5 \times 10^{-1}$
  (c) $4 \times 10^{-4}$ (d) $5.4 \times 10^{-2}$
  (e) $8 \times 10^{-6}$ (f) $6.8 \times 10^{-11}$
  (g) $3.46 \times 10^{-1}$ (h) $9 \times 10^{-2}$
  (i) $5.6 \times 10^{-3}$
**3** (a) 0.35 (b) 0.06 (c) 0.00072
  (d) 0.0022 (e) 0.0000135 (f) 0.00000533
  (g) 0.00000000088 (h) 0.00000044 (i) 0.4999

## Exercise 8Q

**1** (a) $9.6 \times 10^{13}$ (b) $1.722 \times 10^4$ (c) $8.4 \times 10^{-3}$
  (d) $1.476 \times 10^{-12}$ (e) $2.91 \times 10^{-1}$ (f) $1.47 \times 10^{-9}$
  (g) $2.83 \times 10^{30}$ (h) $1.0 \times 10^3$ (i) $7.84 \times 10^6$
  (j) $1.0648 \times 10^{-5}$
**2** (a) $2.1 \times 10^8$ (b) $2.4 \times 10^{-5}$ (c) $2.133 \times 10^{-1}$
  (d) $6.378 \times 10^1$ (e) 5.2 (f) $4.416 \times 10^{-3}$
  (g) $2.684 \times 10^4$ (h) $1.463 \times 10^{-9}$
**3** Approximately 500 s or 8 min
**4** (a) Earth
  (b) $5.91 \times 10^3$ km (5910 km)
  (c) $1.949 \times 10^4$ km
  (d) 6.543 times

## Mixed exercise 8

**1** (a) £3150 (b) £7200
**2** £24
**3** £224.97
**4** 8.1 miles per litre
**5** £1111.11
**6** (a) £114.89 (b) £177.87 (c) £41.70
**7** £1820
**8** (a) $1.4 \times 10^8$ (b) $1.94 \times 10^6$
**9** £1.40 × 10^7
**10** 362.88 kg
**11** $3.38 \times 10^8$ km²

# Chapter 9 Functions, lines, simultaneous equations and regions

## Exercise 9A

**1** (a) 1 → 0 (b) 1 → 5 (c) 1 → 8
  2 → 2   2 → 8   2 → 10
  3 → 4   3 → 11   3 → 12
  10 → 18   10 → 32   10 → 26
  (d) 1 → 0 (e) 1 → 1.5 (f) 1 → 2
  2 → 3   2 → 2   2 → 2.5
  3 → 6   3 → 2.5   3 → 3
  10 → 27   10 → 6   10 → 6.5

## Exercise 9B

**1** (a) $y = x + 2$ (b)

| $x$ | 0 | 1 | 2 | 3 | 4 | 5 |
|---|---|---|---|---|---|---|
| $y$ | 2 | 3 | 4 | 5 | 6 | 7 |

(c)

2 (a) $y = x + 4$

| $x$ | 0 | 1 | 2 | 3 | 4 | 5 |
|---|---|---|---|---|---|---|
| $y$ | 4 | 5 | 6 | 7 | 8 | 9 |

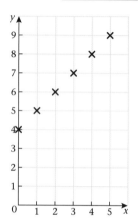

(b) $y = 2x + 3$

| $x$ | 0 | 1 | 2 | 3 | 4 | 5 |
|---|---|---|---|---|---|---|
| $y$ | 3 | 5 | 7 | 9 | 11 | 13 |

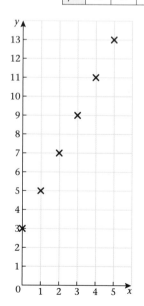

(c) $y = 3x + 2$

| $x$ | 0 | 1 | 2 | 3 | 4 | 5 |
|---|---|---|---|---|---|---|
| $y$ | 2 | 5 | 8 | 11 | 14 | 17 |

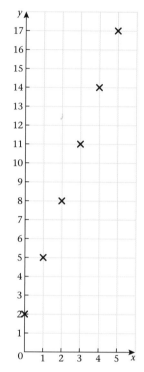

(d) $y = 2x$

| $x$ | 0 | 1 | 2 | 3 | 4 | 5 |
|---|---|---|---|---|---|---|
| $y$ | 0 | 2 | 4 | 6 | 8 | 10 |

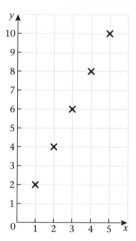

3 (a)

| $x$ | 1 | 2 | 3 | 4 | 5 |
|---|---|---|---|---|---|
| $y$ | 4 | 7 | 10 | 13 | 16 |

**(b)**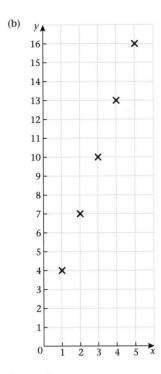

**(c)** $y = 3x + 1$

**4 (a)**

| $x$ | 1 | 2 | 3 | 4 | 5 |
|---|---|---|---|---|---|
| $y$ | 3 | 5 | 7 | 9 | 11 |

**(b)**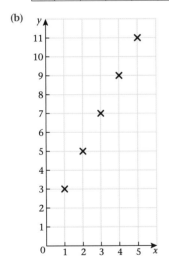

**(c)** $y = 2x + 1$

**5 (a) (i)**

| $x$ | 1 | 2 | 3 | 4 | 5 |
|---|---|---|---|---|---|
| $y$ | 3 | 5 | 7 | 9 | 11 |

**(ii)**

| $x$ | 1 | 2 | 3 | 4 | 5 |
|---|---|---|---|---|---|
| $y$ | 2 | 4 | 6 | 8 | 10 |

**(b) (i)** $y = 2x + 1$      **(ii)** $y = 2x$

## Exercise 9C

**1 (a)**

| $x$ | 0 | 1 | 2 | 3 | 4 |
|---|---|---|---|---|---|
| $y$ | 0 | 4 | 8 | 12 | 16 |

**(b)**       **(c)** 14 miles

**2 (a)**

| $x$ | 0 | 5 | 10 | 15 | 20 | 25 |
|---|---|---|---|---|---|---|
| $y$ | 0 | 8 | 16 | 24 | 32 | 40 |

**(b)**

**(c)** 21 km (20.8 to be exact)
**(d)** 9 miles (8.75 to be exact)

**3 (a)**

| $x$ | 0 | 1 | 2 | 3 | 4 | 5 | 6 |
|---|---|---|---|---|---|---|---|
| $y$ | 0 | 3 | 6 | 9 | 12 | 15 | 18 |

(b)

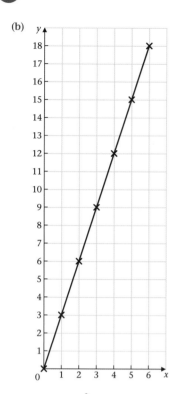

(c) 5 buckets ($4\frac{2}{3}$ to be exact)

**4** (a)

| $x$ | $\frac{1}{2}$ | 1 | $1\frac{1}{2}$ | 2 | $2\frac{1}{2}$ | 3 | $3\frac{1}{2}$ |
|---|---|---|---|---|---|---|---|
| $y$ | 1 | $1\frac{1}{2}$ | 2 | $2\frac{1}{2}$ | 3 | $3\frac{1}{2}$ | 4 |

(b) A joint of lamb cannot weigh 0 kg.

(c)

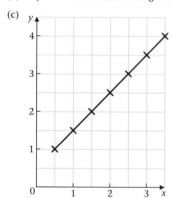

(d) About $2\frac{3}{4}$ hours

## Exercise 9D

**1** (a)

$y = x + 6$

(b)

$y = 2x + 5$

(c)

$y = 3x + 1$

(d)

$y = 3x - 4$

(e)

$y = -2x + 3$

(f)

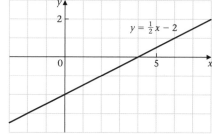

$y = \frac{1}{2}x - 2$

**2** $y = 3x + 1$ and $y = 3x - 4$
**3** (a) $y = \frac{1}{4}x + 1$ and $y = \frac{1}{4}x - 1$
   (b) Coefficients of $x$ equal
**4** (a) (0, 5)         (b) (0, −2)
   (c) (0, −5)      (d) (0, 4)
**5** $y = 4x + 3$       **6** $y = 5x - 3$
**7** $y = 3x + 5$       **8** $y = mx + c$
**9** $c = 4$; (0, 4)    **10** $c = -3$; (0, −3)
**11** (a) (0, 1)       (b) 5
**12** (a) $y = \frac{1}{3}x - 4$   (b) (0, −4)

**13** (a)

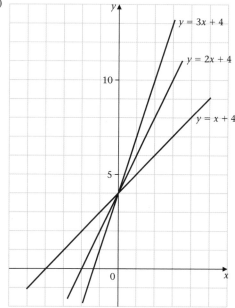

$y = 3x + 4$
$y = 2x + 4$
$y = x + 4$

(b) all (0, 4)
(c) Lines with higher coefficients are steeper.
**14** (a) 3     (b) 3     **15** (a) $\frac{1}{2}$    (b) $\frac{1}{2}$

### Exercise 9E

**1** (a) (i) 5   (ii) (0, 4)   (b) (i) 2   (ii) (0, −7)
   (c) (i) $\frac{1}{4}$   (ii) (0, 9)   (d) (i) −4   (ii) (0, −3)
   (e) (i) 9   (ii) (0, 8)   (f) (i) −2   (ii) (0, 7)
**2** (a) (i) −2   (ii) (0, 3)   (b) (i) 3   (ii) (0, −5)
   (c) (i) $\frac{1}{2}$   (ii) (0, −4)   (d) (i) $-\frac{1}{3}$   (ii) (0, 2)
   (e) (i) $\frac{3}{5}$   (ii) (0, −2)   (f) (i) $-\frac{3}{4}$   (ii) (0, 3)
**3** $y = 6x + 7$
**4** (a) $y = 2x + 5$
   (b) $y = \frac{1}{2}x - 1$
   (c) $x + y = 8$ or equivalent
   (d) $5x + 2y + 10 = 0$
**5** (a) 3    (b) $y = 3x + 2$
**6** $y = 4x + 7$    **7** $y = -3x + 11$
**8** (a) 4    (b) $y = 4x + 3$

### Exercise 9F

**1** (a) $-\frac{1}{5}$  (b) $-\frac{1}{2}$  (c) −1  (d) $-\frac{4}{3}$  (e) $\frac{2}{5}$  (f) $\frac{7}{2}$
**2** (b)    **3** $y = -\frac{1}{3}x$   **4** $y = -x + 6$   **5** $y = \frac{5}{2}x - 9$
**6** (c)    **7** $y = -\frac{3}{2}x + 10$    **8** $y = \frac{3}{4}x - 5$

### Exercise 9G

**1** (a) $(2, 2\frac{1}{2})$   (b) $(3\frac{1}{2}, 5)$   (c) $(3, 6\frac{1}{2})$
   (d) (3, 4)   (e) $(6, 8\frac{1}{2})$

### Exercise 9H

**1** e.g. (1, 9)   **2** (b), (c), (d)   **3** e.g. (5, 2)
**4** (b), (c), (d)   **5** $x = 3, y = 1$
**6** (a) $x = 2, y = 1$  (b) $x = 4, y = 2$  (c) $x = 4, y = 1$
   (d) $x = -3, y = 4$  (e) $x = 3, y = -1$  (f) $x = 4, y = 3$

## Exercise 9I

**1** $x = 3, y = 2$ **2** $x = 4, y = 1$ **3** $x = 2, y = -1$
**4** $x = -2, y = -3$ **5** $x = \frac{1}{2}, y = 1\frac{1}{2}$ **6** $x = 2\frac{1}{2}, y = -1$
**7** $x = 7, y = -1\frac{1}{2}$ **8** $x = \frac{3}{4}, y = -3$ **9** $x = -1, y = -2$

## Exercise 9J

**1** $x = 4, y = 1$ **2** $x = 3, y = -2$ **3** $x = -3, y = -5$
**4** $x = 3, y = 2$ **5** $x = \frac{1}{2}, y = -4$ **6** $x = 5, y = 3$
**7** $x = -7, y = -4$ **8** $x = 3, y = -5$ **9** $x = 2\frac{1}{2}, y = 1$
**10** $x = 1\frac{1}{3}, y = -1$

## Exercise 9K

**1** $a = 2.5, b = 4.5$ **2** £5 per hour **3** 29 and 37
**4** £9.30 **5** 18 **6** $a = 5, b = -5$
**7** £3 **8** 11p **9** 300 kg
**10** (a) $a = 7, b = -2$
(b) (i) $3\frac{1}{2}$ (ii) $(0, -5\frac{1}{2})$

## Exercise 9L

**1**

**2**

**3**

**4**

**5**

**6**

**7**

**8**

**9**

**10**

**11**

**12**

**13** $x \leq 1$ **14** $x + y > 3$ **15** $y > x$ **16** $2x + y > 4$

**17**

**18**

**19**

**20**

**21**

**22**

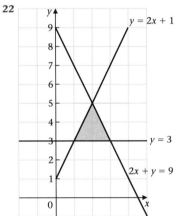

**23** $y \leq 5$, $x \leq 4$, $y \geq -\dfrac{5x}{4} + 5$

**Mixed exercise 9**

**1** 17, 21

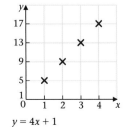

$y = 4x + 1$

**2** (a)

(b)

(c)

**3** (a) $y = 3x + c$ $(c \neq -2)$    (b) $y = \frac{1}{2}x + k$ $(k \neq 1)$
   (c) $y = a - 2x$ $(a \neq 5)$
**4** $(\frac{1}{2}, 5)$
**5** (a) $y = 9 - \frac{1}{3}x$    (b) $y = 6 - \frac{1}{3}x$
**6** (a) 7, $(0, 3\frac{1}{2})$    (b) $-1\frac{1}{2}$, $(0, 3)$
   (c) 2, $(0, 5)$    (d) $-1$, $(0, -2)$
**7** (a) $p = 4$, $q = -1$    (b) $x = 4\frac{1}{2}$, $y = -3$
**8** (a) $y = 2x + 6$    (b) $y = 6 - \frac{1}{2}x$
**9** (a)

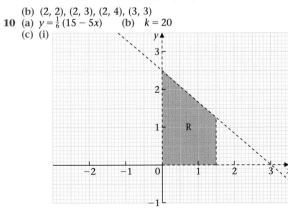

(b) $(2, 2)$, $(2, 3)$, $(2, 4)$, $(3, 3)$
**10** (a) $y = \frac{1}{6}(15 - 5x)$    (b) $k = 20$
   (c) (i)

(ii) $(1, 1)$

# Chapter 10 Presenting and analysing data 1

## Exercise 10A

1
```
4 | 5, 9
5 | 3, 4, 5, 5, 6, 7, 7, 8, 8
6 | 0, 0, 0, 2, 2, 3, 4, 4, 5, 6, 7, 8
7 | 0, 3, 4, 5, 7
8 | 2, 3          Key: 5 | 3 means 53 years
```
mode = 60, median = 62, mean = 63.07

2
```
2 | 5, 8, 8,
3 | 0, 1, 4, 7, 7, 7, 8, 9
4 | 1, 2, 3, 5, 5, 6, 6, 6, 7, 7, 9
5 | 0, 2          Key: 2 | 5 means 2.5 kg
```
mean = 4.01 kg, median = 4.15 kg, mode = 3.7 kg and 4.6 kg

3
```
44 | 7, 7, 8, 8, 9, 9, 9, 9
45 | 0, 0, 1, 2, 3, 3, 3, 4, 5, 6, 7, 7, 7, 9
46 | 0, 1, 2, 2, 3, 3     Key: 44 | 7 means 44.7 s
```
mode = 44.9 s, 45.3 s and 45.7 s
median = 45.3 s

## Exercise 10B

1 (a) (i) 34  (ii) 28.5  (iii) 26.4
  (b) Mean is lowest – the '4' depresses its value compared to the mode and median.
  (c) 31, 25.5, 23.4
2 (a) 32.6
  (b) No – because the ages are so spread out
3 'Average' could be mean, median or mode.
  The mean will be distorted by the small number of very high earners.

## Exercise 10C

1 (a) 287  (b) 258  (c) 319
2 (a) 19  (b) 11  (c) 40.5
3 (a) 51.06 g  (b) 50.89 g  (c) 51.19 g

## Exercise 10D

1 0, 20, 26, 12, 8, total $f$ 45, total $fx$ 66. Mean 1.47, Mode 1, Median 1
2 Mode 0, Median 0, Mean 0.5
3 (a) 2 goals  (b) 3 goals  (c) 3.2 goals

## Exercise 10E

1 (a) 7  (b) 2
2 (a) £9  (b) £4
3 (a) $4\frac{1}{2}$  (b) $2\frac{1}{2}$

## Exercise 10F

1 (a)

| Class interval | Frequency $f$ | Middle value | $f \times x$ |
|---|---|---|---|
| 1–5 | 16 | 3 | 48 |
| 6–10 | 28 | 8 | 224 |
| 11–15 | 26 | 13 | 338 |
| 16–20 | 14 | 18 | 252 |
| 21–25 | 10 | 23 | 230 |
| 26–30 | 3 | 28 | 84 |
| 31–35 | 1 | 33 | 33 |
| 36–40 | 0 | 38 | 0 |
| 41–45 | 2 | 43 | 86 |
| Total: | 100 | Total: | 1295 |

  (b) 13 words
2 11.8 years
3 (a) 61–100  (b) 61–100  (c) 69.3

## Exercise 10G

1 Not necessarily. Drapeway Ltd may have a few very high wage earners which will push up the value of the mean.
2 On average students did better on Paper A (higher median). There was a bigger spread of marks on Paper A, with the spread of the middle 50% of candidates being over $2\frac{1}{2}$ times that on Paper B.
3 Club 2 has an older median but a smaller spread. Generally there are more older people in Club 2 but because the spread in Club 1 is larger, it may have some members who are as old as the Club 2 members.

## Exercise 10H

1 (a), (b)

  (b) No, the 3 month average is steady at 7 or 8.
2 (a)

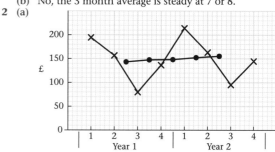

  (b) The gas bills are rising slowly.
3

The number of passengers fell slowly between the beginning of 2003 and the end of 2005.

## Exercise 10I

1

The greater the distance travelled the smaller the depth of tread.

**2** (a)

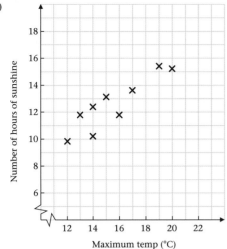

(b) As the number of hours of sunshine increases, the maximum temperature increases.

## Exercise 10J

**1** (a)

(b) High negative correlation      (c) About 9 km

**2** (a)

(b) There is strong positive correlation between rotational speed and wind speed
(c) About 76 rev/min
(d) 4 m/s is far outside the range of data given, so the relationship may have changed.

**3** (b) (i) 14 to 15 hours      (ii) 14°C to 15°C

## Mixed exercise 10

**1** (a)

| 7 | 6 7 7 7 8 8 9 |
|---|---|
| 8 | 0 0 0 0 2 3 5 6 7 7 8 |
| 9 | 0 0 5 5 5 5 5 5 5 8 |
| 10 | 0 1 5 6 6 8 8      Key: 7 | 6 means 76 kg |

  (b) (i) 95 kg      (ii) 88 kg      (iii) 89.6 kg
      (iv) 32 kg      (v) 15 kg

**2** 19

**3** (a) 162 kg, 167.1 kg
  (b) (i) median  (ii) Yes. Not affected by the larger values.

**4** (a) 30            (b) 6, 2
  (c) 2             (d) No. The mode is better.

**5** (a) $300 < w \leqslant 500$
  (b) 18 800 g
  (c) You do not know where the weights fall in each interval. The midpoint of each class interval is used to represent the class interval.
  (d) About 470 g

**6** (a) £67.50, £65.25, £63.75, £62.75, £62, £60.50, £59.75, £59.25, £58.50
  (b) Generally decreasing.

**7** (a) 12, $13\frac{2}{3}$, 15, 18, 16, 10
  (b)

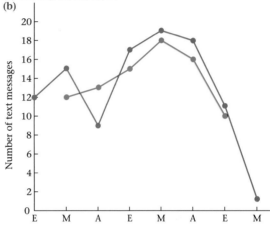

  (c) Increasing trend until Sunday morning, then decreasing trend.

**8** (a)

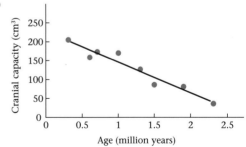

  (b) Strong negative correlation. Points close to a straight line.
  (c) About 90 cm³

**9** (a)

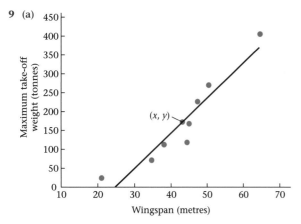

(b) (i) 43.2 m, 169.8 tonnes
(c) About 24 to 65 metres

**10** (a)

|  | Median | IQR |
|---|---|---|
| Male | 22 | 10 |
| Female | 25 | 8 |

(b) Smaller median for males, but larger IQR.
So not enough evidence to conclude a significant difference.

# Chapter 11 Estimation and approximation

## Exercise 11A

**1** (a)

　46.383
◄── 46.3826
　46.382

　　(b) 46.383

**2** (a)

| Name | Time |
|---|---|
| R. Grey | 1 min 45.48 sec |
| M. Hobson | 1 min 45.48 sec |
| T. Knight | 1 min 45.48 sec |

(b) M. Hobson, T. Knight, R. Grey
**3** (a) 137.3　(b) 0.6738　(c) 5.0　(d) 9.00
(e) 17.994　(f) 2.0097
**4** (a) 95.047　(b) 9.760　(c) 10.91　(d) 176.0

## Exercise 11B

**1** (a) 3.17　(b) 965　(c) 16　(d) 10
(e) 55.764　(f) 55.90
**2** (a) 196.161　(b) 196　(c) 196.16　(d) 200
(e) 196　(f) 200　(g) 200　(h) 196.1614
**3** (a) 43 670　(b) 44 000　(c) 40 000
**4** (a) 1940　(b) 4450　(c) 9800　(d) 86 000
(e) 1000　(f) 60 000
**5** (a) 0.003　(b) 0.000 88　(c) 0.0090　(d) 0.0009
(e) 0.01　(f) 0.0004
**6** (a) 0.007　(b) 0.066 67　(c) 0.000 0029
**7** (a) 0.39　(b) 0.039　(c) 39.4　(d) 40 000

## Exercise 11C

(Note: there are alternatives to questions 1 (i) and (ii), and 3.)
**1** (a) (i) $9 \times 10$　(ii) 90　(iii) 82.7896
(b) (i) $4 \times (2 - 0)$　(ii) 8　(iii) 7.3875
(c) (i) $40 \times 4$　(ii) 160　(iii) 160.7296
(d) (i) $(2000 \times 300) + 400$　(ii) 600 400
(iii) 633 086
(e) (i) $\dfrac{200 \times 75}{50}$　(ii) 300　(iii) 294.831 3152
(f) (i) $\dfrac{0.6 \times 0.02}{0.04}$　(ii) 0.3　(iii) 0.262 550 588
**2** (a) 8.5　(b) 40.488　(c) 4.6706　(d) 134.3632
(e) 76.704　(f) 8.0736
**3** (a) 7 or 8　(b) 6　(c) 9 or 10　(d) 3
(e) 7 or 8　(f) 10　(g) 7 or 8　(h) 8
(i) 7　(j) 3　(k) 10　(l) 3 or 4
(m) 13　(n) 175　(o) 3 or 4

## Exercise 11D

**1** (a) 3.85 cm–3.95 cm　　(b) 17.6195 m–17.6205 m
(c) 52.95 cm–53.05 cm　　(d) 1.0295 m–1.0305 m
(e) 28.5 m–29.5 mm

**2**

| School | Attendance to the nearest 100 | Lowest value of range | Greatest value of range |
|---|---|---|---|
| Southpark | 1400 | 1350 | 1450 |
| Westown | 400 | 350 | 450 |
| Eastgrove | 800 | 750 | 850 |
| Northbury | 1200 | 1150 | 1250 |
| Southone | 2100 | 2050 | 2150 |

**3** 4 min 7.555 sec to 4 min 7.565 sec
**4** 16.5 miles to 17.5 miles

## Exercise 11E

**1** (a) (i) 0.2335 km　(ii) 0.2345 km
(b) (i) 0.3185 s　(ii) 0.3195 s
(c) (i) 0.5445 kg　(ii) 0.5455 kg
(d) (i) 0.7945 km　(ii) 0.7955 km
(e) (i) 9.4165 s　(ii) 9.4175 s
(f) (i) 3.4585 g　(ii) 3.4595 g
**2** (a) 29.5 cm　(b) 18.45 cm, 18.35 cm
**3** (a) 3.65 cm　(b) 15.0 cm, 14.6 cm
(c) 3 s.f. ($4 \times 3.7 = 14.8$ lies midway between the bounds of the perimeter)
(d) Yes, 3 s.f.
**4** (a) 99.5 m
(b) (i) 14.75 seconds　(ii) 14.85 seconds
(c) (i) 6.700 336 7 m/s　(ii) 6.813 559 3 m/s
(d) (i) 6.76 m/s
(ii) Midway between the answers in (c)
**5** (a) 5.65 cm, 5.55 cm
(b) 120.5 cm　　119.5 cm
(c) 6042.32 cm$^3$　　5781.94 cm$^3$
**6** (a) 8 450 000 km$^2$, 8 550 000 km$^2$
(b) 21.83 people/km$^2$, 21.46 people/km$^2$
**7** (a) (i) 815　(ii) 805
(b) (i) 2.935　(ii) 2.925
(c) (i) 278.632 478 6　(ii) 274.275 979 6
(d) 276.5 to 4 s.f.
(There are alternatives; the quoted answer is the mean of the upper and lower bounds.)

## Mixed exercise 11

**1** (a) 9.5　(b) 0.046　(c) 7.70　(d) 7.43
**2** (a) 424　(b) 0.2147　(c) 11 000　(d) 90 000

**3** (a) $60 \div 1$      (b) $3 \times 2$
   (c) $110 - 80$      (d) $60 + 20$
   (e) $(20 + 4) \div (3 + 5)$      (f) $8 \times 4 \div (4 + 5)$
**4** (a) $15.25$ km  (b) $15.15$ km
**5** (a) $29.25$ cm$^2$  (b) $0.538$
**6** (a) $r : 1.75, 1.65$;
      $R : 31.05, 30.95$
   (b) $29.2$

# Chapter 12 Sequences and formulae

## Exercise 12A

**1** $2, 4, 6, 8, 10$      **2** $3, 4, 5, 6, 7$
**3** $10, 13, 16, 19, 22$      **4** $13, 11, 9, 7, 5$
**5** $6, 9, 14, 21, 30$      **6** $2, 11, 26, 47, 74$
**7** $4, 9, 16, 25, 36$      **8** $1, 8, 27, 64, 125$
**9** $2, 4, 8, 16, 32$      **10** $-2, 4, -8, 16, -32$
**11** $\frac{1}{2}, \frac{1}{4}, \frac{1}{8}, \frac{1}{16}, \frac{1}{32}$      **12** $1, 3, 6, 10, 15$
**13** $1, \frac{1}{2}, \frac{1}{3}, \frac{1}{4}, \frac{1}{5}$      **14** $\frac{1}{2}, \frac{2}{3}, \frac{3}{4}, \frac{4}{5}, \frac{5}{6}$
**15** $17$

## Exercise 12B

**1** $8$    **2** $12$    **3** $17$    **4** $7$    **5** $12$
**6** $9$    **7** $21$    **8** $8$    **9** $7$    **10** $20$

## Exercise 12C

**1** $n + 2$    **2** $2n + 3$    **3** $4n + 3$    **4** $10 - n$
**5** $14 - 2n$    **6** $10 - 3n$

## Exercise 12D

**1** $-11$   **2** $53\frac{1}{8}$   **3** $30.2$   **4** $26.3$   **5** $5$
**6** $47.8$   **7** $223$   **8** $-45$   **9** $100.152$   **10** $-43$
**11** $47.4$   **12** $195.5$   **13** $-65$   **14** $82$   **15** $9.09$
**16** $10.8$   **17** $3.44$   **18** $1.30$   **19** $9.71$   **20** $23$

## Exercise 12E

**1** $18$   **2** $5.40$   **3** $22$   **4** $0.8$   **5** $4$
**6** $4.5$   **7** $-8$   **8** $-1\frac{1}{4}$   **9** $6$   **10** $7\frac{1}{2}$
**11** $5$   **12** $12.6$   **13** $7$ or $-7$   **14** $3.99$   **15** $4.2$
**16** $27.6$   **17** $201$   **18** $15.3$   **19** $1.5$   **20** $4.8$

## Exercise 12F

**1** $x = q - p$      **2** $x = t - 7$      **3** $x = b + a$
**4** $x = \frac{1}{5}w$      **5** $x = \frac{p}{n}$      **6** $x = 3f$
**7** $x = md$      **8** $x = \frac{bc}{a}$      **9** $x = \frac{p + q}{n}$
**10** $x = \frac{5 - b}{a}$      **11** $x = \frac{c - h}{d}$      **12** $x = \frac{p - q}{5}$
**13** $x = \frac{b - a}{3}$      **14** $x = m(p - n)$

## Exercise 12G

**1** $I = \frac{V}{R}$      **2** $l = \frac{A}{w}$      **3** $d = \frac{C}{\pi}$
**4** $w = \frac{V}{lh}$      **5** $u = v - at$      **6** $t = \frac{v - u}{a}$
**7** $h = \frac{C}{2\pi r}$      **8** $R = \frac{100I}{PT}$      **9** $l = \frac{P - 2w}{2}$

**10** $h = \frac{A - 2\pi r^2}{2\pi r}$    **11** $x = \frac{y}{3}$    **12** $T = \frac{PV}{k}$
**13** $x = \sqrt{\frac{y}{5}}$    **14** $x = \sqrt{\frac{E}{k}}$    **15** $r = \sqrt{\frac{A}{\pi}}$
**16** $n = \frac{2S}{a + d}$    **17** $a = \frac{2S - nd}{n}$    **18** $x = \sqrt{\frac{y}{k}}$
**19** $h = \frac{3V}{\pi r^2}$    **20** $r = \sqrt{\frac{3V}{\pi h}}$    **21** $a = \sqrt{c^2 - b^2}$
**22** $b = \sqrt{\frac{a^2 + 8}{4}}$    **23** $s = \frac{gt^2}{2}$    **24** $L = \frac{gT^2}{4\pi^2}$
**25** $y = \sqrt{1 - x^2}$    **26** $u = \sqrt{v^2 - 2as}$    **27** $x = \sqrt{\frac{a^2w^2 - v^2}{w^2}}$
**28** $x = \sqrt{\frac{9 - y^2}{9}}$    **29** $x = \frac{y - 5}{y + 1}$    **30** $u = \frac{vf}{(v - f)}$

## Exercise 12H

**1** $P = \frac{V^2}{R}$      **2** $s = \frac{1}{2}gt^2$      **3** $A = \frac{\pi d^2}{4}$
**4** $a = rw^2$      **5** (a) $A = \frac{P^2}{16}$  (b) $P = 4\sqrt{A}$
**6** $x = \frac{y^2}{4a}$      **7** $A = 2\pi r^2 + \frac{2V}{r}$      **8** $F = \frac{2A}{l} + l$

## Mixed exercise 12

**1** (a) $108, 147$      (b) $3n^2$
**2** (a) $27, 31$      (b) $15, 12$
   (c) $32, 64$      (d) $28, 36$
**3** $t = \frac{v - 30}{7}$     **4** $g = \frac{4\pi^2 a}{T^2}$     **5** $r = \sqrt{\frac{A}{4\pi}}$
**6** $y = 2x + 5$     **7** $v = \frac{fu}{u - f}$     **8** $u = \frac{D - kt^2}{t}$
**9** (a) (i) $g = 10, t = 20$    (ii) $2000$
   (b $2748.12$
**10** (a) $r = 7, h = 11, \pi = 3$; $1617$ cm$^3$
   (b) $1860$ cm$^3$
   (c) $1891.88$ cm$^3$
**11** (a) $f = 4(v - 55)$  (b) $v = \frac{1}{4}f + 55$

# Chapter 13 Measure and mensuration

## Exercise 13A

**1** (a) $3.35$ m, $3.45$ m      (b) $4.55$ m, $4.65$ m
   (c) $15.24$ m$^2$, $16.04$ m$^2$
**2** (a) $194.46$ km      (b) $190.55$ km

## Exercise 13B

**1** (a) $52.5$ cm$^2$, $31$ cm
   (b) $80$ cm$^2$, $48$ cm
**2** (a) $(6x + 8)$ cm    (b) $7$      (c) $136$ cm$^2$
**3** (a) $4$ cm      (b) $16$ cm$^2$
**4** $62\,500$ m$^2$
**5** (a) $30$ cm$^2$      (b) $6$ cm$^2$      (c) $45$ cm$^2$
**6** (a) $4x - 5$      (b) $8.5$
**7** (a) $40$ cm$^2$      (b) $36$ cm$^2$      (c) $30$ cm$^2$
**8** (a) $70$ cm$^2$      (b) $8.75$ cm
**9** $9.49$
**10** (a) $105$ cm$^2$      (b) $14$ cm$^2$      (c) $66$ cm$^2$
**11** $58.4$ cm$^2$      **12** $2.4$ cm

## Exercise 13C

**1** (a) $31.42$ cm, $78.54$ cm$^2$
   (b) $50.27$ cm, $201.06$ cm$^2$
   (c) $37.70$ cm, $113.10$ cm$^2$

**2** (a) 15.71 m   (b) 19.63 m²
**3** $\pi r^2 = 2\pi r$, $r^2 = 2r$, $r = 2$ (or 0)
**4** (a) 2.39 cm   (b) 17.94 cm²   **5** 37.85 cm
**6** (a) Area   = 39.27 cm²
         Perimeter = 25.71 cm

   (b) Area   $= \dfrac{25\pi}{2}$ cm²

         Perimeter $= (10 + 5\pi)$ cm
**7** (a) 181.70 cm   (b) 1666.19 cm²

## Exercise 13D

**1** (a) 125 cm³   (b) 1728 cm³   (c) 54.872 cm³
**2** (a) 10 cm   (b) 600 cm²
**3** (a) 180 cm³   (b) 480.24 cm³
**4** (a) 4 cm   (b) 352 cm²
**5** (a) 504 cm³   (b) 396 cm²
**6** 240 cm³   **7** 12 cm   **8** 576 cm³

## Exercise 13E

**1** (a) 2-D   (b) 3-D   (c) 2-D   (d) 3-D
**2** (2, 1, 3), (4, 3, 1), (5, 2, 12), (27, 3, 11)
**3** $O$ (0, 0, 0), $A$ (4, 0, 0), $B$ (4, 0, 3), $C$ (0, 0, 3), $D$ (0, 2, 3),
   $E$ (0, 2, 0), $F$ (4, 2, 0), $G$ (4, 2, 3)
**4** (a) $O$ (0, 0, 0), $A$ (4, 0, 0), $B$ (4, 0, −3), $C$ (0, 0, −3),
         $D$ (0, −2, 0), $E$ (4, −2, 0), $F$ (4, −2, −3), $G$ (0, −2, −3)
   (b) (i) $(0, -2, -1\frac{1}{2})$   (ii) $(4, -1, -1\frac{1}{2})$

## Exercise 13F

**1** $4\pi r^2$, dimension is 2
**2** $n + m$ must equal 3
   so $n = 0$, $m = 3$ or $n = 1$, $m = 2$ or $n = 2$, $m = 1$ or $n = 3$, $m = 0$
**3** $x + y + x$, length
   $xyz$, volume
   $xy + yz + xz$, area
**4** $\pi a^2 b$, volume
   $\pi b^2 + 2h$, none
   $2ah$, area

## Mixed exercise 13

**1** 1.2 m²
**2** 3 400 000 cm³
**3** (a) 86.625 m³   (b) 119.5 m²
**4** (a) 317.08 m   (b) 5963.5 m²
**5** 50 cm²
**6** 154.06 cm²
**7** 600 cm³, 660 cm²
**8** (a) From $x^2 h = 50$   (b) 3.54   (c) 2
**9** (a) $A$ (−4, 0, 0), $B$ (−4, 0, −2), $C$ (−1, 0, −2), $D$ (−1, 0, 0)
         $E$ (−4, 2, −2), $F$ (−4, 2, 0), $G$ (−1, 2, 0), $H$ (−1, 2, −2)
   (b) (i) $(-2\frac{1}{2}, 0, 0)$   (ii) $(-2\frac{1}{2}, 1, -1)$
**10** Volume, as there are 3 variable dimensions.
**11** (a) 4.35 m, 4.25 m; 3.75 m, 3.65 m
   (b) 16.3 m², 15.5 m²

# Chapter 14 Simplifying algebraic expressions

## Exercise 14A

**1** $x^8$   **2** $y^8$   **3** $6x^7$   **4** $5a^4$
**5** $24a^6$   **6** $48y^5$   **7** $10x^5y^2$   **8** $24a^5b^5$
**9** $a^2b^2c^2$   **10** $18a^2b^3c^5$   **11** $6x^2y^3$   **12** $x^8$
**13** $9a^4$   **14** $8x^6$   **15** $2a^{20}$   **16** $2x^4y^6$
**17** $63x^8$   **18** $14a^{13}b^6$   **19** $36x^2$   **20** $27x^6$

## Exercise 14B

**1** $x^3$   **2** $3a^3$   **3** $6xy^3$   **4** $x^{-2}$
**5** $a^6$   **6** $\frac{3}{2}a^3x^{-1}$   **7** 4   **8** $x^2$
**9** $5q^2$   **10** $2r^4$   **11** $2e^4$   **12** $3p^5$

## Exercise 14C

**1** 5   **2** 2   **3** 4   **4** $\frac{1}{7}$
**5** $\frac{1}{3}$   **6** 6   **7** $\frac{1}{5}$   **8** $\frac{1}{10}$
**9** $\frac{1}{2}$   **10** 0.4

## Exercise 14D

**1** (a) 2   (b) $\frac{1}{100}$   (c) 4   (d) 32   (e) 81
**2** (a) 125   (b) 32   (c) 32   (d) $\frac{1}{4}$
   (e) 32   (f) 25   (g) $\frac{1}{4}$   (h) $\frac{1}{32}$
   (i) 6   (j) $\frac{9}{4}$   (k) $\frac{64}{49}$   (l) $\frac{1}{125}$
**3** (a) 9   (b) $a^2$   (c) $x^{\frac{3}{2}} y^{\frac{5}{2}}$   (d) $3x$   (e) $\dfrac{2}{x}$
   (f) $\dfrac{a^2}{5}$   (g) $729x^3$   (h) 16   (i) $24y^2$

## Exercise 14E

**1** (a) $\frac{1}{2}$   (b) 0   (c) −3   (d) $\frac{2}{3}$   (e) $\frac{7}{2}$
   (f) $\frac{9}{2}$   (g) 5   (h) 4   (i) 3   (j) $\frac{1}{2}$
   (k) $\frac{3}{2}$   (l) 3

## Exercise 14F

**1** $\dfrac{x}{4}$   **2** $\dfrac{b}{d}$   **3** $4x$   **4** $\dfrac{4t}{3r}$

**5** $3ab$   **6** 2   **7** $\dfrac{(x + 2)}{2x}$   **8** $\dfrac{3}{(x - 4)}$

**9** $\dfrac{x^3y^2(y - 2)}{(y - 6)}$

## Exercise 14G

**1** (a) $\dfrac{3x}{5}$   (b) $\dfrac{y + x}{xy}$   (c) $\dfrac{13}{5x}$

   (d) $\dfrac{11x}{12}$   (e) $\dfrac{7a + 2}{12}$   (f) $\dfrac{x + 17}{10}$

   (g) $\dfrac{(x + 3)}{(x + 1)(x + 2)}$   (h) $\dfrac{2}{x(2 - x)}$   (i) $\dfrac{y - 1}{2(y - 5)}$

**2** (a) 18   (b) $x^2 (x - 1)$
   (c) $12(x - 1)(x + 1)$   (d) $x^3(1 - x)(1 + x)$

**3** (a) $\dfrac{5a}{18}$   (b) $\dfrac{(x - 2)}{x^2(x - 1)}$

   (c) $\dfrac{(x + 2)}{12(x - 1)(x + 1)}$   (d) $\dfrac{x^2 + x + 2}{x^3(1 - x)(1 + x)}$

**4** $\dfrac{2(x + 10)}{(x - 2)(x + 2)}$

## Exercise 14H

**1** (a) $4x(2x + 1)$   (b) $3p(2p + 1)$   (c) $3x(2x - 1)$
   (d) $3b(b - 3)$   (e) $3a(4 + a)$   (f) $5c(3 - 2c)$
   (g) $7x^3(3x + 2)$   (h) $4y^2(4y - 3)$   (i) $2d^2(3d^2 - 2)$
**2** (a) $ax(x + 1)$   (b) $pr(r - 1)$   (c) $ab(b - 1)$
   (d) $q(r^2 - q)$   (e) $ax(a + x)$   (f) $by(b - y)$
   (g) $3a^2(2a - 3)$   (h) $4x^3(2 - x)$   (i) $6x^3(3 + 2x^2)$
**3** (a) $6ab(2a + 3b)$   (b) $2xy(2x - y)$
   (c) $4ab(a + 2b + 3)$   (d) $2xy(2x + 3y - 1)$
   (e) $3ax(4x + 2a - 1)$   (f) $abc(a + b + c)$

## Exercise 14I

**1** $(p+q)(x+y)$  **2** $(x+y)(3-z)$  **3** $(x-y)(5-x)$
**4** $2(a-b)(5+x)$  **5** $(y+2)(x+z)$  **6** $(a+1)(y+2b)$
**7** $(x-b)(1-x)$  **8** $(x-y)(x-z)$  **9** $2(b+1)(a-5)$
**10** $3(a-2c)(1-b)$

## Exercise 14J

**1** (a) $x(x+3)$  (b) $8(x+3)$  (c) $(x+3)(x+8)$
(d) $x(x+6)$  (e) $2(x+6)$  (f) $(x+6)(x+2)$
(g) $x(x-5)$  (h) $8(x-5)$  (i) $(x-5)(x+8)$
(j) $(x+5)(x+3)$  (k) $(x+4)(x-8)$  (l) $(x-6)(x-2)$
(m) $(x+4)(x-3)$  (n) $(x+3)(x+5)$  (o) $(x-7)(x-9)$
**2** $x^2-5x-6$
**3** (a) $-2, -3$  (b) $1, 6$  (c) $-2, -6$
(d) $4, 15$  (e) $4, -6$  (f) $-2, 12$
(g) $3, -16$  (h) $-4, 12$
**4** (a) $(x-4)(x-1)$  (b) $(x+5)(x+2)$  (c) $(x-5)(x+3)$
(d) $(x+3)(x+2)$  (e) $(x-10)(x-1)$  (f) $(y-4)(y+3)$
**5** (a) $(2x-3)(x-1)$  (b) $6(x+2)(x+5)$  (c) $(2y-5)(y+2)$
(d) $2(3a+2)(a+1)$  (e) $(4x+3)(x-2)$  (f) $5(5+4x)(3-x)$
(g) $(5x-1)(x-3)$  (h) $(x^2+2)(x^2+3)$  (i) $2(x^2+4)(x^2+3)$
**6** $(x^n+1)(x^n+8)$
**7** $x(x^{2n}+4)(x^{2n}+2)$

## Exercise 14K

**1** (a) $(x-1)(x+1)$  (b) $(x-5)(x+5)$
(c) $(2x-3)(2x+3)$  (d) $(2x+3)(4x-3)$
(e) $2(p-7)(p+7)$  (f) $2(x-2y)(x+2y)$
(g) $(x+2)^2$  (h) $(x-3)^2$  (i) $2(x+7)^2$
**2** (a) $(x-2)(x+2)$  (b) $x(x-3)$  (c) $(x+1)(x-4)$
(d) $4(x-3)(x+3)$  (e) $2x(2x-35)$  (f) $2(2x+1)(x-18)$
(g) $(x+1)^2$  (h) $x(x+2)$  (i) $2(4x-7)(x+2)$
**3** (a) $(x-4)(x-1)$  (b) $(x+12)(x-3)$  (c) $(x+8)(x-4)$
(d) $(x-1)(2x-5)$  (e) $(4x-7)(x+1)$  (f) $(5x+3)(x-2)$
(g) $(x-1)(x-3)$  (h) $(y+2)(y+5)$  (i) $(x+5)(x-3)$
(j) $(x-7)(x+3)$  (k) $(y+4)^2$  (l) $(2x-5)^2$
(m) $(5x-3)(x-2)$  (n) $(4x+5)(x-1)$  (o) $(5x-3)(x+2)$

## Exercise 14L

**1** $\dfrac{x+2}{2}$  **2** $\dfrac{x-1}{x+4}$  **3** $\dfrac{(x+2)}{(x-2)^2}$  **4** $\dfrac{(x+9)}{(x+1)}$

**5** $\dfrac{(x+2)}{x}$  **6** $\dfrac{4}{(x+1)(x+2)}$  **7** $2$

## Mixed exercise 14

**1** (a) $x^4$  (b) $y^{12}$  (c) $m^8$  (d) $6r^3t^6$
**2** (a) $2p(p-2q)$  (b) $(p+q)(p+q+5)$  (c) $(x+1)(x+6)$
**3** (a) $3x(x+2y)$  (b) $(x-5)(2x-7)$
**4** (a) $\dfrac{3}{(y+2)}$  (b) $\dfrac{3}{(x+1)}$

**5** $\dfrac{(2x+3)}{(x-1)}$

**6** $\dfrac{(5x-4)}{(x^2-1)}$

**7** (a) $p^9$  (b) $x^5$  (c) $y^2$
**8** (a) $\frac{1}{9}$  (b) $6$  (c) $9$  (d) $3\frac{3}{8}$
**9** (a) $(3x-1)^2$  (b) $\dfrac{(2x+3)}{(3x-1)}$

**10** $\dfrac{5(x-3)}{(x-2)(x-1)}$

**11** $\dfrac{(2x-5)}{(2x-1)}$

**12** $p=3$ or $-3$, $q=-6$ or $30$, $r=9$
**13** (a) $7p$  (b) (i) $xy$  (ii) $x^2y^2$
**14** (a) $3$  (b) $7$  (c) $-2$

# Chapter 15 Pythagoras' theorem

## Exercise 15B

**1** (a) $13\,cm$  (b) $15\,cm$  (c) $12.5\,cm$  (d) $7.5\,cm$
**2** (a) $11.4\,cm$  (b) $35.5\,cm$  (c) $7.2\,m$  (d) $20.8\,m$
**3** $26\,cm$  **4** $14.14\,cm$

## Exercise 15C

**1** (a) $9\,cm$  (b) $24\,cm$  (c) $7.5\,cm$  (d) $10.5\,cm$
**2** (a) $6.3\,m$  (b) $35.5\,cm$  (c) $8.7\,cm$  (d) $21.2\,cm$
**3** $24.4\,cm$  **4** $12.4\,m$
**5** $9.80\,m$  **6** $129.7\,km$

## Exercise 15D

**1** (a) $x=13\,cm$  $y=19.85\,cm$
(b) $x=6\,cm$  $y=12.04\,cm$
(c) $x=9\,cm$  $y=50.8\,cm$

## Exercise 15E

**1** $13$ units
**2** (a) $5$  (b) $4.47$  (c) $11.31$  (d) $14.87$
(e) $5$  (f) $12.08$
**3** $5.83$ units

## Exercise 15F

**2** (a) obtuse  (b) acute  (c) obtuse  (d) right
(e) obtuse  (f) obtuse

## Exercise 15G

**2** (a) Yes  (b) Yes  (c) Yes  (d) No
(e) Yes  (f) No

## Exercise 15H

**1** $15.26\,cm$  **2** $18.31\,mm$
**3** (a) (i) $13\,cm$ (ii) $17.72\,cm$ (iii) $20.81\,cm$  (b) acute

## Exercise 15I

**1** (a) $x^2+y^2=16$  (b) $x^2+y^2=49$
**2** (a) $x^2+y^2=25$  (b) $x^2+y^2=144$  (c) $x^2+y^2=225$
**3** $x^2+y^2=169$
**4** Any eight of: $(5,0), (0,5), (-5,0), (0,-5)$
$(3,4), (3,-4), (-3,4), (-3,-4)$
$(4,3), (4,-3), (-4,3), (-4,-3)$

## Mixed exercise 15

**1** $12.4\,cm$  **2** $6.24\,m$  **3** $30.8\,km$
**4** $x=26\,cm, y=15.0\,cm$
**5** $13.6$ units
**6** $7^2+8^2<11^2$, so obtuse
**7** Only (b) is a Pythagorean triple, as $10^2+24^2=26^2$
**8** $20.8\,cm$
**9** (a) $13\,cm$  (b) $23.3\,cm$  (c) $23.9\,cm$
**10** $5$  **11** $x^2+y^2=16$  **12** $x^2+y^2=289$
**13** No. For example, they can be similar triangles or semi-circles.

# Index to Books 1 and 2

You can find pages 291–552 in Book 2.

You can find pages 291–552 in Book 2.

You can find pages 291–552 in Book 2.

You can find pages 291–552 in Book 2.

You can find pages 291–552 in Book 2.

You can find pages 291–552 in Book 2.